¡Hola, amigos!

D1537023

¡Hola, amigos!

A Plan for Latino Outreach

Susana G. Baumann

Foreword by Yolanda Cuesta

Latinos and Libraries Series
John L. Ayala and Sal Güereña, Series Editors

 LIBRARIES UNLIMITED

AN IMPRINT OF ABC-CLIO, LLC
Santa Barbara, California • Denver, Colorado • Oxford, England

Copyright 2011 by Susana G. Baumann

All rights reserved. No part of this publication may be reproduced, stored in a retrieval system, or transmitted, in any form or by any means, electronic, mechanical, photocopying, recording, or otherwise, except for the inclusion of brief quotations in a review or reproducibles, which may be copied for use in classroom, educational programs, and not-for-profit settings, without prior permission in writing from the publisher.

Library of Congress Cataloging-in-Publication Data

Baumann, Susana G.
    ¡Hola, amigos! : a plan for Latino outreach / Susana G. Baumann ; foreword by Yolanda Cuesta.
        p. cm. — (Latinos and libraries series)
    Includes bibliographical references and index.
        ISBN 978-1-59158-474-2 (acid-free paper)   1. Hispanic Americans and libraries.   2. Library outreach programs—
United States.   I. Title.
    Z711.92.H56B38   2011
    027.6′3—dc22   2010032711

ISBN: 978-1-59158-474-2

15   14   13   12   11   1   2   3   4   5

This book is also available on the World Wide Web as an eBook.
Visit www.abc-clio.com for details.

Libraries Unlimited
An Imprint of ABC-CLIO, LLC

ABC-CLIO, LLC
130 Cremona Drive, P.O. Box 1911
Santa Barbara, California 93116-1911

This book is printed on acid-free paper ∞

Manufactured in the United States of America

"Ten Reasons for Multicultural Library Services" from Raison d'être *for Multicultural Library Services* reprinted with permission of International Federation of Library Associations and Institutions (IFLA).

To my children Laura and Luciano
To those who have yet to visit a library

Contents

Series Foreword

We are pleased to present to the library community a new series on Latino library services. Latinos and Libraries contributes to the relatively new field of serving Latinos in libraries in the United States. Because the literature in this field is somewhat thin, this series answers the call to add scholarship to this field of library endeavor. Our expectations are that, through the Latinos and Libraries series, we will bring new information to the area of serving Latinos, and that readers of this series will become more educated and informed about topics relevant to the Latino community.

This series covers public, academic, and special library issues, services, questions, problems, and solutions. In our attempt to be comprehensive we have enlisted various library practitioners in the field of library service to Latinos. These librarians, library directors, and library and information science professors represent a wide spectrum of library endeavors.

The authors also represent a wide range of Latino national origins and backgrounds, including Chicano/Chicana, Colombian, Peruvian, Puerto Rican, Mexican, and Anglo. These practitioners have written and will continue to write articles and monographs on Latino library service, and we are honored to include their contributions in this series.

The publisher and editors of Latinos and Libraries have been working diligently and thoroughly in presenting this wide-ranging and in-depth coverage of library service. Our hope is that you will be pleased with the coverage and with the continuing addition of literature to the field, including the premier title of the series *¡Hola, amigos! A Plan for Latino Outreach* by Susana G. Baumann, which presents a systematic approach to outreach for Latino communities.

Thank you to the publisher of the series and for its dedication to expanding the literature in the field of Latinos and libraries. There is more to come.

John L. Ayala and Sal Güereña
Series Editors

Foreword

One of the most rewarding experiences of my consulting career was being selected to write the curriculum for the Spanish Language Outreach Project developed by WebJunction and funded by the Gates Foundation. My role was to write the curriculum and train a corps of trainers who would then present the curriculum throughout the United States. It was in one of these train-the-trainer sessions that I met Susana Baumann. As I presented the curriculum, I could see Susana nodding her head in agreement, smiling at some of the comments and examples, and amplifying the concepts with her own stories and illustrations. During the course of the training, I realized that Susana and I shared a similar passion, conviction, and urgency to help organizations, especially libraries, connect with the Latino community and culture we both represent and love. Susana's experiences as an immigrant from Argentina, and mine as a Tejana whose family has lived north of the Rio Grande since the 1700s, are a good example of the diversity and complexity of the U.S. Latino community public libraries must serve. There are Latinos in your community with backgrounds and experiences similar to ours and many others whose lives in the United States are being shaped daily by their proficiency in English, their ability to move about the community freely and safely, their knowledge about what help is available for them, and a myriad of other factors. This diversity demonstrates the beauty and challenge of helping libraries connect with their Latino communities—a challenge Susana helps you with throughout this book.

As a consultant and trainer, one of my biggest frustrations is being unable to provide the ongoing help and support my clients and workshop participants need in order to effect change. Due to the realities of limited staff and the pressures of covering public service desks, most library training events are limited to four to six hours of contact time—barely enough time to introduce the issue and its consequences, present basic concepts and alternatives, and provide brief experiential opportunities. Susana's book provides the support and guidance you need to continue to build your knowledge of the Latino community and to refine your plans for reaching out to them long after a training workshop is over and you have returned to the realities of serving the public.

Many concepts and principles in this book resonate with me, but none more than the emphasis on equity of access. For decades, Latino library advocates have battled the assumption of library managers and staff who do not see Latinos in their libraries or who see low circulation of Spanish language collections—that Latinos do not read and do not use libraries. The consequence of this assumption has been that services to Latinos have often been relegated to a lower priority to be addressed only when project funding or staffing becomes available. Serving Latinos is treated as a special effort instead of acknowledged as reaching a significant segment of the community whose needs must be met within the basic array of library services. Instead of asking ourselves the fundamental question of why we don't see Latinos in great numbers in our libraries, we tend to want to move quickly to the specifics of the how—how can we get Latinos to come to the library? This book will help you understand the why and will give you the tools to implement the how through an in-depth discussion of the demographics, cultural differences, perceptions, and barriers that impact the Latino community's ability and willingness to use the library.

This book is much more than an advocacy tool or a call to action, although it is filled with statistics, data, and talking points to help you make the case for serving Latinos. It is a practical and comprehensive approach that goes deep into the Latino culture and provides you with the tools, strategies, and techniques you need to connect with your Latino community. It articulates clearly and persuasively the basic outreach concepts practiced by successful Latino library practitioners, yet it stretches the perspective and thinking of even the more experienced. For those familiar with WebJunction's Spanish Language Outreach curriculum, this book will help you move to the next level of understanding and implementation. Do not let the comprehensive approach overwhelm you; instead, find the chapter that fits your particular situation, take the time to thoughtfully answer the questions and probes Susana provides to stimulate your thinking, and use the detailed and helpful forms that accompany every chapter of the book. Covering everything from general advocacy tools to cultural implications to specific marketing tactics, Susana applies her considerable marketing and outreach expertise to serving Latinos in libraries and scores a hat trick.

Yolanda Cuesta
Cuesta MultiCultural Consulting and Training
Sacramento, CA

Acknowledgments

This book was born out of the exchange of knowledge with and contribution of hundreds of library employees who attended my training sessions because they believed language and cultural barriers shouldn't be obstacles to welcoming Latino patrons into their libraries. I have seen them passionately and compassionately talking about their convictions for a better world inside and outside the library—values I share.

In addition, I want to thank Roz Reisner, former Program Coordinator at Central Jersey Regional Library Cooperative (CJRLC), for her initial support and friendship. She introduced me to the library world as well as the publishing world, two steps that were instrumental in bringing this book into fruition. Sadly, at the time this book went into production, the CJRLC (along with other library cooperatives in New Jersey) was dissolved, after 25 years of service, due to budgetary cuts.

A special thank you to Yolanda Cuesta, who graciously agreed to write the foreword of a book that was *en pañales* (in baby diapers) when we met at the WebJunction Spanish Language Outreach Institute in Seattle in 2007. By showing her trust, she gave me the confidence to finish this work—maybe without even knowing it.

Along the way, many people contributed to my writing, but I especially need to mention Bridget Daley, friend and colleague, for her patient and insightful reading of this manuscript, which turned it into "readable English," and her many and accurate devil's advocate comments. My daughter, Dr. Laura I. Catelli, PhD, was also a sounding board for discussing many elements of this work, especially those chapters related to her specialty in Latin American Colonial Studies. Barbara Ittner, my editor, has been particularly patient in directing my first steps as a published author.

Working outside an institutional environment is not easy, so I also express my gratitude to all those institutions and librarians that helped me with research and resources, sent me information about their programs and services, and nurtured my way along these chapters with their encouragement and friendship. A special thanks to Queens Borough Public

Library, New York, for the courtesy of giving permission to reprint excerpts of their website mission statement and vision and values statements. Likewise to the Ocean County Library of New Jersey Board of Trustees for allowing the use of excerpts from their website mission and diversity mission statements.

Finally, I thank my family and friends, who are spread out across three continents. Moments of doubt and discouragement during all these years of reinventing my identity in America were dispelled because of their support and faith in my ability to succeed.

Introduction

Equity of access to library services for underserved populations is not a new concept in the library environment. Moreover, since dramatic demographic changes took place in our country in the last decades, the delivery of equal access and service has required added efforts from libraries and library personnel encountering language and cultural barriers while serving migrant minorities.

Throughout the history of immigration, libraries have played an instrumental role in aiding new immigrants to become a part of our society (Novotny 2003), bridging the language and survival gap by including language-acquisition programs, encouraging literacy improvement, and acting as community service referrals. Recently, however, these efforts have been affected by the turmoil of an immigration debate and the overwhelming numbers of immigrants to be served.[1]

> Throughout its history, the United States has had a mixed relationship with immigrants, welcoming them when they are needed and passing restrictive laws when too many came too quickly. It appears that when the percentage of foreign-born moves upward from 10 percent, the country has an intensive immigration debate. (Murray 2007)

In addition to this situation, which has divided the nation in a sterile debate, immigration rates have been, until recently, the highest since the 1850s. Between 1990 and 1997, the annual national immigration rate—including all countries of origin—oscillated between 1 million to 1.2 million a year and peaked between 1999 and 2000.[2] In 2001, it started declining, returning to 1.1 million a year in 2003. Estimates in 2004 showed a slight increase to 1.2 million (Passel and Suro 2005).

Latinos encompass approximately 50 percent of immigrant numbers. Latino immigration increased substantially between 1990 and 2000, with a peak at the end of the decade, increasing the already established Latino population to an estimated 43 million Latinos living in the

United States according to the U.S. Census Bureau estimates for 2006. A 2006 Pew Hispanic Center fact sheet reports that unauthorized immigrants represented between 10.7 and 11.5 million people (Pew Hispanic Center 2006). However, "not only has the economic downturn in the United States eliminated many of the jobs that used to lure immigrants, human rights groups say, but also the federal government has stepped up efforts to stop the underground railroad of migrants, building mammoth fences in several border towns and flooding the region with hundreds of new Border Patrol agents equipped with high-tech surveillance tools" (Mckinley 2010).

Latino immigration is intertwined with this country's history. The United States developed new relationships with Mexico after the Texas Revolution that ended in 1836 and the Mexican American War of 1848, while the 1898 Spanish American War changed relationships with Cuba and Puerto Rico.

The Mexican American War peace treaty caused half of the Mexican national territory to be incorporated into the United States's geography. The consequence of this geographical addition of Mexican land has been the presence of 13 generations of Mexicans living in the United States. Mexican immigration—and that from other Latin American countries—was also encouraged by government agricultural programs, such as the *Braceros*[3] programs between 1942 and 1964, that allowed the admission of Mexican farm workers to labor in farms in the United States.

Puerto Rican and Cuban immigration waves constituted the main Caribbean Latino influx into the United States before citizenship was given to Puerto Ricans in 1917 and before the Cuban revolution of 1959, which caused Cubans to seek political asylum in this country.

In 1900, when the United States population amounted to 76 million inhabitants, approximately 500,000 were of Latin American origin (Saenz 2004). One hundred years later, the Latino population is almost 100 times larger and comes from 19 different countries in South, Central, and North America and the Caribbean.

This population is diverse in terms of cultural and regional differences, levels of education, and socioeconomic achievement. The reasons Latinos came—and continue to come—to America in pursuit of the American Dream are also diverse. However, most Latinos share Spanish as a common language, almost 85 percent follow the Roman Catholic religion (which has greatly influenced their cultural heritage with common values that bond them deeply), and many see *el Norte* as their hope for survival and dignity.

As Latinos enhance the social and economic fabric of this society, deep cultural transformations take place, not only in the way this community inserts itself into the host culture but also in the way the host culture reacts to this insertion. Feared by some, welcomed by others, Latinos have created the largest cultural impact in the history of the United States. This cultural impact assumes a variety of modalities and has a different dynamic, more than any other wave of immigration to this country.

This process, defined in terms of acculturation or acculturative process, refers to the degree Latinos are influenced by mainstream American culture almost immediately upon arrival (Ainslie 2002).

The term *acculturation*[4] has been used to describe the changes that result from the contact of two cultures, the result of such changes (Kottak and Kozaitis, 1999), and the dynamics between immigrant populations and the host culture that receives them (Bourhis et al. 1996). Although ambiguous, this term has been used, redefined, and adapted to a variety of disciplines, such as anthropology, psychology, sociology, literature, and, lately, marketing.

In this context, I will use the term *acculturation* to name the interchange of influence between two cultures without a subordination of one another, a definition that has also been called biculturalism or multiculturalism (LaFromboise, Coleman, and Gerton 1993). When one of the cultures becomes dominant, I use the term *assimilation*, which has also been defined as incorporation or fusion (Berry 1998).

In terms of understanding acculturation as the result of cultural adaptation from one culture to another, I also support the term *transculturation* (Ortiz 1983), a two-way exchange of cultural characteristics that develops new configurations in both cultures. The changes in Latino marketing paradigms in the last decade are a living proof of this theory (Korzenny and Korzenny 2005). Finally, *retroculturation* or *reculturation* refers to the attempt of third-generation (and subsequent) Latinos to reclaim values and behaviors related to their background of origin (MacNeil and Grassin 2003).

A last word on terminology used in this book is related to the terms *Latino*, *Hispanic*, and *Anglo-American* or *Anglo*. *Latino* and *Hispanic* are used interchangeably despite the preferences of members in this community. The term—either *Latino* or *Hispanic*—used in the sources of reference is given preference; for instance, most government sources use the term *Hispanic*. I use the word *Latino* as a personal preference because of its more inclusive nature.[5] When referring to a U.S.-born citizen, I might use the term *Latino American* or mention the generational gap—Latinos of first, second, or third generation. Also in this context, the term *Anglo-American* (or *Anglo*)—although not the most representative term of white Americans—is used primarily in direct contrast to *Hispanic* or *Latino* and is not limited to persons of English descent but is generally applied to any non-Hispanic whites.[6]

Latinos and Library Services

Public libraries in most Latin American countries are found in large cities, some of them in magnificent buildings—the archives of each country's history and cultural heritage. There are few public libraries, and most do not include a lending system because of small budgets and modest resources. Users need to stay at the library to see most materials, and photocopying is allowed only in certain cases. Few libraries have enough copies of fiction books to organize book clubs or lend them to their members. Private libraries that offer a fee-based lending system can be found in Latin America. Most Latin Americans who like to read are used to purchasing their reading materials, and owning a large personal library is a sign of high social or intellectual status.

For the hard-working population, however, books are not of easy access. Lack of economic accessibility and low literacy levels make other materials—such as magazines, newspapers, and graphic novels bought at the typical newsstands that can be seen in many cities on corners or near public transportation stops and stations—preferred by the general population.

Public libraries are considered places for students and scholars to gather academic information. Adults might visit a library to find a specific document or information in reference books or archives, but the fact that the lending system is so reduced makes it difficult for people to think of the library as a resource.

For the same reasons, many public schools lack a school library. Private schools tend to have better libraries and equipment. In the last decades, the use of computers has increased library use, especially for academic libraries in schools and universities. The proliferation of cyber cafes, or *locutorios telefónicos* (small stores that offer the use of public phones and computers for a small fee), creates competition for public libraries in large cities.

Library resources vary from country to country. For instance, the Mexican *Red Nacional de Bibliotecas Públicas* (RNBP)—a national network of public libraries—was established in 1983. It is the most extensive library system in Mexico. Regulated by the *Consejo Nacional para la*

Cultura y las Artes (Conaculta), a government agency depending on the Mexican Department of Education, it is federally, state, and locally funded. The RNBP includes 7,010 public libraries of different types and dimensions, such as the central public library in Mexico D.F., central state public libraries, and regional and municipal branches. There are 2,236 such locations in 2,451 municipalities. Basic services are on-site borrowing, limited checkout services, literacy and reading workshops and activities, and guided visits. Some branches also offer computers, Braille collections, videos, magazines, and newspapers.

Although it looks good on paper, the system has several problems. For instance, the number of Mexico's public libraries (2,236) available to a population of over 108 million Mexicans results in each location serving an average of 48,300 people (compared to the number of U.S. public libraries estimated at 20,082[7] serving an average of 15,300 people).

Services are focused on children's needs (Chávez 1969), and only in recent years have some locations been connected to international library networks. Decreasing numbers of professionally educated librarians and insufficient library school programs are significant barriers to offering quality services (Carrión 1977; White 1969). These libraries are aided by U.S. library organizations such as the American Library Association (ALA)—for instance, through the use of ALA's standards on bibliographic information, library furnishing, and library education and management—and REFORMA (the National Association to Promote Library and Information Services to Latinos and the Spanish-Speaking)—which has recently offered workgroups, exchanges of library faculty and students, and access to U.S. postgraduate programs—but much more needs to be done.

The situation in Central American countries is even more staggering. In addition to few existing education library sciences programs in the region, a small number of libraries, impoverished collections, and little resources to attract users to libraries, Central America now confronts the digital divide. Guatemala, El Salvador, Honduras, and Nicaragua lead with illiteracy rates ranging from 36 percent in the first to 24 percent in the last country, while Costa Rica and Panama trail behind with rates around 5 and 8 percent. The number of public libraries per country is 150 for Guatemala (population of 12 million), 16 for El Salvador (population of 6.8 million), 106 for Honduras (population of 6.6 million), 56 for Costa Rica (population of 4.1 million), 86 for Panama (population 3.2 million), and an unregistered number for Nicaragua (population 5.5 million).[8]

According to the International Federation of Library Associations and Institutions (IFLA), 3,942 public libraries can be found in South American countries (1999 data); however, this information is incomplete as data was collected from UNESCO (United Nations Educational, Scientific, and Cultural Organization), reporting only for Argentina, Bolivia, Chile, Venezuela, and French Guinea. Library service points are estimated at 5,000 for South America compared to North America with 125,000; Asia, with 85,000; and Europe, with 440,000 service points.[9]

For these reasons, Latinos have little tradition in library services, at least not the way library services are rendered in the United States. The American library system is a solid, extended institution that offers a lending policy of many materials, a variety of services beyond borrowing books, and a presence in practically every small town in America.

A Word on the Latin American Publishing Industry

The Latin American publishing industry, on the other hand, suffers from the economic trends in each country. The educational systems, despite the good intentions of governments to encourage education and literacy, do not have enough resources to count on.

According to a UNESCO report from 2000,[10] half of the countries in the world produce a yearly average of less than one book per inhabitant. Of the rest, 30 percent produce between one and three books while 20 percent print four or more books per person. Around 60 percent of countries possess less than 50 textbooks per 1,000 inhabitants, while in 20 percent of countries there is an average of more than one textbook per inhabitant.[11]

A report from the Buenos Aires city government[12] shows that the publishing industry in Latin America is headed by Argentina, with 17.6 percent of the total production, followed by Mexico, 15.3 percent; Colombia, 11.9 percent; and Chile, 4.5 percent. Latin America produces 44.3 percent of books written in Spanish while Spain publishes 55.7 percent.[13] The survival of these industries depends on the impact of economic and social crisis in each country.

Mexico's publishing companies, for instance, were affected in the last decades by *el tequilazo* (the country's economic crisis of 1995), which resulted in the elimination of government subsidies. According to data from the *Cámara Nacional de la Industria Editorial Mexicana* (CANIEM), the organization that groups publishers in that country, the impact was such that of 423 publishing active companies in 1991, only 237 survived through 1999. In the 1991–2001 decade, the industry diminished from over 21,000 to over 15,000 titles published per year (Sánchez Ruiz 2003, p. 412).

In addition to photocopying and pirate editions, one of the major causes of the Mexican publishing industry's devastation is, ironically, the import of books from the United States. In 2000, 1,784 Spanish translations of English books were sold in Mexico. Another cause has been the change in technology, which left many companies unable to upgrade their printing equipment to the digital era.[14]

What This Book Is All About

This book aims to help library personnel recreate ideas, remove impediments, and improve their outreach services to Latinos regardless of language or cultural barriers, age, location, country of origin, gender, and any other characteristic that defines this group within the library's community. Understanding Latinos' behavior regarding library services and literacy issues in their countries of origin is essential when dealing with cultural barriers between Latinos and the library system.

Libraries that have crossed those barriers with diligent outreach strategies and a thorough comprehension of Latino culture have experienced an overwhelming response from members of this community, so I encourage you to do the same. Some of the difficulties libraries and their staff have encountered while interacting with Latinos are the following: (1) new immigrants do not use the library because they might be unaware of the services or, in the case of undocumented immigrants, because they might be concerned about confidentiality issues; (2) established immigrants might still be not aware of library services or, if they are, may use the library in a limited fashion; (3) highly educated Latinos might use the library more regularly but have other resources available, such as personal computers at home and work and the economic capability of buying books and other materials; and (4) these barriers and habits change according to the nationality of origin, level of education, time of residence in the United States, age, and socioeconomic status of Latino library patrons.

The purpose of this book is to present a plan template to help libraries come up with goals, strategies, and tactics to develop or improve outreach services to Latinos. The template can be used at any moment of the outreach process. Libraries around the country are at different stages of their outreach efforts to Latinos, so the template is flexible enough to incorporate programs that are already in place or start from the very beginning. Overall, the template—a series of worksheets and tables found at the end of each chapter—can be used at different times and for different types of efforts, from planning to internal training and from branding efforts to promotional mini-campaigns.

Also, with practice and time using these tools, you will find that the template's basic structure can be utilized with any group with language and cultural barriers in the library environment. The information you need to fill in will change, but the steps to follow are basically the same.

I chose the word *outreach* in the title because it has a not-for-profit connotation while *marketing* is used more for commercial purposes, but in the text both terms are used interchangeably. The book draws ideas from 17 years of marketing experience in additional fields, from corporate to nonprofit and government organizations, and from 8 years of training and consulting with public and school libraries around the country. Traditional and social marketing principles and techniques have been applied and adapted to the library outreach environment. Outreach from a marketing point of view might offer a fresh look based on market competition rather than the passive logistics traditional in library services. With whom do libraries compete? For one, libraries compete against the Internet, bookstore chains, and all sorts of mass media, including audio and video materials that have invaded the market.

However, in the case of the Latino community, libraries compete against established behaviors, limiting beliefs, and the lack of tradition in library services. For that reason, I used concepts and ideas from social marketing—a term first coined by Philip Kotler and Gerald Zaltman (1971) that became a discipline in the 1990s—to create a plan for advancing a social cause, idea, or behavior. In part, I have chosen this approach because social marketing is used to sell behavioral change (Kotler, Roberto, and Lee 2002), and a large part of your work with the Latino community entails changing their habits and views regarding library services.

A fundamental difference between commercial marketing and social marketing, although using the same principles, is based on the fact that commercial marketing pursues a financial gain versus an *individual or societal gain*. In addition, the concept of *competition* used by both approaches differs. Social marketers work with the predominance of a social problem, people's readiness for change, and the organization's ability to reach that audience.

Social marketing will help you address the Latino community's current behaviors—your real competition—in addition to competing with other organizations offering similar services or products (Kotler, Roberto, and Lee 2002).

In this work, I also use concepts from cultural marketing (Korzenny and Korzenny 2005) as a tool to target individuals whose behavior, habits, and beliefs differ from the overall dominant market. Latinos constitute a group significant enough to create population and paradigm shifts in the general market.

In writing this book for the library environment, I have relied on the experience and guidance of library experts who have led the way for many years. However, an important part of this book are the concerns, questions, and solutions I have exchanged with library personnel—front-liners as well as decision makers—in my face-to-face training experience, whose comments and suggestions have always been illuminating and insightful.

Although to many this book might look like it only addresses the needs of recent immigrants, their language and cultural barriers, their fear of information disclosure, and their general unawareness of library services, in truth many Latinos who have lived in the United States for a long time are still unfamiliar with library services or do not take complete advantage of those services. Others still believe libraries are for students and scholars or prefer to buy their reading materials.

Many still speak Spanish at home—although are bilingual in their workplace—and prefer to be addressed in that language. Marketing research shows that almost 62 percent of Latinos living in the United States have a fair to good command of the English language (Korzenny and Korzenny 2005). Most speak Spanish at home, but 84 percent agree that learning English is an advantage and a necessity if they want to stay and succeed in this country. Therefore, Latinos navigate among these bicultural trends. Creating trust and long-term credibility in your institution as the source of information they need will make them feel respected for their cultural differences and preferences and embraced as part of your community.

¡Hola, amigos! A Plan for Latino Outreach offers a step-by-step course of action to guide small- and medium-sized libraries in pursuing a deeper knowledge of their Latino target audiences, developing a solid knowledge of their organizational strengths and weaknesses, and planning and carrying out more effective, systematic outreach strategies to build long-lasting relationships with Latino patrons. Although larger organizations might find new ideas and strategies, they might also need professional support due to the complexity of their organizations and the amount of personnel they hire. Those systems usually cover large demographic areas, which are also complex to serve.

Chapter 1 of this book, "Changing the Outreach Outlook," presents ideas about reframing the present concept of outreach to a new perspective, thus placing emphasis on who needs library services the most. Libraries confront difficult challenges in serving Latinos and need increased support from their communities, their government officials, and the community itself to accomplish their goals. A good first step is to encourage your staff's participation in the plan ahead and discuss the benefits all parties involved receive by pursuing these steps.

Based on these ideas, chapter 2, "Your Organization's Vision," elaborates the role of your library's organizational chart. An explicit commitment to serving diverse populations made by some libraries around the country has led the way in bridging the informational gap. The basic concept of a plan for Latino outreach, and guidelines to discuss your organization's tools and procedures, are provided in this chapter.

Because this is a considerable responsibility to be undertaken by libraries alone, chapter 3, "Assessing Strategic Partnership Opportunities," discusses how to involve other organizations and businesses in your community that pursue similar purposes—serving or reaching out to the Latino population. Ideas for exchanging information, resources, and activities are also discussed in the context of collaborating with the community and promoting leadership.

The relevance of knowing your Latino audience cannot be emphasized enough, as it will define your services, strategies, and resources. Chapters 4 and 5, "Getting to Know Your Latino Patrons" part 1 and part 2, provide tools and procedures to research your Latino community both from a demographic and a psychosociocultural perspective (Korzenny and Korzenny 2005, p. 11). Additionally, ways to compare and interpret the data to your organization's advantage are provided.

Chapter 6, "Positioning Your Library and Its Resources," elaborates on the need to create a clear image of your organization, your programs, and your services in the minds of your Latino customers. Evaluating and preparing your internal and external resources is the first step to compel your Latino customers to act and use the programs and services your library offers. It will also build credibility in your organization and sustain your outreach efforts. You will need to do both when dealing with a community that, for a number of reasons, is unaware of or lacks tradition in using library services as offered in the United States.

Outreach activities discussed in chapter 7, "Planning and Implementing Your Outreach Activities," will help expand services in your area as well as increase awareness about your

Latino community. The goal of organizing and conducting outreach activities involves developing ideas to attract specific groups of Latinos according to their characteristics and needs, to continue generating interest, and to prioritize services.

As with any other business venture, a steady and loyal clientele requires persistent promotional efforts, without which all other hard work will go to waste. Chapter 8, "Promoting Your Library," addresses general promotional strategies for your library services, which in marketing equates to branding efforts, and specific promotional strategies, which equates to your sales efforts. This dual promotional attempt, which seems quite an accomplishment, is based on a social marketing approach encouraging behavioral change through enticing messages and effective promotional strategies.

Chapter 9, "Evaluating Results and Procedures," helps you assess the progress and growth of your organization over time as a vital part of your Latino Outreach Plan. The evaluation aims at your organization's internal and external results and examines outcomes as well as procedures to adjust your course of action and find solutions for any challenges or obstacles found.

Finally, chapter 10, "Your Plan for Latino Outreach," offers blank template versions of all worksheets and tables used in previous chapters and other worksheets that will help with the details of the task at hand. The formats are simple, but the complexity of your plan will be defined by the size of your target market, the availability of your resources, and the commitment of your organization to this plan for Latino outreach.

Notes

1. For a brief history of immigration laws in the United States, see Murray (2007).
2. Since 2000, legal immigrants to the United States comprise approximately 1,000,000 per year. Of these, 600,000 already lived in the United States but changed their immigration status. Legal immigrants are at their highest level since 1910. Undocumented immigrants arriving each year might number at least 700,000 (Pew Hispanic Center 2005).
3. The *Bracero* program (1942 through 1964) allowed more than 4.5 million Mexicans to obtain temporary agricultural work in the United States. See National Museum of American History, "Opportunity or Exploitation: The Bracero Program," http://americanhistory.si.edu/ONTHEMOVE/themes/story_51_5.html (accessed October 29, 2009).
4. *Dictionary of International Terms in Literary Criticism,* a cooperative project initiated by the International Comparative Literature Association (ICLA), http://www.flsh.unilim.fr/ditl/ACCULTURATION.htm (accessed October 29, 2009).
5. The use of the terms *Hispanic* and *Latino* continues to be a source of debate. Hispanic implies a direct connection to a Spanish heritage while Latino represents all people coming from different countries who speak romance languages.
6. "In parts of the United States with large Hispanic populations, an American of Polish, Irish, or German heritage might be termed an Anglo just as readily as a person of English descent as a catch-all term for non-Hispanic whites." *The American Heritage® Dictionary of the English Language,* 4th ed., s.v. "Anglo," http://dictionary.reference.com/browse/Anglo (accessed November 20, 2009).
7. International Federation of Library Associations and Institutions (IFLA), "Global Library Statistics 1990–2000," http://www.ifla.org/III/wsis/wsis-stats4pub_v.pdf, page 6 (accessed November 3rd, 2009). This document is a first attempt to provide a snapshot of the world's libraries.
8. Data from the Central American Seminar on the IFLA-UNESCO Manifestos for Public and School Libraries and Internet (San José, C.R., 2007) [Reports by the directors and coordinators of the college, public, and school libraries of Central America]. Universidad Nacional (UNA), Heredia, Costa Rica, cited in "Toward Information Literacy in Central America," a presentation by Alice Miranda-Argueda at the World Library and Information Congress: 73rd IFLA General Conference and

Council, August 19–23, 2007, Durban, South Africa. In addition, Miranda-Argueda stated that "IFLA has supported projects to foster the training of in-service personnel and the development of documentation and information services. IFLA was a pioneer in the region in organizing events, including the IFLA-UNESCO Manifesto (Costa Rica, 2007), Library Associations (El Salvador, 2002), Parliamentary Libraries (Costa Rica, 1996), and Public Libraries (Nicaragua, 1995). In addition, it has contributed to research projects on topics of interest for Central America, along with scholarships to fund participation in the Annual Conference of IFLA, etc. However, these isolated contributions which are not related to academia have a reduced scope. At the Central American Seminar on the IFLA-UNESCO Manifestos that was held this year in Costa Rica, the urgent need to create an educational and training program on Information Literacy was pointed out by participants." Miranda-Argueda is the former director of the School of Library Sciences, Documentation, and Information of Universidad Nacional (UNA) Costa Rica, periods 1990–1993 and 2001–2006, http://archive.ifla.org/IV/ifla73/papers/083-Miranda-Arguedas-trans-en.pdf (accessed July 27, 2010).

9. IFLA, "Global Library Statistics 1990–2000," September 2003, http://www.ifla.org/III/wsis/wsis-stats4pub_v.pdf (accessed November 3, 2009).

10. United Nations Educational, Scientific, and Cultural Organization (UNESCO), *Facts and Figures 2000*. Paris: UNESCO Institute for Statistics, 2000, p. 33.

11. Ibid.

12. Gobierno de la Ciudad de Buenos Aires, "Estadísticas de la Industria Editorial," http://www.buenosaires.gov.ar/areas/produccion/industrias/observatorio/estadisticaslibros.php (accessed November 3, 2009), an effort from the City of Buenos Aires government to maintain publishing industry statistics in Argentina.

13. Ibid.

14. Within this scenario, the government of President Fox announced in 2002 that the Mexican secretariat of public education would grant 500 million pesos (approximately US$50 million at the time) to the literacy program *Hacia un país de lectores,* which was seen as a political joke by many members of the Mexican academic and intellectual community.

Chapter 1

Changing the Outreach Outlook

Overview

In the Introduction of *From Outreach to Equity,* Satia Marshall Orange and Robin Osborne (2004, p. xi) dive into the core of the outreach issue: "Historically, our solution to addressing the information needs of the 'under-' or 'un-served' populations is through library outreach services. . . . These outreach services often take place off-site; are often dependent on special funding; are often administered by special staff. It is time for new ideas and language to help us reach our goal."

The problem, in part, is in dichotomous thinking, as manifested in the library administrator's language: "regular" users versus "unserved" or "underserved" populations; "regular" library services versus "outreach" services; "annual budget" versus "soft money." Developing outreach for the diverse populations currently living in the United States is not an easy task, and only a change in the way libraries see these efforts will ensure realistic results. Moreover, the traditional logistics of library services—clients coming to libraries—is changing as well. Outreach thus becomes a priority to ensure continuity of library services.

With changing demographics and the global movement of population masses, libraries in the United States have been called once again to duty. As in the past, libraries are instrumental in easing the acculturation of immigrants looking to improve their lives and those of their children. However, in the present, the challenges libraries confront are monumental. Not only has the Latino population grown rapidly in the last few decades, but has also changed demographically and geographically because of economic and political factors such as employment opportunities and immigration-friendly states. Latinos represent a different type of immigration—one that is here to stay but under its own circumstances, with changing needs and wants of its constituents. In addition, language and cultural barriers represent obstacles in the interaction between library personnel and Latinos. For these reasons, libraries need to take on a different role in their communities. This chapter shows that, although outreach is often seen as a requirement, it really presents a powerful *opportunity* for libraries to get involved in their communities, expand their staff's personal and professional horizons, and reap the benefits of increased funding and activity.

The Complex Environment of Outreach

When referring to library services, the concept of outreach needs to be reframed so that it is based upon equity rather than disparity. In other words, the question you need to ask is "Who *needs* library services the most?" rather than "Who *uses* library services the most?" Only when this change is made, will libraries be ready to provide equal access and deliver equal service because services will not be determined by logistics or materials but by prioritizing the way library services reach their audience.

Marshall Orange and Osborne cite a very comprehensive definition of outreach as "a program of library services designed to identify, contact, and serve persons who are educationally disadvantaged; members of ethnic or minority groups in need of special library services; unemployed and in need of job placement assistance; living in areas underserved by a library; or blind, physically handicapped, aged or confined in institutions."[1]

Outreach in such a complex environment must be broken down further to accommodate the different needs of, for instance, individuals who are educationally disadvantaged and for whom English is a second language, such as Latinos. Members of the Latino community, like their English-speaking counterparts, might also be unemployed and in need of job placement, might live in areas underserved by a library, might be confined in institutions, might be elderly or physically handicapped, or might otherwise have special needs. The point is that Latinos at large have the same problems, needs, and expectations as the general population.

However, the reasons Latinos and other foreign-born minority patrons do not use libraries like English-speaking patrons do might be different. The big dividers we need to address are the language and cultural barriers that prevent Latinos from using libraries to the same extent as other members of the community.

Latino Outreach . . . What For?

Why do we want to serve these underserved populations? How do we want to serve them? When I ask these questions in training sessions, answers come unclearly and tentatively. Most library employees know they want to do it—after all, they are attending the workshop—but for many, their outreach goals are not yet clear.

Consider an analogy from another context. Mexican food has become a regular part of almost any restaurant menu that serves American traditional, contemporary, or gourmet food. A large part of the American public has incorporated spicy Mexican-inspired food into their dietary preferences. Yet when it comes to books and services in libraries, it is difficult to incorporate Latino interests as a regular service. It seems that we need to have a separate dining room for our Latino patrons—a separate menu—and we cannot figure out a way to feed them every day!

"When viewed as a tag for those who are not regular [users], outreach sets up a model of 'otherness' that seems to diminish the value of the services and the individuals associated with them. Outreach is often defined by group difference without recognizing the similarity of ongoing needs of that group" (Marshall Orange and Osborne 2004, p. xiii).

How do we deal with this paradox of providing a service to a targeted group without engendering a sense of otherness? It is important to recognize the critical role of outreach as building a bridge to provide Latinos with the opportunity to become a well-integrated part of this society, its language, and its culture. This instrumental role will tend to eliminate the minority stigma that Latinos—and other groups—carry. In this effort, libraries must be well equipped, well informed, and culturally competent to deliver equity of access.

Worthwhile efforts *are* being made, and they should be continued and expanded. Hispanic Heritage Month, for instance, is a valuable time of year during which many libraries celebrate special cultural achievements and the values of a diverse community that is part of our society. However, Hispanic Heritage Month programs would be even more meaningful if done in the context of a year-round activity that celebrates and integrates that culture into our system and provides the necessary information and opportunities to welcome Latinos into the benefits and responsibilities of this society.

From Outreach Advocates to Outreach Professionals

The weight of such a task cannot be carried or even supported by library staff's individual advocacy. Any one person can serve as an advocate for any number of issues, and the importance and benefit of individual efforts should not be underestimated. Advocacy can consist of a simple statement or a costly advertising campaign, a well-strategized chain of telephone calls or word-of-mouth dissemination. However, in the library environment, advocacy that is solely left to employees' good will and personal choice lacks real weight in achieving results and merely loses continuity. Moreover, even the enthusiastic energy of library personnel can crash against an often-repeated complaint: "Managers and supervisors welcome our ideas but give us no time or funding to carry them out."

Outreach then becomes the odd job nobody wants—not only because outreach serves the special needs of certain populations, but also because it creates the inequality it tries to address when segregated from regular library services.

However, when library personnel, directors, board members, and administrators look at their libraries as their own small businesses, transforming profit pressure into service pressure with all the advantages and responsibilities of a nonprofit, government organization, professionalizing outreach becomes a must—or, at least, a strategic goal to be prioritized.

Outreach then turns into an effective tool to serve those who need library services the most, and the traditional passive logistics of library services change into a dynamic marketing strategy aimed at reaching outside the library walls and into the real world. Professionalizing outreach strategies serves the purpose of increasing services and funding for all, and "sameness and difference are no longer seen as mutually exclusive but rather complementary" (Marshall Orange and Osborne 2004, p. xiv).

Professionalizing outreach also allows individuals to make career choices enabling them to become leaders in their communities with the certainty of a job professionally done. Some colleges and universities around the country offer coursework on outreach in their library science plans of studies. Support and recognition of career choices are fundamental in motivating employees to pursue their personal and professional interests while working in any environment, and libraries should not be any different.

From Center of Information to Community Builder

In this era of information, libraries are uniquely positioned to look for, gather, and deliver information. Traditionally, libraries have provided a wealth of information to the communities they served, with relatively simple logistics. No massive advertising campaigns, no heavy pressure on the final consumer, and, generally speaking, no celebrities offering their products.

Times are changing, demographics are changing, and the way we conduct business in many aspects of our lives is changing, too. Schools, for instance, have had to adapt to changing and challenging environments when they were hit with new Latino immigration waves. Their goals might be different, but the effort of thinking outside the box and finding new strategies to achieve their goals is the same. Schools had to engage in the bilingual-education controversy, define their own goals, develop curricula to include non-English-speaking students coming in at any age and any level, and still manage to achieve official standards.

Libraries are positioned to assume a central role in supporting social change necessary to generate collective power for the powerless and the underserved. Because of their service responsibility and the amount of information libraries carry, they are instrumental in ensuring—together with other organizations in their community—that "new Americans" will go through the acculturation process in the best, smoothest way possible. Library leadership in the community is also a way to ensure the future of one of our most valuable institutions.

RAISON D'ÊTRE FOR MULTICULTURAL LIBRARY SERVICES

The International Federation of Library Associations and Institutions (IFLA), the leading international body representing the interests of library and information services and their users, developed the following reasons to support the right of every individual in our global society to access a full range of library and information services. IFLA also promotes international cooperation to share "experience in library services to multicultural populations in view of the necessity to ensure that every member in our global society has access to a full range of library and information services."[2]

Section on Library Services to Multicultural Populations[3]

Ten Reasons for Multicultural Library Services

1. A library's mission is to serve its community, which in many cases is multicultural and multilingual, or becoming increasingly culturally diverse.
2. Multicultural and multilingual library services ensure equality of service and access to information.
3. In an era of globalization with more ease in trans-border communication and travel, individuals need to learn about other cultures, languages, and peoples, which fosters appreciation for different experiences and broadens people's outlook on life.
4. Information that is provided in languages and through accessible channels to diverse communities enables their democratic participation in civil society.

(continued)

What Latinos Can Do for Libraries

Demographic changes act as cultural and economic *jalapeños*—they spice everything up! An increasing immigration influx creates social and cultural paradigm changes due to the immigrants' need to rebuild a new identity that will fit in the receiving social structure.

Empowered Latinos bring an added value to your organization: a loyal customer base that will advocate for the library internally and externally. Lately, Latinos are becoming actively involved in politics. According to the National Association of Latino Elected and Appointed Officials (NALEO),[4] there has been an increase in Latinos serving in elected office—from 3,743 in 1996 to 5,129 in

2007. In the highest levels of office, the growth is over 50 percent. Between 1996 and 2007, the number of elected Latinas increased by 74 percent. Latino elected officials are serving in nine nontraditional Latino states—Alaska, Georgia, Kentucky, New Hampshire, Missouri, North Dakota, Oklahoma, South Carolina, and Virginia. This means libraries have the opportunity to cultivate a support base, build a customer base for the future, and politically support their own livelihood.

As per Carla D. Hayden, ALA President, 2003–2004, "By finally embracing equity of access we will be affirming our core values, recognizing realities and *assuring our future*" (Marshall Orange and Osborne 2004, p. xi [emphasis added]).

> *(continued)*
>
> 5. Information provided in languages and through channels appropriate to diverse user communities also promotes multiple types of literacy, which facilitates the acquisition of new knowledge and skills to ensure equality of opportunity in all realms of civil society.
> 6. Information on one's own heritage as well as others' reinforces one's own culture and promotes understanding of other experiences and perspectives respectively, and contributes in the development of a more harmonious society.
> 7. The world's knowledge, creative forms of expression, and cultural practices are documented in diverse formats and languages, thus the offering of a multicultural collection should be made available for all to access.
> 8. The learning of different forms of creative expression, work, and problem-solving leads to fresh insights and opinions which can result in novel ways in which to innovate, act, and solve problems.
> 9. Providing information about and for a library's multicultural community demonstrates that community members and their cultures are valued.
> 10. Libraries are spaces for intellectual and recreational engagement, and libraries offering multicultural and multilingual services and collections become community spaces that bring people together.

Reasons to Market Library Services to Latinos

At this point in history, new immigration legislation is being debated, a wall dividing Mexico and the United States is being built, borders are being guarded by disturbed citizens such as the Minuteman Project,[6] and U.S. Immigration and Customs Enforcement (ICE) is doing its job diligently. Therefore, some library directors and other personnel may be hesitant to cater to the Latino population.

Except for some regions in the United States that have had Latinos for

> In 2007 and 2008, I conducted several training sessions in California, Pennsylvania, and Florida. During those sessions, I informally surveyed[5] 342 library employees about how libraries benefited from reaching out to Latinos. The following answers were mentioned:
>
> - Makes the institution relevant in the community
> - Empowers Latinos and provides leadership opportunities
> - Strengthens the foundation of democracy
> - Reinforces libraries' service role
> - Increases circulation and funding
> - Forces institutions to upgrade logistics
> - Presents new challenges to developing business
> - Creates new advocates for library services
> - Assures the future of libraries

a long time, many Americans became aware of the reality of the numbers with the 2000 U.S. Census. Although Latinos have lived in the United States for many generations, they are now frequently being asked to justify their presence in the United States more than any other immigrants in order to receive government services.

In their work *Serving Latino Communities,* Alire and Ayala (2007) offered an excellent case for including Latinos in the library environment with abundant statistics and demographics, a strong sense of the social and political implications, and a lot of common sense. As information professionals, they said that libraries should look at demographic changes and the impact of those changes in planning activities and services so that Latinos, as any other group in the community, have equal access to information.

Latinos are culturally diverse; younger than the general population; poorer than other minorities (but with a burgeoning middle-class sector); and, despite the fact that they do not achieve high levels of education (around 12% nationwide have completed a four-year degree), over 80 percent of this population is somewhat bilingual.

The main reason libraries should market their services to Latinos is simply because they are a substantial part of the community. However, there are many grounds that make it imperative, even urgent, to increase efforts toward this goal. Those in the community at large or the library community who disagree with the idea of marketing library services to the Latino community tend to do so based on the following ideas:

1. **Myth:** Libraries should not offer service to Latinos in the United States because most of them are undocumented or living illegally in this country.
   Fact: Less than one-quarter of the Latino population in the United States is undocumented.
   - Latinos represent an average of 16 percent of the U.S. population—almost 48.4 million, according to 2009 U.S. Census estimates.[7]
   - Estimates indicate that the number of undocumented Latino immigrants living in the United States declined from 2007 to 2009 to 11.1 million (approximately 22.9%).[8]
   - Moreover, of the approximately 1,000,000 legal Latino immigrants added to the United States each year, 600,000 already live in the United States but change their immigration status (Passel 2005).
   - These statistics show the eagerness of this community to become an established part of our society. Many libraries are extending their services to Latino populations; however, the funding and commitment to continuous service to attract this population still has a long way to go.

2. **Myth:** Undocumented Latinos do not pay taxes.
   Fact: Documented *and* undocumented Latinos represent a powerful economic driving force at a national level who pay federal, state, and local taxes and push forward regional and states economies.

Major American corporations began to turn their attention to the Latino market in 2000, when the group's buying power was estimated at $500 billion per year. According to the Selig Center for Economic Growth, the estimated buying power of Latinos in 2007 was $863.1 billion, an increase of over 8 percent from 2006, concentrated geographically. This buying power translates to sales taxes paid at rates ranging between 7.25 percent in

California (where 27% of the population is Hispanic or Latino) to 2.9 percent in Colorado (where 19.5% of the population is Hispanic or Latino).[9]

For instance, in Colorado, the Bell Policy Center, in its report *State and Local Taxes Paid in Colorado by Undocumented Immigrants,* estimated that in 2005, between $159 million and $194 million (including state and local sales, income, and property taxes) was paid by undocumented immigrant households; this number represents between 70 and 86 percent of Colorado's state and local government costs for the provision of federally mandated services provided to this population.[10]

In North Carolina,[11] Latinos paid $756 million in taxes in 2006 and spent $817 million in state expenses. Despite a burden of $102 per head, the positive economic impact of Latino spending in North Carolina was estimated at $9.19 billion in 2004, which attests to nearly 90,000 new jobs, a study at the Kenan-Flagler Business School found (Kasarda and Johnson 2007, pp. i–ii).

Not every state has this sort of report, but national studies indicate the level at which undocumented immigrants pay taxes and create economic growth in the United States. The White House's Council of Economic Advisers stated in its "Immigration's Economic Impact" report key findings that "on average, U.S. natives benefit from immigration. Immigrants tend to complement (not substitute for) natives, raising natives' productivity and income." It also reports, "careful studies of the long-run fiscal effects of immigration conclude that it is likely to have a modest, positive influence."[12]

The same report advises that immigrants also contribute to the solvency of programs such as Social Security and Medicare in the long-term.[13] Moreover, in the 2008 annual report on Social Security released by the Federal Government in March of that year, the program's trustees noted that undocumented workers are expected to augment the program throughout the upcoming decades because of two reasons: first, they pay taxes during their work lives but do not collect benefits later; second, undocumented workers are entering the United States at ever younger ages and are expected to have more children. This will result in "a substantial increase in the number of working-age people paying taxes, but a relatively smaller increase in the number of retirees who receive benefits—a double boon to Social Security's bottom line," according to a 2008 article in the *New York Times* ("How Immigrants Saved Social Security" 2008).

Another way to look at the fiscal issue is to learn about property taxes and the effect of Latino homeownership. Although still lagging behind the national average of 69.1 percent, Latino homeownership has increased to 49.7 percent in the last 10 years, according to the Congressional Hispanic Caucus Institute.[14] This rate means this portion of the Latino population pays property taxes directly, while others pay it indirectly through renting properties.

As indicated by the aforementioned Selig Center study, 6.8 percent of 22.9 million businesses in the United States are owned by Latinos, which represents a 31 percent increase between 1997 and 2002—triple the national growth rate of 10 percent for all businesses in the United States during that period. This increase means that 1.5 million Latino business owners pay business and sales taxes, creating dynamic regional economies. And state and local taxes are the main funding source for many, if not most, U.S. public libraries.

3. **Myth:** Materials and services need to be offered in Spanish because Latinos do not want to learn English.

   Fact: According to a 2006 Pew Hispanic Center report (January 2008),[15] 36.3 percent of native-born Hispanics speak only English at home, 50.4 percent speak English very well, and 13.4 percent speak English less than very well.

The National Association for Bilingual Education, through the Bilingual Education Act,[16] reports that studies consistently show that higher levels of academic achievement are attained when English-language learners develop their native-language skills, increasing their opportunities for bilingualism and bi-literacy—important skills in today's global economy.

Likewise, bilingual education expert Kenji Hakuta of Stanford University[17] asserts that bilingual instruction's most fundamental hypothesis is that skills and knowledge learned in the native language transfer to English. Therefore, knowledge learned in Spanish transfers to English without requiring relearning concepts. In fact, research supports that previous knowledge in a student's first language greatly facilitates literacy skills in the second language,[18] which means that efforts to increase Spanish literacy will support the easier acquisition of a second language in children and adults.

4. Myth: Other waves of immigrants assimilated faster than Latinos.
   Fact: While most European immigrants assimilated over a long period—almost 100 years—in only the last 20 years, the influx of 27 million immigrants from countries in Asia, Latin America, the Caribbean, and Africa has created an extraordinary change in cultural and language paradigms.

Certainly, the increasing demand for ESL (English as a Second Language) classes and survival-skills instruction presented by the new waves of immigrants in the 1980s and 1990s represents a challenge because of the large numbers of newcomers and the language and cultural barriers implied.[19]

In "The Role of Libraries in Providing Services to Adults in Learning English," Shelley Quezada (1991) speaks about the important role libraries have historically played in the United States in literacy education. Some libraries, she says, first provided ESL and adult literacy classes for European immigrants coming into the United States at the beginning of the 20th century. Since then, main library tasks in serving immigrants have been literacy support, ESL instruction, and citizenship education.

Presently, however, trying to educate such a large immigrant population with low literacy levels and little understanding of library services requires a continuous activity that imposes a heavy weight on library employees' workloads. In addition, even if the government would fully fund this effort according to the population in need, there would still not be enough trained teachers and educators, locations, and materials to absorb such fast population growth.

5. Myth: Latinos will never become part of the United States' social fabric as other immigrants did.
   Fact: The acculturation process of Latinos in the United States not only is becoming a strong social component but is also influencing many aspects of this society, at different levels and degrees—what has been called the Latinization of the United States.[20]

It is common knowledge that, historically, America has been a land of immigration. From 1820 to 1860, immigrant influx came mainly from Great Britain, Ireland, and Western Germany. Until 1890, these countries, along with the Scandinavian nations, continued to provide immigrants. However, from 1890 to 1910 (until World War I) the majority of new immigrants came from Austria, Hungary, Italy, and Russia. According to demographer Audrey Singer,[21] from 1900 to 1930, the foreign-born population increased steadily, then declined during the U.S. depression years.

Immigration restrictions during World War II diminished levels of European immigration for the next 40 years until the Immigration and Nationality Act of 1965 opened up immigration from other regions, causing a boom in the 1980s and 1990s. The foreign-born population more than doubled during those decades—rising from 14.1 million to 31.1 million—due to immigration from countries in Asia, Latin America, the Caribbean, and Africa.

Due to such growth, immigrants need to adjust to a new reality while the hosting population becomes rapidly diversified. This process of give-and-take, of mutual adjustment and knowledge, is often altered by the fear of the unknown, the concern among all populations (both the hosting population and the newcomers) that cultural identities will be lost or transformed.

According to a 2007 report of the Pew Hispanic Center (Waldinger 2007), most Latino immigrants reveal moderate levels of connection with their home country—reflected in their degree of transnational activities, such as traveling back home, and their cultural behaviors. The report concludes that they maintain some connections to their country of origin by sending money or calling their families frequently. Latinos have a positive view of life and political traditions in the United States and hold a less favorable assessment of other aspects, such as morals, the report said.

Latino immigrants who have been in the United States for decades are less connected than recent immigrants. This type of connection is also related to their origin. Colombians and Dominicans are more actively involved than Mexicans, and Cubans have the least contact. Those who have been in the United States longer are more ready than newcomers to declare this country their homeland and to describe themselves as Americans (Waldinger 2007).

6. **Myth:** Latinos are not interested in education.
   Fact: Latinos encounter a broad range of difficulties when trying to pursue their education in the United States. Despite efforts of immersing Spanish-speaking Latino children in English classes—or perhaps because of those efforts—Latinos still lag in educational achievements compared to the general population and other minority groups.

In addition to language barriers, Latino adults and young adults often find it difficult to continue their education because of financial limitations. If teens and young adults living at home (especially between 16 and 25 years of age)[22] do not work to contribute to the household income, it creates economic hardship in the family; therefore, work may interfere with or even take precedence over school.[23]

Spanish-speaking students and their parents often struggle with the school or college application process and its financial opportunities—unavailable to them if they are undocumented, even if they receive their high school diploma—or the revalidation of studies performed in their countries of origin. Most foreign degrees are not considered equivalent to those of American colleges and universities and are usually assessed by independent evaluators. For instance, a six-year professional degree in an area of expertise, common in many Latin American universities, might be evaluated as equivalent to a bachelor's degree in the United States.[24]

Professional and entrepreneurial immigrants might have some advantages over their counterpart immigrant workers, such as higher educational degrees or business experience in their countries of origin, but only if they master the English language. Even so, they encounter difficulties in finding a job, pursuing a career, or starting a new business.[25]

When 342 library employees were asked how Latinos benefit from libraries services, they responded that Latinos gained the following benefits:

- Increased educational opportunities
- Increased employment opportunities
- Access to vital information for survival
- Access to free recreational materials
- More assimilation/acculturation opportunities
- Additional socialization opportunities
- Social, political, and economic empowerment
- A greater sense of belonging

Aside from English-language issues, some segments of the Latino population also show low literacy levels in their native language. When I arrived in the United States in 1990, I thought to myself, *"El que no sabe leer y escribir en este país va muerto"* (Whoever is illiterate in this country is dead meat).[26] I perceived a society based on the power of literacy and the written language—although illiteracy levels are still considered high in the United States.[27]

Low literacy levels are extensive in some Latin American countries. A number of immigrants come from countries where literacy is a luxury or from areas where large indigenous populations speak native languages, many of which do not have a written format.[28]

According to a Central Intelligence Agency report (1999), although educational efforts have improved recently in Latin America (the population of students there rose 30% between 1980 and 1992[29]), other segments of the population, such as adult learners from indigenous populations and the poor in general, still find themselves excluded from educational opportunities (Seda-Santana 2000).

While Americans are accustomed to a highly functional literate society based on written communication in almost every aspect of life, many Latinos come from low-functional societies based on verbal/oral communication and solidarity networks. In addition to poverty and meager opportunities, additional causes for illiteracy, such as learning disabilities, may go unnoticed because of improper, late, or nonexistent procedures for diagnoses.

U.S. public libraries are instrumental in leading adults into literacy and, consequently, helping their children become avid readers (Alire and Archibeque 1998, p. 36), so it is to the library's advantage to offer services geared to the Latino population. In addition, bilingual programs in which children and parents can teach each other both languages—English and Spanish—provide great support to Latino children's development while encouraging their parents to learn a second language.

Moreover, migrating to another country and into a different culture entails a great degree of isolation and solitude, especially at the beginning until some degree of acculturation is achieved. Latinos and other immigrant groups tend to get established in geographic clusters, where others from their same place of origin have been residing for some time and might help them cross that gap.

Socially, the primary activities shared by Latinos and their families are church services and family gatherings. A great goal for public libraries is to become a third friendly option where individuals and families will find a place of recreation, social encounter, and identification with the new culture—a place where they belong.

Personal and Professional Benefits for Your Staff

In addition to providing benefits for your customers, you must find personal and professional benefits in this task—benefits that will keep you going in times of difficulty and give you something to look forward to in the future. In addition to the benefits your organization perceives in funding, staff development, and cultural and professional expansion and opportunities we already mentioned, personal benefits might include individual preferences and interests, experiences, and/or your own ethnic background. For example, you may be interested in the culture and language of Latin America; may have traveled to Latin American countries or studied them in previous years; you or your family may be from Latin America; you may be related to or acquainted with people of Latino origin; or you may just have a personal or professional inclination toward this culture.

> When 342 library employees were asked what they saw as the personal and professional benefits of reaching out to Latinos, they answered that they found opportunities for the following:
>
> - For advocacy
> - To professionalize and systematize outreach activities
> - To build a diverse workforce
> - For personal growth and expansion of one's own horizons
> - To challenge one's own comfort zone
> - To develop career choices and personal choices
> - To gain recognition for a job well done
> - For accountability and "service pressure"
> - To contribute to the future of our libraries and our means of employment!

Overall, as with the other challenges you have faced in your library career, you need to put passion and dedication into this effort, becoming an expert at what you do. Only then will you be totally committed to yourself, your organization, and the Latino community you serve.

I have summarized these ideas discussed by your colleagues in Worksheet 1.1. In chapter 10, please find a blank version you can complete with questions to help you and your organization discuss and discover the current and potential benefits a plan for Latino outreach brings to all members of your local community. This worksheet will help you clarify and reflect on the benefits of marketing library services to your Latino community. Think of the benefits this effort brings not only to your local Latino community, to your organization, and to you personally, but also to your local community at large according to the ideas developed in this chapter. Be specific, and try to bring details from your local situation. You will find this worksheet and memory joggers in chapter 10 to be the first step toward your Plan for Latino Outreach.

The ideas conveyed in this chapter revolve around the need to exchange the traditional otherness approach of outreach in the library environment for a new concept of integration. In other words, when a library develops an overall plan for marketing the resources it offers to the public, the ways in which it markets to Latinos—or to any other population faced with language and cultural barriers—will come all the more naturally to the table because the tools and procedures will be in place. The next chapters provide the tools and procedures necessary to help you achieve these goals and benefits.

Notes

1. Marshall Orange and Osborne (2004, p. xii), citing "Libraries, Library Systems, Trustees, and Librarians: Title 8, Section 5, L" of the New York State Law and Regulations of the Commissioner of Education.

2. IFLA, "Library Services to Multicultural Populations Section," September 29, 2009, http://www.ifla.org/en/about-the-library-services-to-multicultural-populations-section (accessed October 4, 2009).

3. IFLA, "Raison d'être for Multicultural Library Services," September 29, 2009, http://archive.ifla.org/VII/s32/pub/s32Raison.pdf (accessed October 4, 2009).

4. National Association of Latino Elected and Appointed Officials (NALEO), http://www.naleo.org/directory.html (accessed November 2, 2009), a nonpartisan leadership organization representing more than 6,000 Latino elected and appointed officials.

5. The questions appearing in side boxes in this chapter were asked at training sessions. The survey was informal and was never published.

6. Jim Gilchrist is the founder of the Minuteman Project, a citizen border-patrol group that tries to prevent undocumented immigrants from crossing the Mexican border. James Gilchrist, "Minuteman Project," http://www.minutemanproject.com/ (accessed October 4, 2009).

7. U.S. Census Bureau, "Population Estimates: National—Characteristics," http://www.census.gov/popest/national/asrh/NC-EST2009-srh.html and "Facts for Features" CB10-FF.17, July 15, 2010, http://www.census.gov/newsroom/releases/archives/facts_for_features_special_editions/cb10-ff17.html (accessed September 13, 2010).

8. Lately, the Pew Hispanic Center reported as almost two-thirds smaller the amount of undocumented immigrants coming to the United States. Pew Hispanic Center, "U.S. Unauthorized Immigration Flows Are Down Sharply Since Mid-Decade" September 1, 2010, http://pewhispanic.org/reports/report.php?ReportID=126 (accessed September 13, 2010).

9. U.S. Census Bureau, "State and County Quick Facts: State of Colorado," http://quickfacts.census.gov/qfd/states/08000.html (accessed November 4, 2009).

10. Robin Baker and Rich Jones, "State and Local Taxes Paid in Colorado by Undocumented Immigrants," The Bell Policy Center, June 30, 2006, p. 1, http://www.thebell.org/PUBS/IssBrf/2006/06ImmigTaxes.pdf (accessed October 4, 2009).

11. "Of Meat, Mexicans, and Social Mobility," *The Economist*, June 15, 2006, http://www.economist.com/displaystory.cfm?story_id=7063472 (accessed November 4, 2009).

12. "Immigration's Economic Impact," The White House's Council of Economic Advisers, June 20, 2007, p. 1, http://www.scribd.com/doc/341987/02023cea-immigration-062007 (accessed October 29, 2009).

13. Ibid., p. 2.

14. Congressional Hispanic Caucus Institute, "Bridging the Latino Homeownership Divide: Congressional Hispanic Caucus Institute Expands National Housing Initiative," 2006, http://www.chci.org/news/pub/bridging-the-latino-homeownership-divide-congressional-hispanic-caucus-institute-expands-national-housing-initiative (accessed November 4, 2009).

15. Pew Hispanic Center, "Table 19: Language Spoken at Home and English-Speaking Ability by Age, Race, and Ethnicity 2006," in "Statistical Portrait of Hispanics in the United States, 2006," 2006, http://pewhispanic.org/files/factsheets/hispanics2006/Table-19.pdf (accessed November 4, 2009).

16. *Improving America's Schools Act of 1994*, "Title VII—Bilingual Education, Language Enhancement, and Language Acquisition Programs," Public Law 103–382, 1994, http://www.nabe.org/files/TitleVII1994.pdf (accessed November 5, 2009). The Bilingual Education Act was repealed and replaced by the No Child Left Behind Act (http://www.nabe.org/advocacy.html) in 2001 (accessed November 5, 2009).

17. Kenji Hakuta, professor of Education at Stanford University and director of its doctoral training program in bilingual education, received his training under Roger Brown and Jill de Villiers at Harvard University, where he received his PhD in Experimental Psychology. Hakuta is the author of works on Japanese, Spanish, and English and has written extensively on different aspects of bilingualism.

18. C. Goldenberg, "Teaching English Language Learners: What the Research Does—and Does Not—Say," *American Educator* 32, no. 2, pp. 10–11, http://www.aft.org/pdfs/americaneducator/summer2008/goldenberg.pdf (accessed November 5, 2009).

19. In *Serving New Immigrant Communities in the Library,* Sondra Cuban alleged, "Immigration, now dominated by populations from non-European countries . . . brings up many language learning and education issues" (Cuban 2007, pp. 15–18).

20. *Latinization* of America is a term used in several media referring to the rapid growth of the Latino population and its influence on the American landscape regarding racial and ethnic mix, language influence, political trends, and economic power.

21. Singer is an expert on international migration and an immigration fellow at the Brookings Institution Metropolitan Policy Program, http://www.brookings.edu/experts/s/singera.aspx (accessed November 5, 2009).

22. "Working age Latino immigrants tend to be mature adults; about 1-in-10 is between the ages of 16 and 24. By contrast, 4-in-10 working age second generation Latinos are between the critical ages of 16 and 24, reflecting the native-born youth boom." Pew Hispanic Center, "Work or Study: Different Fortunes of U.S. Latino Generations," May 29, 2002, http://pewhispanic.org/files/reports/9.pdf (accessed November 5, 2009).

23. "Nearly three-quarters (74%) of all 16- to 25-year-old survey respondents [to this study] who cut their education short during or right after high school say they did so because they had to support their family." Pew Hispanic Center, "Latinos and Education: Explaining the Attainment Gap," October 7, 2009, http://pewhispanic.org/reports/report.php?ReportID=115 (accessed November 5, 2009).

24. There is no single authority in the United States for the recognition of foreign degrees and other qualifications, depending on the criteria of the admitting school or college, prospective employer, or state licensing boards, according to the U.S. Department of Education, "Recognition of Foreign Qualifications," http://www.ed.gov/about/offices/list/ous/international/usnei/us/edlite-visitus-forrecog.html (accessed November 5, 2009).

25. A mastery of the English language is essential at that level of education. I personally met immigrants from Peru and Mexico who, despite their professional degrees in, respectively, business administration and biochemist engineering, were holding house-painting jobs with a local contractor in New Jersey. Their poor English prevented them from working in their fields of expertise, and they had not found opportunities to acquire the language at a professional level in a short period.

26. Translation is approximate. "Dead meat" was an expression I learned a few years after I arrived in the United States. The expression *"ir muerto"* is very common in Argentina to express that someone has no chance of doing or getting something.

27. Around 20 percent of the population is believed to be functionally illiterate in the United States, National Institute for Literacy, Almanac of Policy Issues (Undated, added August, 2003) http://www.policyalmanac.org/education/archive/literacy.shtml (accessed November 5, 2009).

28. Latin America and the Caribbean's literacy levels relatively good performance—measured by conventional methods—masks huge disparities within and between nations. Countries like Argentina, Trinidad and Tobago, Bahamas, Cuba, and Uruguay have illiteracy rates of less than 5 percent but 13 percent of Brazilians and almost a third of Guatemalan adults cannot read or write. UNESCO, "Literacy in Latin America and the Caribbean," http://portal.unesco.org/education/en/ev.php-URL_ID=8519&URL_DO=DO_TOPIC&URL_SECTION=201.html (accessed November 5, 2009).

29. Central Intelligence Agency, "The World Factbook," https://www.cia.gov/library/publications/the-world-factbook/ (accessed July 7, 2005).

WORKSHEET 1.1   Benefits and Challenges of Latino Outreach

Goal: To develop awareness among staff regarding the benefits and challenges of providing services to Latinos.

A. Make a list of benefits to your organization, to the Latino community, and to your staff:

YOUR ORGANIZATION

Makes the institution relevant in the community

Reinforces libraries' service role

Increases circulation and funding

Forces institutions to upgrade logistics

Presents new challenges to developing business

Empowers Latinos and provides them with leadership opportunities

Strengthens the foundation of democracy

Creates new advocates for library services

Assures the future of libraries!

YOUR LATINO COMMUNITY

Increases their educational opportunities

Increases their employment opportunities

Provides access to information vital for survival

Provides access to free recreational materials

Offers acculturation opportunities

Expands their socialization opportunities

Empowers their social, political, and economic development

Presents them with an opportunity to "belong"

STAFF/YOU

Creates opportunities for advocacy

Professionalizes and systematizes outreach activities

Strengthens diversity in the workforce

Increases professional and personal growth and expands horizons

Challenges staff's own comfort zone

Develops career choices and personal choices

Provides recognition for a job well done

Outlines accountability and "service pressure"

Contributes to our libraries' future and our means of employment!

B. Choose two benefits to the library, to the Latino community, and to staff/you that particularly interested you! Describe briefly why those interested you.

C. Now think of a list of challenges. Develop a "contrast list." A contrast list reflects your ideas of how challenges can be solved.

CHALLENGE:	SOLUTION:
Community members' complaints to our area	*Look at benefits that local Latinos bring*
Some resistance from staff	*Increase diversity training opportunities*

See chapter 10 for worksheets as reproducible pages for training purposes.

Chapter 2

Your Organization's Vision

Overview

In making a passionate case for the role of library directors, Dinah Smith O'Brien, from the Plymouth Public Library, Massachusetts, encouraged library leaders to become involved in the needs of the community their library serves and aware of how that community perceives their institution. "Reach out to your staff with the training they need to do good community outreach, and reach out to your community with good library services. . . . If you talk the talk of a library leader, you must also walk the walk. Outreach begins at the top. Outreach begins with you" (Smith O'Brien 2004).

In my experience, those institutions whose management makes a true commitment to serving Latinos are the ones that stand out. No matter how dedicated library staff might be, if there is no support from the institution in the form of policies, funding, and strategies to facilitate their actions, their efforts will likely have a minimal outreach impact.

However, strong commitment to working with diverse communities also needs to be nourished from the bottom up, not just mandated from the top down. Staff members—those in the trenches—are constantly in contact with the wants and needs of the community. They see and live the everyday problems and opportunities, and it is crucial that they be empowered to persuade management to get things done (see Figure 2.1).

As described in chapter 1, an orderly approach to serving Latinos in your community requires a planned initiative. Some preparatory steps need to be taken before effective planning can begin. This chapter introduces the concept and essential elements of a Plan for Latino Outreach. It also walks you through the preparation stages for launching your plan by providing tools to analyze your organization's vision and mission, launch a Committee

Board members	Board members
Library directors	Library directors
Management/Administrators	Management/Administrators
Library personnel, interns, volunteers, etc.	Library personnel, interns, volunteers, etc.
COMMITMENT STARTS FROM THE TOP DOWN	COMMITMENT IS NOURISHED FROM THE BOTTOM UP

FIGURE 2.1   Human Resources Involvement in the Library Environment

for Latino Outreach (CLO), and develop an internal communication process among colleagues and co-workers. It also suggests ways to get everybody involved in this initiative.

Is a Plan for Latino Outreach Really Necessary?

In chapter 1, we covered the benefits of working with the Latino community. In order to follow a systematic approach to achieving those benefits, you need to go through a planning process that will incorporate the library's mission statement, help your organization define its vision for marketing services to Latinos, identify goals, devise strategies to achieve those goals, monitor the development of those strategies, and evaluate success. You need a Plan for Latino Outreach.

This outreach plan needs to be a part of your organization's strategic plan, which sets forth the organization's vision and goals for the next five to seven years. An organization might need several outreach plans to focus on specific areas, and all need to respond to a master marketing plan that sets the main guidelines for that specific organization.

Your Plan for Latino Outreach might be a part of a Diversity Outreach Plan that sets strategies for all ethnic and other diverse populations in your community. You need to add specific strategies—including goals, products, promotional tactics, and so forth—for specific audiences that are part of your community. These decisions will depend on the demographics you serve. In the same way, and for clarification purposes, your Plan for Outreach to Persons with Physical Disabilities might be a part of a Special Needs Population Outreach Plan—as shown in Figure 2.2.

Your Plan for Latino Outreach includes specific goals, strategies, schedules, auditing and evaluation tools, and resources. All this information becomes part of a living document shared by all members of your organization to which all will contribute and for which all will be responsible. From board members, directors, and branch managers to human

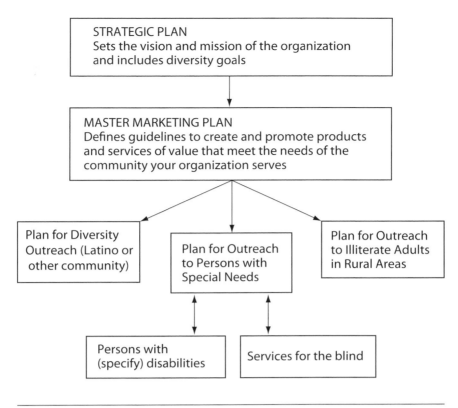

FIGURE 2.2 Master Marketing Plan

resources, administrative, and professional library personnel, everybody should be familiar with and have ample access to this document, which will become the heart and soul of your commitment to serve the Latino community.

Whether your organization is small or large, developing a Plan for Latino Outreach will allow you to accomplish the following:

- Set goals and strategies for marketing your library services to Latinos
- Obtain important information regarding the Latino community you serve
- Evaluate and maximize both your internal and external resources
- Prioritize and make decisions regarding the focus of your promotional efforts and outreach activities
- Foresee and overcome cultural and language barriers that are obstacles to performing your services efficiently
- Leverage community partnerships with other public and private entities that serve this community
- Assess the progress and growth of your Latino membership and their use of library services over time
- Find new funding resources, and tap more deeply into existing ones
- Comply with national and state goals for underserved markets in an efficient, orderly way

The planning process will also help you analyze your organization's strengths and weaknesses, identify internal and external opportunities and threats, and position your library to play a relevant role among the Latino community you serve.

Essential Elements of a Plan for Latino Outreach

Your Plan for Latino Outreach should be concise and practical; otherwise, people will not use it. It should contain additional documentation to reinforce the decisions and strategies you will follow as a result of having done your homework (such as conducting a market analysis, identifying and describing products and services, determining promotional and outreach strategies, and much more). However, the plan itself should function as a road map—a summary of those ideas collected along the way, the input of your staff and advisors, and the information you will find and use to reach your goals.

In order to start and implement a plan for Latino outreach—or marketing plan—you need to accomplish set goals:

1. Define your organization's mission and vision.

Your library's formal mission statement defines the institution's fundamental purpose—its reason for existence. On the other hand, its vision statement articulates your goals and future aspirations about serving your Latino population with your products and services: guided by the mission, where do you envision the library going?

2. Conduct a market analysis.

Based on your research, your market analysis examines your Latino population profile, its composition and needs, to better understand the audience to whom you will direct your outreach efforts.

3. Assess external resources.

Your external resource assessment researches and prioritizes community partnerships, funding sources, and other forms of public and private support. It also evaluates external opportunities and threats that might affect the successful achievement of your plan.

4. Assess internal resources.

A look at your internal resources appraises your organization's collections, materials, and services and defines a course of action to improve, expand, or sustain the appropriate customer service. It also finds strengths and weaknesses in these resources and defines solutions in order to match your Latino community needs.

5. Position your resources.

Create a clear image of your programs and services in the mind of your Latino customers—ideally, an image that will compel them to use the programs and resources your library offers based on your community profile. You also need to identify the priorities among the groups in your local Latino community and respond to those priorities according to available resources.

6. Promote your library.

Generate promotional strategies to attract and retain Latino customers, from branding efforts to promoting specific programs and events with mini-promotional campaigns.

7. Manage and evaluate your plan.

Outline timetables, budgets, and benchmarks, and review and evaluate your results to continue, adjust, or redefine your marketing strategies.

These essential elements of a plan for Latino outreach have been adapted and simplified from traditional and social marketing plans to fit the needs of libraries and librarians whose marketing experience might be random and unsystematic. The idea of this plan is to give some order to your thoughts and efforts and, hopefully, an easier procedure you can follow.

Your Organization's Vision and Mission

As previously stated, your organization must have a clear vision and mission defining the role of your library, the audiences to be served, the products and services to be offered, and the needs you endeavor to fill.

Your vision makes an inspiring statement. It expresses a clear and powerful image of the ideal impact you hope to make by carrying out your organization's mission and goals. Many organizations find their vision by responding to the following question: "How would my community—and the world—be different if we entirely accomplished our mission?" Think in terms of the values of your cause, such as dignity, fairness, inclusiveness, respect, and integrity. For example, "An inclusive community without illiteracy," or "A community that respects and shares cultural differences through education."

A mission statement, however, talks about the more specific steps your organization takes in order to reach your vision. A clear mission statement should be customer oriented and provide strong direction to the organization. Most libraries would agree that their mission refers to the pursuit and accessibility of knowledge; meeting their patrons' educational, recreational, and cultural needs; guaranteeing the freedom to read as the building block of a democratic society;[1] and, in our changing world, providing access to electronic resources with the same purpose. However, how do libraries guarantee that those needs are met when members of the communities they serve have language and cultural barriers that prevent them from fully accessing and benefitting from those services?

A mission statement needs to address those issues clearly. Many organizations are afraid of political incorrectness when drafting their mission statements, resulting in very brief phrases that say little about their intentions. Others make generic statements with all-inclusive views. Remember, your institution's mission statement explicitly defines your business and what it offers. If your mission statement is generic, then it not only serves little purpose, but it also suggests the institution is likely targeting a generic market, when in reality your audience is not homogeneous. A mission statement is the voice of your library, and it speaks loud and clear about your organization's intentions.

A good first step in embarking on your Plan for Latino Outreach is to analyze your organization's vision and mission statements and evaluate how involved your organization really is in serving the segments of your community that offer language and cultural challenges.

What Your Library Stands For

In order to re-examine—and perhaps redefine—your vision and mission statements, you need to ask simple questions:

1. Do your organization's mission and vision statements mention any diversity purposes?
2. If yes, how are they expressed?
3. What actions is your organization taking in order to achieve these purposes?
4. How does your organization show its commitment to these purposes?

In this chapter I provide two examples of actual public library mission statements that include a diversity purpose—throughout the nation, there are other examples that similarly guide library systems and demonstrate this commitment to diversity.

Both examples talk about diversity in general terms as well as catering to the various communities they represent. These mission statements create clear goals for action. As a result, the organizations in these examples generated a variety of services for non-English speakers.

Institutional Mission Statement Case Study: Queens Library, New York

---

QUEENS LIBRARY, NEW YORK

Mission Statement

"The mission of the Queens Library is to provide quality services, resources, and life-long learning opportunities through books and a variety of other formats to meet the informational, educational, cultural, and recreational needs and interests of its diverse and changing population.

The Library is a forum for all points of view and adheres to the principles of intellectual freedom as expressed in the Library Bill of Rights formulated by the American Library Association" (adopted January 1991).

Queens Library's commitment to diversity continues to be expressed in its *Vision:* "As Queens Library enters its second century, it will be universally recognized as the most dynamic public library in the nation. This recognition will arise from: the Library's dedication to the needs of its diverse communities; its advocacy and support of appropriate technology; the excellence of its collections; the commitment of its staff to its customers and the very highest ideals of library service."

And it comes up again, prominently, in its *Values:* "Customers: We believe that meeting the needs of our diverse customer base is first and foremost." This commitment can also be seen in two of its four strategic directions:

Queens Library "serves as a destination for the informational, educational, cultural, and recreational needs and interest of our diverse customers and communities."

"People in Queens consistently receive quality library service provided by dedicated, knowledgeable, experienced, and diverse customer-oriented staff."[2]

1. What is the diversity purpose of Queens Library?

"To provide quality services, resources, and lifelong learning opportunities through books and a variety of other formats to meet the informational, educational, cultural, and recreational needs and interests of its diverse and changing population."

2. What action is Queens Library taking in order to achieve that purpose?

Queens Library "has become the destination for the informational, educational, cultural, and recreational needs and interests of its diverse customers and communities," and provides "quality library service by dedicated, knowledgeable, experienced, and diverse customer-oriented staff."

3. How does Queens Library demonstrate its commitment to that purpose?

With the Library's dedication to "the needs of its diverse communities; its advocacy and support of appropriate technology; the excellence of its collections; the commitment of its staff to its customers and the very highest ideals of library service."

The Queens Library's commitment to diversity is expressed as a goal of revitalization—almost a celebration of the times in which we are living—and reflects a sense of the library's pride in its pledge. The organization shows its commitment to foreign-language speakers in many ways. Its Web site and advertising materials are translated into six different languages. Extensive programming, collections, and activities for several communities speaking those languages are organized by location and branch. Their "New Americans Program" includes international language collections of books, periodicals, CDs, CD-ROMs, and videos in a variety of subject areas, such as romance novels, computer books, cookbooks, biographies, best sellers, martial arts novels, and parenting guides. Public programs assist new immigrants in adapting to life in America and celebrate the culture of the diverse ethnic groups in Queens. The organization also offers multiple resources and information appropriate for the borough's demographics.

For the Latino community specifically, the library offers activities such as health workshops, computer classes in Spanish, ESOL (English for Speakers of Other Languages) classes, Spanish and bilingual *hora del cuento* (story time), an annual Latin-American fair, presentations by Latino authors, citizenship classes, and a professional employment search, just to mention a few. As you see, the variety of offerings covers literacy and survival skills as well as social and health-related issues. Visit their Web site, http://www.queenslibrary.org, and click on the "Español" link at the top left to view the library's Spanish-language home page.

Please look at the frequency and variety of activities offered throughout the year, including but not limited to *Programas Latinos*.

Diversity Committee Mission Statement Case Study: Ocean County Library, New Jersey

Consider another example, this time a Diversity Committee mission statement rather than an institutional mission statement. The value of this example is the intense activity the Ocean County Library System engaged in to create an effective structure that has facilitated a solid internal commitment at all levels of the organization. This commitment launched an institution-wide participation in the library's diversity purpose.

OCEAN COUNTY LIBRARY SYSTEM, NEW JERSEY
Diversity Committee Mission Statement

"Committee members provide active leadership for the Ocean County Library System in fostering an understanding of diversity issues and in assuring a welcoming environment to all customers and staff members regardless of age, class, gender, ethnicity, mental/physical ability, race, religion, or sexual orientation. We are committed to promoting library services for all of the county's diverse populations. We are accomplishing this through the creation of guidelines, staff training, outreach to our communities, the development of programs and exhibits, and the recruitment and retention of qualified and diverse library personnel. Our goal is to have a positive and lasting effect on every individual who deals with the Ocean County Library by reflecting our values outwards to staff and customers and enabling them to expand their horizons in an atmosphere of safe exploration."[3]

---

1. What is the diversity purpose of the Ocean County Library System (OCLS) Diversity Committee?

"Provide active leadership for the Ocean County Library System in fostering an understanding of diversity issues and in assuring a welcoming environment to all customers and staff members regardless of age, class, gender, ethnicity, mental/physical ability, race, religion, or sexual orientation." Promote library services "for all of the county's diverse populations."

2. What action is OCLS's Diversity Committee taking in order to achieve that purpose?

"The creation of guidelines, staff training, outreach to our communities, developing programs and exhibits, and recruiting and retaining qualified and diverse library personnel."

3. How does OCLS show its commitment to that purpose?

"By reflecting their values outwards to staff and customers and enabling them to expand their horizons in an atmosphere of safe exploration."

Note that the purpose of the Diversity Committee's mission statement is different from a library's institutional mission statement in that it speaks more specifically about the actions of the committee and not the library's goals in general. In other words, the library's mission statement represents institutional diversity goals while an outreach or diversity committee charter sets more specific guidelines for outreach strategies.

Under the slogan "Connecting People, Building Community," the Ocean County Library's Diversity Committee formed in February 1997 to develop a diversity training program based on the library's strategic plan and its mission to "connect people of all ages, backgrounds, lifestyles, and cultures to the information and materials that best suit their needs."

Under the guidance of a private company dedicated to diversity training, OCLS developed a plan encompassing three phases: Phase One began in September 1998 with a system-wide scan. Eighty-one volunteers from the general staff, the library's administrative team, and the Library Commission participated in affinity focus groups; all levels of the organization were represented and addressed the internal resources issues. In April 1999, representatives from community groups and organizations actively concerned with diversity issues participated in focus groups held at the Toms River and Lakewood Branches, thus focusing on external resources.

The project's Phase Two, completed by the end of 2000, included diversity training for four groups: the Diversity Committee, the Administration Team, supervisors, and support staff. Phase Three provided ongoing follow-up, support, and consultation days for planning and commitments. In addition, the Diversity Committee completed a demographic report based on the 2000 Census by region and branch. This report acknowledges the racial and ethnic diversity of Ocean County and ensures the system continues to provide library programs, services, and collections of interest to the diverse populations they serve.

The outcomes of that planning process are impressive. The Diversity Committee has been very active in offering training to a variety of library workgroups, such as youth services providers and public relations teams, and in developing more in-depth diversity training for its supervisory staff, the committee itself, and members of the administrative team. Staff members have also been invited and encouraged to attend cultural awareness sessions related to Latinos, Orthodox Jews, African Americans, and Muslims that included the participation of community leaders and experts in the field.

A new position, Outreach Services Librarian, was created in October 2001 to lead outreach to diverse communities and carry out the Diversity Committee's proposals. Other outstanding results of these activities include the active participation of the administrative level as an integral part of the Diversity Committee, an enthusiastic staff willing to participate in foreign-language acquisition training sessions, and a yearly diversity program now shared throughout the system and with other libraries.[4]

In 2003, the committee held a Diversity Summit for Branch Managers that resulted, after overcoming some obstacles, in the Diversity Plan for Branch Managers, a document that focuses on three system-wide goals from the OCLS current Strategic Plan:

1. Every resident uses and champions the Library.
2. The Library is a catalyst for growth and change.
3. The Library is the focal point of the community.

Branch managers included staff diversity training in their plans and developed activities using their newfound knowledge of the community they served.[5]

In summary, a clear mission statement is both a beacon that guides your institution in its purposes and a touchstone that helps you evaluate results down the road. A good mission statement is customer focused, includes all members of the community, and serves as the basis for selecting and evaluating three- to five-year long-range goals.

As you can see in the two previous examples, both organizations have extensively developed and made public their diversity purposes, supporting their commitment to the diverse populations they serve with solid ideas and well-defined actions.

Worksheet 2.1 will help you assess your organization's vision, mission, and goals related to diversity and, more specifically, to Latino outreach efforts.

Launching a Committee for Latino Outreach (CLO)

These two sample mission statements show that clearly defined and articulated goals and structure are instrumental in achieving results. Worksheet 2.1 should help you clarify your ideas of what an organization's commitment to diversity entails.

It can be difficult to change or update an organization's mission statement; doing so requires a good deal of involvement from different levels of your organization, and institutional bylaws may dictate that a certain formal process is followed. However, you can take action by launching a CLO and defining the committee's charter.

Launching a CLO and creating an internal communication process are the two preparation phases to defining your Plan for Latino Outreach. If your organization already has a Diversity Committee or an Outreach Committee, then you can establish your CLO as a subcommittee with its own particular goals.

A CLO is the first approach to professionalizing Latino outreach, and the committee defines its own goals and charter. The function of the effective CLO is both advisory and as a working committee. It acts as the board of directors of every Latino outreach effort and helps you in the following:

- Defining a clear charter for your Committee for Latino Outreach
- Creating an outreach plan to accomplish the goals the committee sets forth
- Planning and programming library outreach activities
- Ensuring the financial viability and accountability of your efforts
- Interpreting and representing the Latino community to the organization
- Representing the organization among Latinos
- Giving and receiving feedback from the Latino community
- Recommending training goals and procedures for committee members and coworkers
- Advocating internally and externally for Latino outreach
- Overseeing and assessing the plan's success, evaluating results, defining changes, and refining strategies and tactics

Members of the CLO could include staff from all levels of the organization. CLO members are usually recruited from library employees who are interested in outreach efforts as a personal choice but will be the seedbed to recruit the best and the bravest, who will eventually be professionalized. CLO members need not be permanent but should make a commitment to a certain term and a specific activity.

Ideally, the CLO should also include outreach professionals. Achieving paid positions to work specifically on outreach activities in the face of budget cuts—when you are shorthanded for regular library activities—is not an easy task. However, as you read in their mission statement, the Ocean County Library System was able to add such a position over time. This might be more feasible for medium and large systems than for small libraries with very limited budgets. Yet if it becomes your CLO's goal to create this key position or department in your organization, this goal could become as important as hiring a reference librarian or a children's specialist, depending on the demographics you serve.

You can also try to recruit outreach specialists from the community you serve to participate as members of your extended CLO, and idea we will discuss shortly. Look for professionals with experience in marketing to the Latino community as well as corporate diversity professionals and those with experience in community outreach in the nonprofit environment. They might become permanent members of your extended CLO, or they might volunteer in an advisory capacity as consultants or participate at certain stages of the committee's development. Most importantly, you need individuals who are sincerely dedicated advocates for your library, who can develop well-informed, do-able ideas and make them happen. For instance, they might be willing to help you develop outreach personnel internally, and your staff might become more eager and enthusiastic if they feel supported by someone with experience and that their efforts are getting results.

Outreach personnel need to be adequately trained and compensated. This will create opportunities for current employees who are eager to advance and will provide effective ways of creating employment around the library environment, such as students looking for paid internships, candidates seeking part-time positions in library services, and similar opportunities.

In the final analysis, all your employees need to be engaged in Latino outreach efforts and play a part in one way or another. Just supporting your effort by not interfering or resisting is a plus. And remember, most people work for two reasons: money and recognition. If you cannot reward them monetarily, increase their job satisfaction by publicly recognizing their efforts. Personal fulfillment is essential for those who choose to work in the nonprofit field, and you can make one or the other—or both—the incentive to attract members to your CLO.

The Basic Structure of a CLO

The structure of your CLO is simple, strong, and efficient. It is both an advisory and a working committee: as a group, its members not only have a vision but also need to do some work. (Ideally, other staff members and volunteers eventually will help carry out the plan.) Effective committees are comprised of individuals with a broad range of knowledge, experience, and interests. You need to assess your potential candidates' strengths and abilities to perform the tasks at hand—at least when selecting the committee's first members—and recruit candidates who will fill gaps in expertise and library connections. Having different levels of experience and areas of interest represented is recommended: a good mix will bring a more dynamic synergy to the table.

The CLO's size and the frequency of its meetings will be determined by the size of your organization, the different stages of the CLO's development, and the availability of its members. It will also change as the different tasks and goals are accomplished and the committee reaches a better understanding of the Latino community it serves. In time, the committee will recruit new members, will set policies and procedures, and will regularly review its own structure.[6] General responsibilities of all members include the following:

* Defining the CLO's charter
* Creating and implementing the Plan for Latino Outreach and monitoring its progress

- Making decisions and executing tasks as needed
- Representing the CLO and advocating for the institution in the library community, the Latino community, and the community at large

It is recommended that the CLO have three executive positions: chairperson or president of the CLO, secretary or vice chair, and treasurer or administrator (the CLO probably will not manage funds on a day-to-day basis, but it will need to ensure there are enough funds to cover activities). However, these are suggested positions and designations. You and your committee can decide upon a different model based on the library's existing committees or your preferences. Suggested responsibilities of each member follow. (The descriptions of these responsibilities are generic, and positions might include additional duties or tasks necessary to operate the CLO.)

Chairperson or President's Responsibilities

1. Overseeing the CLO's operation and ensuring the achievement of its charter
2. Acting as a link and building the relationship between the CLO and management
3. Reporting CLO activity to the chair of the diversity committee, if the CLO is a sub-committee; the office in charge of public service or public relations; or the library director
4. Evaluating the development, direction, and organizational strength of the committee and executing its operation

Vice Chair or Secretary's Responsibilities

1. Assisting in chair's duties and acting in his or her absence
2. Conducting special assignments such as committee members' development and overseeing public relations and media
3. Setting committee meeting agendas and keeping meeting minutes and other records of the CLO's activity

Treasurer or Administrator's Responsibilities

1. Managing the CLO's actions related to financial responsibilities
2. Ensuring adequate funding for CLO's activities and working directly with the library's financial department personnel
3. Implementing financial procedures for the CLO
4. Making appropriate financial reports available to the CLO and the library system

In addition, your CLO will need people to lead subcommittees that will arise as the result of the committee's activities. For example, subcommittee areas could be market research, strategic partnerships, funding, internal resources, programming, promotional strategies, and any others that are needed and practical.

1. The market research subcommittee designs, develops, decides, and implements the best strategies for conducting research to define the library's demographic environment and provides initial and sequential reports on the local Latino community's ethnic diversity.
2. The strategic partners subcommittee identifies contacts and establishes strategic partnerships with local and/or regional organizations and companies serving the Latino community in the library's area. It also establishes an extended CLO, or La-

tino Advisory Committee, comprised of Latino leaders in the community who may not be able to dedicate the time for active regular participation in the CLO but who are willing to serve in an advisory capacity.

3. The funding subcommittee, together with the treasurer or administrator, is in charge of ensuring funding for Latino outreach activities through dedicated budget lines and other organizational resources and/or securing new and alternative funding sources by organizing fundraising activities or leveraging support from strategic partners.

4. The internal resources subcommittee is responsible for assessing and enhancing the library's products and services based on an audit of the library's holdings and the findings of the market research subcommittee; evaluating and strengthening the image of the library, including its facility or facilities, to make it Latino-user friendly; and working to ensure that all CLO members and library employees are ready and capable to interact with Latino customers by proposing and implementing customer service training and development.

5. The programming subcommittee plans, designs, and implements cultural and educational programs that celebrate the beliefs, traditions, and lifestyles of the Latino community, with the purpose of attracting and engaging its members to library services and activities and empowering them by sharing their culture and accomplishments with the community at large.

6. The promotional strategies subcommittee, one of the linchpins of the CLO's operation, is in charge of internal and external communication about the CLO's activities. This includes keeping staff members and volunteers apprised of the committee's mission, vision, plans, and accomplishments and promoting the library and its Latino outreach programs and services externally to a variety of constituencies—not limited to the Latino community—through public relations, library service awareness, and institutional branding efforts. It is in charge of developing and implementing membership, branding, and marketing campaigns through traditional media as well as alternative promotional tactics, distribution channels, and the community.

With this basic understanding of the people you'll need to recruit for your CLO, you now are ready to assess the potential candidates within your library. Worksheet 2.2 helps you pre-qualify each candidate with just a few ideas of their professional and personal interests. Brainstorm with colleagues about the people that had shown interest or who would be a good fit for this project. You might find that there are only two or three people willing to initiate the committee. If that is the case, do not get discouraged—that is a good start. You will not need all subcommittee leaders or chairs in place at the beginning of your planning process. If you cannot find support within your own branch (or even if you do), try contacting colleagues at other branches within your system, and establish a network of CLO members. They might bring to the table resources you do not currently have, and vice versa.

Additionally, members of your CLO do not need to be Latino or of Latino background; essentially, they must bring to the effort a sincere passion and interest in serving this community and must be open and eager to being trained in its cultural intricacies.

Set up a time for meeting each candidate and introducing them to each other and to the idea of the CLO. When you approach each candidate about the possibility of serving on the CLO, ask about his or her personal and professional interests in the Latino community. Talk to candidates about their relevant accomplishments and connections and the way you envision them contributing to the committee's efforts with their particular skills and qualifications. Be sure to explain the role and responsibility of the committee in general, as well.

Due to your own enthusiasm, you might be tempted to encourage people to take over something they are not sure about. Just be patient; some of your co-workers might want to see where and how the CLO is going before they join.

Make a list of potential ideas for discussion about the CLO and the good qualities that make your candidates suitable for each position. You can have informal discussions one-on-one, or you might discuss the ideas in small groups so you can sense the group's synergy.

Some topics for discussion are the following:

1. Their personal and professional interest in and experience with the Latino community
2. Their interest and commitment to joining this outreach effort
3. The responsibilities and expectations of a CLO member and other related ideas developed in this chapter
4. Their relevant contacts and connections with community leaders and others
5. The type of position on the CLO in which they see themselves best fitting

After a number of informal meetings, invite them to be part of the CLO and officially launch the committee. You might want to have some formality, such as inviting your director, management and/or trustees, and other co-workers and presenting the new structure and its members. Making it official will add a sense of commitment to your plan.

This structure will provide a modus operandi for your Latino outreach efforts, but, most importantly, it will give you—the CLO members—visibility and recognition within your organization and externally in the community.

The approach I've used for starting the CLO assumes you and a group of co-workers are taking responsibility for this initiative with the library management's blessing. However, your library system might have procedures in place for starting committees and selecting members. Please research these options, and follow your organization's procedures if this is your case.

The Extended CLO Structure: Your Latino Advisory Board

In addition, you can invite leaders of your community to become part of an extended CLO structure—a Latino Advisory Board (LAB) that meets with the CLO members periodically or as needed and acts as a link to the community. You can look for potential candidates in the corporate world, social service agencies, small businesses, and in other nonprofits, especially those dedicated to education, health, and community development. The LAB keeps you grounded, gives you advice on how to provide assistance to Latino customers, advocates for the library's services within the community, and brings information about its needs and wants. Designate one person in your CLO structure—perhaps the vice chair or secretary—to act as a liaison between the CLO and the LAB members. Chapter 3 covers how to approach and work with community leaders in more detail.

Your CLO's Charter

In order to define your CLO's charter, you need to clarify some ideas about your business. Answering the questions in Worksheet 2.3 will define the direction of your efforts and help you create your charter. These answers will also give you an idea of where you think you stand and what you think are the most pressing issues regarding your commitment to working with your local Latino customers.

You have an a priori definition of what you already have and what you need to improve or expand; you can begin creating your CLO's charter, highlighting the answers in Worksheet 2.4 and condensing the result into a paragraph or two, as we did in our example.

Do not be too concerned about creating the perfect statement as you will probably revise it down the road. Every action you define in Worksheet 2.4, "Your CLO's Charter," becomes a goal that will be the basis for later defining a marketing strategy. For instance, if you say: "Expand library services for the local Latino population," then you will have to create a strategy to: (1) define those library services; (2) define and implement the expansion of those services; and (3) attract local Latinos into those services (including Spanish-speaking, bilingual, and English-speaking individuals of Latino background). For now, your goals are general, but they will become more precise as you continue to define and design your strategies.

Creating a Communication Process

The second preparation phase to your Plan for Latino Outreach involves creating an internal communication process that will link your CLO's activities with your organization and engage staff members and volunteers in the process.

In forming the CLO, you will need to establish a formal communication link between the committee and library leadership for purposes such as reporting on the CLO's activities and progress and requesting authorization for meetings, events, funding, and so forth. The CLO chairperson or president should act as the liaison, reporting to a management staff designated by your director, with a clear understanding and agreement on the terms and frequency of your communication process.

In addition, establish procedures for communicating with all library personnel. The purpose of this communication process is to accomplish the following:

- Generate discussion among your staff members and volunteers about the benefits of working with Latinos and generate ideas for potential training to support Latino outreach efforts
- Voice concerns related to customer service, collection needs, and services that can be improved, and suggest solutions
- Raise awareness of and promote CLO activities and recruit potential new members

Your organization likely already has an effective internal communication tool in place, such as a periodic employee/volunteer newsletter, an intranet, or an e-mail digest sent to all personnel. The CLO may be able to piggyback onto that tool or use it as a model to create something similar but with its own identity.

Your CLO might want to create an internal motif and slogan to attract potential members and include those in all communication elements. Your emblem might be related to the current logo of your organization with added content related to diversity or Latinos, such as a word in Spanish (¡Bienvenidos! Welcome!), or a totally different emblem that represents the ideas of the new CLO. Likewise, your slogan might relate to goals in your library's strategic plan but might also represent the new ideas you created for this charter. If you do adopt an emblem for the CLO, it is important that all communication tools also include the library's logo, as well, to underscore the message that the CLO is an institutional initiative, not a side project.

Possible tools you can use in your internal communication process include the following:

- Memos with your CLO emblem and/or slogan on library letterhead
- A printed newsletter or e-news blasts, scheduled at regular intervals
- Your intranet, if you have one
- Progress reports delivered during staff meetings
- Brown-bag lunchtime gatherings highlighting success stories and opportunities for staff involvement
- A creative approach that generates enthusiasm

These ideas will help you encourage and inspire your colleagues and co-workers to build your communication process by proposing the following actions:

1. Share a success story or satisfied patron testimonial related to customer service to Latino community members.
2. Submit a review of a new Spanish or bilingual printed material or DVD in the library's collection.
3. Post questions (and answers) regarding Latino cultural issues.
4. Report operational or materials needs.
5. Announce opportunities for staff diversity training and/or Spanish-language classes.
6. Research and share ideas for activities and services other libraries offer to Latinos.
7. Report CLO activities and invite staff to participate.

(For guidelines on how to implement each of these actions, see Worksheet 2.5 in chapter 10.)

The goal of this communication process is to keep your co-workers informed about the CLO's developments, to generate enthusiasm, and to recruit them into your efforts. In other words, stir the pot!

Your Organization's Participation

When working on your CLO, keep in mind that in order to succeed, the effort cannot be made by just a few individuals. You need the involvement of the whole organization.

Becoming an organization that is competent in cultural diversity requires a commitment from the organization as well as the individuals that work in it. Pledging to a long-term Plan for Latino Outreach must be the promise from every member in your internal community—the library environment—at all levels. Each organization's particular circumstances will create unique demands and require different degrees of staff involvement, but essentially two elements are critical to the success of your Latino outreach efforts:

- Your staff's team approach embracing the benefits of working with the Latino community previously discussed
- Your staff's firm belief that these goals are as important as any other goal in the organization's strategic plan

Making the commitment to market services to Latinos is just one side of the coin. The other is training your organization in learning the intricacies of Latino culture and understanding the role of culture in marketing to Latinos and, specifically, to your local Latino community.

Therefore, the ideal situation would be one where (1) all individuals involved in library services (from trustees to volunteers) agree with the goals of serving a Latino community; and (2) they all become somehow knowledgeable of cross-cultural marketing—in other words, interacting with a group of people with different cultural imagery, behaviors, values, and beliefs.

However, what if not all individuals in your library community agree with these goals? Inside pressure against these efforts can be devastating to your initiative.

Professional development training is a key factor that enables an organization to become competent in cross-cultural interaction. Successful companies invest time, energy, and money in training their workforce because the people factor can become a dragging force in business performance. Employee turnover, absenteeism, and low morale are only some of the well-known human factors that can negatively affect an organization's performance. In addition, cultural barriers that have not been addressed internally can also have detrimental effects resulting in low circulation or service ratings, a poor reputation, loss of patrons, and detachment from the community.

In order to fulfill your commitment to working with the Latino community, the organization as a whole needs strong guidelines that can be applied both internally and externally—in your library environment, your Latino community, and your community at large—and must sustain those guidelines with an outreach plan. Fortunately, training and professional development need not to be expensive or fancy, just effective. You can set up train-the-trainer sessions, group discussions, surveys, celebration days, or other creative ways of encouraging staff members, volunteers, and trustees to talk about themselves and the Latino community they serve, developing cultural competency in the process.

Your Bilingual Staff

More than due to the materials found in a library, Latinos return to the library because of the way library personnel show interest in and care for their problems and needs. Helping your library personnel interact with Latino patrons—whether Spanish-speaking, bilingual, or deeply acculturated individuals—is extremely important because relationships are very important in this community. It is crucial to create some type of genuine connection.

While training librarians in Occupational Spanish and Latino culture around the country, I have found a general agreement that it is okay to make an effort to learn *some* Spanish to communicate with patrons but what libraries *really* need is Spanish-speaking personnel. Where can libraries find qualified personnel to meet this need?

Only 3.1 percent of Hispanics are employed in education, training, and library services (Kochhar 2007), while a small portion—less than 5 percent (Nguyen 2005)—of degrees in library science go to Latinos every year. In addition, Latinos have the highest dropout rate in education nationally[7] and an increasing disadvantage in completing higher education (Fry 2004). So is the situation hopeless?

Recruiting and retaining employees is already a challenge in the library environment. There is concern about economic hardship and a loss of employees in the next few years related to massive retirement of baby boomers, although libraries are trying to retain baby boomers as senior volunteers or part-time workers.[8] Demographic changes in the population—with Latinos as one of the largest and fastest-growing minorities—and political, economic, and technological trends are changing the library environment and human resources needs (OCLC Online Computer Library Center, Inc. 2005).

Part of your outreach success in bringing Latinos into libraries does involve the presence of Spanish-speaking personnel.[9] However, a truly culturally competent organization is one in which any employee is able to create a personal relationship with any patron, no matter what culture or ethnicity they come from and no matter what language they speak or do not speak. Once staff members become aware that personal relationships are more important to their Latino patrons than language barriers, they can better assist them, even if they are only able to speak some Spanglish or do not speak any Spanish at all.

Today Latinos are a significant minority in our country, and, in some areas, bilingualism is a reality. Serving Latino and Spanish-speaking patrons with similar individuals in your workforce might be ideal, but it brings up a number of other issues and challenges heard from librarians over the years.

1. Staff believes that services can ideally be delivered to minority patrons in their community when the organization has enough employees mirroring that community. However, in order to deliver equity of access, employees mirroring each ethnicity, race, or national origin would need to be hired—an economically and practically impossible goal.
2. Latino library employees have complained that sometimes they are not promoted or advanced in their careers because their language skills are necessary for the daily operation of the library at a particular function. This might not always be the case, but the perception exists.
3. Latino employees have also suggested that they feel a lot of pressure to adequately serve the Latino community and take responsibility for the well-being of their Latino patrons.
4. Not all Latinos are aware of the cultural differences among different Latino populations, nor do they share the same interests, levels of education, and socioeconomic backgrounds. In addition, a Latino librarian who has achieved a graduate degree at a U.S. college or university is most likely native born; if born outside the United States, it is likely he or she has been in this country long enough to have acquired a certain level of acculturation or assimilation as compared to recently immigrated potential customers. Therefore, these differences in nationality and level of acculturation might become barriers between them and Latino customers.
5. Sometimes, library staff also feel that non-Latino employees rely on their Latino co-workers for interacting with Spanish-speaking patrons, which prevents the rest of the employees from benefiting from the professional—and personal—growth of becoming culturally competent individuals in a culturally diverse organization.
6. Regardless of efforts made by national organizations such as REFORMA, progress in recruiting Latino students to ALA-accredited programs continues to be small (Ramírez Wohlmuth 2000).
7. Latino patrons are still treated as outsiders with special needs instead of patrons with needs and values in common with others.

Language and cultural behaviors might be difficult to overcome, but offering appropriate services presents even more challenges. Many libraries have expressed their concern about the difficulties in recruiting Spanish-speaking personnel, even at an administrative level. Why is it hard to find Latino employees to work in the library environment?

When Hiring Diverse Personnel Is a Challenge

Due to the scarcity of libraries in Latin America, many Latinos might not see this field as a career option. Cultural issues having little to do with the job itself might also be in play.

According to author and career counselor Dr. Jean Kummerow (2000), when choosing a career people are influenced by four different factors:

1. **Cultural factors,** such as worldviews, identity issues, family values, and class structure preconceptions and stereotypes, obstruct or make it difficult for some people or groups to hold particular jobs. Comparable to the glass ceiling for women in the work environment, there are additional barriers for Latinos and Latinas to access jobs in the library environment: this is what Rhonda Ríos Kravitz calls the "adobe ceiling" (2000, p. 28). In Latino cultures, certain jobs might be considered too academic, and parents might be afraid of losing their children's respect if they became too smart (Gil and Inoa Vázquez 1996). Also, librarianship as a career option might be seen as distant, lacking opportunity, or simply unknown to the potential candidate.

2. **Gender factors,** which include gender bias and discrimination within the same Latino culture, create strong obstacles for career decisions. In more traditional Latino cultures, women might not be allowed by their father or husband to work a full-time job or a traditional man's job. Women might be directed to short-term careers related to feminine or nurturing qualities, such as cosmetics and hair styling, artistic disciplines, or, in the best case, teaching and nursing. In 2007, men accounted for 74 percent of the science and engineering labor force, and Latinos in these fields were most likely to be working as technicians, generally for lower pay.[10] Husband and children are typically a first priority in a Latino woman's self-realization, and job and professional development are secondary, competing with the Latina's devotion to family and household chores (Gil and Inoa Vázquez 1996). Of course, you might be able to rely on the "Ñ generation" (Valdés 2000), the new Latinas—usually U.S.–born, mostly acculturated younger females who are willing to take risks.

   On the other hand, men might be directed by parents and socially influenced by peers toward manly jobs that require strength and physical activity. An inclination to an academic or artistic career might be seen as an unmanly choice by some social groups. The 2007 ALA report "Diversity Counts" (Davis and Hall 2007) stated that in 2000, only 597 Latino males were credentialed in the profession as compared to 1,541 women.

3. **Efficacy factors** play a role in career selection and relate to a person's belief in his or her own ability to be successful in a certain profession, job, academic endeavor, or specific subject. This also includes credibility issues, such as trust in certain types of organizations, institutions, or workplaces.

   Working in government institutions might bring issues of confidentiality, especially if there are different generations present in one household with differing immigration status—including U.S.–born children from undocumented parents[11] or different immigration status among family members. In this case, positive information about career possibilities, the scope of professional development, and job opportunities will allow a potential candidate to make an informed choice. Young adults might also see working at a library as boring and unglamorous compared to other professions or vocations, so creating a healthy habit of using the library at a young age is instrumental in library services development.

4. **Traditional career factors** are usually key for people of different educational and socioeconomic backgrounds. Traditional degrees that involve many years of school and high tuition (e.g., medical doctor, lawyer, or engineer) are not a realistic choice for low-income Latino families, while middle- and upper-class families and individuals will be inclined to these professions. Because of the vertical structure in Latin American society, traditional professional careers are seen as possibilities only for rich people, and mostly males.[12] Overall, 55 percent of the Latino population in the United States works in jobs not requiring a formal education, such as construction, manufacturing, health care support, transportation, material moving, personal care and service, building and grounds cleaning, food preparation and serving, farming, fishing, and forestry, while only 13 percent of Latinos work in activities that require a college degree as we will see in chapter 4. Promoting library studies early in high schools and offering scholarships and funding opportunities might create a pool of potential candidates to access the library profession.[13]

Can a White Person Be a Diversity Leader?

This question might be a little shocking. Regardless of race or ethnicity, people from different backgrounds have a genuine interest in promoting diversity. However, white people might experience exclusion by some people of color, who may distrust the motives of a white person who promotes diversity or feel the person does not have the credibility to be a diversity leader[14]—I have personally experienced this issue because I'm a white Latina from Argentina. Country of origin or nationality might be another obstacle to diversity leadership. Some people of color might consider themselves natural diversity leaders because they have resided for a long time in a community or because they feel they have seniority in diversity issues. Such a situation can bring frustration and discouragement to your staff.

If this occurs, it is necessary to review the elements that make us all diverse, which are not limited to race, color, or national origin. Gender, age, abilities, religion, sexual preferences, and other variables make us all diverse in many ways. Acquiring diversity competency in the workplace not only has to do with issues of *disparities,* but also with issues of *equality.* You need to find out how you can bring everybody to an equal playing field so all have the same opportunities. Discover the issues in your workplace, and bring them to an open discussion in the training context.

A productive way to promote diversity leadership and support your staff in becoming diversity leaders is to encourage them to participate in the community they serve. The next chapter expands on ideas about bringing the library outside its walls to build true community partnerships, assess the help you need, and sustain long-lasting working relationships with other leaders in your community.

Notes

1. ALA Council and the Association of American Publishers (AAP), "The Freedom to Read," Adopted June 25, 1953, with subsequent amends http://www.ala.org/ala/aboutala/offices/oif/state mentspols/ftrstatement/freedomreadstatement.cfm (accessed July 28, 2010).

2. Queens Library, New York, "Mission Statement," updated December 19, 2003, http://www.queens library.org/index.aspx?page_nm=Mission+Statement (accessed November 24, 2009). Queens Library is an independent, not-for-profit corporation and is not affiliated with any other library system.

3. Ocean County Library System, New Jersey, "Diversity Committee Mission Statement," approved by the Ocean County Library Commission, February 2000/Updated September 2001 and August 2002, http://theoceancountylibrary.org/About/Diversity-Plan.htm#mission (accessed November 24, 2009).

4. For additional information, please visit the "Valuing Diversity" page at the Ocean County Library System Web site at http://theoceancountylibrary.org/ (accessed November 24, 2009).

5. For additional information, please visit "Diversity Plan for Branch Managers 2006–2007" at the Ocean County Library System Web site at http://theoceancountylibrary.org/About/Diversity Plan.pdf (accessed November 24, 2009).

6. For more information on procedures and guidelines for the committee's role and development, please see additional sources in the Bibliography.

7. Pew Hispanic Center, "Latino Teens Staying in High School: A Challenge for All Generations," January 2004, http://pewhispanic.org/files/factsheets/7.3.pdf (accessed November 24, 2009).

8. Paula M. Singer, PhD, "Retaining & Motivating Excellent Library Employees," Infopeople Webcast, March 6, 2006, http://infopeople.org/training/webcasts/webcast_data/115/retaining_moti vating.pdf (accessed November 24, 2009).

9. In *Serving Latino Communities*, Alire and Archibeque (1998, pp. 141–43) sustain that the best-case scenario is to hire Latino personnel.

10. Mark Mather, "2007 Occupational Profiles Reveal Wide Gender, Racial Gaps in Science and Engineering Employment," Population Reference Bureau, December 2008, http://www.prb.org/Articles/2008/sloanoccupationpages.aspx (accessed November 24, 2009).

11. The last immigration amnesty was the Immigration Reform and Control Act (IRCA) of 1986, which means that some immigrants have resided in this country without documentation for over 20 years. Also, not every immigrant took advantage of this amnesty at the time.

12. Even middle- and upper-class women in Mexico, for instance, are rarely included in top management and executive positions in family businesses or corporations. Between 2003 and 2005, as a freelance writer for *US Industry Today* (http://mag1.olivesoftware.com/activemagazine/welcome/USIT/VirtualMag.html), an industry magazine covering all sectors of manufacturing and shipping, transportation, and distribution, I conducted telephone interviews with over 200 high-level executives of major Mexican corporations. Only two corporations were led by women.

13. Programs such as LIS Access Midwest Program (LAMP)—a successful initiative of a regional network of academic libraries and information science schools dedicated to promoting library careers—and funding opportunities to increase numbers of students within the field of library and information science (LIS) are instrumental in enticing minority students to choose this path.

14. Dr. Patricia Arredondo addresses this issue in "Operationalization of the Multicultural Counseling Competencies," AMCD Professional Standards and Certification Committee, 1996, p. 3, http://www.tamu-commerce.edu/counseling/Faculty/salazar/OperationalizationOfTheMulticul turalCounselingCompetencies1996.pdf (accessed January 4, 2010).

WORKSHEET 2.1   Your Mission and Vision

Goal: Analyzing your organization's vision and mission statements can bring into discussion how you and your co-workers understand diversity and outreach goals.

A. First, look at your library's mission and vision statements and the institution's strategic plan. Do they include specific reference to offering inclusive services or serving a broad community? Do they mention terms such as "diverse," "diversity," "underserved populations," "disadvantaged," "cultural competency," "equality of access," "immigrants," "non-English-speaking populations," or other such terms? These are common keywords, but the statement could express the same idea in other ways.

B. Look at your library's vision or diversity statement and "fish" for values described. Not all libraries have a vision or diversity statement—if yours doesn't, the planning process provides an opportune time to develop one.

C. Answer the following questions:

1. What are the diversity purposes of your organization, and how are they expressed?

2. What actions is your organization taking in order to achieve these purposes?

3. How does your organization show commitment to these purposes?

4. What ideas would you like to add or change in your mission statement?

5. What new actions should be taken to increase support of diversity purposes?

6. Is the mission statement customer focused and concerned with the diversity in your community?

7. What new goals or pursuits—expressed in a charter statement—could be added or expanded to the present ones?

8. Who will be supporting these new goals?

See chapter 10 for worksheets as reproducible pages for training purposes.

 From *¡Hola, amigos! A Plan for Latino Outreach* by Susana G. Baumann. Santa Barbara, CA: Libraries Unlimited. Copyright © 2011.

WORKSHEET 2.2   Committee for Latino Outreach (CLO) Board Members

Goal: Encourage co-workers and colleagues to become active members of your Plan for Latino Outreach in a balanced and productive team.

FOR THE POSITION OF CHAIRPERSON/PRESIDENT

Name *Elisa Garcia-Maguire*

Current position *Branch manager*   **Location** *Little Haven City South Branch*

Personal or professional interest *Has developed strategic partnerships with local rural worker organizations and bilingual literacy programs*

Qualification for this particular position *Leadership, commitment to the library's mission, outreach and diversity, bilingual, respected by staff and management, congenial, active advocate for the Latino community*

Availability *For consideration*

NOTES

_____

_____

_____

_____

_____

See chapter 10 for worksheets as reproducible pages to complete information for every position in the CLO.

WORKSHEET 2.3   Latino State of Affairs

Goal: Review your organization's capabilities and intentions regarding the local Latino community.

1. How many Latino customers does your library presently serve (estimated), and what fraction of the local Latino community do they represent? Do you need to attract more members of this community, or do you just want to sustain the numbers you already serve?

2. What geographical area does your organization serve? Do you need to expand your geographic reach?

3. Who are your present Latino customers?

4. Who are your potential Latino customers?

5. What products and services does your library currently offer to the Latino community?

6. Which products or services would you like (or see the need) to create, expand, or improve?

7. What is unique in your organization that will attract Latino customers to your products and services? Describe facts and values (for instance, "free services" is a fact; "staff commitment to work with Latino customers" is a value).

See worksheet in chapter 10 for expanded questions; feel free to add your own ideas.

 From *¡Hola, amigos! A Plan for Latino Outreach* by Susana G. Baumann. Santa Barbara, CA: Libraries Unlimited. Copyright © 2011.

WORKSHEET 2.4   Your CLO's Charter

Goal: Define your service purpose and the goals to be achieved through this Plan for Latino Outreach.

---

1. What are the service purposes of your CLO to the Latino community? Some action words you can use include provide, expand, increase, create, foster, promote, and assure.

    The service purpose of the CLO is to provide and assure access to quality informational, educational, and recreational resources and learning opportunities to the Latino communities.

2. Who are the recipients of these efforts in your Latino community?

    The beneficiaries of the CLO's efforts would be (enter a brief description of the local Latino community as you know it): *the local Latino communities that reside in the geographical area of Little Haven City and its suburbs, from those who have been established here for over three generations to those who have recently set foot in our area. We also recognize that, among this community, there are different backgrounds and generational gaps that constitute a vibrant and diverse cultural heritage.*

3. What actions do you propose the CLO undertake in order to fulfill your purposes? Trigger words include create, attract, outreach, develop, recruit, advocate, improve, expand, etc.:

    We plan to create culturally appropriate programs and services that respond to their changing educational, cultural, and recreational needs and interests. Our library will attract them as the distinctive place where they can fulfill those needs and expand their interests. We will also help them integrate into the cultural heritage of Little Haven City.

4. How does your organization show its commitment to those purposes? (Commitment of time, personnel, technology, collections, facilities, funding, etc.)

    We commit to growing, funding, and developing internal and external resources including dedicated diversity-oriented personnel, access to technologies and collections, culturally suitable programs and services, and a friendly and welcoming physical and professional environment.

5. Summarize these ideas in a paragraph or two. Do not be too concerned about creating the perfect statement as you will probably revise it down the road.:

Charter Statement

The purpose of the Committee for Latino Outreach is to provide and assure access to quality informational, educational, and recreational resources and learning opportunities for the local Latino communities that reside in the geographical area of Little Haven City and its suburbs.

From ¡Hola, amigos! A Plan for Latino Outreach by Susana G. Baumann. Santa Barbara, CA: Libraries Unlimited. Copyright © 2011.

We plan to create culturally appropriate programs and services that respond to their changing educational, cultural, and recreational needs and interests—due to their different backgrounds and generational gaps—and help integrate this vibrant and diverse population into the existing cultural heritage of Little Haven City. For that purpose, we commit to growing funding and developing internal and external resources including dedicated diversity-oriented personnel, access to technologies and collections, culturally suitable programs and services, and a friendly and welcoming physical and professional environment.

NOTES

_____

_____

_____

_____

_____

_____

_____

See worksheet as reproducible page in chapter 10.

 From *¡Hola, amigos! A Plan for Latino Outreach* by Susana G. Baumann. Santa Barbara, CA: Libraries Unlimited. Copyright © 2011.

Chapter 3

Assessing Strategic Partnership Opportunities

Overview

Common knowledge advises, "If there is a problem in the community, the solution is in the community." When members of a community work together, developing skills to address common problems, they are usually the most able to identify those problems and work toward solutions.

As mentioned previously, corporations and nonprofit organizations, such as libraries, differ in many ways, including financial resources. They also approach marketing to a Latino audience differently. Your library's nonprofit status gives you some advantages. In the corporate environment, marketers would virtually have to steal, cheat, and bribe to get the competition's marketing campaign information, which is carefully guarded. They spend thousands of dollars hiring agencies to manage confidential information such as the way the company perceives its markets, the philosophy with which it markets its products, how it interprets the data and information resources, and how it operates the data in order to become more attractive to the consumer.

In the nonprofit environment, however, a wealth of information is available to you for research because a library's mission is to service the community, and it is not driven by profit. If a corporation calls local schools to find out about their demographics, most likely they will not get an answer, but a school more often than not will share some information with you if they have it and it does not involve confidential issues.

Moreover, for-profit corporations may be willing to cooperate with you in different ways because your library can help further the company's diversity or volunteer work goals. The contribution they make to your cause—be it a gift-in-kind or a monetary contribution—may be tax deductible or help their corporate image. A corporation may want to exchange information and solutions for problems they might have internally, such as information for their Latino employees related to problems in the workplace or at home. This exchange might be of mutual benefit to the for-profit partner as well as the library.

I chose the term "strategic partnership" to identify working agreements that benefit all participating community members, either individuals or organizations. Working with strategic partners involves the opportunity to advance an organization's insertion in the community they serve. You will not be alone in this effort, and, if you decide to participate, probably you will be welcomed to countless meetings, fundraisers, and community efforts of all kinds.

This chapter helps you identify your strategic partners and determine who are the best partners for each effort, when you can request their help, and how you can reciprocate the effort. You do not want to burn their cooperation, nor you want to burn your outreach efforts and your own staff. I will also expand on the concept of a Latino Advisory Board and how leaning on them will help you carry on your efforts with ease.

Where to Look and How to Start

> Not all efforts should be on your shoulders!

Strategic partnerships are not new to the library environment. Many libraries and library systems have developed and worked with them for a long time with great success. However, it might be the first time your local library is engaging in this type of venture for the Latino community. Although many ideas and goals might be similar, you should keep in mind some specific issues.

When considering strategic partners, you will be surprised by the amount of organizations that might agree to work with you in different ways. Many publications offer lists of such organizations in different fields and areas,[1] but where do you start?

To establish your priority list, consider three distinct types of external help that you might be able to look for (and find!):

- Strategic partners
- Community leaders
- Market channels

Let us see what each of these partnerships means to you and to the community you serve.

Strategic Partners: An Opportunity for Resource Exchange

Diverse community needs cannot be addressed by a single organization, private or public. All members of the community must work together to provide a supportive environment and aid each other, providing the resources their partners lack. This is called a strategic partnership, a working agreement in which members from different backgrounds and areas of the community consent to develop mutually beneficial projects.

The advantages of these agreements include the opportunity to share resources, learn from and aid each other in achieving their goals, augment marketing and communication resources and channels through which to deliver their message, develop mutually beneficial programming, and establish or strengthen long-term credibility in the target community for both organizations.

Building such a work agreement can be challenging because organizations often have different agendas or demands. Also, personal opinions and conflicting approaches can delay and even obstruct a happy ending. In addition, you might have to work with cultural differences if the issue arises. So it is mandatory that you have some cultural competency training under your belt *before* you get into such a commitment.

Although you might be targeting the Latino community at this time, successful strategic partnerships need to represent the different racial, ethnic, and cultural components of each community. Today, your efforts may be with the Latino community; tomorrow, they will be focused on the Asian, the aging, or the gay and lesbian communities. A multicultural approach to strategic partnerships takes care of many overlapping dimensions you would like to target. You will find illiterate, aging, gay, and blind individuals in the Latino and Asian communities as well as the English-speaking community.

Your goal is to create long-term partnerships with people you can get to know well and with whom you can find common ground. Also, each strategic partner brings a different resource or skill to the table.

Another approach to partnerships is to look around your community to see if any already exist. Decide if you want to join in or start a new one. If you put the word out, organizations will likely contact you. Strategic partners might be organizations that have a stake in reaching out to the Latino community in general or for a specific project in particular.

Do not wait for invitations to participate at community affairs or activities. Focus on the activity you want to develop and see who your strategic partners are regarding that particular service. You might want to look in the areas of health, education, human services, housing, and family resources, to name a few.

Tomar el Toro por las Astas *(Take the Bull by the Horns)*

If your organization makes a bold decision in favor of proactive strategic partnerships, preparation tasks are as important as outreach programming or developing new services. You need to know as much about your strategic partners, community leaders, and market channels as you know about yourself. Deadlines, busy times of the year, outreach goals, community programs, marketing habits, and schedules are just some of the information you will need from your strategic partners to work with them without disturbing their development.

Some natural strategic partnerships seem to succeed repeatedly, such as working with local Hispanic/Latino or pro-Hispanic/Latino nonprofit and government agencies. You do not need to work with all of them at the same time. Set your priorities according to your outreach goals, and request their participation.

Establish a liaison with one contact person who will keep you posted about the agency's developments, their needs, and how you can work together. They probably have the most data about the local Latino population, and they are or probably know the Latino leaders in the area—their board members are probably some of them. In exchange, offer services. For instance, some of these agencies lack a large conference room where they can offer presentations and activities, and, depending on the location, your library might become an extension of their own facilities.

Your local school system is another unique possibility for information and partnership. As we will see in our next chapter, the Latino population is young, and according to the U.S. Census, their birth rate is higher than the white/Caucasian population so your local school system is a likely place to meet Latinos and learn about the local demographics. Attend PTA (Parent Teacher Association) meetings and teachers meetings whenever possible so you can gather as much information as possible. Ask the school how they would like the library to support their efforts in receiving new Latino students and parents. You might access a large number of Latino homes in your community through the school system and Head Start programs.[2]

The third important partners are local hospitals and free clinics in your area. They collect information about health, but most hospitals and clinics have little time and/or budget to develop targeted educational and prevention campaigns. The lack of insurance among minorities is not the number one cause of health disparities; rather, it is the lack of information related to health issues and low health literacy.[3] Libraries can and must help remedy this situation.

Most hospitals and sometimes clinics have monthly or quarterly community meetings and many have established Community Advisory Boards (CABs), committees where diverse members of the local community bring their concerns and ideas about local health issues. Become a part of it. By participating, you will find out what their needs are and how you can support their activities in exchange for information about health issues in your community—general statistics—so you can gather materials and offer educational events at your library.

At this stage, collecting and providing information is the most important task!

Community Leaders: Your Source of Information

In order to establish successful strategic partnerships, you will need the assistance of community leaders or community advisors, individuals of Latino background or those who work with the Latino community on a continuous basis who can advise you on the community's needs and wants. These individuals might be heads of community groups and associations, nonprofit and government agencies, faith-based organizations and churches, and/or local business owners.

When talking to community leaders, consider that they might represent only a *portion* of the Latino community you are trying to target. They might be well-known, but they do not necessarily represent the community at large, especially if your demographics vary in age and country of origin. For instance, a Latino community organization that originally provided aid to Puerto Ricans in the New York/New Jersey area might not completely represent the interests of the later Mexican immigration that came to the Northeast. Sometimes community leaders tend to personalize information according to their own agendas, political views, or personal preferences.

For this reason, you will need to go to institutions and organizations, and to community and church events, to discover the natural leaders, those individuals the Latino community respects because they have developed leadership and guidance by doing good. They might not necessarily hold a position or be involved in an organization, but everybody in the community knows these people for one reason or another. Never count on just one source of information—make sure all members of your Latino community are represented.

Also, remember that the needs, problems, and perspectives of recent immigrants might be quite different from the issues of those who have been a part of the United States for generations. For instance, the use of libraries or knowledge of library services might be familiar to someone who has lived locally for a long time or who has no reason to be threatened by confidentiality issues. However, someone who is unfamiliar with library services might be negative, indecisive, or may even give the impression that members of the community do not need to use the library when asked how the library could help solve some of their problems or achieve their goals.

One of the first questions to ask community leaders is about their knowledge and/or familiarity with library services, if they have used the library for their own benefit and in what ways. If they are not familiar with your organization and its services, then it is a good idea to introduce them to library services and your outreach goals before starting the interview.

Even if they are familiar with it, invite those community leaders you have chosen as your advisors for a guided tour of your library so they can get a first-hand look at its offerings. Explain to them the intentions of your outreach plan, what you already have, and your goals, and ask for their suggestions on how to achieve those goals. Observe the way they behave in the library environment, and ask them to advise you about what they see as physical and cultural barriers for Latino library users. More acculturated Latinos will probably be more comfortable and capable of finding their way around or asking questions. They might have a different perspective from a recent immigrant, someone not used to library services or unfamiliar with the setting.[4]

Another consideration when talking to community leaders is the cultural aspect of communication. It is often hard for people to express their feelings, talk about their habits, or give clear ideas about certain subjects, especially if the interview involves personal topics such as thoughts, beliefs, or convictions. In some Latino cultures, people even tend to agree or say what they think the interviewer wants them to say (Korzenny and Korzenny 2005). They might believe it is rude to disagree with you, or they may tell you they do not know much about something you are asking.

Yolanda Cuesta, from Cuesta MultiCultural Consulting,[5] has done a terrific job at designing and providing tools for libraries to contact community leaders and develop interview skills. You can find additional information on her work at the WebJunction Spanish Outreach Program of the Bill and Melinda Gates Foundation.[6] We have also reproduced her *Guide for Conducting Community Leader Interviews*—with permission—in chapter 10.

Cultural Aspects of the Interview Process

If you have ever prepared a questionnaire about the local Latino community, you might find that generic questionnaires usually result in a chaotic amount of responses that take some effort to interpret and organize. In cultural marketing research, "focused interviews," a technique applied to focus groups,[7] might be useful to organize questions related to a subject matter and previously inform the interviewee about the topic at hand. Strengths and weaknesses of this technique are described in Table 3.1.

Focused interviews are used to collect qualitative data in a setting that allows an interviewee to talk about his or her views on a particular topic. The focus of the interview is the research goal at hand, and usually the interviewer announces the topic to the interviewee ahead of time, in a previous contact (by phone or e-mail). Be precise with your topic; for instance, if you need to find out about the demographics, clearly state, "I need to discuss with you the demographics of our local Latino community, such as country of origin, time of residence in our community . . ." (and give all the variables you need to discuss) or "I have done some research about the demographics of this area, but I need you to help me confirm

TABLE 3.1   Strengths and Weaknesses of the Focused Interview

Strengths of Method	Weaknesses of Method
1. Efficient connection between interviewer and interviewee	1. Method depends on the interviewer's ability to understand the topic and come up with questions during the interview
2. Simple way of getting information about behaviors, beliefs, etc. (nonquantifiable)	2. Level of clarity and eloquence of the interviewee
3. People are able to talk about the topic at hand in detail	3. Interviewer's unconscious guidance to interviewee's answers
4. Depending on the interviewee, little direction from the interviewer may be needed	4. More time consuming to conduct than surveys
5. The interviewer can discuss complex questions and expand questions based on responses about which the interviewer had no prior knowledge	5. Expensive if done in large groups
	6. Difficult to repeat exactly
6. No preset questions that could leave important information out of the interview	7. Personal nature of interview may make findings difficult to generalize
7. Easy to record (video or audio tapes)	

Adapted from "AS Sociology of AQA," http://www.sociology.org.uk/as4aqa.htm (accessed November 15, 2009).

if I'm on the right track." Your interviewee might not have precise numbers, so you will need to do some research on your own, but they might know about the history of the community, when and why they settled there, and more.

Try to build a connection with the interviewee as in a conversation. Ask questions when it feels appropriate. Prepare questions before the interview, but also ask questions that occur to you during the session. You will need to do some previous research in order to ensure you have some fluency on the interview topic.

You must first be somewhat familiar with the cultural background of your community leaders to create the right kind of questions. A lack of knowledge of the interviewee's cultural habits, behaviors, and beliefs may result in asking poor questions and getting poor answers (Korzenny and Korzenny 2005, p. 14). As an example, if your interviewee is Mexican American and has been established for a long time in your area, his or her views and perspectives about the community might greatly differ from those of a Cuban immigrant established in the 1960s. The latter had a different immigration experience—including reasons for coming to the United States, level of education, and worldviews—while Mexican Americans born here and whose families have been part of this country for a long time might see the same topics very differently.

Interviewing several local community leaders will give you a broad sense of their worldviews, expectations, and goals. Start the interview by asking about their personal story: how they became a part of this country and the local Latino community and how they got involved with its population. Librarians are usually concerned about asking personal questions, but you will find out that Latinos love to tell you their story. Some disclosure about you—about your family or children and how you became interested in Latino culture—will start a bond that can take the relationship a long way. A warning: do not tell a Cuban leader that you love spicy Mexican food! Their preferences in food are very different, and it might make you look a little off.

Market Channels: Help Promoting Your Efforts

Market channels are businesses and organizations that can help you attract customers. They have the ability to aid you in your efforts to reach the community they also serve. Market channels are small businesses on the Latino side of town—groceries, video stores, restaurants, clothing stores, and any other business owned by Latinos or places Latinos shop or go for other needs (such as insurance, health care, car purchases and repair, and so forth) as well as utility companies, large supermarkets and department stores, fast-food businesses, public and private transportation, and more.

The difference between market channels and strategic partners is the active role the strategic partner will play in developing a project, program, or event to fulfill the Latino community's needs. Market channels will only aid you in your promotional efforts.

You may find that some organizations or businesses have multiple roles as community leaders, market channels, and strategic partners, or even all three roles at times. Those roles might be interchangeable and temporary or permanent. You might be able to define a priori those potential roles, but it will be up to them to determine the role they play each step of the way.

Choosing your market channels carefully will determine your success in promoting your activities, outreach events, and services. Choose market channels where competition is light because you do not want your information to get lost in the midst of other information. If you are going to use the community bulletin board of a supermarket as your market channel, your information might be competing with many other announcements, and the public may not see it. Chapter 8 expands on these concepts through a discussion of promotional efforts.

The importance of market channels in promoting your efforts to reach the Latino community (or any other community) is a key element in your success. Organizations often do not take full advantage of free promotional channels, and all the planning and programming effort might go to waste if the information does not get to the targeted audience.

How to Proceed

When seeking strategic partners, community leaders, and market channels, cast a wide net. Do not leave anyone out—you will find a memory jogger list in Worksheet 3.1, "Researching Potential Strategic Partners." Remember that reaching this community might not only be *your* challenge, but it might be everybody's challenge. The leadership of the local public library may start a movement toward integrating this community to the everyday life of a town, city, or rural area.[8]

Consider creating a database just for this use. Microsoft Access is an excellent tool for this purpose, and it is usually included in your Microsoft Office software package, but you can also use the new 2007 Business Contact Manager Database in Microsoft Outlook. You can store the complete information of several contacts, write notes to yourself, set up meetings with your strategic partners, print letters, and follow up with the frequency of their input. Your library may already have a central database that can be used for this purpose, or you may simply use your e-mail address book to set up e-mail distribution lists and mail merges.

Once you detect potential helpers, let them know you are interested in targeting the local Latino community to offer your services. Inform your potential partners, community leaders, and market channels of your intentions in a friendly letter with a brief one-page description of your plan: you have already defined goals, a mission statement, and an internal outreach committee. Your general proposal, which is both a request *and* an offer of collaboration, should include your intentions, ideas of topics or activities that might help establish a mutually beneficial working relationship, and a request for their input. Tell them you will contact them at a defined future date—no longer than two weeks after the first contact—with more specific information about programs and projects.

At this point, you want to know more about your potential helpers. If you are targeting strategic partners—those with a more active role—find out who is the community liaison in each organization, either corporate or nonprofit. It might be a public or community relations officer, a diversity director, an outreach coordinator, someone in human resources, or a program coordinator. Once you find out who they are, work with them; that is their job. You may be surprised at how many corporations dedicate volunteer work to diversity.[9] If they also consent to be one of your market channels, for promotional purposes, they might allow you to include a promotional teaser in their mailings every now and then—for instance, utility companies and some government agencies involved with community services might agree to it. Be sure to explain further how they can serve to get the word out and augment the library's limited marketing resources. Remember, you are a nonprofit organization, and their effort might have a donation value that can be tax deductible. There are always opportunities, and you must find ways to use them.

Remember to reward their efforts. Suggest an honorary membership at the library for their continuous support, provide information they might need, or, most importantly, plan joint efforts.

As suggested in Worksheet 3.1, consider your local scene and where Latinos go for services, help, work, or play. In large cities, limit your list to the library service area, and work with those market channels included in that area; in small towns, include businesses and organizations that are in immediate contact with your potential clients, especially if the community is clustered in a particular part of town.

Employers can be a great potential resource for channeling information. Large or small, almost every employer has a cafeteria, small lunchroom, or kitchen where employees take breaks and spend some time during the day. Look for businesses that employ a substantial number of Latinos. Many businesses have personnel statistics that can help you. Once they agree to cooperate with you, find out their demographics and decide your course of action.

Ask the company about issues that might be of interest to their Latino employees and what information the library might be able to provide. Information exchange is sometimes crucial in subjects related to the workforce and the workplace, such as safety, family issues, absenteeism, sexual harassment, addictions, and more. You might provide information on these subjects in exchange for posting your information at their sites, coordinating a small presentation at lunchtime about library services and programs, or participating in job fairs or activities within the organization. It might be of such interest to some employers to sponsor ESL or computer classes at their facility that they might fund the endeavor.

Other important issues to help with market channels:

- Ask to post fliers or posters on their premises.
- Distribute door hangers for community center programs.
- Ask to include information in their mailings.
- Use them as your third-party credibility to advertise your activities.
- Train your staff to carry and distribute information at their locations.

- Supply them with information that enables them to talk about the services you offer.
- Consider having an annual or biannual gathering with your and their staff to foster teamwork.
- Do not forget to say thank you. For those who make a meaningful contribution to your organization's efforts, acknowledge their support in promotional materials that might relate to the program(s) they support or sponsor.
- Send them a copy of your achievements so they see your service is growing.
- Keep them in the loop!

If you are reaching out to small businesses, be sure your expectations are realistic. Small business owners are usually so busy that they have little time to dedicate to these efforts, but they might help by displaying information, announcing events, and offering promotional items or discounted or even free catering for events. Do not discount anyone. Let them know of your effort, and allow them to help in the best way they can. It will be free advertising for them to participate in your events, and small businesses are always looking for ways to save a buck!

Worksheet 3.2 in chapter 10 will help you contact and assess potential strategic partners and evaluate their role and participation in your outreach plan.

Talk to the Media

Although working with media outlets is really one of your promotional strategies, this great opportunity to become strategic partners with the local Latino media and work with them in a different way needs to be mentioned here. Please consider the following ideas:

1. Read local and national trade magazines and online news sites that talk about diversity and the Latino market. Check Web sites such as the National Association of Hispanic Publications, Inc. (NAHP),[10] but keep in mind that not all local publications are represented in their member list.
2. Subscribe to magazines, newspapers, and Web site and blog feeds (through RSS and Atom) that market to your target audience—that is, the Latino group you are trying to attract to your services—especially content that is bilingual or in Spanish. Make them a part of your library's permanent collection and your everyday activity. You will find which market channels are interested in your Latino community.
3. Do Internet and local Yellow Pages research to find local business that market to your target community—these companies will either promote specific products to serve the community or state *"Se habla español"* (Spanish is spoken).
4. Watch Spanish television and take note of companies and organizations marketing to Latinos.

Chapter 8, "Promoting Your Library," expands on these promotional strategies and offers guidelines to approach the media and other promotional outlets.

Why, How, and When to Participate

When thinking about your strategic partnership opportunities, define different ways to participate. Some ideas will come from your strategic partners, who might have suggestions about how and when you will be able to participate with them, an important reason for attending their community meetings and events.

Organizing activities with your strategic partnerships not only brings benefits to your institution in outreach but also in training, funding, development, and all other areas your library might want to explore. At the 71st IFLA General Conference and Council in Oslo, Norway, the Hamilton Public Library of Ontario, Canada, declared that strategic partnerships showed aspects of libraries of which you might not even be aware.[11] Here are some of their ideas:

1. Reputation: Your library's values, as expressed in your mission statement and vision, are valued and respected by other partners.
2. Credibility: The very existence of public libraries speaks for libraries as institutions that deliver what they promise.
3. Trusted judgment: Libraries are perceived as fair and ethical organizations without a political agenda but with a strong commitment to their communities.
4. Infrastructure: The large infrastructure of a public library can support partnerships in different ways—in-kind, funding leverage, research expertise, and so forth.
5. Staff involvement: Partnership development is a responsibility of senior staff positions. However, staff's information skills are relevant in different information-related environments. Partnerships can also create job opportunities (through donors, funding, etc.).
6. Respected skills: Librarians are well-respected and are sought for their expertise in the areas of traditional library skills, information technology, and new information environments.

With these ideas in mind, here are some examples of possible participation you could offer:

Sponsor a Community Activity by Helping with Logistics

At times, your participation may involve simply helping with logistics for a sponsored activity, lending your facilities, or publicizing an event. An organization might be planning an event where you could bring information related to a specific subject matter, provide materials or articles, or offer follow-up activities. For instance, while I was the director of an educational center, we organized the "First Latino Blood Drive in New Jersey" together with the American Red Cross of Central New Jersey. The event was publicized with flyers and posters in local schools and the free clinic in town. We distributed them across the Latino neighborhood in restaurants, stores, and grocery stores. It was also publicized in different local newspapers, especially those in Spanish. It was announced at the Spanish mass at local churches several times during that month. The drive was set up at the local church facility, starting before the Spanish mass so people could attend after the service. The promotion was a huge success, with 75 people participating in the drive in a small town of approximately 600 Latino families.

While donors were waiting to donate blood, we offered them information about our center and its activities. Information about health-related issues and HIV/AIDS was also provided at the site. It was an educational and positive experience for all participants. Balloons and entertainment were provided for children who were waiting for their parents, and adults also received giveaways.

Organize an Intervention

An intervention is a direct action you could take to change a negative situation in the Latino community you serve. For example, is there community concern regarding high rates of domestic violence, teen suicide, high school dropouts, or other issues? This information might be revealed through your marketing analysis, contact with your strategic partners, word of mouth, or hospital statistics showing that these are problems in your area.

Your entire intervention effort might be to simply raise awareness of the problem among the community and provide extra information at the library about where individuals can find help. Research and get the best materials you can find on the subject in Spanish. Display a brochure in Spanish offering library materials and a helpline at your partners' facilities, and concentrate your efforts on distributing the brochure. Make sure materials and services are offered in Spanish and English, especially if your population is not bilingual. Make the library the center of attention for a problem that has to do with the community's education and literacy levels while you expand awareness about community concerns—for Latinos and for the community at large.

If the nature of the topic is private or confidential, place your materials in a protected or reserved place where people will feel comfortable reviewing them. When Latinos or Latinas show up to request the materials, explain that the services are free and confidential, and make yourself available to answer questions. Show empathy and compassion but no pressure. While they might not take the materials the first time, if they find a friendly environment and Spanish-speaking personnel, they might come back for additional information.

Lend Your Facilities

Occasionally we hear stories about how public libraries can be a useful presence in the community by providing learning experiences. As suggested in chapter 1, placing public libraries at the center of community activities might give libraries a new role and, at the same time, allow them to provide a meeting place for organizations that lack a place to discuss, treat, and solve sporadic community affairs. Here is an example of the important role the public library could play in a community.

Latino workers in a town in New Jersey used to stand on a certain downtown street waiting for jobs, as they do in many other locations around the country—the famous "muster rows." Neighbors and law enforcement personnel found the behavior annoying and unsafe[12] for the town and decided to prohibit the practice. Reasons given were that potential employers picked them up in trucks, generating traffic problems in the area, overcrowding, loitering on the streets, and littering. The workers had some concerns, too. Workers would stand outside in any weather condition—cold, snow, rain, or heat—for long periods of time. Sometimes workers were picked up but never returned to the site, and other unsafe situations occurred.

With the help of local organizations, community leaders decided to meet to discuss a course of action. They wanted to maintain the muster row as an employment opportunity but at the same time comply with the new regulations. The workers could not find a public place to hold their meetings. Eventually, a local church allowed them to meet in its front hall.

As a result, the workers organized a workers' association called CASA (House), which continued to meet regularly at that church and is working toward employment and lifestyle improvements for this Latino community. Not only have they organized a workers' registry—for both workers and employers—but they also have organized ESL classes in the church's basement with volunteer teachers from the same community. The local newspaper played an instrumental role in helping publicize these activities, and a local photographer documented the process. Donations were also collected to pay expenses and materials for the ESL classes and to help some families financially when they lost work.

This story provides an excellent example of a great opportunity for a local public library to step in and offer its facility for such meetings. Latinos would have the opportunity to immediately get acquainted with the library. It would be a natural place to gather information about a course of action, their rights, and how they could contact other organizations that went through the same process. The library could capitalize on the meetings by offering library cards and introducing families to library services, and the library could continue hosting classes and events—a great opportunity to become the community leaders libraries should and are entitled to be!

Participate in and Support Community Activities

Asking your employees to participate in a local fair, festival, or community gathering might sound like an extra burden to their already busy lives. However, these venues may be ideal opportunities for reaching Latinos. If you have professionalized your outreach personnel, your diversity committee should be working like a charm, and you will have decided which opportunities to take advantage of and how you are going to participate at community activities, so it should be seen as an exciting opportunity, or at least the natural course of doing business, rather than a cause of additional stress.

Many towns have at least one community event during the year. Big cities offer countless opportunities for community activities. Choose the ones you feel will bring the best opportunities for you to reach out to the Latino community, and participate in those events. Latino community parades are celebrated each year and have continuity, but there are also health fairs and music festivals, among others.

Learning from Existing Efforts

Before starting activities with your strategic partnerships, do some research on existing efforts, such as the following:

1. YALSA (Youth Adult Library Services Association) has a committee called Partnerships Advocating for Teens (PAT), whose goal is "to explore, recommend, initiate and implement ways of working with other organizations that work for youth."[13] In 2009, YALSA presented a program called "It Takes Two: School and Public Libraries, Partnerships That Work" at the Chicago ALA Conference.[14] Also, please see library consultant and media specialist Tasha Squires's 2009 book *Library Partnerships: Making Connections between School and Public Libraries,* where she describes the relevant role of libraries in sharing ideas, resources, and programs offered by schools as a way of achieving community goals.
2. In his paper "Public Library Partnerships: Mission-Driven Tools for 21st Century Success," Glen E. Holt (1999), director of the St. Louis Public Library, explains how

appropriate partnerships can improve library services, and even their business operations, and provides an overview and an action outline about how to use partnerships for advancing libraries' institutional mission.

3. Also read "Public Library Partnerships Which Add Value to the Community: The Hamilton Public Library Experience," by Beth Hovius, Director of Public Service and Collections at the Hamilton Public Library, Ontario, Canada.[15] Hovius makes a detailed description of partnerships her institutions have been involved with as well as the benefits and learning experiences of each one.

These resources might not provide the exact examples you need to work with your Latino community, but they will certainly give you ideas on how and where to find your potential strategic partnerships.

You can find a list of national Latino organizations at directories such as LaRed Latina,[16] Fundsnet Services Online,[17] and the Hispanic Employment Program.[18] Find out if any of these organizations have a chapter in your area, and contact them to establish a strategic partnership.

Staff Participation in Strategic Partners' Activities

As important as determining your strategic partners is deciding the type of participation you will have with these partners or at these partners' activities. The type of participation referred to in this section is related to the imperative need to professionalize outreach activity within the library environment.

Making these tough decisions might not be in your realm or even in the realm of your CLO, but bringing the discussion to your organization's management is. If your organization decides to ignore some of its local population, then this is a decision for which your organization must take responsibility, but it is preferable to masking outreach efforts with a little here and there, frustrating employees and making little impact on the community you serve.

Asking your library personnel to leave brochures in the community is simply not enough. You want to ensure that your efforts are strategic and organized and that the information reaches its target audience. If your information distribution is based purely on willingness, you will wear out your staff and your contacts because the effort will be inconsistent, unsystematic, and sporadic.

For the same reasons, you cannot always rely on your personnel's good disposition to attend a community meeting or an activity at the hospital, sacrificing free time with family or other personal activities. So, too, you cannot expect your staff to stand at a community fair for hours or make announcements at the Spanish mass on a Saturday afternoon if it adds an extracurricular activity to their already busy schedules. Most libraries are short-handed, and staff members already wear many hats, so it is not reasonable to burden them with even more responsibilities.

The true success of any effort is consistency and dedication, and people need money and recognition for their efforts. Outreach efforts cannot only depend on the enthusiasm of a few; success requires the decision of all.

If you are effectively short-handed or lack the budget to develop outreach activities, your first task is to create the conditions that will enable you to do outreach. That decision, again, must be made at the higher levels and might become the first step in your outreach plan after assessing your organization goals and defining your priorities within the context of your population.

To know the nature of the task you confront, the amount of effort it entails, and the time, human factor, and funding it will require, you also need to know in depth who your Latino customers—current or potential—are. Getting to know your Latino patrons is not such a difficult task if you follow some of the guidelines provided in the next chapters.

Notes

1. Some examples of these lists can be found in Alire and Archibeque (1998, p. 167) and "Resources for Identifying Community Leaders," WebJunction Spanish Outreach Program, http://www.Web Junction.org (accessed November 30, 2009).
2. "Head Start is a national program that promotes school readiness by enhancing the social and cognitive development of children through the provision of educational, health, nutritional, social and other services to enrolled children and families." From "Mission Statement," U.S. Department of Health and Human Services, Administration for Children and Families, Office of Head Start, http://www.acf.hhs.gov/programs/ohs/ (accessed November 30, 2009).
3. U.S. Department of Health and Human Services, "Healthy People 2010," http://healthypeople. gov/Data/midcourse/html/execsummary/progress.htm (accessed November 29, 2009).
4. The ethnographic approach described in chapter 5 will help you overcome these barriers.
5. For more information on Yolanda Cuesta, Cuesta MultiCultural Consulting, and the WebJunction Spanish Outreach Program, visit http://www.WebJunction.org.
6. WebJunction Spanish Outreach Program, "Empowering Library Staff to Meet the Technology Needs of Spanish Speakers, 2003–2007," http://www.webjunction.org/slo (accessed November 30, 2009).
7. Robert Merton (1910–2003), American sociologist, developed this interviewing approach. See his work *Social Theory and Social Structure,* published in 1949 with edits in 1957 and 1968. For additional information on focused interview techniques, see Livesey (2005) or the online version at http://www.sociology.org.uk/as4aqa.htm (accessed November 15, 2009).
8. For an excellent account of a collaborative community effort, see Sundell (2000).
9. *DiversityInc.,* a trade magazine published in New Jersey, yearly ranks the top 50 companies for diversity nationwide. See http://www.diversityinc.com (accessed November 30, 2009).
10. The National Association of Hispanic Publications, Inc. (NAHP) is a nonprofit, nonpartisan trade advocacy organization representing the leading Spanish-language publications serving 41 markets in 39 states, the District of Columbia, and Puerto Rico, with a combined circulation of over 23 million. See http://www.nahp.org/member_publications/index.asp (accessed November 30, 2009).
11. Adapted from "Public Library Partnerships Which Add Value to the Community: The Hamilton Public Library Experience," by Beth Hovius (lecture, World Library and Information Congress: 71st IFLA General Conference and Council, "Libraries—A Voyage of Discovery," Oslo, Norway, August 14–18, 2005), http://archive.ifla.org/IV/ifla71/papers/041e-Hovius.pdf (accessed November 30, 2009).
12. "Hispanic Day Laborers Sue Freehold, Claiming Right to Gather to Seek Work," *New York Times,* December 31, 2003, http://www.nytimes.com/2003/12/31/nyregion/hispanic-day-laborers-sue-freehold-claiming-right-to-gather-to-seek-work.html (accessed November 30, 2009).
13. Young Adult Library Services Association, "It Takes Two: School and Public Libraries, Partnerships That Work, ALA Program, Chicago," YALSA blog, the official blog of the Young Adult Library Services Association, http://yalsa.ala.org/blog/2009/07/22/it-takes-two-school-and-public-libraries-partnerships-that-work-ala-program-chicago/ (accessed November 30, 2009).

14. Partnerships Advocating for Teens (PAT) Committee Description, http://www.ala.org/ala/mgrps/divs/yalsa/aboutyalsab/partnerships.cfm (accessed July 29, 2010).

15. See Note 11

16. LaRed Latina, a forum that disseminates sociopolitical, cultural, educational, and economic information about Latinos, is available at http://www.lared-latina.com/pros.html (accessed November 30, 2009).

17. Since 1996, Fundsnet Services Online has provided grant writing and fundraising resource assistance to those in need of funding for their programs and initiatives. See http://www.fundsnetservices.com/latorg.htm (accessed November 30, 2009).

18. Hispanic Employment Program, Reference Page http://www.hepm.org/index.cfm?page=main&frm=article&id=1 (accessed July 29, 2010).

WORKSHEET 3.1   Researching Potential Strategic Partners

Goal: Research all potential organizations in your local community that might be involved or interested in targeting your local Latino community.

1. Where do Latinos in your community shop?

2. Where do Latinos in your community go for services?

3. Where do Latinos in your community go for help?

4. Where do Latinos in your community work?

5. Where do Latinos in your community play or seek entertainment?

NOTES

_____

_____

_____

_____

Chapter 4

Getting to Know Your Latino Patrons: Part I

Overview

Educator and former librarian Sondra Cuban starts her Introduction to *Serving New Immigrant Communities in the Library* by acknowledging, "For generations, librarians have faced the great challenge of meeting the needs and interests of their changing ethnic communities. However, today's immigrants contend with different societal issues than did those in the past, and they test library services in new ways" (Cuban 2007, p. 1). Nothing fits this statement so well as the case of the Latino community.

In 2002, Latinos became the largest minority in the United States. In 2008, one in six residents was of Latino origin, and they comprised more than 15 percent of the total population.[1] The Latino population is the second fastest-growing population after Asians in every region of the country, and its growth rate is projected to remain that way until 2025. This population growth has no precedent in this country's history.[2]

In addition, the Latino community's cultural, economic, and educational diversity post a challenge for libraries marketing their services to this community. The importance of knowing who your audience is cannot be emphasized enough as it will define services, strategies, and resources.

This chapter introduces tools and procedures to develop the first stage of a market analysis—a Latino community market profile. The second stage, a Latino community cultural perspective, will be developed in the next chapter. This chapter also presents a brief scope of the Latino demographics in the nation and some characteristics for each region.

Also included in this chapter are suggested questions you can ask to find vital local information, and this chapter explains how different variables work together and have an impact on library services. Finally, I provide some useful worksheets and examples on how to interpret the data and apply this knowledge to define market segments.

In addition, I analyze and comment on sources of information, practical ways in which you can research those resources, and how you can use data to your advantage.

Your Market: A Moving Target

> Do not rely on assumptions or wishful thinking.

Success in reaching your Latino market is directly related to how knowledgeable you are of your target audience and its preferences and behaviors. It is also important to know how ready your potential customers might be to use your services.

Companies spend significant amounts of money on marketing research to plan marketing strategies before presenting a product. They also test the product after it has been released on the market to follow the product's performance and how the market responds to it.

Many excellent works for the library environment[3] have been published with concepts, ideas, and tips on how to gather information and assess the needs of the Latino community that libraries serve. A good combination of information gathering and other fundamental strategies, such as direct experience and observation, will help you and your CLO reach your market analysis' goals. And do not exclude the possibility of hiring marketing and outreach professionals if your budget allows!

If your organization lacks a market analysis, you need a good starting point to know who is in your target community and what their wants and needs are. Without hard data to back up your plan, your marketing strategy is aiming at a moving target.

Even if you—or your organization—have done previous market research, you need to regularly research your current and potential Latino patron base in order to remain familiar with the changing demographic trends of your local Latino target market. The U.S. Census shows that Latino settlements change every five to ten years. Localities in some states have seen their populations grow 200 and 300 percent in the last decade.[4]

One piece of advice: do not fall into the "analysis paralysis" pit. Gathering data is only the platform from which you will launch your outreach effort and not a goal in itself. Developing a market analysis should not be a difficult task if you follow some basic guidelines.

The Goals of Market Analysis

In today's busy marketing environment, consumers are bombarded with communication about products and services. The businesses most likely to succeed are usually those that have a better understanding of their consumer's needs and wants and position themselves as fulfilling a unique niche. These businesses must show they have advantages over the competition so their targeted consumers think of them as a first choice when looking for the type of product they offer. How can libraries become the first choice when Latinos think about obtaining information, looking for knowledge or enjoyment, or learning new skills? You need to know who your patrons are, learn about their needs and wants, and attract them to your services.

Your task is no different from that of any other business trying to find out valuable information about their target audience in order to successfully develop and market products or services.

The first step of your market analysis requires that you develop a market profile of your local community. It requires doing research into basic demographic data. I have selected a number of variables for this approach that often have the greatest impact in defining the needs of your local community. Combining some of these variables gives you a better understanding of how your Latino community behaves, what they need from you and your organization, and how you can plan to approach them with your products and services.

Once you have gathered this basic information, you need to identify segments or groups according to different demographic variables—such as age, gender, or country of origin—to answer questions such as the following: Do young Latinos from different countries of origin behave in the same way? How do Mexican women act differently from Puerto Rican women in relation to issues such as marriage and raising a family? There are many more questions of a similar nature you can also ask.

The next step in your research, discussed in chapter 5, will be to gain a greater understanding of your Latino market's cultural behaviors as influenced by variables such as an individual's social class, social norms and behaviors, lifestyle, use of time, gender roles, leadership, relationship with money, beliefs about life and death, health and religion, parent-child relationships, and more. Defining market segments and their cultural behaviors (Korzenny and Korzenny 2005, pp. 12–15) is vital to your planning process because it will help you reduce your risk of marketing the wrong product(s) or marketing to the wrong segment(s), thus wasting your money and efforts.

While demographic information is easy to gather and is usually readily available, as you'll see in the next section, cultural research entails gathering information about lifestyles, values, and behaviors across and within cultures, which might be a little more challenging, especially in a group as diverse as the Latino community.

Most market profile models work with quantitative demographic variables—such as percentages of Mexicans, Cubans, and Puerto Ricans; percentages of females or males; and so forth. I discuss the underlying reasons why the data is needed as well as how to interrelate the data to build information that helps you identify market segments, an important part of your market analysis. I also explain how each of these variables affects the makeup of your target audience and how the variables interact with each other.

Keep in mind two common mistakes. The first mistake is assuming your organization knows what Latino patrons need by following general guidelines of services to other groups in your library. For instance, some libraries spend money on a wonderful Spanish collection that does not serve their local Latino community needs, either because literacy levels are not high enough, the type of material does not relate to the cultural background or national origins of local Latinos, or it does not address the literary needs of that particular community. This approach is usually ineffective. I discuss this topic in chapter 6.

Second, you cannot market your services to your Latino market the same way you do to your general market, not only because of the existing diversity among Latinos themselves but also because of the cultural differences that exist between the general market and Latinos. Therefore, you will need to be culturally aware of those differences before you market your services appropriately.

Conducting a market analysis will help you accomplish the following goals:

1. Gain an understanding of your Latino market's behaviors, beliefs, and preferences
2. Identify market segments within your Latino community

3. Learn your market segments' level of readiness (how ready they are to use library services)
4. Prioritize service to market segments according to needs, wants, and resources

A market analysis is a two-step procedure to get to know your target audience. The first step entails developing a market profile of your Latino audience in both demographic and cultural dimensions. The second step requires carrying out a community needs assessment, which will be covered in chapter 6.

Market Profile

The first step of developing a market profile requires gathering and interpreting basic data or demographic information about your local Latino community because it has the greatest impact in defining the needs of your local community. These demographic variables include information about country of origin, socioeconomic status, immigration status, age, gender, levels of education, family composition, group size, income, occupation, and time of residence in the United States. These variables are introduced because of their relevance to library planning purposes. Each variable is discussed in terms of its following characteristics:

1. Short summary of national trends
2. Variable significance and how it relates to other variables
3. Suggested questions for the library professional to ask when doing market research

Latino Demographic Data

Most Americans became aware of the reality of Latino demographics after the 2000 U.S. Census results were published. Their presence had been known—especially in those areas where Latinos have been established for generations—but their numbers were surprisingly overwhelming.

The 2000 U.S. Census estimated the U.S. Hispanic[5] population at 35.3 million—approximately 12.5 percent of the total U.S. population[6]—increasing by more than 60 percent between the 1990 Census and the 2000 Census. During the period between 1950 and 1996, the total U.S. population grew more that 75 percent. Throughout the same period, the Hispanic population increased more than 600 percent.[7] It is estimated that by 2050, the Hispanic population will constitute 30 percent of the nation's inhabitants, or 132.8 million (Lytwak 1999). Nearly one in three residents of the U.S. will be of Hispanic origin by 2050.

Latinos increasingly fuel the population growth of key states. According to a study by the U.S. Census Bureau,[8] between 1990 and 2000, Hispanics increased by over 100 percent the populations of 22 states, including North Carolina (from 1.2 to 4.7%), Arkansas (0.8 to 3.2%), Georgia (1.7 to 5.3%), Tennessee (0.7 to 2.2%), and Nevada (10.4 to 19.7%). California, Texas, and Florida gained 3.3 million, 2.3 million, and 1.1 million Hispanics in that order, which represent the largest numerical increases.[9]

More recent information from the Pew Hispanic Center and the "Statistical Portrait of Hispanics in the United States, 2007," is shown in Table 4.1.

TABLE 4.1 Change in the Hispanic Population, by State: 2000 and 2007

	2007	2000	Change 2000–2007	Percent Change (%) 2000–2007
California	13,219,347	10,928,470	2,290,877	21.0
Texas	8,591,352	6,653,338	1,938,014	29.1
Florida	3,751,186	2,673,654	1,077,532	40.3
New York	3,146,959	1,527,145	395,699	25.9
Arizona	1,893,171	1,292,152	601,019	46.5
New Jersey	1,379,047	1,117,604	261,443	23.4
Colorado	967,536	735,769	231,767	31.5
New Mexico	872,626	759,343	113,283	14.9
Georgia	733,510	434,375	299,135	68.9
Nevada	643,358	393,397	249,961	63.5
North Carolina	636,442	377,084	259,358	68.8
Washington	611,369	444,718	166,651	37.5
Pennsylvania	564,880	399,736	165,144	41.3
Massachusetts	519,190	428,530	90,660	21.2
Virginia	488,589	333,482	155,107	46.5
Connecticut	411,349	330,952	80,397	24.3
Michigan	394,878	319,463	75,415	23.6
Oregon	391,561	273,209	118,352	43.3
Maryland	346,990	230,992	115,998	50.2
Utah	307,132	214,750	92,382	43.0
Indiana	301,599	201,203	100,396	49.9
Ohio	282,603	218,350	64,253	29.4
Wisconsin	267,563	191,097	76,466	40.0
Oklahoma	262,223	186,340	75,883	40.7
Kansas	246,966	173,746	73,220	42.1
Tennessee	211,797	142,732	69,065	48.4
Minnesota	207,602	116,692	90,910	77.9
Missouri	169,739	118,235	51,504	43.6
South Carolina	168,322	94,652	73,670	77.8

(*Continued*)

TABLE 4.1 (*Continued*)

	2007	2000	Change 2000–2007	Percent Change (%) 2000–2007
Idaho	148,133	100,271	47,862	47.7
Arkansas	145,918	85,303	60,615	71.1
Louisiana	135,077	92,836	42,241	45.5
Nebraska	133,666	80,204	53,462	66.7
Rhode Island	122,812	89,870	32,942	36.7
Alabama	121,552	111,634	9,918	8.9
Iowa	115,934	72,152	43,782	60.7
Hawaii	101,865	87,853	14,012	15.9
Kentucky	87,175	56,922	30,253	53.1
Mississippi	51,921	37,811	14,110	37.3
Delaware	50,559	37,301	13,258	35.5
District of Columbia	48,941	44,092	4,849	11.0
Alaska	39,061	25,742	13,319	51.7
Wyoming	36,753	29,751	7,002	23.5
New Hampshire	32,707	21,536	11,171	51.9
Montana	23,624	18,568	5,056	27.2
South Dakota	23,275	10,718	12,557	117.2
West Virginia	18,223	10,101	8,122	80.4
Maine	14,322	12,925	1,397	10.8
North Dakota	9,094	7,429	1,665	22.4
Vermont	6,254	5,260	994	18.9
Total	45,378,596	35,204,480	10,174,116	28.9

Source: Pew Hispanic Center tabulations of 2000 Census IPUMS (Integrated Public Use Microdata Series) and the 2007 American Community Survey (1% IPUMS): "Statistical Portrait of Hispanics in the United States, 2007," http://pewhispanic.org/files/fact sheets/hispanics2007/Table-13.pdf (accessed December 1, 2009).

Independent sources state that the Census left out a large number of Latinos living and working illegally in each state, which would place the Hispanic community as the largest minority group in the country. The Pew Hispanic Center estimates that over 10 million undocumented immigrants live in the country.[10] This addition positions the United States as the second most populated "Hispanic" country in the world—after Mexico, whose population is approximately 111,211,789 (estimated as of July 2009).[11]

Country of Origin

Summary of National Trends

According to a 2004 survey brief by the Pew Hispanic Center,[12] there is an important diversity between the origins of the Latino population in different states. Five states with large Latino populations were surveyed, representing 69 percent of the total U.S. Latino population, including California (31%), Texas (19%), New York (8%), Florida (8%) and New Jersey (3%). The Latino population in California and Texas is overwhelmingly Mexican (84% and 83%, respectively), the report said, with a minor presence of Central Americans in both states (9% and 5%, respectively).

The majority of Latinos in Florida are Cuban (41%), followed by Puerto Ricans (18%), Mexicans (17%), and South Americans (13%). In New York and New Jersey, Latinos are represented by Puerto Ricans (33% and 30%, respectively), Dominicans (31% and 21%, respectively), and South Americans (13% and 21%, respectively).

Totals of each country of origin are shown in Table 4.2, which indicates a great predominance of Mexicans followed—way behind—by Puerto Ricans and other populations of Latino or Hispanic origin.

TABLE 4.2 Nativity, by Detailed Hispanic Origin, 2007

Nationality	Total	Percent (%)
Mexican	29,189,334	64.3
Puerto Rican	4,114,701	9.1
All Other Spanish/Hispanic/Latino	2,880,536	6.3
Cuban	1,608,835	3.5
Salvadoran	1,473,482	3.2
Dominican	1,198,849	2.6
Guatemalan	859,815	1.9
Colombian	797,195	1.8
Honduran	527,154	1.2
Ecuadorian	523,108	1.2
Peruvian	470,519	1.0
Spaniard	353,008	0.8
Nicaraguan	306,438	0.7
Argentinean	194,511	0.4
Venezuelan	174,976	0.4
Panamanian	138,203	0.3

(Continued)

TABLE 4.2 (*Continued*)

Nationality	Total	Percent (%)
Costa Rican	115,960	0.3
Other Central American	111,513	0.2
Chilean	111,461	0.2
Bolivian	82,434	0.2
Other South American	77,898	0.2
Uruguayan	48,234	0.1
Paraguayan	20,432	0.0
Total	45,378,596	100.0

Source: Pew Hispanic Center tabulations of the 2007 American Community Survey (1% IPUMS): "Statistical Portrait of Hispanics in the United States, 2007," http://pewhispanic.org/files/factsheets/hispanics2007/Table-6.pdf (accessed December 1, 2009).

Country of origin or nationality plays an important role in the assimilation or acculturation process and interacts with issues of identity. Mexicans have been defined as less likely to assimilate despite being part of this country for over a century. They tend to keep issues of identity close to their heart. When asked, 62 percent of Mexicans identify themselves by their nationality of origin, against 57 percent Puerto Ricans and 41 percent of Cubans (de la Garza et al. 1992).

Variable Significance and How It Relates to Other Variables

Where are your local Latino groups coming from? Latinos coming from distant countries probably had money, documents, and a visa to enter the country, and they are usually—but not always—members of higher social classes, more educated, and with a higher economic level. Many Latinos coming from bordering territories might have used alternative routes not requiring documentation. Coming to this country as an agricultural worker versus as a professional will define different behaviors in relation to social mobility; attitude toward education, literacy, and technology; and geographical mobility—the ability to go back and forth to their country of origin or move around inside the United States.

If your local Latino population belongs to the same region in their country of origin, it might result in a more homogeneous group with which to work. For instance, people coming from Puebla, Mexico, are more likely to have common traits and traditions, native stories and legends, symbols, and so forth. Puerto Ricans from New York will show different behaviors from those coming from the island of Puerto Rico.

Country of origin also might define—or be related to—reasons for coming to the United States, immigration status, socioeconomic status, and level of education.

Suggested Questions When Doing Research

- Where are your potential or current Latino patrons coming from?
- What regions in each country are they from?
- What year did they migrate to the United States?

- How was the political and/or economical situation in their country of origin at time of immigration?
- What other reasons (such as attractive U.S. legislation, working visas, employment opportunities, and low-cost lifestyle) attract them to live in your community?

This first step is crucial in defining the services you will market and the level of readiness of your market to receive those services. For instance, a Cuban professional with 30 years or more of residence in the United States might have a solid knowledge of library services while a recent migrant worker might require offerings related to Spanish or English literacy and vital information regarding immigration status.

Race and Racial Tension

Summary of National Trends

Each country in Latin America is defined by a racial mix derived not only from the influences of the colonial conquest (Spain, Portugal, England, the Netherlands, etc.) but also the characteristics of the aboriginal population and the successive slavery and immigration waves from other continents.[13] Those racial mixes, however, do not guarantee a seamless racial integration among each country's inhabitants, much less among those of different countries. In addition, immigrants face issues of racial interaction with local groups in the United States (whites, African Americans, Asians, Native Americans, etc.).

Several authors (Fuch 1990; Gans 2004; Wilson 2003) have sustained that race is a detrimental factor in how Latinos assimilate or acculturate to this country and how the host culture "allows"—or not—their assimilation or acculturation process. Racial tension among Latinos of different nationalities, among Latinos and local racial and ethnic groups, or between established groups and new Latino immigrants is common due to several factors that include the following: 1) a sense of belonging and seniority embraced by the established groups or minorities; 2) different perceptions of each other's racial and ethnic groups; 3) the language and cultural divide and a resistance from both parties to bridge that divide; 4) established groups fearful of a decline in the current civic and social structure; and 5) the transitional aspects of neighborhoods' ethnic transformation.

In addition, although Latinos have a high interracial marriage rate (30%),[14] class and race divisions in Latin America do exist. They might not follow the ways Americans describe and define race (Fox 1996, p. 23), but in most Latin American countries, white minorities are usually more educated, with higher social mobility and economic power, while mixed racial groups and indigenous groups are less educated, poorer, and have lower social mobility.

Variable Significance and How It Relates to Other Variables

Race as a variable interacts with country of origin, literacy levels, and language ability. These variables may determine the level of hardship your local population goes through in the assimilation or acculturation process. You need to be familiar with the racial tensions that affect your local Latino community and the factors that are at play to avoid interference with your planned activities.

Suggested Questions When Doing Research

- Is the local Latino population homogeneous in relation to issues of race and racial background?

- Are there antagonistic groups in the local community in relation to historic issues (for instance, territorial conflict between two countries that share a geographical limit)?
- How does the local community receive recent immigrants?
- Is the perception of the established English-speaking population that immigrants are taking jobs away?
- Are recent immigrants becoming victims of scams, robbery, and exploitation?
- Are established groups of immigrants from one country discriminating against immigrants from other Latin American countries?

These and other conflicts might be addressed by carefully planning the services and activities offered to the diverse groups in your community and by establishing strategic partnerships with community leaders representing different nationalities in your local community, a variety of social agencies, and the local government.

Geographic Mobility

Summary of National Trends

Geographic mobility is related to two different activities: 1) internal geographic mobility, or the immigrants' patterns of relocation within the United States; and 2) external geographic mobility, or the opportunity to go back and forth to their countries of origin.

In the last decade or so, external and internal mobility have changed old patterns of relocation—proximity to major international airports, clusters in urban neighborhoods, and family reunification—to new ones. Different factors, such as work availability, services, friendlier states, and location in rural areas farther from urban environments, affect these changes.

Work availability might define seasonal geographic mobility. For instance, Latinos involved in the horse racing industry travel with the horses to different locations according to seasonal demand. In the same way, since the 1960s, changes in the meatpacking industry[15] originated great internal geographic mobility in the states of Colorado, Minnesota, Iowa, Nebraska, Texas, Utah, and North Carolina.

Variable Significance and How It Relates to Other Variables

Internal geographic mobility affects or delays Latinos' acculturation/assimilation process as it can prevent the family's permanent insertion in a local community. External mobility is affected by the family's socioeconomic status—which includes the ability to financially support long-distance travel and relocation. It is related to family composition—for instance, a family of five needs a substantial amount of money and time off from work and school to travel back home, a luxury only established immigrants might have. It is also related to their occupation—seasonal agricultural or construction workers, for instance, might usually leave in late November and return around the month of March every year, depending on the type of crop or project in which they are involved.

Immigration status also has an impact on external geographic mobility: some undocumented Latino immigrants might be unwilling to travel back to their countries of origin for fear of being caught at the border, while others might do it on a regular basis, especially those living in bordering states.

Suggested Questions When Doing Research

- How long have your local Latino families been established in this area? How many generations (or years)?
- Are there recently established families as well? How long have they been around?
- Are recently established Latinos in your area coming from outside the country, or are they relocating from other states (which means they might be more familiar with the system and, consequently, more ready to use library services)?
- If they are internal migrants, where are they coming from? A city or a rural area? Gateway states? (Gateway states are those considered the first places Latin American immigrants arrive and include California, Florida, New York, Illinois, New Mexico, and Arizona.)
- If coming from outside the country, are they seasonal workers? What times of the year are they engaged in work?

Internal geographic mobility will define your changing demographics and the community needs assessment of your local Latino community, which you need to update every five years. It will also define the knowledge and readiness of your local community about library services. Your external geographic mobility will define the type of services, schedules, and general dynamic of services offered during the year. Migrant workers sometimes bring their families with them, and children lack educational continuity when they change schools several times in a school year.

Seasonal work will affect the continuity of any service that needs fixed schedules (ESL or computer classes, for instance) but will increase the presence of Latinos during certain times of year, when you would be able to focus on programming your activities. Parents working summer schedules might require children's activities at your local library.

Socioeconomic Status/Social Mobility
Summary of National Trends

Latino immigration differs from other waves of immigration in having less opportunity for social mobility (Gleeson 2005). Reasons include coming from a very class-structured, increasingly unequal society (Torres-Rivas 1983)—even encompassing pockets of servitude in some regions of Latin America—which defines a "class mentality" among poor Latinos[16], and language inability, which includes not only a lack of English ability but also native or Amerindian languages spoken as first languages or mother tongue. Some of these languages do not have a written format. These concepts are expanded upon in chapter 7.

The type of jobs they perform, usually in agriculture and services, and their geographical mobility, impedes permanent settlement and stability. Compared to former waves of immigration into the United States, which slowly assimilated into the fabric of society in a span of over 100 years—especially for those who never went back to the "old country" (Cuban 2007; Takaki 1994)—Latinos find it more difficult to move up the social ladder.

According to a 2000 Pew Hispanic Center study, Latinos are concentrated in occupations that rank among the lowest in socioeconomic status.[17] Fifty-five percent of Latinos were engaged in occupations falling in the bottom third of the socioeconomic scores (along with 44 percent of blacks), while only about 30 percent of whites and Asians work in these occupations. However, only 13 percent of Hispanics and 17 percent of blacks were employed in the seven highest-ranking occupations, while whites and Asians doubled these rates—26 percent and 32 percent, respectively.

Variable Significance and How It Relates to Other Variables

Socioeconomic mobility relates to income and occupational mobility, but time spent by immigrants in the United States is an important factor for their ability to move upward. These variables are discussed later in this chapter. Different groups in your community might have dissimilar opportunities for social and economic mobility related to their immigration status and country of origin. You need to find out where they are starting from and how other variables interact to increase or hold back social and economic mobility among the Latino community you serve.

Suggested Questions When Doing Research

- What type of economic insertion do local Latinos have in your community?
- If they are recent immigrants, what type of occupation do they have in your community? Are there local groups with the same background to receive them at first (called "clusters," those groups provide shelter and share housing and opportunities with newcomers)?
- If they have been established for a longer time—two or more generations—how has their social mobility been affected and in how much time? (For instance, you can find out if their children or grandchildren have gone to college, acquired better job opportunities, moved to different geographic locations or still live in the same location, etc.)
- If established for a long time, are Latinos of the second and third generations—that would be first and second generations of Americans—integrated to the local community?
- Are they still working in the same industry and type of activity, craft, or job as their parents or grandparents?
- What is the percentage of Latinos (male and females) pursuing higher education? What is their background?
- Have local families developed small businesses and/or professional offices in the area (lawyers, doctors, real estate brokers, restaurants, groceries, etc.)?
- Is there an established Latino middle class in your area?

With this information, you will find a better panorama of who is who in your community and how you need to define services for each segment. While it is true that Latinos from middle and upper classes living in the United States are rather well educated, speak English well, and are familiar with American culture, those who do not speak English well are not necessarily from lower classes, uneducated, or undocumented. Find out if these customers might be ready for library services, and emphasize their ability and eagerness to learn and become knowledgeable about the system.

Immigration Status

Summary of National Trends

Immigration status is a strong variable that defines services and promotional strategies and affects immigrants' response to library services. Official data from the Department of Homeland Security's Office of Immigration Statistics (Massey 2005) show the national origins of documented migrants. Among legal immigrants to the United States, 25 percent are from Mexico, 11 percent are from the Caribbean, and 12 percent are from the rest of Latin America, comprising 48 percent of the total 9.1 million legal immigrants that arrived between 1991 and 2000. Also in 2000, 69 percent of the 7 million undocumented immigrants residing in the United States were from Mexico, 2 percent were from the Caribbean, and 12 percent were from elsewhere in Latin America. Many immigrants enter the country legally and then become undocumented because of visa expiration or an inability to change their immigration status.

In 2007, the Woodrow Wilson International Center for Scholars published results for its "Key Findings from the 2006 Latino National Survey." The survey included 8,634

TABLE 4.3 Generations and Citizenship Status

Generation and Citizenship Status of Interview Subjects (in percentages nationally and by state)					
	Gen 1	Gen 2	Gen 3	Gen 4+	Citizen	Noncitizen
Nationwide					57.0	42.9
Arizona	56.5	16.3	13.1	12.9	61.4	38.4
Arkansas	81.4	5.5	5.9	5.7	39.5	60.5
California	67.7	15.1	8.3	8.3	56.8	43.2
Colorado	58.5	8.5	16.4	14.9	60.3	39.7
D.C.	75.2				45.0	55.0
Florida	72.0	9.7	3.8	1.5	67.4	32.6
Georgia	81.9	7.4	3.1	4.9	32.9	63.1
Illinois	65.8	16.0	6.6	6.1	61.6	38.4
Iowa	62.0	12.3	11.8	11.8	54.4	45.6
Maryland	86.6				45.0	55.0
Nevada	75.9	15.6	7.1	4.0	49.4	50.6
New Jersey	68.3	12.1	5.5	1.1	60.8	39.2
New Mexico	43.7	9.3	27.1	19.1	72.6	27.4
New York	56.2	7.4	8.4	6.5	67.1	32.9
North Carolina	85.5	7.1	1.8	2.4	34.3	66.7
Texas	56.4	12.5	15.3	15.0	63.4	36.6
Virginia	80.7				47.9	52.1
Washington	66.5	10.4	10.0	9.4	55.3	44.7

Source: "Redefining America: Key Findings from the 2006 Latino National Survey. Weighted Demographic Tables—Nationally and by State," Woodrow Wilson International Center for Scholars, http://www.wilsoncenter.org/index.cfm?topic_id=1427&categoryid=170E04BB-65BF-E7DC-4B8C5CB1C8E70BC0&fuseaction=topics.events_item_topics&event_id=201793 (accessed December 1, 2009).

respondents from 15 states. This study of Hispanic demographic trends indicates great changes in the Latino community since 1989, the last year of the survey.

Table 4.3 indicates that higher numbers of first-generation immigrants are settling in the new, fastest growing states such as Arkansas, North Carolina, Georgia, Nevada, Maryland, and Virginia, thus increasing the amount of illegal immigration in those states.[18] Trends also show that the substantial immigrant population moving to these new states is the result of anti-immigrant sentiment and policies developed in longer established or traditional Latino-populated states, such as Arizona and Colorado.[19]

Even though California, Florida, and Texas continue to be gateway states with a high incidence of first-generation immigrants, communities tend to be more established in those states where the population has been settled for longer and where there is a higher percentage of older Latinos: in Arizona, the fourth generation is 12.9 percent of the immigrant population; in New Mexico, 19.1 percent; in Colorado, 14.9 percent; and in Texas, 15 percent. The states that have been populated by immigrants the longest also show higher degrees of citizenship, which means that a higher percentage of first-generation immigrants acquire legal status in their lifetime.

The Pew Hispanic Center (Passell 2007) reports that the percentage of legal foreign-born residents who became naturalized U.S. citizens in 2005 rose to 52 percent—a 14 percent increase since 1990. Annually, the average number of naturalizations increased from less than 150,000 in the 1970s to more than 650,000 since the mid-1990s.

In 2005, the same source informs that among all 36 million foreign-born residents, 35 percent were naturalized citizens, 33 percent were legal noncitizens, and 31 percent were unauthorized migrants. The amount of all legal foreign-born residents who became naturalized U.S. citizens rose to 52 percent that year—the highest level in the past 25 years and a 14 percent increase since 1990—showing an increased tendency that those who are eligible do apply for citizenship. But most importantly for library services, 8.5 million legal resident immigrants were eligible for naturalization.

Also, keep in mind those special situations that involve some immigrants from Latin America. For instance, the U.S. government offers temporary protected status (TPS) for natives of three Latin American countries: El Salvador, Honduras, and Nicaragua. These countries' natives acquired TPS because of "ongoing armed conflict, an environmental disaster, or other extraordinary and temporary conditions," according to the U.S. Citizenship and Immigration Services.[20] Immigrants from those countries, legally or illegally entering the United States, are not forced to go back, but they have to complete paperwork each time their TPS expires. Lately, natives of Haiti have been designated as eligible for the TPS visa.

Immigrants can also achieve legal permanent residence through the Legal Immigration Family Equity Act (LIFE) or a family member who is a legal citizen; adoption or marriage; the diversity lottery; employment; the registry provisions of the Immigration and Nationality Act, which allow a person who has been present in the United States since January 1, 1972, to become eligible to obtain lawful permanent residence even if they are illegally in the United States now or initially entered the country illegally; through a religious organization; and through investment.[21]

Each year, the Diversity Visa (DV) Lottery program makes 50,000 immigrant visas available through a lottery to people from countries with low rates of immigration to the United States. Countries such as Mexico, Canada, China, India, and the United Kingdom are excluded. Of such visas, 5,000 are allocated for use under the Nicaraguan Adjustment and Central American Relief Act (NACARA), which began with the Diversity Lottery program of 1999.[22]

Variable Significance and How It Relates to Other Variables

The variable of immigration status is related to country of origin, the opportunities and limitations of each nationality, socioeconomic status, who and how they enter the country, and time of residence in the United States—the longer time in the country, the more possibilities to obtain some sort of documentation. It also is affected by events occurring in the immigrant's country of origin at the time of emigration—which, in some cases, help (e.g., political refugees)—and the conditions under which the immigrant stays in the United States (for instance, the difference between a student who comes with a temporary visa and is offered employment to stay and a temporary worker who decides to stay after his or her working visa is expired).

Suggested Questions When Doing Research

- What is their country of origin and related immigration status? (For example, Puerto Ricans are U.S. citizens while immigrants from other countries might not be.)
- Are they established or recent immigrants? If recent immigrants, how long since they came? What type of job do they perform, or what industries are they engaged in? Are employers willing to sponsor their immigration status?
- If they have been in the area for over 10 years, what is the immigration status of their family? (The status might be mixed and could include children born in the United States and/or undocumented parents and grandparents.)
- What are their needs for information in relation to their immigration status?

By taking advantage of this information[23] and finding out who in your community is ready to take the steps to become permanent residents or citizens, you might develop an opportunity to offer information and citizenship classes at the library. However, you need to know your stats and set measurable goals in order to position your resources, staff, and budget. This is a hot subject in the Latino community, and if you create expectations, you had better be ready to respond to those expectations!

Age

Summary of National Trends

Statistics show that Latinos are a younger population than whites, African Americans, and other established minorities.[24] Hispanic children under 5 years old represent 10.5 percent of the general Hispanic population while children under 5 years old represent only 6.7 percent of the general population. Hispanics comprise 22 percent of children under 18. Hispanic children will represent 39 percent of the population in 2050, compared to 38 percent of single-race, non-Hispanic whites.[25] Hispanics 65 and older represent 4.8 percent of the Hispanic population and 12 percent of the general population. Data in numbers of Latinos by age group and sex are presented in Table 4.4. Note that Latino males are a majority in the youngest ages, most probably because of the higher number of first-generation male immigrants. (The source does not differentiate native-born from foreign-born Latinos in this table.)

Age at immigration of those born outside the United States has a direct impact on second language acquisition[26] and literacy ability. The 2002 National Survey of Latinos (Brodie et al. 2002) categorized four groups: age 10 or younger, 11 to 17, 18 to 25, and 26 or older.

TABLE 4.4   Hispanic or Latino Population by Age and Sex, 2000

Hispanic or Latino Origin Population Selected Age Groups	Both Sexes	Male	Female
Under 18 years	12,342,259	6,334,844	6,007,415
Under 1 year	771,053	394,611	376,442
1 to 4 years	2,946,921	1,505,820	1,441,101
5 to 13 years	6,185,947	3,160,636	3,025,311
14 to 17 years	2,438,338	1,273,777	1,164,561
18 to 64 years	21,229,968	11,100,077	10,129,891
18 to 24 years	4,743,880	2,598,352	2,145,528
25 to 44 years	11,639,545	6,147,220	5,492,325
45 to 64 years	4,846,543	2,354,505	2,492,038
65 years and over	1,733,591	726,874	1,006,717

Source: U.S. Census Bureau, "Census 2000 PHC-T-8. Race and Hispanic or Latino Origin by Age and Sex for the United States: 2000," Table 8, February 25, 2002, http://www.census.gov/population/cen2000/phc-t08/tab08.pdf (accessed December 1, 2009).

Of these four categories, the highest percentage of immigrants pertains to the 18–25 group (37%) and 26 and older (34%). Those who immigrated at a young age—10 or under—may have had more similar experiences to Latinos born in the United States, are more likely to speak English—18 percent are English dominant and 70 percent are bilingual—and would have been through the American educational system at some point, with a higher percentage of high school and college education than those who arrived at an older age.

Variable Significance and How It Relates to Other Variables

The age variable of your population interacts with other variables such as immigration status, time of residence in the United States, country of origin, and geographic mobility. Age is also defined by your local population or target audience belonging to the first, second, third, or fourth generation of immigration. For instance, aging Latinos who are first-generation immigrants to this country are more likely to plan their retirement in their country of origin. Several factors influence this decision, such as low retirement savings or social security contributions, cost of living in the United States, reuniting with family members (aging parents, siblings, and extended family and friends), and dismemberment of the family composition in the United States.

Suggested Questions When Doing Research

- How old are the different groups or market segments in your local Latino population? (School registration might be an indicator of extensive established young families in the area, as would the birthrate at the local hospital or your town's Office of Vital Statistics. You can also check church attendance and hospital statistics for older Latinos.)

- What issues in relation to family are of concern in your local Latino community? Are there health issues related to age (from teen pregnancy and suicide rates to aging chronic diseases) for which the library can provide information and/or awareness?
- How does age relate to working matters such as safety, benefits, rights, and obligations for which the library can provide information?
- How does age relate to issues of literacy and educational opportunities for those involved in the workforce, looking for employment opportunities, or pursuing a higher education?
- What are the literacy rates—in English and Spanish—in the young Latino population (age 26 and under)?

The future of the labor force, from blue collar to professional and management employment; education and educational opportunities; an increase or decrease in income levels and employment opportunities; and access to information and technology are just some of the areas where libraries can help this young, growing community continue to position itself in key areas of American life.

Gender

Summary of National Trends

There are 46.9 million Hispanic adults in the United States. The number of Hispanic males in 2008 was 107 per every 100 Hispanic females in contrast to the overall population with 97 males per every 100 females.[27] Women represent 48 percent of all Hispanics, according to U.S. Census Bureau 2007 estimates, which continues the same trend of the past decade.[28]

According to a Pew Hispanic Center analysis of data from the U.S. Census Bureau and the United Nations (Fry 2006), women constituted a large share of legal immigrants to the United States but have been surpassed by an increasing flow of undocumented male immigrants.

Contrary to global trends, the United States added increasing numbers of undocumented male immigrants at rates greater than both female immigration and legal immigration rates. The report shows that in March 2005, 52 percent of the 11.1 million undocumented immigrants were male adults, while only 48 percent were females. Gender composition in U.S. migration trends shows a unique characteristic different from trends in other countries around the world.

However, even in 1989, California reported[29] the appearance of Latino single young females and working mothers in Latino migration trends. Although California has always presented occupational opportunities for immigrant women in domestic work, sweatshops, and agriculture, these opportunities have expanded greatly in the state's economy. Due to textile and shoe manufacturing companies fleeing to China, the female Mexican skilled labor force migrated to the United States from these collapsed industries in the northern part of Mexico. In other cases, employment opportunities in field and food processing operations for women increased up to 40 percent of the agricultural work force. A large number of these women were not only working wives but also single unmarried females or heads of single-parent households. These trends also affected women from Central American countries.[30]

Latino women have a higher fertility rate, at 84 births per 1,000 compared to 63 births per 1,000 of non-Hispanic women; are equally likely to be married (54%), although immigrants are more likely to be married than native-born Hispanic women; and are younger than the non-Hispanic white population, especially those born in the United States.[31]

Latino women are also less educated than non-Hispanic women. Around 36 percent have less than a high school education, and nearly half of all Latino immigrants (49%) have less than a high school education.[32]

Findings also state that Latino women are more likely to be employed in blue-collar occupations—cleaning and maintenance, food preparation, production, and personal care and service occupations—than non-Hispanic women. They are twice as likely to live in poverty compared to non-Hispanic women. Finally, 55 percent of native-born Latinas report they speak English very well while 73 percent of immigrant Hispanic women say they do not speak English very well.[33]

According to a 2005 Pew Hispanic report,[34] Hispanic male and female workers greatly differ in their occupational attributes: 49 percent of males worked in construction and production occupations in 2000 while 61 percent of females worked in service and sales occupations. Hispanic women are also more likely to be in professional occupations than males, said the report.

Variable Significance and How It Relates to Other Variables

As you see, information about the gender demographics of your population will relate to age, family composition, education levels and literacy ability, occupation, socioeconomic status, and time spent in the United States. "Nuyorican" (New York Puerto Rican) single mothers with small children will have very different needs and responses to library outreach than third-generation Mexican American working young women with no children. Keep in mind these levels of acculturation/assimilation when offering services to this population, as well as to support your offering with logistics.

Suggested Questions When Doing Research

- How many Latino females and males are there in your community (region, neighborhood, town, etc.)?
- What ages are they? (Try to estimate different groups: children, teens, young adults, adults, and seniors.)
- What is the marital status of each gender? (Remember, Latinas tend to live with companions and give birth at an early age, and many are single mothers.)
- Do Latino females in your community have children? How many, and what age?
- What is their country of origin, and what is their generational gap?

Information about gender demographics will allow you to have a better understanding of issues that are specific to males and females among your local Latino community. It will help you plan services, information, and materials to specifically fit the needs of these market segments and work around their work schedule and/or family obligations. This stage of your market research is related to quantified data. The next chapter expands on gender cultural behaviors.

Levels of Education

Summary of National Trends

Demographics in relation to Latino levels of education in the United States show that of the population aged 25 years and older—which constitutes the larger group of Latinos living in this country—only 28.2 percent have a high school diploma, and only 12.6 percent obtain a college degree. The gap is even greater between native-born and foreign-born Latinos: while 31.5 percent of American Latinos achieve a high school education, only 25.8 percent of those born outside the United States do so.[35]

According to the 2006 National Survey of Latinos report on education,[36] Latinos have a generally positive view of local schools, teachers, and educational institutions, and they represent that they are involved in their children's education. However, they express concern that teachers are not able to bridge the cultural gap in the classroom, resulting in unfair treatment to Latino students.

Levels of education shown in Table 4.5 follow the educational trends of states that have had Latino populations the longest—such as Florida, New Mexico, New York, and New

TABLE 4.5 Latino Levels of Education

	None	Less Than Eighth Grade	Some High School	GED	High School Grad	Some College	Four-year degree	Grad School
National	2.7	20.2	18.0	2.9	22.2	19.2	8.7	6.2
Arizona	1.4	18.7	19.6	2.7	22.3	22.1	8.0	5.2
Arkansas	3.3	24.9	22.0	3.2	24.4	13.0	6.8	2.5
California	3.6	20.6	18.6	2.9	22.0	20.1	6.7	5.5
Colorado	1.7	17.4	18.6	3.3	26.9	17.1	9.3	5.6
D.C.	3.6	14.5	19.6	0.0	12.1	27.9	9.7	12.7
Florida	1.6	14.5	13.2	2.6	21.1	23.2	14.1	9.8
Georgia	3.7	23.9	19.2	3.2	20.3	14.4	8.3	7.0
Illinois	3.8	20.8	16.6	2.8	22.9	18.3	8.9	5.8
Iowa	2.2	24.8	17.8	2.9	22.9	19.3	6.2	3.9
Maryland	3.7	21.8	15.3	2.8	18.3	19.9	13.8	10.3
Nevada	2.1	20.7	20.7	3.4	25.7	17.0	5.6	4.9
New Jersey	3.2	15.6	18.0	1.0	23.0	20.3	12.3	6.6
New Mexico	1.7	15.9	15.8	3.9	22.8	22.9	12.3	7.2
New York	1.4	17.5	17.3	2.9	23.5	21.0	8.9	7.6
North Carolina	2.6	26.1	21.4	2.4	22.2	14.4	6.3	4.6
Texas	2.6	21.6	18.4	3.7	20.8	18.5	9.7	4.7
Virginia	2.4	19.9	16.0	2.0	15.1	20.8	14.6	9.3
Washington	5.4	20.4	18.4	2.8	20.3	20.8	8.1	4.0

Source: Redefining America: Key Findings from the 2006 Latino National Survey. Weighted Demographic Tables—Nationally and by State," Woodrow Wilson International Center for Scholars, http://www.wilsoncenter.org/index.cfm?topic_id=1427&categoryid=170E 04BB-65BF-E7DC-4B8C5CB1C8E70BC0&fuseaction=topics.events_item_topics&event_id=201793 (accessed December 1, 2009).

Jersey—as having the highest levels of education (between high school graduates and some college). Washington, DC; Maryland; and Virginia have a higher-educated population, probably according to job-placement requirement. States with the highest percentages of Latinos with graduate degrees are Washington, DC; Maryland; Virginia; and Florida (where the Cuban population is the highest educated). The numbers plunge dramatically in other states. Table 4.5 does not, however, itemize levels of education according to first-, second-, third-, or fourth-generation Latinos.

College Attainment

According to the 2005 report "Recent Changes in the Entry of Hispanic and White Youth into College" (Fry 2005), the college graduation gap is wider between Latinos and white college students than the very considerable differences in high school completion.

The study finds two trends in relation to graduation rates: (1) even well-prepared Latinos end up attending postsecondary institutions that are less selective; and (2) even when well-prepared Latinos go to the same kinds of schools as their white peers, they have lower graduation rates.

For students beginning at community colleges, white youth are nearly twice as likely as Latinos to finish a bachelor's degree. Gaps are also significant among those starting in the four-year college sector (Fry 2004). According to the report "Federal Policy and Latinos in Higher Education: A Guide for Policymakers and Grantmakers" (Santiago and Brown 2004), the majority of Latinos in higher education (75%) are concentrated in few states—California, Texas, New York, Florida, and Illinois—with over 50 percent of all Latinos enrolled in California and Texas. About 45 percent of these undergraduate students are enrolled in about 230 institutions of higher education identified as Hispanic-serving institutions (HSIs), which represent only 7 percent of all postsecondary institutions.[37]

However, a 2009 report from the Pew Hispanic Center found that the number of young Hispanics going to college is increasing (Fry 2009). From 1970 to 2007, the number of Latino youth beginning college studies increased sharply from 25 to 40 percent. Latino first-time, full-time freshman enrollment grew by an average of 24 percent in seven states: California, New York, Arizona, New Jersey, Florida, Texas, and Illinois. The biggest increase—greater than 50 percent—was in Florida. Nevertheless, the majority of Latinos in higher education are enrolled in two-year institutions as part-time students, while the majority of white, black, and Asian/Pacific Islander students are enrolled in four-year institutions (Fry 2005).

College graduate numbers continue to be small: Latinos earned 5 percent of masters degrees in 2001, 3 percent of doctoral degrees, and 5 percent of first-professional degrees in 2001—compared to whites of whom 70 percent earned a masters, 61 percent a doctoral degree, and 74 percent first-professional degrees (Santiago and Brown 2004).

¡Excelencia in Education!,[38] a nonprofit organization that promotes policies and practices that support higher educational achievement for Latino students, reports that 63 percent of Latinos registered in college education in the period 2003–2004 received financial aid. Female enrollment was 60 percent compared to 40 percent of males, 86 percent of all students were U.S. citizens, possibly second generation or naturalized, and 12 percent were resident aliens—possibly first-generation immigrants. Of those enrolled, 48 percent were of Mexican origin, 16 percent were Puerto Rican, and 3 percent were Cuban (other countries not reported). Regarding their parents' levels of education, 49 percent had achieved a high school level or less, 40 percent had a bachelors degree or less, and only 12 percent had an advanced degree. Income levels for these families showed 24 percent at less than $40,000 a year and 23 percent at over $40,000; 25 percent of students were economically independent earning $20,000 or less, and 29 percent earned over $20,000.

As you can see, all these variables work together to give you a better idea of the educational status of your local Latino population and where you should focus your efforts. Does your local Latino community follow national trends? What are the local levels of education attainment, and how can your library services encourage your Latino population to persist in its education? You need to know the facts in order to plan ahead.

Latinos Online

Latinos lag behind white and non-Hispanic blacks in their use of the Internet. An increasing 56 percent of Latinos go online compared to 71 percent of non-Hispanic whites and 60 percent of non-Hispanic blacks. Lack of personal computers and limited English ability explain the gap in Internet use between Hispanics and non-Hispanics. Among adult Latinos using the Internet, 78 percent are English-dominant (76% of whom are bilingual) compared with 32 percent who are Spanish-dominant. Seventy-six percent of U.S.–born Latinos use the Internet compared with 43 percent foreign-born, and 89 percent of Latinos with college degrees go online compared to 31 percent who did not obtain a high-school diploma (Fox and Livingston 2007).

Being Mexican is associated with a decreased probability of going online, according to the study. The report states that only 52 percent of Latinos of Mexican descent use the Internet.

Variable Significance and How It Relates to Other Variables

What is stopping Latinos from using the Internet? You need to see the variables combined, such as levels of education, language ability, income or economic levels (which allow families to own a computer at home and pay for services), age, and family composition. The same issues are related to the level of and opportunities for education. Time in the United States has a great impact on how Latinos see education and educational opportunities after living in the United States and becoming more acculturated or assimilated, as do country of origin and socioeconomic status.

Suggested Questions When Doing Research

- What are the levels of education of Latinos in your community depending on their country of origin? (In Mexico, for instance, secondary or high school education is only mandatory since 1993, and it is offered in a three-year cycle. Most countries in Central and South America have mandatory basic elementary and free public education. Colombia adds mandatory education until 15 years of age. Some countries, such as Nicaragua and Peru, offer multicultural and linguistic programs that preserve local indigenous cultural manifestations. Argentina, Venezuela, and Uruguay have mandatory elementary and high school systems.)[39]
- What are the higher levels of education in your community? (Check time in the United States and generational gap—first, second, and third generation—and also check in community colleges and universities in your area for alumni directories and present registration. Also check in the industrial, governmental, and corporate employment in your area.)
- What level of technology readiness and computer ability does this community carry? (Check the type of work they perform and the industries they work in to gain

insight into their need to develop computer and technological abilities. Also, check the age of your population, as younger Latinos are more in tune with technology advances.)

Level of education is an instrumental variable to consider in defining with precision library services, level of materials and information, and literacy services, either in English or Spanish. Consider the fact that many recent immigrants come with the purpose of finding work in blue-collar activities—farming, fishing, construction, landscaping, and services—which require low literacy levels in both languages.

Language Ability

Summary of National Trends

Information about the language ability of Latinos varies according to different authors and sources. According to a new analysis of six surveys conducted this decade among more than 14,000 Latino adults, the Pew Hispanic Center reports that most Hispanic American adults born from immigrant parents are fluent in English. However, only a few of their parents report to be skilled English speakers (Hakimzadeh and Cohn 2007). The surveys show that only 23 percent of Latino immigrants speak English very well, while 88 percent of their children born in the country speak English very well. This ability increases to 94 percent for later generations.

Bilingual Latinos tend to use their languages differently depending on the setting. About 60 percent of bilingual Hispanic workers report speaking more English in the workplace while 29 percent report speaking only Spanish.

Although other sources such as the U.S. Census Bureau report different data, these disparities are based on the variance in cross sections of information, size of surveyed population, differences in the way each report defines the variables, and geographical cross sections of the information, among others. A general tendency, however, is to call first-generation immigrants a "lost generation"[40] in relation to language ability because the main goal of this generation is to make ends meet, while the successive generations' higher degree of acculturation or assimilation favors the acquisition of the English language.

No matter what source you use, knowing a great deal about the local population your library serves is the only way to guarantee you will provide the services they require, especially when some of the national studies do not provide direct data comparisons.

Variable Significance and How It Relates to Other Variables

When language ability is combined with income and occupation, English-dominant Latinos show a tendency to increase their income levels close to the national average of whites (29% make over $50,000), and 66 percent work in white-collar occupations.

When language ability combines with country of origin, Puerto Ricans are the most English-dominant group—39 percent of the Puerto Rican population is fluent in English or speaks English very well—and Dominicans are the least English-dominant group at only 6 percent. Cubans, Central Americans, Colombians, and Mexicans are more likely to be Spanish-dominant groups.

Language ability is also affected by levels of education, literacy, and time of residence in the United States. Table 4.6 shows that children who immigrated at an early age are more likely to become bilingual or English dominant than those who came at later ages.

TABLE 4.6   Primary Language among Foreign-Born Latinos, by Age at Immigration

	Age at Immigration to the United States			
	10 or less	**11–17**	**18–25**	**26+**
English dominant	18	4	1	2
Bilingual	70	31	15	10
Spanish dominant	11	66	84	89

Source: Pew Hispanic Center/Kaiser Family Foundation, "2002 National Survey of Latinos, Summary of Findings," December 2002, http://pewhispanic.org/files/execsum/15.pdf (accessed December 1, 2009).

Suggested Questions When Doing Research

- What groups are English dominant or Spanish dominant in your community?
- If a large group is first generation or recent immigrant, are there low literacy levels in Spanish?
- What are the different groups' levels of readiness in relation to their ability to learn English?
- What type of work are these groups involved with, and does this work require English-language ability? (You can talk to local employers about their workers' required language ability and how they communicate with them.)
- Are native languages other than Spanish spoken in your local Latino community? (Community leaders might be aware of this.)
- What is the language ability and age of children in the local community? (Recent teenage immigrants might need more help from alternate sources of education, such as the library, than children born in the United States who start learning English-language skills at an early age, although children born of Spanish-speaking parents might need additional help with homework.)

Knowing the language ability of Latinos in your community is important because it will aid in defining your collection acquisition and service programming. It will affect internal and external resources. It will also define this community's readiness for library services and their ability to communicate and improve literacy—in English and Spanish—through non-systematic education in the library setting.

Family Composition

Summary of National Trends

According to a study on demographic growth from the Pew Hispanic Center,[41] the U.S. population reached 300 million in 2006. One hundred million people have been added to the population since 1966. The fact sheet breaks down the U.S. population by race/ethnicity and nativity at the 200-million and at the 300-million mark. The study reports that in 1966, Hispanics represented only 8.5 million (or a little over 4%) of the total 200 million people living in the United States compared to the estimated 44.7 million (or a little over 22%) of the total 300 million in 2006, which accounts for 36 percent of the added population. Latin

American immigrants and their relatively high fertility rates were determinant in this increase, according to the report.

Immigrants from all origins and their U.S.-born children accounted for 55 percent of the population's increase since 1966. Latino immigrants and their children were by far the largest group, at about 29 million persons (52%); white immigrants and their progeny increased by approximately 10 million (18%); and black immigrant populations and their children increased by almost 4 million (7%). Of the 29 million Latinos added in the last decade, 12 million were immigrants' U.S.-born children, according to the Pew estimates.

According to a report from the U.S. Census Bureau (Ramirez 2004),[42] over half of the Hispanic population in the United States aged 15 and older were married, 34 percent were never married, and approximately 14 percent were separated, widowed, or divorced in 2000.

Among Hispanic groups, the report found Cubans were the most likely to be married, followed by South Americans, Mexicans, and Spaniards. However, Cubans were also more likely to be separated, widowed, or divorced than any other Hispanic group. Over one-third, or 38 percent, of Puerto Ricans and Central Americans were never married in 2000.

The average Latino household size is four persons compared to the general population, which is 2.59, according to the 2000 Census.[43] New immigrants tend to group in houses to share expenses and find support in a social network system. Normally, established families host new immigrants from a pool of relatives and acquaintances from their original region or locality, frequently for long periods until the new immigrants are established.

However, some states are reporting changes in these localization patterns, with a growing presence of immigrants from, for instance, the Mexican states of Oaxaca, Tlaxcala, Yucatan, Chiapas, and Guerrero—states without a long tradition in migration. Consequently, these immigrants lack the support system others had. Many of these immigrants belong to Mexico's indigenous populations, may not be fluent in Spanish, and show lower levels of education, which creates a much harder process of adjustment to the hosting culture.

Another aspect to consider in family composition is the fertility rate of Latinas compared to non-Latinas in the United States, as already explained. A higher rate of Latino fertility—especially in Mexican women—has been considered a political threat because of the birth increases of Latino children in U.S. territory (Chavez 2004). In 2005, the U.S. Census Bureau reported that birth rates for the population of Hispanic origin had kept steady since 1997 at around 14 percent, while the white and black population rates had decreased from 12.2 to 11.5 percent and 17.4 to 15.7 percent, respectively. Mexican women tend to have the highest fertility rates, while Cubans have the lowest.[44]

Latino teen birth rates in the United States increased 30 percent between 1980 and 1992 while non-Latino rates increased by only 6 percent. A 2004 study[45] focuses on Latinas ages 15–19 and 20–24, both never- and ever-married young mothers, and their ability to sustain themselves and their living arrangements given the high levels of poverty in this social group. Since then, teen pregnancy rates have decreased for all demographic groups. Although the average decrease for all population was 28.5 percent, Latino teens' rates only decreased around 15 percent.[46]

Puerto Rican mothers are less likely to be married and less likely to live with parents or other adults. They face deeper levels of poverty and are more likely to be enrolled in welfare. Cuban mothers, on the other hand, report the highest household incomes and the lowest rates of welfare aid of any group. Mexican and Central and South American mothers follow a similar pattern to Anglo Americans in relation to marriage and living arrangements, although their poverty rates are much higher.

Variable Significance and How It Relates to Other Variables

These differences in economic and social outcome are usually related to immigration status; levels of education and language ability; knowledge of the welfare system, as in the case of Puerto Ricans, who might be more familiar with laws and regulations in the United States; family composition; and family support.

Keep in mind that issues such as fertility rates and teen pregnancy might also be related to high school dropout rates and decreasing employment opportunities for young Latinas.

Suggested Questions When Doing Research

- How many Latino families live in your community?
- How many single female and male Latinos live in your community?
- How many Latino single mothers live in your community? What is their country of origin? Age? Number of children? (You might be able to get unofficial estimates from schools' data without breaking confidentially issues.)
- What are the families' sources of livelihood? Do both parents or only one or the other work?
- Are there families living under the poverty level? Are there children living under the poverty level?
- What type of housing, educational, and health care assistance do they get? (Check with information obtained in the next topic, "Income.")

Check if these topics apply to your local Latino community, and find out if there is an opportunity for your library to develop educational and informational activities about these topics by partnering with other organizations in your community. Work your schedules around these families' working schedules and transportation issues.

Income

Summary of National Trends

In 2006, the median household income for all households in the United States was $48,451, while the median household income for Hispanic households was $38,747, according to a 2006 report from the American Community Survey (Webster and Bishaw 2007).[47] The median earnings for Hispanic men were $27,490 while Hispanic women had median earnings of $24,738, the report said.

According to the report "2006 Census Poverty and Income Data,"[48] Latinos had the biggest drop in poverty rates (–1.2%) in 2006 of all minority groups. Although median household income increased for all groups—except non-Hispanic whites—when adjusted according to inflation, median income is still less than in 2000. Latinos had an annual increase of 1.7 percent in median income.

Table 4.7 shows that median family income among Hispanic groups varied from a high of $53,000 for Spaniards—immigrants from Spain or of Spanish background—to a low of $28,700 for Dominicans in 1999 (Ramirez 2004).

The same study reports that among Hispanic groups, men and women of Spanish origin had the highest median earnings ($39,600 and $30,900, respectively), while men and women from Central American had the lowest ($22,400 and $18,600, respectively).

TABLE 4.7   Hispanics' Median Family Income, 1999

All families	$50,046
Hispanic	$34,397
Mexican	$33,516
Puerto Rican	$32,791
Cuban	$42,642
Central American	$34,150
South American	$42,824
Dominican	$28,729
Spaniard	$53,002
Other Hispanic	$34,703

Source: U.S. Census Bureau, "Summary File 4: 2000 Census of Population and Housing" (Families classified by Hispanic origin of householder. Data based on sample. For information on confidentiality protection, sampling error, non-sampling error, and definitions, see www.census.gov/prod/cen2000/doc/sf4.pdf) (accessed December 1, 2009).

More than 22 percent of the Hispanic population in the United States lives in poverty, compared with 12.4 percent for the total population. The poverty rate among Latino groups ranged from 27.5 percent for Dominicans to 14.6 percent for Cubans and 12.8 percent for Spaniards.

Poverty by age shows that more Hispanics under 18 years of age lived in poverty in 1999 than the general population under age 18—a ratio of over one in three compared with one in six. Dominicans and Puerto Ricans under 18 showed the highest levels of poverty. In addition, 19.6 percent of the Hispanic population 65 years and older lived in poverty compared with 9.9 percent of the total older population.

Variable Significance and How It Relates to Other Variables

These numbers drag far behind the general population rates and might relate to levels of education, occupation, language ability, immigration status, generational gaps, and time of residence in the United States. As you can see, it is important to know where your Latino patrons or potential patrons are from because there are large inequalities in economic power, which eventually prohibit access to better education, employment opportunities, and social mobility.

Suggested Questions When Doing Research

- What percentage of your Latino population lives in poverty?
- What nationalities are more affected by poverty in your local area?
- What generation of Latino Americans (second generation and over) are more affected by poverty?
- In your community, what occupations keep Latinos under the poverty level?
- What is the percentage of Latino children living in poverty in your town (community, region, and/or neighborhood)?

- How does it affect their school performance? How can your library help compensate for a lack of homework help, language illiteracy, learning disabilities, lack of home computers, and other concerns?
- How are Latino teens in your community affected by poverty?
- How can your library help with educational opportunities for adults and young adults?

Levels of poverty have an impact on the ability of parents to seek and access educational opportunities for their children because of increased time at work—low-paying jobs require a longer work schedule to make ends meet—and their own lack of educational opportunities, which can be transmitted to their children. Your library can aid in bringing information to their homes and providing concrete help after school hours in research, literacy, and reading skills.

Occupation

Summary of National Trends

In 2006, the Census reported 19,613,000 Latino workers in the United States (see Table 4.8). The Hispanic labor force grew from 6.1 million to 16.7 million in the last two decades of the century. Latinos represent 13 percent of the labor force in the United States, higher than any other minority. However, this growth has not seen corresponding rate increases in earnings and employment. Both rates lag behind those among whites or blacks (Kochhar 2005).

The yearly median household income for Latinos differed by around $10,000 from the general population in 2006, usually with more individuals contributing to the household (Webster and Bishaw 2007). The gap is the result of Latinos' concentration in nonprofessional service occupations, such as building, ground cleaning and maintenance, and food preparation and serving. Since 1990, "whites have increased their representation in professional occupations while Hispanics trended towards construction and service occupations" (Kochhar 2005). What does this mean? The effect is a growing labor force that is continuously impoverished, resulting in less self-sustainability, increased state burden, and less social mobility.

Although Latinos are seen as primarily agricultural workers—and many foreign-born workers are—Latinos have been part of the formal labor market for generations—in health care, janitorial services, apparel and laundry services, food processing, and construction. Latinos have also participated in the building of the U.S. railways, mining, garment, meatpacking, construction, and automobile industries. However, Latinos lag behind general wages in part due to the obstacles they face in becoming part of unionized industries and the spurning of Latinos from labor movements (Trumpbour and Bernard 2002).

The occupational status of Mexicans and Puerto Ricans ranks lower compared to whites while Cubans are comparable to whites (Kochhar 2005). Occupation varies in relation to country of origin, as shown in Table 4.8, among Mexicans, Puerto Ricans, Cubans, and other Hispanics (South and Central America). Notice that as occupational status decreases in rank, the participation of Mexicans in these activities or occupations increases.

In terms of more skilled workers, Latino professionals work in a variety of economic sectors: 30 percent in nonprofit, government, or academia; 27 percent at publicly held Fortune 1000 companies; and 30 percent in private businesses, according to the Hispanic Alliance for Career Enhancement survey.[49]

TABLE 4.8 Employed Hispanic or Latino Workers by Sex, Occupation, and Detailed Ethnic Group (in Thousands)

Category	Total		Mexicans		Puerto Ricans		Cubans		Other Hispanics	
Year	2006	%	2006	%	2006	%	2006	%	2006	%
Total, 16 years+	19,613	100	12,477	64	1,484	7	778	4	4,874	25
Men	11,887		7,863		782		452		2,790	
Women	7,725		4,614		702		326		2,083	
Management, professional, and related	3,337	17	1,830	14	375	15	227	30	1,095	32
Service	4,649	23	2,978	23	320	21	121	15	1,230	26
Sales/office	4,154	21	2,435	19	407	27	200	25	1,112	26
Natural resources, construction, and maintenance	3,893	19	2,818	22	147	10	107	14	821	21
Production, transportation, and material moving	3,580	18	2,416	19	235	15	123	16	806	22

Author's selection of data from original source. Includes persons of Central or South American origin and of Other Hispanic (or Latino) ethnicity not shown in source. Percentages by occupation might not add up to 100 percent due to rounding.

Source: United States Department of Labor, Bureau of Labor Statistics, "2006 Household Data Annual Averages, Labor Force Statistics from Current Population Survey," http://www.bls.gov/cps/cpsa2006.pdf (accessed December 1, 2009).

According to this survey, Latino professionals tend to be loyal to their employers if satisfied with their jobs, prioritizing opportunities for career development within the company over compensation. Thirty-seven percent of Latino professionals have been at the same job more than two years and 25 percent for more than five years. However, when asked about promotions and salary increases, 25 percent responded they have never been promoted regardless of time at their present job, and 42 percent responded they had not received a salary increase within the last 12 months.

Variable Significance and How It Relates to Other Variables

Closely related to the income variable, occupation not only defines earnings and employment projections in a developing economy, but it also determines social status and mobility beyond economic outcomes. Most occupations held by Hispanics rank low in most indicators of socioeconomic status, such as earnings, educational requirements, and skill levels.

Suggested Questions When Doing Research

- Do Latinos in your community follow national trends?
- What generation of Latinos lives in your community, and what sectors of the economy do they work in?

- How do these occupations affect their economic and social mobility? (For instance, if they work in occupations with a high rate of turnover and constantly have to move, it is hard to get established and increase their occupational opportunities.)

Working with your local government and employers will provide the necessary information on your Latino labor force and determine their need for your services. Also, it will bring opportunities to develop strategic partnerships, provide information, and generate regional economic growth.

Time of Residence in the United States

Summary of National Trends

Studies show that while the socioeconomic status of foreign-born Hispanics is low when they arrive, in the first five years of residing in the country, it slowly improves with time spent in the United States.

TABLE 4.9 Socioeconomic Status Scores for Hispanics by Place of Birth and Years since Arrival in the United States, 2000

Country	Males	Females
Mexico		
≤5 years	17	17
6–10 years	18	18
10–20 years	21	20
20–30 years	24	24
>30 years	30	29
Puerto Rico		
≤5 years	27	28
6–10 years	27	28
10–20 years	28	29
20–30 years	31	31
>30 years	34	33
Cuba		
≤5 years	28	27
6–10 years	30	29
10–20 years	32	30
20–30 years	38	37
>30 years	46	42

Author's selection of data from original source.

Source: U.S. Census Bureau, "The Occupational Status and Mobility of Hispanics," 2000 Census PUMS files, December 15, 2005, http://pewhispanic.org/files/reports/59.pdf (accessed December 1, 2009).

The data in Table 4.9 show that Mexican immigrants who have been in the United States for five years or less attain a low socioeconomic score, but after living in the United States for over 30 years they score higher rates. This shows improvement, but they still lag behind the average of 35 for the general population and the average of 37 for whites.

Cuban immigrants start high on the scale relative to other Hispanics, and those who arrived 20 years ago now have scores comparable to whites or higher than the U.S. average. It should be noted, however, that not all of this increase is necessarily a sign of progress with years spent in the United States. At least some of this outcome could be the result of the higher skill levels of Cuban immigrants who arrived earlier. Therefore, higher occupational attainment—regardless of years spent in the United States—could be the result of their reasons for immigrating to the United States.[50] According to a 2007 report from the Pew Hispanic Center (Kochhar 2005), Latino workers' wage distribution has progressed in the last 10 years. Latino immigration has changed the profile of the U.S. labor force in a span of 25 years. In 1980, Latinos represented only 6 percent of the labor force while by 2005 they had increased to 15 percent.

Since 1995, a percentage of Latinos working in the United States moved from the low end toward the middle, the report says. Employment showed a 112 percent growth in the high-middle range compared to a 57 percent increase in the lowest range of wage distribution. Despite this progress, foreign-born workers still lag behind in low-wage jobs in relation to native-born workers. Latinos were still a majority in the low-wage force between 1995 and 2005.

TABLE 4.10 Distribution of Employment across Wage Classes, 2005 (Foreign-Born Workers by Place of Birth and Year of Entry, 2005, in Percentages)

| | Hourly Wage Class | | | | | |
	Total*	Low	Low-middle	Middle	High-middle	High
Place of birth						
Mexico	100	40	29	19	8	4
Caribbean	100	26	26	22	13	12
Central America	100	26	26	22	13	12
South America	100	23	23	23	16	15
Year of entry						
Before 1970	100	13	19	20	18	31
1970–1979	100	18	19	21	19	23
1980–1989	100	22	22	22	17	17
1990–1999	100	29	26	19	12	14
2000–later	100	40	24	16	9	11

*Percentages may not total 100 percent due to rounding.

Source: Pew Hispanic Center, tabulations of Current Population Survey data, "1995–2005: Foreign-Born Latinos Progress on Wages," August 21, 2007, http://pewhispanic.org/files/reports/78.pdf (accessed December 1, 2009).

Foreign-born Latinos represented 36 percent of low-wage workers in 2005, well above the average of 20 percent for the labor force as a whole. However, this represented considerable progress from the 42 percent rate in 1995.

As shown in Table 4.10, this variable—distribution of employment across wage classes—works together with place of birth and year of entry. Immigration status also plays a role in foreign-born workers' ability to negotiate wages.

Table 4.10 shows that despite the progress in wage distribution, the trend looks gloomy, as 40 percent of Latino workers earned low wages compared to 11 percent in the high-wage level in 2000, while 13 percent of Latino workers earned low wages and 31 percent earned high wages before 1970. This trend might have been affected by the peak of immigration—legal and illegal—in the period from 1999–2000 (Passel and Suro 2005).

Variable Significance and How It Relates to Other Variables

The amount of time Latinos have resided in the United States is an important variable that affects many aspects of Latino demographics, such as their social and economic mobility, levels of education, and language ability. Study of this variable also defines trends—that is, patterns of how Latinos tend to move around, behave, work, and become acculturated. It also affects the way they find new work opportunities in and ease of traveling to friendly states, not only in the first generation but in second-, third-, and fourth-generation behaviors. Time in the United States also affects health and educational outcomes [51] and even levels of crime, poverty, and imprisonment (Zehr 2009).

These trends affect how libraries determine what type of services to offer and set long-term planning goals.

Suggested Questions When Doing Research

- What is the trend in relation to the time of residence in the United States in your local community?
- What is the nationality of origin—if first generation immigrants—of your local Latino community? What is their national background if born in the United States?
- If recent immigrants, have they been in your community for more than 5, 10, 15, or 20 years? (Remember, your demographics might change every five years.)
- What generational gap do they belong to? What are the percentages of each generation? (This answer will vary if you are in a gateway state or a new immigration state. It is important to know the number of individuals and families to which your library needs to respond.)
- How has time of residence in the United States affected the type of work they do or industries they work for, levels of education, social mobility, and health outcomes in your community? (You will need to talk to your community leaders, schools principals, hospital directors, and other leaders in the community who might know and share this type of data with you.)

Library services in this case will address acculturation issues and direct services and information according to the needs of the different Latino generations that are part of their communities. Your library needs a different outreach approach when the majority of your population has resided locally for a long-time—even if they come from another state, consider their complete time of residence in the United States—or are recently established immigrants, with a lesser degree of acculturation or assimilation.

TABLE 4.11   Latino Market Profile Key Findings—A Summary

Country of origin	Defines social mobility; attitude toward education, literacy and use of technology; and geographical mobility. Plays an important role in the acculturation process and interacts with issues of identity.
Race and racial tension	Although Latinos have a high interracial marriage rate (30%). Class and race divisions in Latin America are a reality. Racial tensions might have an impact on your local Latino community. Factors at play might be related to differences in countries of origin, differences in social and economic status, and racial tensions with other groups in your community.
Geographic mobility	This variable is related to two actions: (1) internal geographic mobility and (2) external geographic mobility. New patterns of relocation within the United States, such as work availability, friendlier states, and changes in the economic structure or settling far away from urban concentrations, are affecting internal geographic mobility. The ability to financially support long-distance travel and immigration status has an impact on external geographic mobility.
Socioeconomic status/social mobility	Latinos have less opportunity for social mobility. Reasons include coming from a very class-structured society; the type of jobs they perform, usually in agriculture and services; and geographical mobility that might impede total acculturation.
Immigration status	Only around one-fifth of Latinos are undocumented in the United States. Immigration status varies with countries of origin: while some countries are excluded from immigration alternatives such as the green-card lottery, others have special protection laws (NACARA). Requests for naturalization have increased in the last decade.
Age	Latinos are a younger population. Age of population is related to the immigration status (children are less able to emigrate without documentation), time of residence in the United States (older immigrants tend to return to their place of birth),, country of origin (fertility rates are higher in some populations), and geographic mobility (younger immigrants tend to move more frequently than older ones).
Gender	The United States added increasing numbers of undocumented male immigrants higher than both female immigration and legal immigration. However, some states report the appearance of skilled single young females and working mothers from Mexico and Central America working in domestic work, factories, and agriculture.
Levels of education	The Latino population 25 years and older lag behind their white and African American counterparts in high school and college achievement. Latino parents are concerned with the way the educational system treats Latino students due to the cultural divide in the classroom.
Language ability	Sources show different data regarding the English or Spanish dominance of Latinos. The first generation is usually Spanish dominant unless the individuals immigrated at an early age. Second and third generations increase exponentially in their English-language ability, especially in the workplace, while many of these individuals use Spanish language at home.
Family composition	Latino families are usually larger than families in the general population. Also, households might shelter other members unrelated by marriage or blood. Single-parent Latinas and pregnant Latina teens are the fastest growing groups in relation to other demographic groups in the United States.

(Continued)

TABLE 4.11 *(Continued)*

Income	Latinos groups' income varies according to background and country of origin. Latino levels of poverty are higher among children and seniors than other groups in the United States.
Occupation	The Hispanic labor force increased 2.5 times in the last two decades of the last century to 13 percent of the U.S. labor force. Latinos concentrate in nonprofessional services, manufacturing, and agriculture but have also contributed in health care services, janitorial services, apparel and laundry services, food processing, and construction.
Time in the United States	Employment opportunities and language ability tend to increase with time of residence in the United States. However, the rates vary according to country of origin and age at time of immigration.

Table 4.11 provides a summary of the variable characteristics we have described so you can have a quick reference when preparing your market research.

In order to help you complete your Latino community—or market—profile, Worksheet 4.1 in chapter 10 brings all the variables together. Fill out the information as best you can with the most predominant groups in your area.

These are common categories to almost every Latino population. Add categories in each variable as you need or see fit to respond to the profile of your local Latino community.

Variables That Work Together

A variable *alone* does not define a market segment and its behavior. On the contrary, variables always affect each other and the resulting trend in that segment's performance. As an example, we have combined the variable *race* with the variables *country of origin, language, and literacy levels,* in Table 4.12 to show how these variables can define differential behavior in market segments.

In Table 4.12, Argentina shows a racial composition of 97 percent white (mostly of Spanish and Italian descent) and 3 percent *mestizos* and natives (mixed of whites and people of Amerindian ancestry, Amerindian, or other nonwhite groups). Literacy levels are at 97.1 percent for both males and females. Languages spoken by the general population are Spanish (official), English, Italian, German, and French (most Amerindian languages are spoken by very small native groups).

Guatemala is a country with a 59.4 percent *mestizo* population—9.1 percent K'iche, 8.4 percent Kaqchikel, 7.9 percent Mam, 6.3 percent Q'eqchi, 8.6 percent of other Mayan population, and 0.2 percent indigenous non-Mayan population. The country is compounded by 21 linguistic communities or ethnic groups including the Achi', Akateko, Awakateko, Ch'orti', Chuj, Itza', Ixil, Jakalteko, Q'anjob'al, Kaqchikel, K'iche', Mam, Mopan, Poqomam, Poqomchi', Q'eqchi', Sakapulteko, Sipakapense, Tektiteko, Tz'utujil, and Uspanteko.[52]

Data reveals literacy levels at 70.6 percent for the total Guatemalan population (male 78% and female 63.3%).[53] Languages spoken are Spanish—spoken by 60 percent of the population—and Amerindian languages—spoken by 40 percent of the population (includes 23 officially recognized Amerindian languages, including Quiche, Cakchiquel, Kekchi, Mam, Garifuna, and Xinca).[54]

TABLE 4.12 Country of Origin, Race, Language, and Literacy Levels Combined

Variable	Categories	Argentina (percent)	Guatemala (percent)
Race	White	97	N/A
	Mestizo white/Ameridian	3	N/A
	Mestizo Amerindian/Spanish and European	N/A	59.4
	Mayan	N/A	40.3
	Non-Mayan indigenous/other	N/A	0.3
Languages	Spanish	99.8	60
	Amerindian languages	0.2	40
Literacy levels	General population	97.1	70.6
	Male	97.1	78
	Female	97.1	63.3

Note: Variables are in percentages. Data is just for exemplification purposes. It does not represent any particular profile population in the United States and does not imply any judgment on the capabilities or skills of each group.

Data source: Central Intelligence Agency, estimates for 2003 from "The World Factbook," https://www.cia.gov/library/publica tions/the-world-factbook/geos/us.html (accessed December 1, 2009).

What does this large educational gap[55] mean to you? If you encounter such large gaps in your local communities, it will force you to rethink service opportunities for these groups while establishing different logistics. The number of different groups and variable combinations will determine your market segments—the smaller groups in your community to whom you need to target your services and promotional efforts.

In order to find variables that work together, the following worksheets are designed to help you discover how particular variables influence the trends and behaviors of your Latino target market segments and, consequently, plan the library services you offer.

Interpreting Your Target Audience Data

To determine what services and information a group might be looking for, you can combine the information you obtained for certain variables, as in the following worksheets. They are filled with information from different sources and offer hypothetical scenarios.[56] I used Worksheet 4.1.1 to develop a short community profile for the local Latino community in Little Haven City, our example location. (Data is just for exemplification purposes. It does not represent any particular population profile in the United States and does not imply any judgment on the capabilities or skills of each group.)

Filling out the information as accurately as possible gives an idea of several variables that would impact library services, and a better understanding of each market segment's needs. You will also be able to assess what issues are more urgent for each group. Then, it is a matter of combining those variables that will show the information necessary to better assess needs.

For instance, Worksheet 4.2 compares the combined country of origin, time of residence in the United States, and occupation variables to see the progression in skills acquired by immigrants in the local area, and in what fashion the library might be able to offer classes that would improve those skills. Notice that people from the same country of origin but from different regions might show dissimilar behavior.

Looking at the interaction of other variables allows you, for instance, to visualize the economic status of the groups, their current work situation, and the progress and size over time of these segments, as seen in Worksheet 4.3. Again, it might help the library make decisions about classes, information, participation at job fairs with strategic partners, resume writing skills classes, and more.

Although the majority of the occupation skills in the four groups belong to the on-the-job (OTJ) training category, group 2 has spent more time in the United States and, for that reason, has increased work opportunities and income range. This also might be affected by the fact that this group's members were originally from an urban setting (Mexico DF) and, therefore, might have higher skills or experience in the labor market. Worksheet 4.3 shows clearly that time in the United States is a positive variable in group 2's skills improvement.

The same group has achieved higher levels of education and, consequently, has achieved higher qualified occupations (administrative/white collar skills), as seen in Worksheet 4.4. This might give the library an opportunity to offer professional classes, such as computer skills or how to start a new business, employment opportunities, and use of databases.

The same group has acquired more English or bilingual language abilities, perhaps over time and on the job (see Worksheet 4.5), which will call for more advanced English classes, maybe some English with Specific Purpose (ESP) classes that focus on an industry or craft.

Group 2 has spent longer in the United States and has achieved legal status in a higher percentage than group 1, a group also from Mexico. However, groups 3 and 4 have also achieved a high percentage of legal status due to specific legislation (TPS and NACARA, the two pieces of legislation that granted temporary and/or permanent residence to Salvadorians and Guatemalans). Group 2 also is the oldest of the groups and is more established (see Worksheet 4.6). This characteristics might call for citizenship classes or additional opportunities to learn English.

If we look at the information vertically, the information about group 2—in this case—will help us determine the level of readiness of the group to use library services—they have lived longer in the United States and have a higher percentage of individuals born in the United States with a higher level of education.

If you look at the information horizontally, you can gather which groups have similar situations, problems, or needs; how they overlap with each other; and what type of common interests they might share that library services can address (see Worksheet 4.7).

In conclusion, for instance, you found that 710 people of 1,125 in this population are Spanish dominant and need language instruction and English literacy so you can establish measurable goals and prepare resources and funds adequately. Is this a number your organization can handle by itself? What type of funding and resources will you need to supply this service, and how long will it take for your organization to implement it (assuming you are not solely responsible for the immigrants' language acquisition and that there are other local resources)? How long will it take the group to achieve results? Are there other organizations in the community that can collaborate with you in this effort? Are there groups among this market segment that have literacy limitations in their native language? Which groups might you serve directly with your own resources while others might be taken care of by strategic partners or other organizations in your community? Do you promote your offerings in the same way to the four groups? Asking and answering these questions establishes a different approach with a higher probability for success than just setting up an ESL class and expecting people to show up.

You can combine any information according to your objectives (for instance, gender, single-parent families, unemployed, etc.). Are you thinking of offering a computer class in Spanish or English? Combine your variables in relation to education, language ability, and computer ability—refer to the Latinos online section. Look also at gender and occupational variables that are dominant in your local community so you know how to set up schedules and logistics—transportation, babysitting, or children's activities. In occupation, look at seasonal schedules to know when is a good time of year to offer your classes and programs.

If you live in a large city, market segmentation is even more important. You will have to work with variables at a branch level and divide your city by your coverage area, the location of your Latino population (perhaps in neighborhoods or *barrios*), or place of work.

Although these assessments might look complicated and time consuming, your organization is already assessing other activities and efforts at the library. For instance, when your organization decides to spend a certain amount on a new database or a reference collection, they probably assess the purchase value against patrons' potential usage. The number of patrons who might use the item, its estimated circulation, and the benefits it will bring to your patrons and other potential members of the community at large might be some of the indicators your organization considers.

Your library might use a systematic approach or just a committee evaluation with an expert recommendation. In any case, this assessment is made based on the knowledge your organization has of all current and potential library cardholders in your local community.

Now you need to incorporate new potential cardholders whom you might not know much about. Once you gather all the information you need, the procedure is basically the same: get recommendations from the experts—your CLO and LAB—about which services, materials, and programs will generate activity among your local Latinos.

How to Learn about Your Demographics

Strategies to gather information in marketing are classified according to the technique and source used to collect the information, the phase of the process where the information is needed or fits, and whether the research data already exists or has been collected for a different purpose (Kotler, Roberto, and Lee 2002, p. 77).

Information might be collected from primary or secondary sources. Information from primary sources—the target consumer—usually is used to collect quantitative and qualitative data that is not yet available for a specific use.

Primary source techniques include (but are not limited to) the following:

Qualitative

- Focus groups/mini focus groups
- One-on-one interviews
- Field observation (ethnographic interviews)
- Informal information gathering

Quantitative

- Data collection from marketing behaviors (purchasing history, credit cards, Internet cookies, etc.)
- Direct mail, online, and telephone surveys

- Field observation (ethnographic interviews)
- Intercept interviews and surveys at location of service

Secondary sources refer to information that has been collected by someone else, for the same or different purposes, and includes the following:

- Prior surveys and studies conducted in the same market segment by others
- Study of information and statistics about similar demographics in other locations
- Literature, publications, Internet information, and databases
- Data collection from marketing behaviors (credit cards, Internet cookies, etc.) conducted by others

We will analyze the advantages and disadvantages of these techniques and strategies in order to help you choose what is best for your effort.

Qualitative Information from Primary Sources

Focus Groups, Mini Focus Groups, and Interviews

These alternatives are usually time consuming. In addition, focus groups, mini focus groups, and one-on-one interviews are activities that need to be conducted by professional interviewers with expertise in cross-cultural or multicultural research. Just because someone is Latino does not mean he or she can moderate or conduct a focus group discussion, just as the fact that a person speaks Spanish does not qualify him or her to be a translator.

In marketing, it is said that you need to know what questions to ask and how to interpret the answers. I call this situation a Plato dilemma: If you do not know what to ask, what would you ask, and if you know what you want to ask, why would you ask?

This dilemma refers to the need to find out more about your audience because you need to know about your audience's cultural background in order to ask intelligent questions. Culture is a construct that depends on human perception and interpretation and because of that is mainly intangible. A researcher who is ignorant about other individuals' culture tends to ask poor or improper questions. In addition, depending on cultural behaviors, individuals might answer with ambiguity, vagueness, omissions, contradictions, biases, and irrelevancies. Results might differ according to levels of education, economic and social status, life experiences, and more. For instance, in some Latino cultures, people will tend to agree or say what they think the interviewers want them to say or will use a more sophisticated vocabulary during the interview, which might mask the purpose of the interview (this is known as the observer's paradox).[57] Corporations usually obtain statistics from large numbers of interviews and extensive amounts of data, and they still make mistakes!

Don't take the entire load on your shoulders; instead, take advantage of your nonprofit status and your community partners. Colleges and universities in the area might have Behavioral Science programs. Talk to them; ask them to embrace your Latino outreach plan and develop focus groups for you as a research activity for their courses. Make a list of the information you need, and let them handle it. Give them a time frame, if possible, but even if gathering the information takes longer, remember you will always be able to use it to adjust and correct your course of action.

Include community leaders and current Latino customers in special focus groups or one-on-one interviews. They might be able to bring information from larger sectors of the community. However, do not forget that community leaders are usually more established immigrants or second- and third-generation Latinos, are usually more acculturated or as-similated, and might have a different vision of library services compared to a recently arrived immigrant.

Quantitative Information from Primary Sources

Intercept Interviews and Surveys at Location of Service

Collecting quantitative information from primary sources can represent a big budget strain because the collection will have to be accomplished by third parties (unless you have the technical capabilities). However, you can set up an adaptation of intercept interviews and surveys at location of service that will provide you with slow but steady information. Libraries should constantly survey all their patrons, Latinos and non-Latinos, in order to improve services. This is part of what we mean when we use the term "service pressure."

Intercept interviews and surveys at location of service should not be extremely long or ask about various subjects at the same time. It is better to focus on one subject at a time, give it a while, and then move to another subject. The more specific the subject matter, the better. If the collected data is not enough, the interview questions and the survey should be reviewed for inaccuracy or problematic cultural issues. Then re-present the interview or survey to your customers at a later time.

These surveys should not be longer than 5 to 10 questions at most and should include a combination of closed, multiple-choice, and open questions depending on the subject matter. Beware of using Likert-type scales (e.g., I strongly agree, I agree . . . etc.) because your Latino interviewees might not be used to this type of grading. Multiple-choice questions should only offer three to four choices. If you have additional options, you would need to formulate a separate question.

Leave open questions to those items where you need feedback for your specific project. For instance, if you are assessing community needs—discussed further in the next chapter—never ask a general question such as, "How can the library serve your needs?" Instead, try asking, "If you go to a library, what do you look for?" which will give you an idea of awareness (how much the interviewee knows about library services), usage (if he or she has been there before), and attitude (if library services are important and useful to the interviewee) toward library services.

You can conduct intercept interviews at public places, malls, fairs, and other places where Latinos gather or transit. You can also reward your interviewees with souvenirs or some other sort of stimulus, such as a temporary library card, a library magnet, or posters. Generally, Latinos tend to be cooperative in this type of interview. However, you will not know your sample's representation (either quantitative or qualitative) unless you include a cross-question—a question related to a different aspect of the interviewee's capabilities. In the previous example, for instance, this might mean asking for his or her level of education. (Ask "What was your last grade in school?" instead of "What is your level of education?") In addition, always ask interviewees if they are willing to share their age in your surveys and interviews.

Secondary Sources

The beauty of secondary sources is that information is already available—you just have to dig it up, and librarians love to do that! Secondary resources save you money and time, and you can exchange information with colleagues and professionals who have done the work before you, for the same or other purposes.

If there is a place where we can look for information, it is a library. Now that all your library personnel are informed through your CLO about their role in this effort and in the outreach plan, it should be pretty easy to make some inquiries regarding demographic information. Useful secondary sources may include the following:

U.S. Census data: You will mostly find information about national, state, and even city and town (up to 25,000 inhabitants) demographics through Census data. Sometimes local information is harder to find, especially related to library use. You might be able to find specific information on countries of origin and additional data on age, foreign-born residents, income levels, ability to speak English, educational attainment, and occupation. This information should give you a general idea of who your target market is; however, you cannot compound segments or subsegments because important additional data might not be itemized.

City government Web sites: Even when viewing the Web sites of the largest Latino-populated cities, not much demographic information was found to help with this type of research. However, town or city vital statistics departments can provide marriage, birth, or death information on the Latino population. This tactic might work in areas where Latinos have lived for a long time, are legal residents, or have married and given birth to children in the United States.

School systems: Contact the local school system through school libraries and find out if they gather any information regarding their students and families. The same resource might be found at universities, community colleges (if they compound statistics), hospitals, Hispanic/Latino agencies and associations, and local or statewide Hispanic chambers of commerce and other business organizations.

Exchanging data with community partners, leaders, and market channels: Chapter 3 explained in detail how to identify and assess your community partners, community leaders, and market channels and how to approach them in order to find information, help for your outreach or promotional efforts, and ongoing community resources. Explain your intention of developing a Latino outreach plan in the understanding that they also work with or serve this community.

Literature, publications, Internet information, and databases: One of the ongoing tasks of the CLO would be to read and research all available literature regarding the Latino market. Subscribe to main magazines in the industry, search for books that talk about Latino culture, and search the Web for sites describing these communities. For a fee, you can also access information from databases published on the Internet by major multicultural market researchers.[58]

Study information and statistics on similar demographics in other locations: Exchange information with other libraries and their community partners in your own state or out of state. Focus on those with a similar basic demographic environment, and ask them if they are willing to share what they have done so far, if they have information and research that profiles their customers, the strengths and weaknesses of their endeavors, and if they would make suggestions on specific projects. Find out who their community partners are and how they have been helpful.

Think of libraries in other states that have been in this struggle for many decades, such as California, Michigan, Florida, Texas, New Mexico, and New York. They might or might not have policies and strategies in place, but it is worthwhile to find out. Through the Internet, it is easy to contact people with a little effort and research.

Once you establish your contacts, try to find a similar immigrant base. You already have your basic local demographics, so you know what you are looking for. If your local Latino audience is mostly Mexicans recently arrived from rural areas to do farming work, you do not want to exchange information with a library serving mostly Cuban middle-class immigrants who have been established in the United States for 50 years.

Tables 4.13 and 4.14 provide a summary of advantages and disadvantages of working with primary and secondary sources. They also provide a quick reference when you need to decide your market research path.

TABLE 4.13 Primary Sources: Advantages and Disadvantages

Primary Source	Advantages	Disadvantages
Focus groups, mini focus groups, and one-on-one interviews	Accurate primary source if done with cross-cultural professional or pretrained staff	Involves time-consuming networking effort within the Latino community
	Local colleges and universities can help design and conduct interviews	Lack of cultural knowledge can lead to asking poor questions
	Community leaders know the problems of the local Latino population	Limited vision of the Latino community (small groups or individuals) or political agendas
	Current Latino customers willing to participate	Current Latino customers unwilling to participate
Field observation	Direct interviewing in houses, streets, or shopping centers in their own community	Limited vision of the Latino community (small groups)
	Structured observation previously prepared (knowing what to observe and how)	Need for pretrained interviewers; lack of cultural knowledge can lead to asking poor questions
	Allows interviewing people of different ages and backgrounds	Might raise confidentiality issues
	Observation in interviewees' own environment, where Latinos might be more open to respond	Need to develop credibility and trust about the interview process
Data collection from marketing behaviors	Constant source of information	Special technological capabilities needed
	Can be outsourced	Interpretation capabilities and trained personnel needed
	Massive	Impersonal for Latinos, expensive for libraries, and not specific for library services
Direct mail, online, and telephone surveys	Constant source of information	Special capabilities needed
	Massive but local; size may be adjusted to Latino target market or market segments	Interpretation capabilities and trained personnel needed; language barrier
	Can survey specific library subject matters	Low rate response (usually around 1–2%); impersonal and expensive

(Continued)

TABLE 4.13 *(Continued)*

Primary Source	Advantages	Disadvantages
Surveys at location of service	Constant source of information	Need extended periods of time and constant surveying
	Can survey specific subject matters by changing survey periodically	Incomplete or inaccurate information
	Current Latino patrons might be willing to participate	Current Latino patrons might be unwilling to participate
	Low logistics	Time and staff needed for classifying and interpreting information
Informal information gathering	Information based on opinions from all walks of life, current and potential customers	Limited information based on a limited vision of library services and cultural background of interviewee

TABLE 4.14   Secondary Sources: Advantages and Disadvantages

Secondary Sources	Advantages	Disadvantages
Prior surveys and studies by others	Great availability through library resources	Lack of specific information on local Latino markets
Information and statistics about similar demographics	Not necessary to be specifically trained in cross-cultural interview process	Lack of accurate information or information too diversified; still need cross-cultural "insights"
Literature, publications, Internet, and databases	Nonprofit status allows libraries to request information from other organizations serving the same Latino community	Need verification of sources' reliability
Data collection from marketing behaviors conducted by others		
Exchange information with other local community organizations	See chapter 3 for exchanging information with strategic partners in your community	Information might not be pertinent to your specific need
Reach out to libraries in other states	A complete list of libraries with Spanish Web sites can be found at http://www.reforma.org/spanishwebsites.htm; the WebJunction Spanish Outreach Program can be found at http://www.webjunction.org/	Basic target audience might not be exactly the same as yours

Trial and Error with an Educated Guess

After following these steps, you still might not be sure the information you have is enough to make decisions about planning and programming activities. Then you will have to act with an educated guess, but this is the least recommended. It takes time, effort, and money, and frequently you do not get the responses you want. Nevertheless, some actions can develop into possible strategies.

For instance, you may assume your local immigrants will be looking for information about how to acquire citizenship or naturalization. However, many Mexican immigrants have been denied the possibility of legal immigration for a long time. They know they cannot get legal status in the United States, especially if they entered undocumented, unless there is a change in the immigration law.[59] So providing information about citizenship is not enticing for this particular group, especially if they are recent, first-generation immigrants—unless they think you are offering "magic solutions."

Now, if your target community has been in the area for over 15 to 20 years and there is a high percentage of property owners—you can find this information at your local property taxes collector—business owners, and commercial activity, then your Latino population might be ready for citizenship classes. Moreover, you'd like to promote naturalization by explaining the benefits of becoming a citizen.

On the other hand, if the local public school gives you data suggesting a very high number of young Latino children, you might want to organize an event focusing on U.S.-born children's access—or limited access—to education, health, public assistance, and so forth. You will be concentrating on a particular issue that is of concern while creating awareness of the need for that type of information, which they probably cannot find for themselves because they might not know it exists.

Also, it is recommended that you follow these guidelines:

- Use common sense (but check your judgment with cross-information).
- Use your intuition (but continue to research!).
- Use multiple sources of information. (It is too risky to use just one source!)

When using your educated guess, give it a little thought and think outside the box! You can use all these strategies in combination because your goal is to gather as much information as possible.

Now, get ready for the next ride; this is just the first part of your market profile. Next, you will learn how to expand into other aspects of your research: the cultural aspects of the different Latino communities and how they differ and interact with each other.

Notes

1. U.S. Census Bureau, "2008 National Populations Projections," http://www.census.gov/population/www/projections/2008projections.html (accessed November 18, 2009).
2. "Latinos represent 51% of population growth in the United States as a whole since 2000," according to Frank Sharry, "Latinos Poised to Shake up 2010 Census, Politicians Beware," November 18, 2009, http://www.huffingtonpost.com/frank-sharry/latinos-poised-to-shake-u_b_362652.html (accessed December 3, 2009). Sharry is the founder and executive director of America's Voice, an organization that advocates for immigration reform.
3. Works include Güereña (1990), Alire and Archinbeque (1998, pp. 18–34), Cuban (2007, pp. 41–61), and Alire and Ayala (2007, pp. 51–80), among others.
4. For more information about population growth in different states, see U.S. Census Bureau, "State and County Quick Facts," http://quickfacts.census.gov/qfd/states/00000.html (accessed December 3, 2009).
5. The term *Hispanic* is used by the U.S. Census Bureau. "The term 'Hispanic' designates a person from a Spanish-speaking country or their descendants" as defined by the Population Resource

Center at http://www.prcdc.org/ (accessed December 3, 2009). The definition of *Hispanic* has been modified in each successive census. For additional information, see Chapa (2000).

6. The Woodrow Wilson International Center for Scholars published results for its "Key Finding from the 2006 Latino National Survey," showing 13.2 percent of the population in the United States as Latino. This is the first national study since 1989. Available at http://www.wilsoncenter. org/index.cfm?topic_id=1427&fuseaction=topics.event_summary&event_id=201793 (accessed December 3, 2009).

7. "Between 1950 and 1996 the driving force behind U.S. population growth dramatically shifted from native-born natural increase to immigration and births to immigrants" (Lytwak 1999).

8. B. Guzmán, "The Hispanic Population, Census 2000 Brief," 2001, http://www.census.gov/ prod/2001pubs/c2kbr01-3.pdf (accessed July 31, 2010).

9. Ibid.

10. Pew Hispanic Center, "Estimates of the Unauthorized Migrant Population for States based on the March 2005 CPS," April 26, 2006, http://pewhispanic.org/files/factsheets/17.pdf (accessed December 3, 2009).

11. Central Intelligence Agency, "The World Factbook: North America: Mexico," https://www.cia. gov/library/publications/the-world-factbook/geos/mx.html (accessed December 3, 2009).

12. Kaiser Family Foundation, "Latinos in California, Texas, New York, Florida, and New Jersey— 2002 National Survey of Latinos Survey Brief," 2004 (Publication #7056), http://www.kff.org/ kaiserpolls/7056.cfm (accessed December 3, 2009).

13. For quick information about each country and its population, please consult the CIA's World Factbook at https://www.cia.gov/library/publications/the-world-factbook/ (accessed December 3, 2009).

14. Latinos' interracial marriage rate in the United States according to the U.S. 2000 Census.

15. "Meatpacking Industry Backs Immigration Reform," *High Plains/Midwest AG Journal,* June 4, 2007, http://www.hpj.com/archives/2007/jun07/jun4/Meatpackingindustrybacksimm.cfm (accessed December 3, 2009).

16. In most Latin American countries, classes are well defined in terms of economic insertion, access to education, and job opportunity. Latin America is a vertical structure, with increasing income inequality, a concentration of wealth in the top 10 percent of the population, and an increase in the low-income or unemployed classes, especially under the neoliberal model. Individuals born in low social classes are rarely able to step up the social ladder. Immigrants see the United States as a horizontal structure with an opportunity for social mobility by applying effort, talent, and hard work. For discussion of this topic, see Portes and Hoffman (2003).

17. Pew Hispanic Center, "The Occupational Status and Mobility of Hispanics," December 15, 2005, http://pewhispanic.org/files/reports/59.pdf (accessed November 18, 2009).

18. For a list of the 100 fastest growing counties in the United States, please see U.S. Census Bureau, "U.S. Census Bureau Table 8: Population Estimates by Counties CO-EST2006-08," http://www. census.gov/popest/counties/CO-EST2005-09.html (accessed December 3, 2009).

19. For instance, the Colorado Constitutional Amendment for the 2005–2006 Initiative cycle, #55, Restrictions on Government Services to Illegal Immigrants. The amendment to the Colorado constitution known as the "Colorado Anti-Immigrant Initiative" concerning the restriction of nonemergency government services to persons who are lawfully present in the United States; restricting the provision of nonemergency services by state and local governments to United States citizens and aliens lawfully present in the United States, except as mandated by federal law; and providing for the implementation and enforcement of this restriction, was submitted to the Colorado Legislative Council on October 27, 2005, and was later barred by the Colorado Supreme Court but overturned by Governor Owens. For additional information see League of United Latin American Citizens at http://www. lulac.org (accessed December 3, 2009). Additional anti-immigrant legislation has been passed in local municipalities such Hazleton, Pennsylvania; Palm Bay, Florida; and San Bernardino, California, and states such as Arizona and Georgia are considering or have passed anti-immigrant bills.

20. Temporary Protected Status and Deferred Enforced Departure, U.S. Citizenship and Immigration Services. More information about the legal requirements for TPS can be found at Immigration and Nationality Act (INA) section 244, 8 U.S.C section 1254a, and in the TPS implementing regulations at 8 CFR Part 244. http://www.uscis.gov/portal/site/uscis/menuitem.eb1d4c2a3e5b9ac 89243c6a7543f6d1a/?vgnextoid=390d3e4d77d73210VgnVCM100000082ca60aRCRD&vgnextc hannel=390d3e4d77d73210VgnVCM100000082ca60aRCRD (accessed July 31, 2010).

21. You can obtain permanent residence in the United States by investing one million dollars or more and providing full-time employment to at least 10 U.S. citizens, according to IMMSPEC, a forms preparation service. See IMMSPEC, "Investment Based Green Card," http://www.immspec.com/ green-card-investment.htm (accessed November 18, 2009).

22. On November 19, 1997, President Clinton signed into law the Nicaraguan Adjustment and Central American Relief Act (NACARA), which provides various forms of immigration benefits and relief from deportation to certain Nicaraguans, Cubans, Salvadorans, Guatemalans, and their dependents, among others. For additional information, see "INS Publishes Final Regulations for NACARA Section 202," 2000. New release from the U.S Department of Justice, Immigration and Naturalization Service, http://www.uscis.gov/files/pressrelease/NACARAFinalRegs_032100v2. pdf (accessed July 31, 2010), and the U.S. Citizenship and Immigration Services (USCIS) portal, http://www.uscis.gov/portal/site/uscis (accessed December 3, 2009).

23. For additional information on immigration requirements, please visit the U.S. Citizenship and Immigration Services Web site at http://www.uscis.gov/portal/site/uscis (accessed December 3, 2009).

24. Latino average age is 26 compared to 35.4 for the general population. See U.S. Census Bureau, "We the People: Hispanics in the United States," December 2004, p. 4, http://www.census.gov/ prod/2004pubs/censr-18.pdf (accessed December 4, 2009). For 2008 data, see comparative tables "Age Data of the United States," http://www.census.gov/population/www/socdemo/age/ older_2008.html (accessed December 4, 2009).

25. U.S. Census Bureau, "2008 National Populations Projections," http://www.census.gov/popula tion/www/projections/2008projections.html (accessed November 18, 2009).

26. The term "second language" is used to describe any language acquired after early childhood. The term "language acquisition" became commonly used after Stephen Krashen contrasted it with formal and nonconstructive "learning." For Stephen Krashen's works, see his Web site at http:// www.sdkrashen.com/ (accessed December 3, 2009).

27. U.S. Census Bureau, Newsroom, "Facts for Features—Hispanic Heritage Month Sept. 15–Oct. 15, 2006, Population," http://www.census.gov/newsroom/releases/archives/facts_for_features_spe cial_editions/cb06-ff14.html (accessed July 31, 2010).

28. Pew Hispanic Center, "Hispanic Women in the United States, 2007," May 8, 2008, revised May 14, 2008, http://pewhispanic.org/files/factsheets/42.pdf (accessed November 18, 2009).

29. "The Challenge: Latinos in a Changing California," in *Continuity and Change in Latin American Immigration: Types of Latin American Origin Immigrants*, report of the University of California SCR 43 Task Force, 1989, http://www.clnet.ucla.edu/challenge/origin.htm.

30. Ibid.

31. Ibid., p. 30.

32. Ibid., p. 30.

33. Ibid., p. 30.

34. Pew Hispanic Center, "The Occupational Status and Mobility of Hispanics," December 15, 2005, http://pewhispanic.org/files/reports/59.pdf (accessed November 18, 2009).

35. Pew Hispanic Center, "Statistical Portrait of Hispanics in the United States, 2007," Table 21, March 5, 2009, http://pewhispanic.org/factsheets/factsheet.php?FactsheetID=46 (accessed November 18, 2009).

36. Pew Hispanic Center/Kaiser Family Foundation, "National Survey of Latinos: Education," January 26, 2004, http://pewhispanic.org/files/reports/25.pdf (accessed November 18, 2009).

37. "Hispanic-Serving Institutions (HSIs) are defined in the Higher Education Act (HEA) as accredited degree-granting public or private nonprofit institutions of higher education with low educational and general expenditures, a high enrollment of needy students, and at least 25 percent total undergraduate Hispanic fulltime-equivalent student enrollment, of which at least 50 percent of Hispanic students are low-income." Ibid., p. 6.

38. Excelencia in Education and the Institute for Higher Education Policy, "How Latinos Pay for College: Patters of Financial Aid (2003–04)," 2005, http://www.edexcelencia.org/pdf/fact_sheet_061207.pdf (accessed November 18, 2009).

39. Centro de Estudios Latinoamericanos, Escuela de Servicio Exterior, Universidad de Georgetown, Base de Datos Políticos de las Américas, "Educación Obligatoria," Estudio Constitucional Comparativo, 2006, http://pdba.georgetown.edu/Comp/Cultura/Educacion/obligatoria.html (accessed July 14, 2009).

40. Although "lost generation" characterizes a group of American writers who showed the disillusionment of Americans after the First World War, the generic term is also used for groups of people disproportionately affected by economic shocks, unemployment, those who died in the war, and first-generation immigrants who did not readily assimilate to the United States.

41. Pew Hispanic Center, "From 200 Million to 300 Million: The Numbers behind Population Growth," October 10, 2006, http://pewhispanic.org/files/factsheets/25.pdf (accessed December 1, 2009).

42. "In Census 2000, Hispanics were asked to mark one of four categories: Mexican, Puerto Rican, Cuban, or other Spanish/Hispanic/Latino. The last category had a write-in option by which a person could provide a specific Hispanic origin group such as Dominican or Spaniard. In order to be comparable with the earlier U.S. Census Bureau report *We the American . . . Hispanics,* the following specific Hispanic groups are included: Mexican, Puerto Rican, Cuban, Central American, South American, Dominican, Spaniard, and Other Hispanic. For information regarding detailed Hispanic groups, such as Colombian and Uruguayan, refer to the technical documentation for Summary File 4 at http://www.census.gov/prod/cen2000/doc/sf4.pdf" (Ramirez 2004, p. 1).

43. U.S. Census Bureau Quick Facts U.S. Population Estimates 2009, http://quickfacts.census.gov/qfd/states/00000.html (accessed July 31, 2010).

44. U.S. Census Bureau, "Live Births, Birth Rates, and Fertility Rates by Hispanic-Origin-Status," http://www.census.gov/compendia/statab/tables/09s0078.xls-2008-12-16 (accessed November 19, 2009).

45. Population Resource Center, "Latina Teen Pregnancy: Problems and Prevention. Executive Summary," prepared in 2002 by Mary C. Dickson and updated by Megan McNamara in March 2004, http://www.prcdc.org/files/Latina_Teen_Pregnancy.pdf (accessed November 20, 2009).

46. Ibid.

47. "Household income includes the income of the householder and all other people 15 years and older in the household, whether or not they are related to the householder. For comparisons of household income, this report focuses on the median—the point that divides the household income distribution into halves, one half having incomes above the median and the other having incomes below the median. The median is based on the income distribution of all households, including those with no income" (Webster and Bishaw 2007, p. 8).

48. National Urban League Institute, "2006 Census Poverty & Income Data," August 28, 2007, http://www.nul.org/policyinstitute.html (accessed December 1, 2009).

49. The Hispanic Alliance for Career Enhancement (HACE) is a national nonprofit organization dedicated to the advancement of Latino professionals that conducts regular surveys among its members related to professional issues among Latinos. More than 500 professionals completed last year's e-mail-administered survey. For additional information see http://www.haceonline.org/ (accessed July 31, 2010).

50. Cuban immigrants came to the United States at four different times: immediately after the Cuban revolution in 1959, during the next decade until the mid-1970s, the so-called "marielitos" who came in the 1980s, and the "balseros," considered the last immigration wave until the present.

51. "Is Becoming an American a Developmental Risk? The Immigrant Paradox," Open Education Free Education for All blog, by Thomas, http://www.openeducation.net/2009/03/22/is-becoming-an-american-a-developmental-risk-the-immigrant-paradox/ (accessed November 20, 2009).

52. Sistema Estadístico Nacional (SEN), Guatemala's Census 2002, "*Marco Conceptual para Enfocar Estadísticas de Pueblos Indígenas,*" http://www.ine.gob.gt/descargas/generoPueblos/Marco_conceptual_pueblos_indigenas.pdf (accessed November 20, 2009).

53. CIA World Factbook estimates for 2003. See the *World Factbook* at https://www.cia.gov/library/publications/the-world-factbook/.

54. Ibid.

55. Guatemalan nonwhite populations do not have the same educational opportunities as they are kept away from educational opportunities by an educational system that does not allow diversity. For additional information on this topic, see Gretchen Kroth, "Roadblocks to Education: Guatemala's Garbage Dump Education System," Counterpunch.org, August 5, 2009, http://www.counterpunch.org/kroth08052009.html (accessed November 20, 2009).

56. Sources used are a combination of data released by the U.S. Census Bureau, http://www.census.gov/; The Pew Hispanic Center, http://pewhispanic.org/; and the 2006 National Latino Survey, http://www.icpsr.umich.edu/icpsrweb/ICPSR/studies/20862 (all accessed July 31, 2010).

57. *The observer's paradox* refers to a situation where the presence of the observer/investigator influences the observation of an event or experiment. The term was coined in 1966 by sociolinguist William Labov (1973).

58. If your organization is looking for a market researcher, I recommend "GreenBook, the guide for buyers of marketing research services," a directory of market research companies with detailed information by location and type of research. GreenBook is a company of the New York American Marketing Association Services, Inc., and can be found at http://www.greenbook.org/AboutUs.cfm (accessed November 20, 2009).

59. The Immigration and Nationality Act (INA) provides for 675,000 legal permanent visas each year worldwide, of which 226,000 are included in the family-based preference system and 140,000 are permanent employment-based visas. Of those, 40,000 go to the lowest level of skills, which is category 3 (Skilled shortage workers with at least two years of training or experience, professionals with college degrees, and 'other workers' who are those 'capable of performing unskilled labor,' and who are not temporary or seasonal.). "Other workers" are limited to 5,000 visas per year. National Council of La Raza, "Basic Facts on Immigration," 2004. http://madreanna.org/immref/basicnclr.pdf (accessed July 31, 2010).

WORSHEET 4.1 Latino Community Profile in Little Haven City (Example)

Goal: Look at the interaction of several variables to understand your local Latino market needs. You can visualize the characteristics of these segments to define what services your organization should offer to be in sync with those needs.

Variable	Specifics	Group 1 Size: 550 people	Group 2 Size: 350 people	Group 3 Size 150 people	Group 4 Size: 75 people
Origin	Country Region	Mexico Puebla	Mexico (DF)	El Salvador (Unknown)	Guatemala (Unknown)
Time in the United States	0–5 years 5–10 years 10–15 years over 15 years U.S. born	40 30 10 20	5 25 35 15 20	20 30 25 10 15	40 15 15 25 5
Age	0–10 11–64 65+	10 85 5	15 75 10	15 72 13	10 88 2
Occupation	Administrative/Professional (skilled) Construction (OJT) Food/Farming (OJT) Production (OJT) Sales Other	 27 25 34 10 4	14 27 10 25 15 9	5 15 25 20 5 30	 35 44 16 5
Income range	Less than $20,000 20,001 to 30,000 30,001 to 50,000 50,001+	70 25 5 	55 30 10 5	70 25 5 	73 15 12
Socioeconomic status	Blue-collar White-collar Other (self-employed)	91 9	62 14 24	90 10	95 5
Immigration status	Undocumented Legal immigrant/Permanent resident Naturalized citizen US born	35 45 20 	15 60 20 5	25 60 (TPS) 15 	30 55 (NACARA) 15
Levels of education	Less than elementary Elementary Less than high school High school Some college Four-year college +	 60 35 5 	 45 35 20	1 64 35 	1 74 25
Language ability	English dominant Bilingual Spanish dominant	5 25 70	23 26 51	12 25 63	3 27 70

Variables are expressed in percentages.

WORKSHEET 4.2 Country of Origin, Time in the United States, and Occupation Combined

Variable	Specifics	Group 1 Size: 550 people	Group 2 Size: 350 people	Group 3 Size 150 people	Group 4 Size: 75 people
Origin	Country Region	Mexico Puebla	Mexico (DF)	El Salvador (Unknown)	Guatemala (Unknown)
Time in the United States	0–5 years	40	5	20	40
	5–10 years	30	25	30	15
	10–15 years	10	35	25	15
	over 15 years		15	10	25
	U.S. born	20	20	15	5
Occupation	Administrative/Professional (skilled)		14	5	
	Construction (OJT)	27	27	15	35
	Food/Farming (OJT)	25	10	25	44
	Production (OJT)	34	25	20	16
	Sales	10	15	5	
	Other (self-employed)	4	9	30	5

NOTES

_____

_____

_____

_____

_____

Variables are expressed in percentages.

 From ¡Hola, amigos! A Plan for Latino Outreach by Susana G. Baumann. Santa Barbara, CA: Libraries Unlimited. Copyright © 2011.

Variable	Specifics	Group 1 Size: 550 people	Group 2 Size: 350 people	Group 3 Size 150 people	Group 4 Size: 75 people
Occupation:	OJT Occupation skills	86	62	60	95
Time in the United States	Less than 10	70	30	50	55
	More than 10	10	50	35	50
Income range	Lower income (less than $20,000)	70	55	70	73
	Higher income (more than $30,000)	5	15	5	2

NOTES

_____

_____

_____

_____

_____

_____

Variables are expressed in percentages.

From ¡Hola, amigos! A Plan for Latino Outreach by Susana G. Baumann. Santa Barbara, CA: Libraries Unlimited. Copyright © 2011.

WORKSHEET 4.4 Time in the United States, Occupation, and Levels of Education Combined

Variables	Specifics	Group 1 Size: 550 people	Group 2 Size: 350 people	Group 3 Size 150 people	Group 4 Size: 75 people
Time in the United States	Less than 10	70	30	50	
	More than 10	10	50	35	55
					50
Occupation	Administrative/Professional (skilled)		14	5	
	OTJ skill	86	62	60	95
Levels of education	Less than elementary				
	Elementary	60	45	64	
	Less than high school				74
	High school	35	35	35	
	Some college				25
	Four-year college		20		

NOTES

_____

_____

_____

_____

_____

_____

Variables are expressed in percentages.

 From ¡Hola, amigos! A Plan for Latino Outreach by Susana G. Baumann. Santa Barbara, CA: Libraries Unlimited. Copyright © 2011.

WORKSHEET 4.5   Time in the United States and Language Ability Combined

Variables	Specifics	Group 1 Size: 550	Group 2 Size: 350	Group 3 Size: 150	Group 4 Size: 75
Time in the United States:	Less than 10	70	30	50	55
	More than 10	10	50	35	50
Language ability:	English dominant	5	23	12	3
	Bilingual	25	26	25	27
	Spanish dominant	70	51	63	70

NOTES

_____

_____

_____

_____

_____

_____

_____

_____

Variables are expressed in percentages.

From ¡Hola, amigos! A Plan for Latino Outreach by Susana G. Baumann. Santa Barbara, CA: Libraries Unlimited. Copyright © 2011.

WORKSHEET 4.6 Age and Immigration Status Combined

Variables	Specifics	Group 1 Size: 550	Group 2 Size: 350	Group 3 Size: 150	Group 4 Size: 75
Age	0–10	10	15	15	10
	11–64	85	75	72	88
	65+	5	10	13	2
Immigration status	Undocumented	35	15	25	30
	Legal immigrant/ Permanent resident	45	65	60 (TPS)	55 (NACARA)
	Naturalized citizen US born	20	20	15	15

NOTES

_____

_____

_____

_____

_____

_____

Variables are expressed in percentages.

 From ¡Hola, amigos! A Plan for Latino Outreach by Susana G. Baumann. Santa Barbara, CA: Libraries Unlimited. Copyright © 2011.

WORKSHEET 4.7   Horizontal Comparison of Variables

Variable	Specifics	Group 1 Size: 550 people	Group 2 Size: 350 people	Group 3 Size: 150 people	Group 4 Size: 75 people
Language ability	English dominant	5	23	12	3
	Bilingual	25	26	25	27
	Spanish dominant	70	51	63	70

NOTES

_____

_____

_____

_____

_____

_____

_____

Variables are expressed in percentages.

From *¡Hola, amigos! A Plan for Latino Outreach* by Susana G. Baumann. Santa Barbara, CA: Libraries Unlimited. Copyright © 2011.

Chapter 5

Getting to Know Your Latino Patrons: Part II

Overview

As indicated in chapter 4, the multicultural diversity of Latinos presents a great challenge when libraries market themselves to this community since addressing this diversity defines services, strategies, and resources.

In their work "Counseling Latinos and *la Familia*," authors Santiago-Rivera, Arredondo, and Gallardo-Cooper (2002, pp. 8–9) talk about the issue in these words: "Multicultural and culture-specific lenses broaden our understanding because they draw on history, anthropology, sociology, political process, economics, and phenomena about human development from both etic and emic perspectives[1]. . . . As attention is given to Latinos as a cultural group, the heterogeneity among Latino ethnic groups and within-ethnic group differences also emerge, leading to further deconstruction of beliefs and stereotypes that have been promulgated as facts."

In other words, understanding in depth the dynamic dimensions of Latino identities is a common need in disciplines as diverse as psychology, sociology, economics, and even marketing. Each discipline has developed cultural perspectives models and tools to study, understand, and apply multicultural competencies to their disciplines and to better comprehend Latino identities from their specific professional angles.

As anticipated, this chapter addresses cultural perspectives from a marketing viewpoint, working on the subjective aspects of culture (Korzenny and Korzenny 2005). Getting to know your Latino patrons from a cultural perspective will increase your opportunities to position your library and your services in your Latino patrons' minds by establishing a fluent, barrier-free communication process.

These descriptions of cultural dimensions are characteristics shared by different groups within the Latino community (Korzenny and Korzenny 2005). These dimensions are construed as common beliefs, behaviors, and lifestyles in Latino culture. However, these pillars of Latino culture vary according to socioeconomic, educational, and other demographic factors. These dimensions are also affected or conditioned by the geography and history of each country and even present regional differences within each country.

In order to give you guidelines from which you can ask questions to become knowledgeable about and familiar with your local Latino community, we have included some descriptions of common cultural dimensions in this chapter. These descriptions offer a broad base of general knowledge from which you can start the second step of your own market profile. By asking questions, you might confirm or reset those beliefs, behaviors, and lifestyle notions. You might also encounter the individual preferences of Latinos.[2]

Also provided in this chapter and the next are tools to help you in the exploratory process of assessing community needs. These are not traditional marketing procedures but simple steps to achieve some understanding of an otherwise not easily attainable goal.

What Marketing Has Done So Far for Latino Culture

As I have often said in my presentations, I did not know I was Hispanic until I arrived in this country in 1990.

Hispanic is a term that has been challenged by scholars and activists for inaccurately including Latin American, European, and even U.S.-born populations under one single category (Dávila 2001). *Latino*, on the other hand, while more inclusive of broader cultural commonalities—such as language and, to a lesser degree, religion—still masks the historical and political circumstances that have affected the way people coming from South, Central, and North America became a part of the melting pot (Gloor 2006).[3] Neither term represents the diversity and complexity of these communities.

The marketing industry was one of the most significant forces in lobbying for a common Hispanic culture or identity. In the 1970s—although efforts can be found before[4]—Hispanic advertising agencies really took off with the idea that all Hispanics shared common values and that just being Hispanic—especially for those involved in marketing and advertising—was synonymous with representing and knowing the Hispanic market (Dávila 2001).

The federal government also took the same approach. The census included the nomenclature "persons of Spanish origin" in 1980, but not until 1990 was the category "Hispanic or Latino origin" included. This was the first time a census category did not gather information only based on a racial profile.

The fast demographic growth of the community also propelled the use of the term *Hispanic* to celebrate and embrace our supposedly common heritage. The origin of Hispanic Heritage Month can be traced to President Lyndon Johnson's initiative in the 1960s—originally Hispanic Heritage Week, which was extended to one month by Congress in 1988.

The high price Hispanics paid—and to some extent keep paying—for this generalization is the "othering" practices of including a large group of people in a marginally ethnic category regardless of economic, educational, racial, or class backgrounds (Dávila 2001). These discriminatory practices tagged the group with the consequential labels and stereotypes: Hispanics or Latinos are hot, sensual, loyal, loud, impoverished, hard working, monolingual, uneducated, and so forth. The list can be endless.

With these stereotypes in mind, we tend to think monolithically about the group. During a workshop at a California library in the summer of 2007, a participant asked me how she could gather Latino participation for an event featuring the Chilean and California-resident writer Isabel Allende. Although she did not express it, I believe her concern was related to attracting stereotyped monolingual, poor, and almost illiterate Latinos to a well-known South American acculturated writer's presentation. Starting with the question, "Who reads Isabel Allende?" one could then look into the vast population of Silicon Valley's capital—approximately 30 percent Latino in a population of over 900,000 people—with the highest median income of any large city in the United States (according to the 2006 Census) and with almost 35 percent of businesses owned by minority women. Within that demography, it should not have been difficult to find Latinas interested in that particular event. She only had to think in terms of the appropriate group or segment of the Latino population who would respond to that incentive. In other words, as with any population, Latinos comprise a vast array of interests and abilities, and the researcher or marketer must broaden his or her view of the Latino man or woman to capture those interests and abilities.

In the 1990s, as Latinos became a "growing buying power,"[5] Hispanic agencies' marketing models changed from a common values base to more pocket-oriented strategies, attempting to focus on the accelerated growth of the Latino market as a result of the increasing wealth and improvement of this community. There was some truth to the model. Studies showed that some sectors of the Hispanic middle class grew by 80 percent during the 1980s and 1990s. One million Hispanic households rose to middle-class status between 1990 and 2000, defined by earnings of $40,000 or more (Valle and Mandel 2003). However, between 1989 and 1997, there was an increase in poverty levels in most Hispanic households, reaching up to 30.7 percent of the population.[6] This marketing strategy focusing on the growth of middle-class sectors hid the economic and social disparities among Latinos in different parts of the nation. Marketers tried to tap deep into corporations' pockets to gain the Hispanic market's attention. However, they were never able to achieve parity with the amount of money corporate clients paid for mainstream advertising.[7]

In the last decade, marketing trends have recognized the Latino market as diverse, multicultural, and multiracial. Known as the acculturation model, marketers emphasized different degrees of acculturation, assimilation, transculturation,[8] and/or retro-acculturation within the Latino market and determined that Latinos connected to products according to their insertion in these different domains. These domains were not necessarily consecutive stages of an acculturative process—the way successive generations tend to integrate into the dominant culture—but depended on and were affected by demographic variables such as age at time of immigration, level of education, language abilities (Santiago-Rivera, Arredondo, and Gallardo-Cooper 2002), time spent in the United States, foreign or U.S. birth, and generational status.

The acculturation model measured the outsider's embracing of mainstream culture values, beliefs, and behaviors and placed him or her in an acculturation rank, which ultimately defined the marketing strategies and tactics followed to target that particular individual. But if we understand acculturation as the interchange of influence between two cultures without subordination of one another (LaFromboise et al. 1993), there is a limit to how much an individual can acculturate without losing his or her original set of values, beliefs, and behaviors, so marketers were really thinking in terms of gradual Latino *assimilation* (Berry 1998).

While a true acculturation model would give Latinos the option of switching from one culture to another as circumstances present—a safe haven—the assimilation model requires not only the actual integration of the outsiders—and the loss of their cultural identity—but also the acceptance of the outsiders by the hosting culture as part of mainstream culture.

The assimilation model failed to recognize the difficulties Latinos faced while trying to embrace mainstream culture and the cultural and discriminatory barriers they needed to overcome. In other words, it did not matter how much they *wanted to belong* but how much they were *allowed to belong*.

Looking for new answers, in 2006 the Association of Hispanic Advertising Agencies (AHAA) launched the Latino Identity Project to explore the deceptively simple question, "What makes a Latino, Latino?" introducing "a new model of Latino cultural identity anticipated to transform the way marketers and advertisers connect with Hispanic customers." The new model, according to marketers, was a significant shift from the overly simplistic way in which Latino customers have been characterized to date—by language, country of origin, and time spent in the United States—to "a set of complex, adaptable, intricate and interrelated values that change through time according to the environment and external stimuli. It is complex, but not complicated. . . . And, while language and acculturation have a role, it is only a supporting role."[9]

The model also proposed that factors such as acculturation levels, ethnic pride, language preference, and socioeconomic status are in fact contextual and not defining factors. Marketers sustained that Latino identity is as complex and fragmented as the general market and cannot be defined with a one- or two-dimensional segmentation model.

On another note, an aspect not widely debated yet in the marketing environment is the dynamic resulting from the reciprocal influence among Latinos of different origin through the exchange of cultural values, beliefs, and behaviors via interracial marriage, social relationships, sharing of neighborhoods and living spaces, the workplace, and the common qualifying experience of being a Latino or Hispanic immigrant. These and other questions are still to be answered.

Cultural Dimensions

Anthropologist James P. Spradley (Spradley and McCurdy 1988) defined culture as the "acquired knowledge people use to interpret experience and generate behavior."

Cultural written and unwritten rules are learned since birth, shared, created, and maintained through human relationships, allowing us to relate to the social group we belong to and differentiate ourselves from other groups. These rules can be grouped in cultural dimensions—categories of human values, behaviors, and beliefs that can be used to describe a culture (Hall 1976). The study of those categories reveals underlying patterns and archetypes—according to Carl Jung's psychology, an inherited pattern of thought or symbolic imagery resulting from past collective experiences that reappear in the individual unconscious—helping people make sense of their shared cultural experience (Spradley and McCurdy 1988). These patterns and archetypes propose generic behaviors from which individual actions are derived, patterned, imitated, or judged. Just like in fiction, cultural archetypes appeal to a segment or group of people who identify with them.

By studying these patterns and archetypes, we might find *trends* of behaviors within certain groups. However, individual behavior is also affected by an array of other factors, such as personality, past experiences, family structure, relationship with parents and siblings, and more, which create differences among individuals within the same cultural group. The risk is then when action is based on generalizations, which can—like a boomerang—have negative consequences as opposed to the intended response.

Common knowledge, for instance, sustains that Latinos do not make eye contact. However, the exact opposite has also been said based on scientific observation (Argyle 1988).[10]

So when you encounter Latino patrons, they might not look at you in the eye because of several factors: (1) it is a sign of respect or fear; (2) they might not understand what you are explaining; (3) they are not agreeing with what you are saying; or (4) they might be afraid of showing a sexual connotation—attraction between a man and a woman. However, the opposite, eye contact, might mean the following: (1) they are acculturated and know eye contact is important to your culture; (2) they are assimilated and it comes naturally to them; (3) they are trying hard to understand what you are saying; (4) they are challenging you; or (5) they come from a population segment in which eye contact is important or expected.

As you see, responses might be related to cultural or personal values defined by the person's degree of acculturation or assimilation, socioeconomic status, or ethnic or national background. Of course, the problem is how to find out which of these situations is taking place. The best answer is to get to know your audience, develop awareness and personal relationships with your patrons, and practice, practice, practice.

Once you become aware of the differences—for example, the reasons why Latinos do or do not make eye contact in the same way as Americans—you will focus less on passing judgment on that particular issue—"that person is or is not looking at me in the eye"—which might make you uncomfortable. That aspect of the interaction will be overcome, and you will be able to focus on the situation at hand without judgment.

It is important, then, to understand some aspects of Latino cultural dimensions—the values, behaviors, and beliefs that can be used to construct an idea of Latino culture. Studying these categories might reveal underlying patterns and archetypes that embrace Latinos in a shared cultural experience. Nevertheless, please keep in mind that these are just generic descriptions. Your job is to know your local Latinos and figure out how to interact with them.

The Latin American Cultural Experience

The major influence in the Latin American cultural experience is related to the clash between native cultures and the religious and political conquest, the strength or weakness of regional indigenous cultures to resist or assimilate, and the way the conquerors imposed on them.

Values, beliefs, and behaviors in areas of strong and advanced cultures—Mayans, Aztecs, or Incas—differ from areas where slaves from Africa were introduced—for instance, the Caribbean and Brazil—or from those regions were the presence of European immigration was later favored—some countries in South America with coasts exposed to the Atlantic Ocean.

In the same fashion, the presence of 13 generations of Mexican American families in the American Southwest produces a very different cultural experience than that of Cubans settled in regions of Florida for over 40 years or the recent internal demographic migration of Nuyoricans[11] into New Jersey and Pennsylvania. Both the incoming and the receiving or hosting cultures interact according to their particular characteristics. In all cases, mutual influence has defined the cultural experiences of both groups.

To study these cultural experiences, some disciplines rely on the individual and his or her context—especially the Latino familial context. Others need to find common ground within large, diverse Latino groups and see how these different groups connect to each other.

An appropriate cultural approach in the library environment might be somewhere in between: it requires working with individuals and families and becoming knowledgeable about the values, behaviors, and beliefs of specific market segments—those smaller portions of the total target market that share characteristics—in order to achieve an active presence of the local library's image in all Latino residents' minds.

Developing a Cultural Approach

In order to develop a reasonable cultural approach for successful outreach, libraries need to become culturally exposed to local Latino communities. In other words, it entails becoming acquainted with specific market segments residing in the vicinity and to whom services will be provided. It involves taking an active role in doing research through primary and secondary sources, talking to community leaders, and getting out and asking questions about local Latinos and their cultures.

Asking questions about lifestyles, values, and behaviors might be difficult if the person conducting the interview is not familiar with Latino culture or with the culture of the interviewee's country of origin, as we already discussed. For instance, it might be difficult to ask how the library can help patrons check out books to a group of low-literate Spanish-speaking working-class individuals who have never been exposed to borrowing materials from a public library and for whom reading a book might be an overwhelming task. It also might be difficult for even educated people to talk about borrowing books from the library when their cultural preference is to buy books.

Answering questions about lifestyles, values, and behaviors also might be difficult for the person or persons being interviewed. As stated before, underlying aspects of culture are made up of assumptions, habits, and beliefs that may not be consciously articulated or taught and, therefore, might be difficult to explain. For that reason, interviewees may give vague responses, may not be familiar with the type of evaluation system you are proposing—such as the use of grading scales—may answer what they think the interviewer wants to hear, or may provide any other "cultural noise" in the communication process.[12]

To help initiate your research efforts, this chapter features a cultural approach based on three levels of performance: an individual level, a group level, and a cultural level. The individual level identifies how members of the culture see themselves within a particular cultural dimension and how they act accordingly. The group level detects the way individuals interact with other members of the group. Finally, the cultural level is the glue that binds everything together by supporting the relationships between individual and group interactions, and the group as a whole, among other culturally distinctive groups.

Descriptions at the cultural level are included in this chapter to help you envision some aspects of the base that sustains individual and group behavior. These descriptions are based on trends described in different studies; in some cases, information that supports the description is also included, but in no way do these descriptions or trends intend to define monolithically a Hispanic or Latino culture. These are just *generic* descriptions of Latino values, beliefs, and behaviors. Differences have been identified whenever possible. In general, except research done on cross-cultural behavior in the workplace,[13] most descriptions are based on field-based research with an ethnographic perspective. Some conclusions have been supported with secondary sources. These descriptions do not cover every aspect of Latino cultural dimensions, and it is not the intention of this approach to be comprehensive in the sense of a sociological or anthropological study. The intention is to provide a broader understanding of ideas that have been discussed and publicized or imposed as *Latino culture*. Some might be stereotypical—stereotypes are never intrinsically positive or negative per se—which is why opposing ideas are presented when possible. However, you will have to find out the particular characteristics of your own local Latino community at the individual and group level, as we stated with demographic variables in chapter 4.

For quick reference, Table 5.1 provides a summary of the descriptions that are discussed later in the chapter.

TABLE 5.1 Cultural Dimensions in Latino Culture

Individual Level	Group Level	Cultural Level
Sense of self	Communication styles	Identity and self-image
Image and appearance		
Body language	Relationship with other members of the community outside the family unit	Individualism vs. collectivism
Use of space	Social protocol	Perception of space/proxemics
Use of time		Perception of time
Generational roles	Relationship with family and extended family	Family values
Parent-child relationship		
Gender interaction	Relationship between individuals of different gender or sexual orientation	Gender roles
	Relationship with peers	
Learning styles	Work principles and practices	Perception of work value, wealth, success, and leadership
Relationship with money and success		
Work habits	Relationship with authorities	
Reasons for immigration		
Health status	Use of the health system and health information	Beliefs about life, death, religion, and the approach to health
Health disparities		
Religious practices and rituals	Religious beliefs and moral values	

Characteristics of Cultural Dimensions
Identity and Self-Image

Much has been said and written about how Latinos identify themselves. In the context of defining race as a social construct (Berger and Luckman 1966), it is common knowledge that Latinos can be of any race. In fact, the race mixture in Latin America includes a wide variety of native groups, blacks, Asians, Caucasians, and beyond.

In 1989–1990, the Latino National Political Survey,[14] a study sponsored by the Inter-University Consortium for Political and Social Research, sampled Latinos living in the United States. They were asked how they identified themselves and were given the following options:

- Place of origin: Those who called themselves Mexican, Puerto Rican, Cuban
- Pan-ethnic names: Those who called themselves Hispanic, Latino, Spanish, Hispanic American
- American: Those who called themselves American or Other

Most respondents chose their own nationality or background: 62 percent of Mexicans, 41 percent of Cubans, and 57 percent of Puerto Ricans identified themselves with their place of origin. Only 10 percent of Mexicans called themselves American while 21 percent of Puerto Ricans and 39 percent of Cubans did so. According to the study, slightly more than half of the respondents were women. Among the national-origin groups, 56 percent of Puerto Ricans, 51 percent of Cubans, and 48 percent of Mexicans were women. Foreign-born men outnumbered foreign-born women; this was especially true among Mexicans.

Overwhelmingly, regardless of nativity, Cubans identified themselves racially as white; majorities of U.S.-born Mexicans and foreign-born Puerto Ricans also identified racially as white. The majority of foreign-born Mexicans and 47 percent of native-born Puerto Ricans, on the other hand, used a Latino referent, such as Latino, *Hispano*, or Mexican, as their racial identification (de la Garza et al. 1992).

Ten years later, "Shades of Belonging" (Tafoya 2004), a report based on the 2000 U.S. Census, found compelling and representative beliefs Latinos share about one aspect of identity and self-image—"sense of belonging"—with a slightly different perspective.

In the 2000 U.S. Census, Tafoya reports, when respondents to the "Spanish/Hispanic/Latino" category were asked about their race, 15 million, or 42 percent, represented themselves as belonging to Some Other Race—SOR—a distinctive view of race, according to Tafoya, that will likely change the way the United States manages the social divide. In addition, 48 percent identified themselves as white; 2 percent as black; less than 1 percent said they were American Indian, Asian, or Pacific Islander; and 6 percent said they belonged to two or more races.

Tafoya concludes that for Latinos, race might represent a measure of belonging. In fact, self-identification as "of white race" increases with those born in the United States, with second and third generations, and with increased civic enfranchisement. Whiteness also converges with higher levels of education, less unemployment, higher economic opportunities, older age, higher percent of registered voters and naturalized citizens, self-identification as being American, and less feeling of discrimination in the workplace. Unfortunately, the study does not represent these results by country of origin or family background.

Individualism versus Collectivism

This aspect, the relationship each individual establishes with the group he or she belongs to, and, more generally, with society, has been defined most commonly by traditional marketing research: "Latinos rate very high on the collectivism end of the continuum" (Korzenny and Korzenny 2005). Nevertheless, according to Hofstede's (2005) scores,[15] different countries in Latin America rank at different levels (see Table 5.2), with scores as high as 46 for Argentina to a low 6 for Guatemala. (With a 91, the United States ranks as one of the highest scores in individualism.)

These trends might influence the way Latinos of different national origin acculturate or assimilate to the hosting culture and the individual's ability to adapt to and survive in an unfamiliar context, to survive outside the immigration cluster, or to aim at more competitive opportunities.

Perception of Space/Proxemics

The distinction between use and perception of personal and community space is necessary for cross-cultural interaction. On one hand, use and perception of personal space includes issues of politeness and appropriate behavior or social protocol. It also includes grooming

TABLE 5.2 Hofstede's Country Individualism Index (IDV) Values in 14-Work-Goals for Some Latin American Countries, Spain, and the United States

Country	Individualism Index	Country	Individualism Index
Argentina	46	Panama	11
Chile	23	Peru	16
Colombia	13	El Salvador	19
Costa Rica	15	Spain	51
Ecuador	8	Uruguay	36
Guatemala	6	United States	91
Mexico	30	Venezuela	12

Source: Geert H. Hofstede, *Culture's Consequences: International Differences in Work-Related Values,* abridged ed. (Thousand Oaks, CA: Sage Publications, 1984), p. 158. (Additional countries in the study are not included in this table.)

habits, body positioning in space, sense of personal space, and other non-verbal messages. Different cultures create distinctive norms for closeness, such as for speaking, conducting business, or courting (Givens 2008).

Latinos' use and perception of personal space have been defined as being more involved with each other than that of Anglo Americans. They are said to interact frequently, casually touch each other with ease, and include friends and extended family in their actions.[16] However, Mexicans and other Central Americans might not interact with other countrymen if they have not been properly introduced based on a high sense of respect among each other (Chong 2002).

Regarding social protocol and use of personal space, for instance, greetings and introductions may vary from country to country. In Mexico, it is customary for the arriving person to greet the others while in other countries, the group will greet the newcomer. For instance, someone who walks into a group of persons eating would say *provecho* or *buen provecho* (enjoy your meal). In Chile, women often greet both other women and men with a kiss on the cheek while in Argentina both men and women kiss each other on the cheek. Urban social protocol is also different from rural social behavior where greetings might be more distant, for example, shaking hands or shoulder tapping. In Mexico, it is customary for men to open doors for women and women to walk in front of men. It is accepted for Colombians to come up to the beginning of a queue despite other people waiting in line, especially if they are elderly (Foster 2002).

Another unique style in social communication is telling *piropos,* a traditional behavior of most Latinos that is used as flattery to beautiful women. The custom comes from Spain, as *piropos* were first publicly used at the beginning of the seventeenth century in writings and poetry. Troubadours and minstrels were in charge to praise or ridicule the heroic feats of the time; many gallant verses and amusing words, even somewhat malicious, can be found as early as in the poem of the *Mío Cid* (1140). The famous classic Cervantes novel *Don Quixote de la Mancha* (published in 1605 and 1615), is plagued with compliments.

This type of compliment puts to the test the creativity of the male courtship and is widely used in every country. Colombians call it *calamitas* or *lisonjas;* Mexicans, *bombas;* Spaniards call them *requiebros* or *halagos;* Chileans like to call them *piropos chilensis.* The extensions of a *piropo* are the witty expressions some Latino cultures use to greet, boast, brag, poke fun at someone, snap back, or even speak in an interchange of words and phrases kin to the Latin American popular ingenuity.[17]

In terms of communal spaces, the use of public places—streets, parks, and plazas—and semi-public places—your front yard and sidewalk—is different in Latino and Anglo culture. For Latinos, these are ambits of encounter, exchange, and enjoyment where they spend time with family, relatives, and friends. Studies on use and perception of community space reveal that Latinos develop a public appropriation of places such as shopping streets and built environments—plazas and material culture such as monuments and cemeteries—with the use of murals, housescapes, and landscapes (Arreola 2004). Research is concerned especially with Latino population distribution, movement and regional patterns, or the historical geographic patterns followed by particular subgroups in time and over time (Arreola 2004).

Perception and Use of Time

Earl Shorris (1992) refers to Latino time's fate by saying: "It is impossible to know what time it is in the Latino world." A great expression to describe the ambivalent use of time in Latino culture, and certainly to differentiate it from the strict, time-oriented Anglo world, Shorris's statement describes the inclination of Mexicans and Mexican Americans to live in the present and in the past while the future is unforeseen or unimaginable.

For most Latinos, present time is more valuable than the future. Latinos focus more on present needs and little change. Therefore, it would be more appropriate to expect them to concentrate on short-term goals rather than long-term ones. Planning for education, family and life events, work and work-related activities, and social activities takes a different perspective from the time-dependent ways of American culture. For example, planning a wedding with one- or even two-year anticipation is not only a foreign but almost a bizarre concept—although in some countries, the influence of U.S. traditions is taking place.

Latinos adapt the passage of time to their needs, and it would be wise not to place a lot of emphasis on fast-moving and closely timed activities at the library. It might create a tense environment for people who grew up in an atmosphere where time was not a critical factor. Family activities and celebrations start around some specific time and continue until the guests are gone, with no set time for ending the activity. It would be rude to ask guests or participants to leave at a certain time. Moreover, family and social events are more successful if they last longer than planned!

Family Values and Familismo

It is widely known that Latinos tend to have close relationships with extended family. But this closeness also implies a close connection and role-defined structure between husband and wife and between parents and children. The qualifier *familismo* derives from a collectivistic worldview where the individual sacrifices for the welfare of the group (Marín and Triandis 1985). *Familismo* implies that the group shares responsibilities for the welfare of the children in kin—including decision making and financial and emotional support, if necessary. The concept extends to children of friends and acquaintances under adult supervision and even in the neighborhood, where adults look after the well-being of children.

Evidence has shown that family closeness does not decrease as a result of the acculturation process that follows immigration (Keefe and Padilla 1987) and that *familismo* is an important value that sustains a positive psychological development of children in transition

(Vega et al. 1993) and lower levels of deviant behaviors such as substance and tobacco abuse among teenagers (Frauenglass et al. 1997).

The concept of *familismo* includes other relationship values: *compadrazgo* (godparenting), grandparenting, and *personalismo. Compadrazgo* is a strong liaison with either members of the family—usually brothers and sisters of both parents—or close friends. They can sometimes be prominent people in the community among certain high-class Latino families. Godparents not only are expected to step up in the parents' absence but are also expected to aid the child in times of need or crisis, are expected to have special deference for the godchild over other children in the family, and are socially considered as those who will continue raising the child in the familial and religious values according to the parents' will. In reality, however, grandparents are more likely to take over raising and educating children if necessary. When the godparents are not members of the family, *compadrazgo* creates a formal bond between the child's parents and the godparents—called *compadres*—and promotes a sense of community (Santiago-Rivera, Arredondo, and Gallardo-Cooper 2002).

Grandparenting can play a central role in Latino families. Although of immense importance, the impact of grandparents on Latino families has received little attention from scientific research and literature (Santiago-Rivera, Arredondo, and Gallardo-Cooper 2002). Their role can vary according to the grandparents' age, gender, social class, financial status, contact frequency, religious beliefs, and geographical proximity to the family and grandchildren. Consequently, the scope of grandparent involvement can vary from a merely social role to a caretaker in the parents' absence—for instance, during working hours—to a custodial grandparenting role. Latino grandparents can be emotionally or geographically distant, but this does not imply they do not have a say in their grandchildren's upbringing. Latino grandparents are mostly always involved in discipline and the maintenance of family rules, directly or indirectly, through advice and even imposition on the child's parents—their own children. In the case of immigrants who leave their children behind, grandparents mostly take on the role of surrogate parents. Because Latinos usually start parenting at an early age and have large families, grandparents might still be young and fit and/or have children their grandchildren's same age.

Personalismo, thirdly, is an interpersonal relationship value oriented to enhance the importance of the person over the task at hand, including time. Latinos build interpersonal relationships with this collectivist worldview in which there is more interest in others than in the self (Levine and Padilla 1980). Family members maintain mutual closeness and dependency, which influences the way Latino families make decisions and perceive and respond to external environments. The case of an Argentinean mother who describes the contradiction of raising her children in the United States, where children "are taught to distrust and not to reach out," compared to her country of origin, where children are taught to "respect and trust others... [where] everyone knows each other and you know their family tree" is a vivid example of *personalismo* (Santiago-Rivera, Arredondo, and Gallardo-Cooper 2002, p. 75).

When these values—*familismo, compadrazgo* (godparenting), and *personalismo*—are severed by migration and distance, members of the family might suffer isolation and loss of identity, feel the lack of a support system, and engage in unusual behavior or suffer related health issues.

Gender Roles

The cultural diversity of the Latino groups coming to the United States is related to demographic variables—as seen in chapter 4—but these variables also affect in subjective ways some aspects of culture. For example, machismo, one aspect of the cultural dimension of gender roles, affects an illiterate woman from rural Mexico differently than an educated, professional woman from urban Mexico. Consequently, services and products offered to these two market segments need to connect with each audience in a different way.

Latino female roles are commonly influenced by the image of the Virgin Mary, a life of motherhood, self-sacrifice, self-giving, and forgiveness. In Mexico, for instance, they are symbolized by regional or local figures from folk legends such as *la Malinche*, representing treason, a victim of the oppressors, or the symbolic founding mother of *mestizos* (the new Mexican people); *la llorona,* the weeping woman; or *las soldaderas*.[18]

Each of these female roles provides an exemplary behavioral model for Mexican women and may differ slightly from female role models in Peru, Puerto Rico, Colombia, or Argentina. The values of motherhood, self-sacrifice, self-giving, and forgiveness, however, are still present. For instance, in Argentina, Uruguay, and Chile, *la difunta Correa*[19] might have similar archetypical values to *las soldaderas* Mexicanas, both representing courage and self-sacrifice for their husbands.

Perception of Work Value, Wealth, Success, and Leadership

There are differences in the way Latinos and Anglo Americans perceive and practice ethics related to the value of work, success, and leadership as well as the culture of wealth. Authors Chong and Baez (2005) emphasized the importance of understanding the generational gap of Latinos at work in order to comprehend the way they perform, relate, and communicate effectively in the workplace. Values such as ambition, loyalty, and leadership, according to these authors, are leading values in the workplace but second to the well-being of their family members; fidelity toward friends, their community, and their employers; and a respect for the work hierarchy chain or positions of authority.

Latinos tend to prefer a collaborative working environment than a competitive one. Nevertheless, there are differences in the way individuals interact in the workplace according to levels of individualism in the workplace (Chong and Baez 2005, p. 17) and time of residence in the United States, which accounts for the level of acculturation and assimilation of mainstream cultural values.

Latinos might talk openly about money and other personal issues to another Latino, even if they just met recently. Conversations about private matters are usually easier among women of the same age or generation once there is built-in credibility, but not among mothers and daughters (again, depending on the level of education and country of origin).

For the same reason that future is an abstract time idea for planning purposes, Latinos are not as used to saving, planning, or investing in long-term monetary commitments as Anglo Americans. Many parents trust their children will take care of them financially as well as physically if the need arises, and most children accept it as a natural duty. The idea of a spiritual or rewarding emotional relationship among members of the family is more important than material wealth, and the center of such well-being might be the family home; ownership of real estate then becomes the pillar of the family tradition for generations. Authors Santiago-Rivera, Arredondo, and Gallardo-Cooper (2002, p. 46) sustain that "For many Latinos, the interrelationship between spirituality and/or religion and cultural practices is extraordinarily close."

Latinos believe in fate but are not determinist. Fate is considered in relationship with good or bad luck, but it does not imply people are condemned to a certain destiny (in earth or heaven), hard to overcome. There is also a tendency among Hispanics to credit achievement to destiny, fate, and other metaphysical or religious circumstances rather than their own ability or talent. Spiritual ideas about fate and faith impact many areas of life including perceptions about the causes and treatment of poor health and illness.

Beliefs about Health, Life, Death, Religion, and the Approach to Health

In order to understand Latinos' approach to health, it is important to keep in mind the diversity of the U.S. Latino population regarding degree of acculturation, time they have spent in the United States, age at immigration, family composition, religious beliefs, degree of religious practice, and so forth. Nationality or country of origin, level of education, and socioeconomic status in their country of origin as well as the hosting country will also have a role in the way Latinos confront health, death, and religious beliefs.

Libraries need to have a clear picture of how specific risk factors and level of acculturation might have deleterious effects on Latinos' health in order to communicate effectively with them and provide the information they need. It is also important to understand how cultural issues may act as protective health factors and how to use preventive messages effectively. Thirdly, delivering the information as a sharing experience enhances the impact of health messages.

In Latino culture, like in many others, the most important health risk factors are alcohol and tobacco use, nutritional habits, and lack of exercise (Chong 2002, p. 68). Work-related higher rates of morbidity and mortality among Latinos are also mentioned as a risk factor because larger numbers of Latino workers are involved in hazardous occupations and industries (Moure-Eraso and Friedman-Jiménez 2001). Rural Latino workers are especially affected by pesticide exposure, sun exposure, injuries, and poor field sanitation, including lack of access to clean water (Azeveda and Ochoa Bogue 2001).

As they become acculturated, Latinos' newly acquired diet becomes a key factor in the prevalence of obesity, diabetes, and hypertension (Alcalay et al. 2000; Sabogal et al. 1987). Fast food, the availability of products with increased sugar content, the change of basic staples (from corn or rice to wheat) and processed sugars and flours affect the immigrants' diet, causing weight gain and related health consequences. According to a 2008 study by the Centers for Disease Control and Prevention,[20] in the past 20 years a dramatic increase in obesity in the United States has taken place. The study shows an animated map of obesity increase from 1985 through 2008 and data by race and ethnicity, in which Latinos have the second-highest obesity prevalence in the country.

Another important factor is a change in lifestyle: for those living in rural or even urban areas—where mass transportation is usual—living, working, and shopping at distances only covered by vehicles takes away their otherwise usual daily activity of walking.

As already explained, Latinos see their world from a family perspective (Chong 2002, p. 70). An individual's degree of acculturation and his or her family composition in the United States are two main components in how Latinos receive health messages. Addressing an individual's health improvement is not generally an effective way to convey a message. However, family well-being should become a major component in the message. If a person immigrated alone or does not have immediate family in the United States, other tactics might apply, such as appealing to the immigrant's desire to see his or her family again in the country of origin or retire to that country of origin in good health—a common goal of elderly Latinos.

Latino culture also assigns major value to the larger collective (Chong 2002, p. 70)—community and friends. Personal behaviors and choices are often guided by opinions and advice from friends and often include building trust, feeling empathy, and caring for the group's welfare. The well-being of the social network becomes a high priority, while competition and achievement are usually less important—again, depending on their degree of acculturation. The well-being of the all is more important than an individual's well-being.

Neighbors constitute an important solidarity network and a source of local information. Libraries could encourage group activities, networking (support groups/telephone/Internet chat rooms), and family interaction to deal with major illnesses and health disparities information.

Another way most Latinos and Latin Americans show social interaction is by supporting their comments with the popular wittiness of *dichos y refranes* (sayings and aphorisms). If analyzed, sayings can tell us a great deal about Latin Americans' beliefs and perspective about life, religion, and fate. Most sayings involve some reflection about God's will—*si Dios quiere, si es la voluntad de Dios,* or *gracias a Dios* (God's willing, if it is God's will, thank God)—and imply being in the hands of God and acknowledging their lack of control over destiny in good or bad times.

Dichos y refranes also refer to common life wisdom passed from generation to generation as well as their way of social communication. An art and a skill, sayings can even express contradictory ideas about Latinos' understanding of life: *al que madruga, Dios le ayuda* (the early bird catches the worm) but also *no por mucho madrugar, amanece más temprano* (not because one gets up early, the sun rises earlier). They also address moral and ethical topics such as the following: *el que a hierro mata a hierro muere* (he who lives by the sword shall die by the sword); *matrimonio y mortaja del cielo baja* (marriage and mortise come from heaven); *abogado, juez, y doctor, cuanto más lejos, mejor* (a lawyer, a judge, and a doctor better farther than closer); *cuentas claras conservan amistades* (transparent business maintains friendships); *no dejes camino por vereda* (do not leave a main road for a sidewalk); *dime con quién andas y te diré quién eres* (tell me who you hang out with and I will tell you who you are); and *en boca cerrada no entran moscas* (flies do not enter in a closed mouth), alluding to the bad habit of gossip. Some of these sayings are almost universally known in most Latin American countries. In addition, each country has hundreds of their own popular sayings and aphorisms, and people use them frequently in everyday life for affirmation or credibility.[21]

As much as the concept of God is present in sayings and aphorism, religious faith is also a powerful resource to deliver health messages. Most Latinos believe problems will be solved with God's, a saint's, or the Virgin Mary's help (Chong 2002, p. 71).

Fatalism might work against those who try to influence Latinos. Fatalistic arguments are not recommended as some Latinos avoid confrontations, and it is difficult to change their belief that an event is predetermined and unalterable (*si Dios quiere; Dios sabe lo que hace*—if it is God's will; God knows what He is doing). With faith and fatalism combined, the challenge is even greater. The best approach is to provide alternatives to extend their viewpoint such as making education a sharing experience with other members of their family and community (Chong 2002, p. 72). Latinos might have a similar approach on issues related to legal and financial matters, work, and family-related situations—such as unfair dismissals, immigration raids, family separation, discrimination, children involved in risky behavior, and mental illness.

Understanding Latino values and the ability to use these values to reach out to your Latino patrons can be useful in capturing your patrons' interest and motivating them to maintain a continuous relationship with your library without overstepping their beliefs and cultural behaviors.

Recognizing the Signs of Culture

Language barriers can also become difficult. If you have traveled to a foreign country where a different language was spoken, somehow you managed to get around and come back. Before leaving, you prepared an itinerary, maybe bought some tourist guides, and tried to learn a couple of basic phrases or even brush up your rusty foreign language from high school or college with an audiotape or two. While on the trip, you managed to ask questions at the hotel, found restaurants where you could eat, explored the places you wanted to visit, and probably shopped around, quickly learning to ask how much something cost in the native language. Overall, you felt grateful when locals were helpful and friendly to you even if you did not speak their language because you were in a vulnerable position. Cultural barriers, however, are much tougher to overcome.

It is human nature to take the path of least resistance to avoid personal effort or confrontation when we feel our daily routine has been compromised by some challenging situation. Maybe we decrease our eagerness for understanding other people, or we drag our feet when it is time for preparedness or just prefer to let someone else do it for us. In addition, cultural barriers are hard to see without proper preparation, but they are easy to experience and create discomfort, fear, and stress.

Learning to communicate between cultures entails several facets, and language is just one of them. Language accounts for only 25 to 35 percent of intercultural communication, which also includes an understanding of beliefs, values, worldviews, behaviors, nonverbal communication (body language), and how people relate to each other (Samovar and Porter 2001).

A major cause of misunderstanding in intercultural communication is a lack of awareness of our own cultural patterns of nonverbal communication while judging others according to our own. Consequently, we might (correctly or incorrectly) interpret others as rude, pushy, aloof, cold, too friendly, or overstated based on how something is said or the way another person acts.

Cultural competence professionals believe in another Spanish saying, *"la caridad empieza por casa"* (charity starts at home). In other words, good practices start with self-awareness of and sensitivity to our own cultural heritage (Arrendondo et al. 1996). We need to be able to identify our own attitudes, beliefs, and behaviors in order to become a nonjudgmental spectator of other cultures' attitudes, beliefs, and behaviors. The best way to learn to interact with other cultures is to own our own. Only when we become conscious about the way we act and react in certain situations, how we relate and communicate with people, how we use the space around us and what makes us comfortable or uncomfortable, what our ethic standards are, or how we behave in the workplace, we are able to perceive and understand how individuals from other cultures interact with us.

Cultural workshops and cultural training are an important activity for all your staff, not only those involved in the Committee for Latino Outreach. Training programs such as those offered by WebJunction, REFORMA, and private consultants are helpful in understanding your potential customers, especially if the training offers customized information for you. However, although there is a wealth of information in your own library, on the Internet, from the publishing industry, or in brochures from other types of local organizations that serve this population, nobody can give you a better idea of their needs than the customers themselves.

Ethnographic Interviews

"People everywhere learn their culture by observing other people, listening to them, and then *making inferences.* The ethnographer employs this same process of going beyond what is seen and heard to infer what people know. It involves reasoning from evidence (what we perceive) or from premises (what we assume)." (Spradley 1979, p. 8)

To discover information about the cultural behaviors, habits, and beliefs of your local Latino customers and have direct experiences from your potential, or current, customers, ethnographic[22] observations—a strategy used to describe people in writing by observing them in their own environment—are recommended. This methodology can also be described as a field study.

Through ethnographic studies based on fieldwork, ethnographers study and interpret culture. Marketing research based on ethnographic methods observes and records interactions that take place among humans in their daily context. Field observation is based on fieldwork—first-hand observation of daily behavior—and can include structured observation and even interviewing in house-to-house surveys. These techniques require fieldworkers of different ages, ethnic backgrounds, presentation, and races usually trained and experienced in a certain number of general data collection procedures and given custom training for each project, usually in the form of briefings, role-plays, and pretests.

Informal or casual observation, also based on this approach, can gather information about relevant audiences and how they behave in real situations. You will need to adapt some of these strategies to your situation to find Latinos in their own environment, such as your staff participating at some of their events or observing them at their workplace, school environment, or church. The benefits of this method are the freedom with which the interviewees behave in their own surroundings and the larger amount of information that can be gathered.

The first method for collecting cultural data is direct, first-hand observation of the target community's daily behavior. Another common method is interviewing members of the community, which may include conversations or short interviews.

Observers—also called informers—can stroll around a certain geographical area, writing down observations related to the physical geography, the people under study, and the general characteristics of the environment. Next, observations about the groups, gender, kinship, and social structure are noted. Languages spoken, changes in language or dialects, means of subsistence, acculturation, and personal values can also be part of the observation. Participants being observed can also take part in the observation through small talk or short, casual questioning. Observers can take notes or make diagrams and drawings on the elements and relationships under observation.

However, it might be difficult for a casual observer—like a non-Latino member of your staff or CLO who is not familiar with the target community—to make all these observations while building credibility with participants to encourage them to share their experiences. For that reason, you might want to take a different approach in terms of ethnographic observation.

First, you have to define a specific topic or subject matter related to the library; your services; the Latino community's cultural values, beliefs, or behaviors; or the image the target community has about library services and then pursue the ethnographic intervention. Then, you need to move on to observation and questioning. Asking general questions about Latino culture or observing without a road map is very difficult to do and is hardly effective.

After the observation and interviewing process, you can transcribe the interview data by using diagrams and symbols, summaries, and statements, and you can review and cross-check answers about local beliefs and perceptions with a Latino community leader or a Latino member of the library. If your research is part of a continuous long-term study of an area or site, these observations can be an instrument for measuring behavioral changes in the individuals or groups observed.

Worksheet 5.1, "A Template for an Ethnographic Interview," has been adapted for the library environment and can be used for different topics and circumstances. It is a generic interview, but you can adapt it to your specific interviewing needs and use it repeatedly. In chapter 10, you will find the same worksheet with more detailed explanations and examples.

The Green Light, Red Light Method

Another way to ensure that your conclusions are accurate is to use an educated guess. You will be using educated guesses at many stages of your strategy, not only when you are using the trial-and-error method. The Green Light, Red Light method will help you carry on to the next step. Always be suspicious of quick conclusions!

When working with a local hospital in New Jersey, personnel came up with the idea of conducting a local nutrition campaign for Latino mothers of children ages 0 to 5 years old. Pediatricians at the hospital had noticed that some Mexican and Central American children of recent immigrants would go from malnutrition to obesity in a matter of months[23] and wanted to develop a campaign to help Latino mothers improve their children's diet, taking into consideration their working schedules. The desired behavior change was to motivate mothers to cook nutritious food for their children instead of feeding them fast food—a common behavior in other communities.[24]

The hospital defined their target market segment as married Latino women, age 21 to 35, with children ages 0 to 5, working out of the house, who enjoy catering to their families. When presented with this definition, the researchers were encouraged to use the green light, red light method as presented in Worksheet 5.2.

This method's idea is to question every assumption you make and find cross-information from other primary sources (such as pediatricians, hospital records, or the moms themselves) to understand how cultural behaviors might help you expand your target segment or find different causes of the problem. The red light column is the *stop and think* column where you insert a statement that challenges your assumption. In this case, the method worked pretty well: the researchers discovered most diet changes were associated with the lack of traditional Mexican ingredients—the predominance of wheat-based instead of corn-based products. Children lacked enough exercise due to their new environment—living in small urban apartments instead of rural areas. They also lacked a playground on their side of town. Another reason was the increase in family income compared to their country of origin, which allowed children to consume more sugar-based products and increased availability and choices of junk food. Other individual reasons were related to particular family situations. To help you research your own cultural topics and situations, you will find a blank copy of Worksheet 5.2 in chapter 10.

Do Your Best, but Do It!

You need to work with these dimensions as if you were creating a new recipe: once you have the basic ingredients, you keep trying with different condiments, adding new ingredients, or changing the oven temperature! Become an expert in cultural information about your Latino community. As you increase your knowledge and understanding of their behaviors and beliefs, you will learn to ask better questions, make more accurate decisions, and increase your chance for success. Once you become familiar with the cultural aspects of the community, you will be able to use your common sense and intuition with *no judgment*. This is the highest stage of cultural competency a person or institution can achieve.

Of course, it is one thing to have the knowledge, it is another to put it into practice in a way that comes natural to you. Human interaction[25] is not easy, and some situations that might occur at your library are presented next.

Live and Learn

Consider some of the nonverbal communication that might arise in the library environment. These behaviors are not uniform in all Latin American cultures and depend on age, gender, levels of education, socioeconomic background, time living in the United States, and levels of acculturation or assimilation. Also, remember that cultural behavior is influenced by the geography and history of each country. Societies such as Mexico, Guatemala, or Ecuador, among others, with a strong influence of indigenous communities, might act very differently from those countries influenced by Spanish or Portugal colonization or extensive European immigration. Here are some examples:

Physical proximity and comfort zones: Authors Pulvino and Lee (1991) call an average distance of 30 to 36 inches between two individuals a "social space" in the United States, between 24 and 30 inches "personal space," and less than 24 inches "intimate space" while Latin Americans generally communicate socially at a distance of 8 to 18 inches. Consequently, at an unconscious level, Latinos might appear to Americans as too pushy or overly sexual while Latinos might think of Americans as distant and cold. In general, Latinos sit and stand much closer to one another than Americans do. Moving away from a customer who feels too close to you—a "close talker," to borrow a term made popular by *Seinfeld*—might be considered insulting.

Body movements and touching: Friendly touching is common in Latino culture; however, it might be perceived as overly friendly by Americans or inappropriate in the professional environment of a library. Latino mothers usually express their feelings with children by hugging and kissing. Women might kiss each other or men. Men might greet each other by shaking hands or with a hug and may even hug and kiss their young sons. There are exceptions, though. For example, people from the Andes region are not very tactile. Men tap each other's shoulders but not much more. Latinos also tend to use hand and arm gestures more often than Americans, which may be interpreted as exaggerated or overly dramatic. If a client extends their hand, be responsive as a welcoming gesture. Children might hug and kiss you once they get to know you. However, Latinos might avoid physical contact just because they see you as an authority figure.

Smiling and talking: Latinos smile in many situations in which Americans will not, especially in the work environment. They might smile even when they do not understand what you are saying or do not agree with you in order to be polite. Also, the tone and pace of a normal conversation among Latinos might seem too loud to Americans. Conversations might be very interactive, and it is not uncommon for people to interrupt each other or finish each other's phrases. A loud discussion or argument might seem threatening or out of control in American culture; however, to a Latino, it may represent caring and interest followed by physical demonstrations of regret, forgiveness, and love (hugs, tears, etc.). Try to follow the lead of your interlocutor in an interaction at the library. Smile back when they smile, especially if you see them acting shy or vulnerable. Be lenient with those who are loud and politely ask them to take it outside or just lower their voices.

Etiquette in greeting or addressing a family or group: Greeting the eldest person or the male representing a group first, and then the female and the rest of the family followed by the youngest children last, is considered customary for Latinos. Also, when families use a third person or their children to interpret for them, try to maintain face and eye contact with the parent or adult involved in the conversation while looking at the interpreter alternatively. If the whole family is present, you might prefer to address the father rather than the mother without excluding her totally from the conversation in recognition of traditional roles. (Also, pay attention to who is posing the questions and respond accordingly.) Begin with small talk, no matter how trivial, by asking about their well-being, complementing the children or the family, and praising the fact that they are at the library—even if you use Spanglish! Going straight to the point immediately—"How may I help you?"—might be seen as impatient and impolite.

Physical stereotypes: Latinos come from 19 different Latin American nations. Latinos come in all sizes and all colors, literally and figuratively—an ample spectrum of races and mixed origins compounds a powerful and ample spectrum of physical features. In addition, some Latinos have lived in the United States for several generations and some have recently immigrated. Do not assume that because someone is short, dark-skinned, or has indigenous facial features they are not a perfectly acculturated, fluent English-speaking United States citizen or because they look fair, blond, and have a German last name that they do not hold the deepest love for their Latino values. Never start a conversation in Spanish unless you have met the customer beforehand. They will be the ones to probably come around and ask you *¿Habla español?* (Do you speak Spanish?).

Attire: We cannot generalize by saying Latino women tend to dress less conservatively than American women as it really depends on their social status and socioeconomic background. Age and country of origin are still strong definers in the way women dress in Latin America. While young women dress to please and be desirable to men (Gil and Inoa Vazquez 1996), older woman are expected to dress more conservatively. More traditional Latin American societies tend to have more strict attire rules. For instance, wearing shorts for males (unless in recreational areas) is considered inappropriate. However, more acculturated Latinos might adopt the customary dress codes of the United States.

Younger Latinos, both male and female, might choose to dress distinctively in order to find some identity in the new context in which they live and struggle. Especially in large cities, clothing trends tend to be inspired by what celebrities and rock and hip-hop stars are wearing—not only for Latinos. Never judge a book by its cover! What might seem to you out of order, too bright or glossy, too short, or exposed might be perfectly normal for members of that community. Try not to let surprise or judgment show in your interaction with these patrons, especially young adults and teenagers.

Overcoming Differences

The aforementioned cross-cultural interactions are only a few of the challenges you might encounter in the library environment. Pleasant communication is always desirable, but, of course, you will find rude, angry, or simply disagreeable customers among Latinos as with any population.

In order to overcome differences, it is necessary to understand your own cultural habits and behaviors and to learn those of the community you serve. This skill can be learned. Use effective intercultural communication, developing skills to communicate with non-English speakers—utilizing an array of tools such as *cheat cards* with Spanish phrases and universal signs—while trying to follow your customers' clues and cues of good communication, all of which will come with practice and experience.

BASIC STEPS TO INTERACT WITH LATINO PATRONS

1. As an organization, know in advance what you want to accomplish with your Latino customers.
2. Acquire some basic Spanish-language skills. Phrases and greetings applicable to the library environment will create rapport and a welcoming environment for all your Spanish-speaking and bilingual patrons. To them, it means you care.
3. Find out information. Get to know your customers, their wants, and their needs.
4. Talk to people who have been there. Latino community leaders and your current Latino patrons can help you get additional information and insights.
5. Read a variety of books and magazines and watch videos, movies, and TV programs that picture Latinos and their communities.
6. Survey your Latino customers frequently about your everyday activities, from how friendly they find the library environment to suggestions for improving your services.
7. Empower them to help you in the communication process.
8. Learn about culturally influenced behaviors and nonverbal communication. It is a great way to get to know yourself as well as your Latino customers!
9. Do not feel embarrassed to use gestures. When a language barrier exists, expressing yourself with gestures or even pictures works and is a completely normal way to communicate.
10. Use other resources at the library. *Cheat cards* with Spanish phrases can aid you greatly, even if you have to display them—instead of speaking them—to your customers. Also, bilingual signs, images, and/or glossaries in Spanish can be of great help.
11. Use computer-generated translation programs available on the Internet to ask simple questions. These can do a decent job when it comes to simple phrases.
12. If your Spanish is limited, ask yes or no questions if possible.
13. Do not hesitate to ask for help when needed (from other Latino customers, co-workers, or visitors).
14. Do not feel embarrassed to make a mistake. Recognize and accept that interpersonal relationships are difficult as it is and that adding the intercultural ingredient does not make it easier.
15. Use humor whenever possible, and do not take yourself too seriously!

Seeking Similarities

During a class, a comment was made about a few Latinas who were married to Irish American men, as it seemed there was some affinity between both cultures. A young American woman of Irish ancestry in the class smiled and raised her hand. She said, "Is it that we both like to drink?"

The stereotypification of both cultures, although a bit uncomfortable, was thought provoking. It made the class think of other values and behaviors they found in common with Latino culture. Some Chinese American and Korean American participants expressed that they found similarities in family values and the shared respect for their aging adults. Participants of Chinese, Pakistani, African, and Korean backgrounds found collectivism—relying on one's extended families or clans for support and protection—in common with some Latin American societies. Those from Italian and Greek cultures, who generally place high value on living in the present and fully experiencing life and the people around them, could relate to Latin Americans in that respect. Catholics descendant from Slavic European immigrants found similarities in family and gender values. And

German descendants could relate to Latinos in interpersonal formality and the use of titles and professional degrees.

"Overall, *all* cultures share a basic common ground in their pursuit of happiness, freedom, and search for a better life for themselves and their progeny. Feeling love for their children, joy and sadness at pivotal moments of life such as birth and death, avoidance of physical and emotional pain, and enjoyment of music, friendship and humor are just some of the commonalities that we can all build upon, not only in the workplace but in our everyday life as well" (Samovar, Porter, and McDaniel 2000, p. 299).

Language and Culture

We spoke about culture and the difficulties that cross-cultural interaction could create in the library environment. Now it is time to talk about language barriers. Culture and language are not entirely separate. In fact, they are so intertwined that frequently it is difficult to express one without the other. Language allows us to convey emotions, thoughts, and expressions that transcend our culture. Language is also valuable in recording our past, our world, and our knowledge. Finally, language is the expression of our identity and a major means of communicating our culture (Samovar, Porter, and McDaniel 2007).

Since language is such an important aspect of maintaining national and cultural identity, the increasing diversity of languages spoken in the United States has created discussion and political turmoil. With the Hispanic population growing significantly nationwide, there have been serious attempts to ban bilingual education (California, Arizona, and Massachusetts have passed legislation to this effect), and some politicians and constituents have expressed fear that the United States will become a two-language nation. Some Americans question the need to allow the use of Spanish language when other waves of immigration have assimilated to the use of the English language. Others adopt the opposite attitude: "I wish grandma would have taught us her mother tongue." Polish, German, Italian, Russian, French, Dutch, Spanish, and other backgrounds make up the rich ancestry of America. However, Americans have been immersed in an insulating, defensive experience for generations, which has created a fearful society (Cornelius 2002).

On the other end of the spectrum, members of the Spanish-speaking community refuse to give up their most precious treasure: the pride of their cultural roots. The majority of Latino immigrants did not leave their countries of origin by choice—many were motivated by social, political, and economic unrest. This is why they usually speak Spanish at home as their primary language even if they speak English at school or work. It is a way to maintain their national and cultural identity in a "both/and" embrace of their native and the hosting culture (Suárez-Orozco and Páez 2002, p. 210).

Spanish will continue to be spoken in Latino households, and it will continue to be nurtured by the constant arrival of new Latino immigrants, a phenomenon that has not occurred with previous immigration waves. Libraries should see this renewal as an opportunity rather than a threat and take advantage of bilingualism—or better yet, multilingualism—as a way to expand the horizons of library patrons.

Se Habla Español (Spanish Spoken)

Marketers place great importance on the use of language because memories and perceptions—the core of our emotional responses—can be evoked by combining language and

POPULAR EXAMPLES OF "MISSED" TRANSLATIONS[26]

1. The translation of the Pepsi slogan "Come alive with the Pepsi Generation" came out as "Pepsi will bring your ancestors back from death" in Taiwan.
2. Scandinavian vacuum manufacturer Electrolux used "Nothing sucks like an Electrolux" in an American ad campaign.
3. In China, the translation of the Kentucky Fried Chicken slogan "finger-lickin' good" suggested to "eat your fingers off."
4. The word "Nova," the name of a Chevrolet car marketed in Mexico, can be misread in Spanish as *no va* or, "it doesn't go."

cultural constructs in a message that customers associate with their own experiences. Words and images can be charged with meaning based on a group's cultural experiences, and they have the power to convey to the customer a positive or negative emotion. So it is vital that your marketing and promotional materials be properly scrutinized before they are released in order to avoid making a mistake—or, worse, a public relations blunder.

Here is an example. While working on a printed multicultural advertising campaign for a Fortune 100 financial company in New York, a number of icons had to be evaluated with accompanying text supporting the company's brochure, which offered financial services to the Latino community. There were reservations about two of the concepts used on the English brochures: the first was a bowl of cherries—referring to the popular American expression "Life is just a bowl of cherries"—which supported the idea that investing early in life would make the investor's mature life pleasant; the second was a fingerprint, with text discussing identity and the personal and unique way each investor could tailor his or her own portfolio.

The expression "Life is just a bowl of cherries" has no relevance to the Latino community, so that message did not convey the idea of happiness or saving for the future. The fingerprint image with the identity text had a negative connotation to the point of being counter-effective. For people who had lived in countries with frequent military and political persecution (between 1964 and 1990, 14 countries in Latin America were under military regimes at different times), fingerprinting represented a scary, negative aspect of their past.

These are just two examples of how text and images are loaded with cultural connotations that cannot always be translated. The bottom line is that word-by-word translation does not work! In the translator's world, there are hundreds, if not thousands, of humorous and sometimes delicate situations where direct translations have caused at least a smile if not a major marketing disaster. Casualties have included using words with sexual connotations for cars, computers, or chocolate candy or just plain senseless translations.

Likewise, trying to adjust library materials and activities that are meaningful to the English-speaking population to a community that has little interest in those materials or no experience in those activities, topics, or subject matters might be a worthless effort.

Dragons, Dreams, and Daring Deeds

In a discussion with a group of librarians in Pennsylvania about their 2005 summer reading program, "Dragons, Dreams, and Daring Deeds," they asked how they could integrate Spanish-speaking children into the activity. The activity, with the title translated into Spanish as *Dragones, Sueños, y Hazañas Heroicas,* focused on "dragons, mythical beasts, the Middle Ages, fairy tales, and fantasy, medieval fairs and feasts, kings, queens, princes, princesses, knights, castles, magical stories, wizards, and wishing wells and provides libraries with the opportunity to explore the entire scope of imagination and books."[27]

Although the title could easily be translated, the activity's imagery was related to a Euro-centric vision of the medieval world that is very popular in the United States. To some Latino children, these stories might be unfamiliar. Children from some Latin American countries might be more familiar with their own stories, fairies, and magical narrations from native legends and folktales. Myths and legends about war, love, death, and nature (especially volcanoes, lakes, flowers, animals, or birds) are popular among people from various Latin American backgrounds, and so are tales about struggles under the Spanish conquest. By introducing children's stories illustrating the historical and cultural contributions of Latinos, the whole group could benefit by the sharing of cross-cultural experiences, comparing concepts and morals of each culture, finding commonalities and differences, and increasing children's—and adults'—worldviews.

For more ideas and information about multicultural programs, please check the following resources: the Alma Project at the Denver Public Schools System,[28] the Wisconsin Department of Public Instruction,[29] and the Center for Children's Books at the Graduate School of Library and Information Science at the University of Illinois in Urbana-Champaign, to name a few.[30]

The Spoken Language

When it comes to selecting materials and topics for a Spanish-speaking audience, there are usually concerns related to the origin of these materials and the universal use of the Spanish language. Can people from Puerto Rico understand people from Colombia or Argentina? Can children from Mexico talk to children from Spain?

To respond to such questions, I always tell my experience when attending some friends' wedding in Scotland. It was a great opportunity to visit that country. The trip was lovely and so was the wedding, but it was hard to believe those people were speaking English (and they were!).

That said, spoken Spanish is as universal as English if you consider and contrast the English language spoken in America, Canada, the United Kingdom (England, Northern Ireland, Scotland, and Wales), Australia, South Africa, and Belize, to name a few English-speaking countries. Whether we are talking about English or Spanish, there are regional differences in the meaning or use of certain words, idiomatic or mixed expressions with native languages, and even different cadence, pronunciation, or intonation.

One of the main differences in spoken Spanish is the use of the pronoun *vos*. *Voseo* is the use of the second person singular pronoun *vos* instead of *tú*. The verb conjugation of *vos* can also be used with *tú* as the subject pronoun, such as in Chile. This change in language usage is known as *Rioplatense* Spanish (in central-eastern Argentina and Uruguay) and is also used in Paraguay, Bolivia, and some regions of Central American countries such as Costa Rica, Guatemala, Nicaragua, Honduras, and El Salvador.[31]

Despite these differences, Spanish-speaking Latinos can be understood by others speaking Spanish. Moreover, it is fun to exchange idiomatic expressions and find which ones are uncommon and which are similar!

Keep in mind, though, that many regions in Latin America speak native languages other than Spanish. According to the Archive of the Indigenous Languages of Latin America,[32] there are hundreds of indigenous languages still spoken today in Latin America—probably between 550 and 700 according to this source. Bilingual efforts and multicultural education are not an exclusive task of people in the United States, where native languages are only spoken by around half a million remaining Native Americans.[33] People with such strong backgrounds in native languages and native cultures are strongly tied to the images, values, perceptions, and interpretations that are cherished within their communities and transmitted from generation to generation.

Also, librarians often ask if there are Spanish dialects. A topic of debate, some linguists sustain that the distinction between language and dialect is more sociopolitical than linguistic (Haugen 1987). If speakers from two varieties of a language can understand each other, then linguists consider those languages to be dialects of one language, each a variation of the language. There are other variations, as well, since language is a dynamic entity that creates differences in the way people speak. A *sociolect*, by definition, is a dialect spoken by a certain social class, while slang, jargons, and creoles are also spoken among a large variety of people from different origins and regions. So there are really no precise rules to define the concept of language and dialect.[34]

Consequently, spoken Spanish is as varied as the people who speak Spanish and the regions where they belong. While it might be a challenge for you to adjust your ear to different pronunciations and usage, following the easy guidelines we discuss next in all your communication materials will ensure your message can be understood by all Latinos in your community.[35]

LANGUAGES SPOKEN IN LATIN AMERICA

The "Atlas Sociolingüístico de Pueblos Indígenas en América Latina" (The Sociolinguistic Atlas of Indigenous Peoples in Latin America)[36] is a complete study of the present situation of native population, language and culture by region and by country. Some 522 populations that speak 420 active languages belonging to 99 different language families were actually found and registered in the region. Examples of these languages are, for instance, people from regions in Venezuela that speak E'ñepa, Kapón, Mapoyo, Yawarana, Makushi, and share languages in the Arawak and Guahibo families of languages with Colombians. Guatemalans speak Quiche, Chinanteco, Kiche, Mam, Garifuna, Maya, and Zapaoteco, with an estimated 20 different variations.[37]

In Mexico, 8 million people speak indigenous languages. They mostly speak Náhuatl, the Aztec empire language, in the states of Puebla, Tlaxcala, Durango, Veracruz, and Guerrero; while Yucatán, Campeche, and Quintana Roo inhabitants speak Yucatec; Ch'ol Zapotec and Chinanteco are spoken in Oaxaca.

The region between Honduras and Nicaragua is known for its Miskito, Pech, and Sumu native languages; while in southern Costa Rica and Panama, indigenous people speak some variety of Chibcha, a language originally from Colombia that extended also into South America up to northern Argentina.

In South America, indigenous languages most spoken are Quechua, Kichwa, Aymara, and Tupí-Guaraní.[38] Over 10 million people speak Quechua in Colombia, Ecuador, and Peru, while almost 5 million speak Guaraní in Paraguay.

The Written Language

Languages have been defined by sociopolitical boundaries and the historical use of a particular language—for instance, the imposition of the Spanish language in Latin America over native tongues through the Spanish conquest.

In its written form, Spanish is universal—compared to spoken Spanish—if standard or neutral Spanish is used. Standard Spanish is a linguistic variety considered an educated standard for native speakers, and is a form of language that conforms to the literary canon and cultural traditions of that language. Standard Spanish not only avoids the use of idioms and regional mannerisms but also uses grammar and vocabulary that are a common denominator to all varieties of Spanish.[39]

Almost any person who has some reading ability in Spanish will understand standard Spanish used in communication materials, textbooks, or nonfiction publications. Fiction, however, might be more tinted with those spoken idioms, expressions, and slang, so it might become a matter of choice for the monolingual reader, who will certainly prefer a Spanish book from their favorite national authors or literature that expresses regional preferences, stories, and characters.

These preferences are well-known by the publishing industry in Latin America, which is not as widely developed as it is in the United States. The publishing leaders in Latin America are Mexico, Argentina, Chile, Venezuela, and Colombia, which have strong ties to publishing companies in Spain. For instance, Grupo Planeta, the largest Spanish publishing company with coverage in Portugal and Latin America, has developed over 20 publishing companies worldwide, with regional extensions in Argentina, Chile, Colombia, Ecuador, Mexico, the United States, Venezuela, and Uruguay, where they offer regionally appropriate literature.[40]

In the United States, there has been a great push in the publishing industry to cater to this new market. Writer and New England correspondent for *Publishers Weekly* Judith Rosen[41] sustained that Spanish-language books are the only category growing in the otherwise flat publishing industry, with double-digit sales growth in the areas of mass merchandisers, price clubs, and music stores. Every major American publisher has created, increased, or expanded Spanish-language programs in the last few years.

Rosen's article, however, brings up an even more interesting point. When interviewed, most American publishing companies agreed that they are increasing their list of Spanish authors as well as the number of Spanish translations of English best sellers, movie tie-ins, and popular nonfiction titles related to self-help, lifestyle improvement, religion, and finances. Rosen says to take note: Latinos seem to want to read what their neighbors are reading, and mass merchandisers are taking advantage of this trend to launch books in both languages simultaneously. This topic is continued in chapter 6 in a discussion of product choices.

Hopefully the guidelines in this chapter will help you ask questions and become familiar with your local Latino community. Cultural knowledge and insights into another culture not only provide you with a broad base of general knowledge from which you can complete your own market profile but also, by comparison, can give you some insights into your own culture. Remember that true cultural competency is the process through which we wear cultural lenses to better see and understand our community. Therefore, this mutual knowledge and understanding will allow all individuals to work and live in a safer, happier, and more rewarding environment.

Notes

1. *Emic* and *etic* derive from the linguistic terms *phonemic* and *phonetic*. An emic perspective refers to the native's interpretation of his or her customs and beliefs. An etic perspective refers to the external researcher's interpretation of the same customs or beliefs from an analytical, anthropological perspective. Anthropologists usually work with both emic and etic interpretations when analyzing human society, although the terms have been largely debated. (Fetterman 2009; Headland et al. 1990).
2. To expand concepts in this chapter and other cultural aspects, I recommend reading "The Latino/a Condition, A Critical Reader" (Delgado and Stefancic 1998).
3. According to Gloor (2006), the melting pot theory has been referred to as cultural assimilation, where people of different cultures and religions are combined in a uniform final product without distinct identities to its components, quite different from the original inputs. The alternative tossed salad analogy encourages the ingredients to retain their cultural identities while contributing to a diverse yet nutritious final product. A third food analogy is that of the ethnic stew, a level

of compromise between integration and cultural distinctiveness (Laubeova 2000). Sociologists, anthropologists, and cultural geographers have criticized the melting pot theory by stating that it produces a society that primarily reflects the culture of the dominant group, also called "Anglo-conformity" (Kivisto 2004, p. 151).

4. According to Dávila (2001), some companies started targeting ethnic markets in the 1940s, but it was not until the 1970s that companies firmly established departments dedicated to target these consumers.

5. A report from the Selig Center for Economic Growth, "The Multicultural Economy, 1990–2009," estimates that the nation's Hispanic buying power will grow from $222 billion in 1990 to $992 billion in 2009, at a compound annual rate of 8.2 percent. (The comparable rate for non-Hispanics is 4.9%.) The Selig Center for Economic Growth (Terry College of Business at University of Georgia) is primarily responsible for conducting research on economic, demographic, and social issues related to Georgia's current and future growth. See http://www.selig.uga.edu/ (accessed January 6, 2010).

6. U.S. Census Bureau, "Historical Poverty Tables," Table 2: Poverty Status, by Family Relationship, Race, and Hispanic Origin, http://www.census.gov/hhes/www/poverty/histpov/perindex.html (accessed January 6, 2010).

7. According to a 1999 Federal Communications Commission study, advertisers on minority-formatted stations only pay around two-thirds of what they pay for general market stations (Teinowitz and Cardona 1999).

8. Cuban ethnographer Fernando Ortiz used the term *transculturation* in 1940 in his study of Cuban culture, *Contrapunteo cubano del tabaco y el azúcar* (Ortiz 1983).

9. Chairman Carl Kravetz speech at 2006 Miami AHAA Annual Conference. See The American Hispanic Advertising Association http://www.ahaa.org/ (accessed January 6, 2010).

10. According to the studies Argyle cited, Latinos make more eye contact, face each other more, and touch more when they speak (p. 58) than other groups.

11. Nuyoricans are Puerto Ricans born or residing in New York.

12. "Cultural noise refers to impediments to successful communication between people of different cultures. Sources of cultural noise include differences in language (e.g., the same words have different meanings), values (e.g., importance of being on time or setting work schedule times in a culture), non-verbal cues (e.g., interpretation of body language), and many others" (O'Connell 1997, p. 67).

13. "Geert Hofstede analyzed a large data base of employee values scores collected by IBM between 1967 and 1973 covering more than 70 countries, from which he first used the 40 largest only and afterwards extended the analysis to 50 countries and 3 regions. In the editions of GH's work since 2001, scores are listed for 74 countries and regions, partly based on replications and extensions of the IBM study on different international populations." ITIM International, http://www.geert-hofstede.com/ (accessed January 6, 2010).

14. The survey objectives called for a national area probability sample of households to yield data about political attitudes and behaviors from one-hour interviews with 800 Mexican, 600 Puerto Rican, and 600 Cuban adults, as well as 700 non-Latinos. A geographic Latino population coverage rate of at least 85 percent was desired for this survey. This means, for instance, that the selection of Puerto Ricans would expand beyond the New York metropolitan area. An overall Latino response rate no less than 70 percent was desired. De la Garza, Falcon, Garcia, and Garcia, "Latino National Political Survey, 1989–1990," http://www.icpsr.umich.edu/icpsrweb/ICPSR/studies/06841 (accessed January 6, 2010).

15. Hofstede's scores are based on five researched cultural dimensions in the workplace culture. In his view, Hofstede (2005) sustains that the nature of this relationship determines not only how individuals see themselves and their immediate group but that it also affects the structure and role of many institutions other than the family.

16. Kathryn Peterson, "Business Etiquette: Working with Hispanic Clients," *Business Connect*, April 2008, http://www.connect-utah.com/articles/business-etiquette (accessed January 4, 2010).

17. For examples of these sayings and proverbs in English, see Zona (1970); Nava (2000); and a beautiful bilingual illustrated edition for children age four to eight by Gonzalez and Ruiz (2002).

18. *La Malinche, la llorona* (the weeping woman), and *las soldaderas* (women who fought side by side with Mexican soldiers) are female archetypes derived from Mexican historical legends and are rooted in the history of the conquest, folklore, or the Mexican revolution of 1910. "Chicano Studies Notes," TBlog, http://chicanostudies.tblog.com / (accessed January 6, 2010).

19. The legend of Deolinda Correa, a woman whose husband was forcibly recruited around the year 1835 by the troops of Facundo Quiroga, describes a woman who followed her husband through the desert of San Juan Province with her baby and died of thirst and exhaustion. Her baby was found alive feeding from the deceased woman's ever-full breast. For more information and stories of other popular saints, see Frank Graziano, "Cultures of Devotion, Folk Saints of Latin America," http://www.culturesofdevotion.com/ (accessed January 6, 2010).

20. Centers for Disease Control and Prevention (CDC), "U.S. Obesity Trends, Trends by State 1985–2008, Overweight and Obesity, Data and Statistics," http://www.cdc.gov/obesity/data/trends.html (accessed January 6, 2010).

21. For additional information about the significance of *dichos y refranes,* please see the Web site "El Refranero Multilingüe," a research project of the Centro Virtual Cervantes (CVC), an Internet site launched by the Cervantes Institute from Spain in 1997 to help disseminate Spanish language and cultures. The site offers translation and equivalency of Spanish aphorisms in more than 10 other languages, including English. http://cvc.cervantes.es/lengua/refranero/Default.aspx (accessed February 15, 2010).

22. Ethnography is a qualitative research method often used in the social sciences to gather empirical data on human societies and cultures. For additional information about ethnographic studies and methods, see Agar (1996), Wolcott (2008), and Fetterman (2009).

23. This study, which was published in the *Archives of Pediatric and Adolescent Medicine* and examined height and weight data for over 8,000 children, showed the weight difference among children of different races. Almost 31 percent of American Indians were obese, while just 13 percent of Asian children were. The rate for whites was 16 percent; for black children it was almost 21 percent; for Hispanics, 22 percent. "Childhood Obesity: The Role of Race," About.com, April 7, 2009. http://familyfitness.about.com/b/2009/04/07/childhood-obesity-the-role-of-race.htm (accessed January 6, 2010).

24. A 2005 CDC study reports that there are a higher proportion of overweight Mexican American children: Among 12- to 19-year-old Mexican American girls, the prevalence of obesity increased from 9.2 to 19.9 percent from 1988–1994 and 2003–2004, when new data was collected. Among 12- to 19-year-old Mexican boys, the prevalence of obesity increased from 14.1 to 22.1 percent. CDC, "NHANES Surveys (1976–1980 and 2003–2006)," http://www.cdc.gov/obesity/childhood/prevalence.html (accessed January 6, 2010).

25. Edward T. Hall pioneered *proxemics*, a means of measuring and analyzing social distances between people as they interact, while Ray Birdwhistell used the term *kinesics* to describe his interpretation of body language—how people communicate through movement, gestures, facial expression, eye contact, posture, and speaking volume. See Birdwhistell (1970).

26. Gathered by TransImage, a multicultural advertising agency, in 1995. For additional phrases see "Advertising Gone Wrong in Translation," http://baetzler.de/humor/ads_gone_wrong.html (accessed January 8, 2010).

27. The Pennsylvania Summer Reading Program Collaborative, *"Dragons, Dreams, and Daring Deeds,"* 2005.

28. The Alma Project is a program that provides multicultural curriculum for early childhood education (ECE) through 12th grade. See http://almaproject.dpsk12.org (accessed January 8, 2010).

29. "Latino Folktales" is an initiative of the Wisconsin Department of Public Instruction with selected children's resources; it is available at http://dpi.state.wi.us/rll/wrlbph/latinofolktales.html (accessed January 8, 2010).

30. "Latino Folktales—2004" is an initiative of the Center for Children's Books at the Graduate School of Library and Information Science of the University of Illinois at Urbana-Champaign

with selected and annotated children's resources by Lisa Weistein. See http://ccb.lis.uiuc.edu/bibliographies/latino_2004.html (accessed January 8, 2010).

31. The use of *vos* (*voseo*) is a linguistic phenomenon in the Spanish language that uses the pronoun *vos* and certain particular verbal conjugations when talking to a speaker, in contrast with other variants of the language in which the pronoun *tú* is used. Two forms of the use of *vos* are differentiated, the reverential use of *vos* (or classical use of *vos*) and the American dialectal use of *vos,* and (a third form) in extinction, the peninsular dialectal use of *vos*. The reverential or classical use of *vos* consists of using the pronoun *vos* to be directed reverentially to the second grammatical person (both in singular and plural), implying the verbal conjugation of the second person plural (v.g. "*lo que vos digáis,*" "*vos me mirasteis*").

The American dialectal use of *vos* or simple use of *vos* proceeds grammatically in a similar way but the conjugation's morphology has suffered different evolutions throughout the continent. Semantically, it has a familial use and is directed to the second person singular. The peninsular dialectal use of *vos*, present in rural zones of the Iberian peninsula's northwest (province of Lugo)—and in isolated areas probably by influence of archaic characteristics of the Spanish language—consists of using the pronoun *vos* instead of *tú* but it conjugates as *tú* in a completely transparent way. "Voseo," Wikipedia, la enciclopedia libre http://en.wikipedia.org/wiki/Voseo (accessed January 8, 2010) (Author's free translation).

32. The Archive of the Indigenous Languages of Latin America is available at http://www.ailla.utexas.org/site/welcome.html (accessed January 8, 2010).

33. For more information about all Amerindian native languages, see Native Languages of the Americas, "Amerindian Language Families," http://www.native-languages.org/linguistics.htm#tree (accessed January 8, 2010).

34. "One might suppose, therefore, that linguists would have a clear and reasonably precise notion of how many languages there are in the world. It turns out, however, that there is no such definite count—or at least, no such count that has any status as a scientific finding of modern linguistics." S. R. Anderson, "How Many Languages Are There in the World?" Linguistic Society of America, 2005, http://www.lsadc.org/info/pdf_files/howmany.pdf (accessed January 8, 2010).

35. "Most of all, it is impossible to form certain grammatical structures in a neutral way due to differences in verb conjugations used (e.g., in Argentina, Uruguay, Paraguay, and Central American countries, 'you' [singular] translates to *vos,* most other countries prefer *tú,* while some Colombians tend to use the formal alternative *usted*—all three pronouns require different verb conjugations). At least one of the three versions will always sound very uncommon in any given Spanish speaking country." Wikipedia, "Standard Spanish," http://en.wikipedia.org/wiki/Standard_Spanish (accessed January 8, 2010).

36. "Atlas Sociolinguístico de Pueblos Indígenas en América Latina" (The Sociolinguistic Atlas of Indigenous Peoples in Latin America), a study by the United Nations' Childrens Fund and Agencia Española para la Cooperación Internacional al Desarrollo (AECID) in Aula Intercultural, an intercultural education portal, a project of the Federación de Trabajadores de la Enseñanza española (FETE—The Teaching Workers' Federation of Spain). See http://www.aulaintercultural.org/article.php3?id_article=3703 (accessed January 8, 2010). (Study is in Spanish.)

37. Ibid.

38. Ibid.

39. "Standard Spanish," Wikipedia, the Free Encyclopedia, http://en.wikipedia.org/wiki/Standard_Spanish (accessed July 31, 2010).

40. For more information, add to the Editorial Planeta URL a period and the two letters representing the country (e.g., www.editorialplaneta.com.ar for Argentina, co for Colombia, mx for Mexico, etc.).

41. Judith Rosen, "The Future of Hispanic Publishing," *Críticas,* May 15, 2006, http://www.criticasmagazine.com/article/CA6332573.html (accessed January 8, 2010).

WORKSHEET 5.1   A Template for an Ethnographic Interview

Goal: To help develop the interviewing skills of your library outreach staff.

Regarding your topic:

Choose a topic for your research (such as a cultural dimension, perception of library services, and behavior or limiting beliefs related to library services as presented in following chapters).

Purpose of the interview:

Give a short explanation about the nature of the interview and the research you are trying to accomplish.

Recording the interview:

You may ask permission to tape the interview if you see the interviewee is at ease with that method.

Keep it simple:

Request the interviewee use every day language.

Looking at materials and images:

Printed material has great visual power, and they will understand the topic right away.

Wrap up the interview:

Review your notes out loud with the interviewee and ask any clarifying questions. Thank him or her for participating. Follo up if necessary.

Questions organized by type:

Descriptive questions
Grand tour questions
Task-related questions
Example questions
Experience questions
Direct language questions
Indirect language questions
Verification questions

Adapted from *The Ethnographic Interview,* by James P. Spradley (Fort Worth, TX: Harcourt Brace Jovanovich College Publishers, 1979).

WORKSHEET 5.2   The Green Light, Red Light Method

Goal: Verify if your assumptions about your target market are correct.

Green Light	Red Light	Action
Married Latino women?	Stop: Marriage is not always a reality in different Latin American countries.	Use hospital records as focus group to determine if there are single mothers in this segment.
Age 21-35?	Stop: Latinas might bear children by 16 years of age, so some children will be missed.	Ask pediatricians if younger mothers visit their offices.
Children 0-5 (preschoolers)?	Stop: Young children (babies 0-2) might be American born and different criteria might apply.	Check with hospital records or vital statistics at the municipal building.
Working out of the house?	Stop: Some Latinas prefer to stay at home with small children.	Check with local day care facilities, or call some mothers from hospital records.
Enjoy cooking for their families?	Stop: Cooking for their families is an obligation (*marianismo*).	Read about Latino mothers' obligations toward their families.
Feeding their children with fast food or similar?	Stop: Most Latinas cook regularly for their families, especially if they are recent immigrants and stay-at-home mothers.	Ask pediatricians if they could provide information from records. Use hospital records for ethnographic focus group.

NOTES

_____

_____

_____

_____

_____

 From *¡Hola, amigos! A Plan for Latino Outreach* by Susana G. Baumann. Santa Barbara, CA: Libraries Unlimited. Copyright © 2011.

Chapter 6

Positioning Your Library and Its Resources

Overview

"Just as Copernicus radically altered how people thought about the world by showing that the earth revolves around the sun, social marketing has moved clients into the center of the universe for the professional serving them. An effective social marketing program focuses on the consumer; all the elements are based on the wants and needs of its target audience rather than on what the organization happens to be 'selling'" (Weinreich 1999, pp. 7–8). With these words, Weinreich provides the key to a new approach in outreach services for all organizations that serve diverse communities. In order to achieve your institution's diversity goals, you need to effectively *position* your library, that is, to *create a clear image of your organization in your Latino customers' minds* —ideally, an image that will compel them to act and use the programs and resources your library offers. In commercial marketing, positioning a product means to differentiate it from the competition, to make it unique. For instance, when you have a headache, what do you take? What brand first comes to mind? Tylenol? Advil? A brand comes to mind because of the product manufacturer's efforts to *position* that product as a first choice with you, the consumer. In the same fashion, how do you position your library so that when Latinos think of information, entertainment, or literacy, *they think of the local library first*?

In the library environment, you are not only in competition with bookstores, newspapers, the Internet, video stores, and other businesses that offer similar products, which constitute your external competition; you must also tackle the significant challenge of overcoming the beliefs, concerns, and habits that Latinos have regarding library services, which will be discussed in this chapter.

The preparation stage for positioning your library is essential to your success. Before starting your promotional efforts, all your resources need to be in place. In preparing to position your library, you need to step back and look at the external and internal factors that might help you define specific goals or projects, guide decision making, or simply affect your course of action. Knowledge of these potential pluses or minuses can give you a greater level of certainty in your planning process, allow you to prepare better for success, and narrow your risk of the unforeseen.

Evaluating internal factors includes considering those resources available to Latino library patrons or potential customers—your collections, materials, and services—in order to define which ones you need to keep, which ones you need to improve or add, and how you can access or create new ones that better serve the needs of your Latino customers. This chapter will teach you a simple procedure that you can use either to analyze your big picture or to dig into specific areas of your resources. It will lead you through the necessary steps to analyze the strengths, weaknesses, opportunities, and threats of your internal and external organizational situation; develop long- and short-term goals; and choose the tasks you want to tackle first according to your priorities and possibilities.

In addition, this chapter offers guidelines on how to find out and assess the needs in your community, ways to present resources to your potential or current Latino customers to encourage them to use your products and services, how to create the necessary incentives to promote your products and services, and how to align your *marketing mix*, a series of factors that will entice your Latino customers to take action!

Getting Ready

> Be assertive, be creative, be thrifty! (What else is new?!)

Developing an outreach plan is not a linear activity. It is more like a squiggly line, with a lot of back and forth, incorporating feedback and direction adjustments. For that reason, make a summary of what you have done so far, and make sure you are ready to position your library and promote it to your Latino patrons—the main purpose of your marketing plan.

By now, you have accomplished the following:

1. Developed a clear mission statement about the diversity purpose of your library
2. Established a CLO; you may have created a CLO charter statement instead of changing your library's mission statement, and you should have defined your CLO members' roles
3. Created an internal communication process that will nurture and sustain your Latino marketing plan and its activities
4. Assessed and established your strategic partners and defined the roles they will play in your plan (some of them are part of your Latino Advisory Board)
5. Completed extensive research about your local Latino community and became familiar with its demographics and market segments
6. Became knowledgeable about your local Latino community's cultural beliefs, values, and habits

Correct preparation through these tasks allows you to get your hands into the next stage of your marketing plan, which involves positioning your library and its resources, promoting and advertising your library and its programs and services, and then evaluating your results.

Guided by the institution's mission statement and/or CLO charter statement—I suggest you review your chapter 2 worksheets at this time—positioning your library gives you a more accurate idea of where you are and where you want to be. It also helps you define priorities to meet the needs of your market segments, which you will identify with a more realistic view. The first step in positioning your library and its resources is to identify your strengths and weaknesses.

The SWOT Analysis

SWOT stands for Strengths, Weaknesses, Opportunities, and Threats.[1] It is advisable to begin any type of strategic planning effort with a SWOT analysis. Try to involve the majority of your employees in this exercise because each will bring a point of view from his or her particular area of action or expertise. Their participation also helps them own the plan and facilitates its execution. After your initial SWOT evaluation, you might want to conduct periodic SWOT meetings—maybe every three years—to reevaluate the planning process or any project or task.

Even after the overall outreach plan has been set forth, you will also want to engage in mini-SWOT exercises while planning individual outreach projects. These exercises will continue to serve as a valuable tool to help you know where to start and what resources you need to get from point A to point B. I give examples on how to proceed, but you will also find blank worksheets in chapter 10 for this purpose. Feel free to adapt them or make your own. These tasks would be a good start for warming up your CLO, but, as suggested, try to be as inclusive as possible with the rest of the staff.

While everybody might understand organizational strengths and weaknesses, organizational opportunities and threats might be less clear. To assess your organization's opportunities and threats, you need to look externally at the environment in which your organization operates. Opportunities and threats mostly come from external forces—your macro-environment (Kotler, Roberto, and Lee 2002, p. 102)—that might not be under your control; however, these uncontrollable forces can affect you. If you plan to either take advantage of an opportunity or get ready to confront a threat, then you can successfully narrow your risk of some unforeseen event affecting your outreach efforts.

An external opportunity, for instance, to attract more Latinos into libraries might be legislation that resolves the status of undocumented immigrants, which in time will diminish the confidentiality fear in your potential users. In contrast, legislation that enforces current immigration laws—such as in the case of the State of Arizona—can act as a threat in attracting undocumented Latinos who fear that enrolling for a library card or registering for a program might put them in legal jeopardy. Economic trends affecting your library might also become a threat (such as budget cuts) but the opposite is true, for instance, if your library gets money to expand the building and has to close or reduce services or move to an area that is not conveniently located for your Latino patrons.

Opportunities might come from a campaign conducted by a community partner, targeting the same market and enabling you to join in on their effort; new technologies and products in the market that can be taught or offered at your facility; or the nomination of a Latino personality to national, state, or local office, who may bring an opportunity to include him or her in your promotional efforts as a role model.

Other SWOT factors might have to do with the following: the location of your facility, other aspects of your organization that add value to your products or services (such as bilingual employees), your social marketing expertise or lack of it, products offered by the competition, your reputation in the Latino community, the Internet (either an opportunity or a threat, depending on how you use it), strategic partners and other alliances in the community, a competitor with innovative products or services similar to yours (such as Google Books or Kindle), and issues with federal, state, and local government.

Please keep the following in mind when doing your SWOT analysis:

- Be realistic!
- Concentrate on evaluating issues today, not yesterday and not tomorrow (although you will discover trends if you compare SWOTs in time).
- Be as specific as possible.
- Do not sweat the small stuff: some areas will be unknown and some will be defined very specifically.
- Keep it short and simple. It is better to have different SWOTs covering different topics than one that gets too complicated!

SWOTs are mostly a subjective matter, and you can gather different information from different members of your organization. Once you have identified key issues in your SWOT analysis, they become the core of your marketing strategic goals supporting your mission statement (or CLO charter statement).

Assessing Strengths and Weaknesses

Your first SWOT analysis related to your local Latino audience will address general ideas such as those that follow. I have included examples (possible SWOTs), but you will have to find your own according to your mission statement or charter statement, and the discussions you held with your CLO members, colleagues, and other members of your community (see chapters 2 and 3).

Let's refresh our example from chapter 2:

The purpose of the Committee for Latino Outreach is to provide and assure access to quality informational, educational, and recreational resources and learning opportunities to attract the local Latino communities that reside in the geographical area of Little Haven City and its suburbs.

We plan to create, outreach, and promote culturally appropriate programs and services that respond to their changing educational, cultural, and recreational needs and interests, due to their different backgrounds and generational gaps, and help integrate this vibrant and diverse population to the existing cultural heritage of Little Haven City. For that purpose, we commit to growing funding to develop internal and external resources including dedicated personnel, appropriate technologies and collections, enticing programs and services, and a friendly and welcoming environment.

In Worksheet 6.1. you will find the main elements of this charter statement that will be the base of this SWOT.

As you see, these are general topics with general comments. Every category might not be filled, or you might need to go back a few times to your initial SWOT as circumstances change. Depending upon which phase of your outreach plan you are working on, your factors and comments might change. In order to dig into more specific areas of your SWOTs, you might want to develop one for each of the areas derived from your mission or charter statement. You could build a SWOT for each of the 15 areas in the example. Also, remember that you will need mini-SWOTS for each particular project or programming you start. SWOTS are a great tool to keep you grounded!

Likewise, your opportunities and threats will have to be related to your macro- and microenvironment as well as your internal situation (see Worksheet 6.2).

Again, you can keep adding your own factors or think of new ones, and you can add a few notes to keep everything fresh in your mind. These lists are tools you will use every time new phases of the project come up, and you will know how to work with them every step of the way. The more you narrow your focus, the more accurate these lists will become.

Working with Your SWOT

Once you have finished these lists, pick three to five high-impact strengths and weaknesses to work on, and start focusing on those. Be realistic about the ones you pick. Do not try to change what is out of your control. For instance, changing the outside of your facility or hiring new personnel might not be realistic at this time. Those might be tasks to tackle in the future when conditions change or new opportunities arise. Focus on using strengths to overcome weaknesses and threats and to leverage opportunities. The following example shows how to take advantage of your circumstances. Working from both lists above, I have selected weaknesses and threats:

Five related weaknesses and threats (WTs):

1. Need to increase Latino cardholders
2. Need to prioritize market segments from market research
3. Need to assess new services needed according to #2
4. Need to overcome some employees' reluctance to learn Spanish
5. Need more cross-cultural training for employees

From both lists, I also selected strengths and opportunities to help overcome those weaknesses and threats:

Related strengths and opportunities (SOs):

1. Current Latino members to help assess new services needed
2. Small but regular budget with which we can provide materials and services for specific market segments
3. Two bilingual part-time employees to become REFORMA members
4. New LSTA (Library Services and Technology Act) grant for offering employees Spanish and cross-cultural training
5. New Latino trustee to help recruit Latino Advisory Board

The next step is to define your marketing strategic goals related to these SOs and WTs. The idea is to enhance the SOs and to build up or work around your WTs.

What can be done?

1. Draw upon current Latino members and new Latino trustee to increase awareness of library services through word-of-mouth, referrals, promotional efforts, and

community events to increase membership, and recruit volunteers for the Latino Advisory Board.

2. Prioritize market segments from market research by assessing needs and/or resources, and add new services in accordance with regular budget.
3. Use part of new LSTA grant to increase cross-cultural and Spanish training for employees.
4. Research alternative sources of funding to support these initiatives.

Now deal with just these few issues at this time, and get ready to define your long- and short-term goals.

Defining Long- and Short-Term Marketing Goals and Strategies

Let us assume your marketing plan will develop over a three-year period, so you need to set specific goals for each different stage according to your SWOT's choices. Next, you will need to put some numbers to your goals, assign responsibilities, and define schedules—that is, to define strategies for each year in preparation for future actions. Your goals should be challenging but achievable and measurable, as shown in Worksheet 6.3.

You will continue to plan each of the short-term goals and strategies in the same way. Stay focused on your first year's goals. Although this seems like a simple plan, implementing it requires a series of steps. You can add goals or choose different goals—but keep in mind that adding tasks will increase your workload, your necessary resources, and your efforts. Keep it simple!

Also, your goals have to be realistic and doable. You can add more goals if you have enough hands and funding. If you are just starting out, focus on just a few like those in these examples. The extent of your goals must relate to your resources, which you will assess next.

If you have already begun your outreach efforts, a good place to start is to evaluate what you have done so far. Your SWOT then becomes an evaluation of your past performances. The procedure is the same, only you will have several layers of strategic goals and, consequently, several planning levels. For instance, you need a SWOT for each of your strategic marketing goals—what has been done and what has been achieved, what needs to be improved, and so forth. Another SWOT will evaluate your human resources—what has been done so far, what you want to see improved, and so on.

Your SWOTs will also give you insights about what venues to pursue. For instance, if you discover in your SWOTs that you have been working exclusively with programming—ESL classes, bilingual story times, or holidays—you will want to emphasize raising awareness about library services in general. If you have been working with a general Latino market, you will want to address your work to specific market segments and assess their needs in order to improve specific services. If you have been focused on services you provide in the library, you will want to develop strategies to take the library out of the building and reach new geographic areas or new audiences. There is always room for improvement!

Take into consideration the size and latitude of your organization. The larger your library system and the larger the geographical area it covers, the more complex and involved your planning process will be. If you have over 10 branches, you will also need to size your plan accordingly. Not all your branches might be in reach of the Latino community due to location or transportation issues. Tackle each task separately, and follow the same simple procedure each time.

Assessing Your Latino Community Needs

Now that you have a clear understanding of your internal and external organizational state of affairs, the next step in positioning your library within a social marketing approach is a two-fold task: first, you need to assess the needs of your local Latino community; second, you need to differentiate your library and your services from your competition (Michman 1991).

What do potential Latino patrons need? What are the concerns, barriers, and problems they need to overcome on a daily basis? What products and services do they look for outside the library and why? You will be asking questions related to cultural subjectivity—that is, how *they* see things from *their* perspective.

Understanding their needs within a cultural perspective will lead you to discover how your products or services might or might not connect with your Latino patrons' needs and what you must overcome in order to make your effort a successful one.

For libraries, learning to develop and sustain a basic community needs assessment is vital for two reasons: (1) libraries must be aware of community needs in order to respond with products and services efficiently and effectively, and (2) Latinos are the fastest growing population, especially in rural America.[2]

Once you learn how to assess community needs, you will be engaged in an ongoing process that produces and upgrades results.

Determine, Assess, Prioritize

In chapters 4 and 5 ("Getting to Know Your Latino Patrons" part 1 and part 2) you defined your market profile with demographics and psychosociocultural information. However, this information does not determine the needs and wants of this community, nor does it tell you what its members know and believe about library services. In addition, it does not describe the benefits and disadvantages your customers perceive (their beliefs) when using or not using library services.

Determining your customers' needs is one of the most important aspects of a social marketing approach. Social marketing focuses on the customer's needs and seeks to find solutions to benefit the target audience and the general society. Chapter 3 develops the idea of interviewing community leaders and focus groups about needs, problems, and perspectives of the community they represent and belong to. (In that chapter, I suggested that you use Yolanda Cuesta's interviewing process for community leaders, which you can find in chapter 10 of this book and on the WebJunction Spanish Outreach Program Web site.)[3]

From those interviews, you probably have a list of problems, comments, observations, and suggestions community leaders gave you, a summary of which might look like this:

The Needs of the Latino Community in Little Haven City

1. Affordable housing
2. Literacy—in English and Spanish
3. Information about rentals and tenant-landlord relationship

4. Information about schools and how PTAs work
5. Help with homework and after-school programs for children
6. Information in Spanish—lack of Spanish television, radio, or newspapers
7. Lack of health literacy and information about common health issues
8. Transportation issues
9. Increase English literacy to improve employment opportunities

Although this list might vary in length and content according to the demographics of your Latino community and the geographical area you cover, these are common issues in Latino communities with recent immigrants or those still in the process of acculturation.[4] If your population has been established longer or for many generations, your list content will vary. You may find a list that includes these elements:

- Employment opportunities
- Résumé writing and interviewing skills
- Alternative education (information about community colleges, schools, and universities)
- International language collections (books, periodicals, and Web sites)
- English and Spanish reading and learning materials (fiction and nonfiction)
- Human and civil rights information
- Voter registration and voting procedures
- Reference information about health—physical and mental—and health literacy
- Community and social service programs (how to find government information)
- Resource guides (Web sites, social networks, directories, etc.)
- Consumer protection and financial education

As you can see, some of these needs are not so different from those of your regular customers. When discussing the needs assessment with library personnel, the library's role in the community comes up often. If you look at the aforementioned lists, you might think there is little your library can do to actually solve problems. However, your needs assessment is related to the information you can provide to the community. You can provide a wealth of information about these and other very needed topics. The concern then becomes how you bridge the information gap.

In order to assess and prioritize your role in the information gap as well as any other service you would like to offer, consider the questions in Worksheet 6.4. You will find this same worksheet in chapter 10. These questions will help you assess and prioritize the issues in your community according to the information you gathered from various sources, including your market research and interviews with community partners.

In order to answer these questions, follow the next steps:

Step 1: From the needs assessment list, choose two or three topics for which you have information readily available (this material should be bilingual and/or translated into Spanish and easily available through the library, through a strategic partner, or through your bilingual staff helping patrons find such information); determine whether you need additional personnel, funding, use of facilities, or strategic partners.

Step 2: From your demographic research in chapter 4, choose the group that is easier to reach, is more open or ready to receive your information, or has a more pressing need for the information you are ready to provide.

Step 3: With the focus on your three-year plan goal, prioritize those needs according to your SWOTs.

The following example uses affordable housing and tenant-landlord information because the housing situation in Little Haven City is pressing due to the real estate crisis. From the demographic analysis, bicultural potential patrons were chosen because they are probably new homeowners or might be at risk of losing their homes to foreclosure. If they have been established over 20 years, they probably speak some English.

In addition, the information about affordable housing and tenant-landlord relationships will be advertised at the library as part of the library's services, focusing on *their problem* and the help the library can provide.

The SWOT illustrates an opportunity to advertise through the new Latino trustee and current Latino cardholders. The LSTA grant can be used to train employees in a bit of Spanish to welcome Latinos to the library and direct them to two bilingual employees who can address their concerns one-on-one or to strategic partners who volunteer at the library.

If the budget can stretch a bit, promotional efforts can be launched with an event that includes leaders of the community—not only Latino leaders but also bankers, government housing agents, local and state representatives, and real estate agents or mortgage brokers who might want to explain alternatives for these community members related to their housing problems. The session can be conducted in English and Spanish. Additional materials could be distributed at that time.

Your first-year planned word-of-mouth campaigns, referrals, and events will have to focus on these types of efforts. Your success stories and press releases will have to tell about these initiatives and information your target community can find at the library about *their problems*.

Go down the list of needs or issues you have, and answer the 10 easy questions in Worksheet 6.4 for each one. You will have then a clear idea of your priorities, resources, and possibilities.

As you see, the focus is not on library services but rather on your customers' needs and how the library can help address them. You can plan several different initiatives during the year, but always keep the focus on your community needs and your goal of raising awareness about library services by following this same procedure.

Who Is Your Competition?

One common pitfall is the belief that if an organization gets the information out, then people will take action and use their services. In reality, this hardly works.

You may have promoted an ESL class and had a waiting list because there were many patrons interested in the class. However, I can almost guarantee the response you had was small compared with the need for English classes in your community. This is not to discourage you; on the contrary, I praise you for your effort. However, this approach goes beyond that to help you sustain such effort.

In social marketing, the goal is to reach every member of the community who needs your services and help them make behavioral changes so they can take advantage of all services. Those coming to your library most likely have a high level of readiness. However, what happens to those who find obstacles and barriers that need to be overcome?

When you interviewed community leaders and some Latino patrons, they probably mentioned Latinos' comments about library products and services. For instance, they might have told you that a group of recent or undocumented immigrant families with low literacy levels and little or no tradition of library services might have the following limiting beliefs, fears, and habits about your services:

1. Fear of legal issues, confidentiality, and undocumented status
2. Lack of trust in institutions
3. Thinking their children do not need to go to college—for many segments, a high school education is enough to get a good job (Borda 2007)
4. Perceive libraries as a boring place only for students and scholars (experience shows even acculturated Latinos might hold this belief)
5. Literacy problems or poor reading habits
6. Working too many hours, with limited or no free time
7. Engaged in seasonal work (from March to November) and moving around or leaving for several months at a time
8. Lack of transportation
9. Family focus on church activities
10. Do not know how to type or use a computer[5]

These are just some examples of your potential customers' limiting beliefs (1–4), obstacles (5–8), and habits/skills (9–10) you have to consider. You might also find specific challenges for each service you would like to offer—fears, lack of ability, lack of interest or lack of knowledge, cultural values, and more. (For instance, lack of reading ability might be a hard obstacle to overcome for an adult Latino male if you are trying to promote "reading to your children," especially if there is a belief that this task belongs to the mother's role.)

These limiting beliefs, barriers, obstacles, and established behaviors of each person or group are, in reality, your competition. To help members of your target community change these behaviors for their own benefit and encourage them to take action, the social marketer needs to understand the belief system, established behaviors, and barriers that prevent these individuals and groups from changing their habits. Your first task, then, is to explore and understand the underlying causes that prevent your potential customers from using your services. Your second task is to respond with a social marketing mind-set—that is, to think not with a service-centered mind but with a customer-centered mind taking into account their preferences, wants, and needs.

Behaviors, Messages, and Obstacles

Some tools have been developed to help you tackle your first task of getting to know your target audience in depth. I will explain how these tools work with the example outlined in the following worksheets. Then, you will apply the same tools in your chapter 10 worksheets. Worksheet 6.5a shows us what your competition looks like.

Evidently, some of your competition has powerful messages, messengers, and obstacles, and your Latino customers need to see that the solution you are offering is attractive and easy to use. Moreover, your solution needs to be attractive enough to overcome these competing behaviors on a continuous basis.

If you do not have enough comments about library services in general or about a specific activity you want to promote, it is strongly recommended at this point that you go back to Worksheet 5.1, "A Template for an Ethnographic Interview," from chapter 10. Use this template to develop some questions for this specific effort or activity, and interview a few people in the Latino community—members of the LAB, current Latino patrons, or a few potential patrons out in the real world. This time, the goals of your interview are the following:

1. Gather information about a specific service, practice, or knowledge you want to provide for this particular group at the library and their previous experience with that service—if any.
2. Grasp what type of visible or invisible barriers, competing behaviors, or opposing messages and messengers they have experienced or perceived.
3. Find out which benefits they look for in this service, how this service might improve their lives, or how you can diminish or ease barriers and competing behaviors.
4. Understand their level of readiness related to the service you want to provide.

Only once you understand what leads your potential Latino customers to behave in an established way will you be able to deal with your real competition. Do not take shortcuts at this important task. Although it is hard to get out of your comfort zone, you will find surprising results when you ask you customers what they need.

How to Overcome Your Competition

You might also consider the following areas when interviewing your potential customers. In order to overcome your competition, there are three benefit areas you might want to address at the interview:

1. The perceived personal benefits, or "What's in it for me?" Your potential customer needs to see real benefits beyond the service offered. You can suggest the benefit "I can communicate with my children," suggesting, for instance, that some Latino teenage children might feel proud of introducing their bilingual parents to their new American friends.
2. Fewer barriers, obstacles, or cost are also benefits that compensate their effort and need to be discussed. Classes need to be in the realistic schedule and transportation possibilities of your target segment to facilitate their involvement. A light snack and beverages at the beginning of the class might entice people to come to class directly from work instead of stopping at home—a temptation to stay—or spending extra money to buy food on the go. Even more, entice some of them to bring a delicious recipe from their country of origin.
3. Social pressure benefits and influencers are related to how the world and other people that influence your Latino customers' decisions perceive the benefits of your customers using these services. In this case, matters of image, prestige, acculturation, safety, and so forth might need to be addressed and could later become incentives for your promotional campaign.

In Worksheet 6.6a you will find examples of benefits you can use to encourage action based on the obstacles and barriers you found.

In summary, you need to increase awareness that being a library cardholder will bring *benefits* to your Latino patrons—"I find all I need at the local library"—and decrease the current habits, obstacles, and limiting beliefs of their competing behavior—"Libraries are not for me."

A word about social pressure or influencers: those people—also called *publics*—your customers look up to might make a difference in your promotional efforts, and you need to consider them in your promotional campaigns. We will expand on this in chapter 8.

At this point, you have completed a situation analysis as follows:

Strategic goal: Reach 3 percent of the local Latino population
Basic need: Lack of awareness of library services
Limiting beliefs, obstacles, and **habits:** (choose three challenges from the aforementioned list of 10 that might be easy to interrelate)

Lack of trust in institutions
Family focus on church activities
Perceive libraries as a boring place only for students and scholars

Based on the analysis of these three challenges, here is a positioning statement example for a general promotional strategy:

[All members of local Latino families] find [enjoyable free activities and useful information] [for the advancement of their lives in the United States] at the local library, [a safe, enjoyable, and welcoming place] where [staff is bilingual and customer friendly].

A positioning statement helps you identify your target audience; their problems, wants, and needs; your value proposition or the solution you offer; the key differentiation of your offering from other similar offerings; and the key benefit your target audience will enjoy:

Your target audience: All members of local Latino families
The service name or category: Enjoyable free activities and useful information
Their problems, wants, and needs: The advancement of their lives in the United States
A key benefit: A safe and welcoming place
The key differentiation: Staff is bilingual and customer friendly

The changeable parts of your positioning statement are included in brackets because if you choose to target other issues, your wording in between brackets would be different. If you choose to target another market segment, then your description "All members of local Latino families" should be replaced by a description of the segment you will target.

Note that this statement is grounded in reality. It's not an image or posture but rather a position that is customer centered (all members of local Latino families), grounded in actual accomplishments (free enjoyable activities and useful information) and relationships (a safe and welcoming place for all where staff is bilingual and customer friendly), and it makes your place, materials, and services unique for that particular audience.

Later, you might base your promotional efforts on this *concept*; however, it would need to be embellished for advertising purposes. Right now, it sets the base for all the efforts you need to make to implement your positioning statement in areas other than advertising. For instance, what can you do to make the library a welcoming place for Latino families? Improve displays of Spanish collections? Set up bilingual signage and make your facility user friendly? Train your staff in a little Spanish? Increase distribution of bilingual newspapers and magazines or music and DVDs? Have activities for the whole family? You have to think of the incentives that are right for your local Latinos . . . what makes them tick!

The statement redefines your community's basic need into a more appealing strategy based on trust, family, valuable information, and fun—values that are cherished by this community.

Let us see another case scenario, this time for a specific outreach activity. A group of Latino teens at the local high school—one of your strategic partners—are behind in reading skills. The school principal has requested the library's help during a summer session so the teens have additional opportunities to improve their reading habits in a more relaxed and fun environment than the school itself. Based on ethnographic interviews conducted among some of these teens, the obstacles in Worksheet 6.5b were encountered.

Some behaviors you might find similar to those of other teens—remember that these are young Latino Americans with probably a good level of acculturation or even assimilation. However, you will see a few differences—for instance, family messages considering reading an unnecessary habit or not encouraging reading because the parents do not speak English.

If the family males are expected to do physical work—to work in an industry or do the same type of job the father does—they might consider reading an unnecessary skill. In addition, some of these teens might have a limited English vocabulary.

By talking with and observing Latino teens, it was concluded that they are very social and cooperative, like to do group activities, usually have great respect for their families, and want to belong or become integrated with other kids. They might prefer certain looks and Latino music, love dancing and having fun, and like to participate in social events. They use cell phones and like to play video games. Like any other teenagers, they love to be the center of attention!

In order to attract this target audience to the library's activity, you need to put your social marketing mind-set to work. What would you offer to make this summer reading program so enticing that they will show up, participate, and keep coming back for more?

You need to think in terms of the benefits they might see in this activity. What is so fascinating about reading? Your answer as a librarian might not be the same as the Latino teens' perceptions, as shown in Worksheet 6.6b.

The way you present improving their reading habits is as a by-product of all the activities, preferences, and habits the target audience enjoys. The promotional idea—Latino Teen Summer Club—is then to go beyond reading skills and offer a comprehensive activity club where the participants will be empowered, actively involved, and rewarded for it!

The club can involve a different activity each week, such as reading and acting in a play, getting dressed in costumes according to a book's characters, or playing games while reading (to improve listening and comprehension). There might be pair or group activities, such as a group competition in researching the library for topics or materials, browsing articles on the Internet, and so forth. There can even be reading sessions outside on the library patio if the weather permits.

It might be important to include a social media project, which can be an excellent promotional tool, as well. For instance, a Facebook page for fans of the Latino Teen Summer Club, sponsored by the library, where they can post their personal pictures and pictures of their activities, chat with each other between sessions, add new friends to recommend to the club, post questions, invite their parents and teachers to see, and so forth, can increase participation. They can also create a photo gallery with their pictures and pictures of their activities to be displayed at the library, and in school when it reopens, to show their achievements.

The positioning statement for this activity is shown in Worksheet 6.7 and summarizes the main aspects we discussed in Worksheets 6.5 (a and b) and 6.6 (a and b).

As you can see, the arguments for a later promotional campaign are being profiled here. You can choose some of these arguments to include in your press releases, flyers, and other promotional materials. Wording and images will have to be creatively developed. You will find a blank Worksheet 6.7 for a positioning statement in chapter 10.

Adopting a social marketing mind-set means changing the way you plan your activity with your potential customers in mind. Instead of doing business as usual, you must ask your customers or potential target audiences what actually works for them and then plan according to your customer's responses.

Marketing a library to Latinos is about relationship building. It is about investing in and building a long-lasting, meaningful connection with Latino patrons rather than making a short-term sale. This means putting effort into getting to know your Latino prospects—more than hosting a fair, festival, or activity.

You will find that once you establish a loyal customer base, your patrons will become your best advertisers, especially in the Latino community, where word-of-mouth is a trusted strategy for passing information. Chapters 7 and 8 continue these ideas, focusing on programming and promotional strategies.

Why You Need to Do Your Due Diligence

The Little Haven City case scenario targets a specific market segment—bicultural immigrants, first generation, fully employed, families with children, and so forth. However, in a diverse Latino market, it is not easy to find approaches that will appeal to a vast majority of your market unless you make some assumptions, and those assumptions might be right—but they are sometimes very wrong. Marketers call this problem "profit pressure," or return of investment (ROI). Every time they spend money targeting a segment, missing the target means that profit is gone. When you must achieve certain economic goals, you cannot afford to miss too many times.

Service pressure should abide by the same concept. For instance, and going back to your short-term outreach goals, if you determined a 3 percent cardholder increase in a calendar year, you will have to target the market as many times as needed to achieve that goal. Understanding the demographics of that market, their preferences, where they are located, and what their needs are will determine your time, effort, and budget. If you achieve your goal in nine months rather than a year, it means less effort and money spent and a better use of materials and services—a positive evaluation of the strategy you used. Moreover, if you do a good job at building relationships with your new patrons overall, you have satisfied customers who will come back for more.

On the other hand, if you miss your target, it means more time, effort, and expense; more adjustments to your original strategy; and a general sense of failure or frustration. An unknown market is like a moving target—you might hit one mark out of ten shots, which is more than you can afford financially and professionally.

By analyzing your new customers' input, you are better able to make decisions related to placing your materials, hiring and training staff, planning and programming events, and deciding the direction of your outreach campaign strategy and fundraising efforts.

The Incentive to *Buy*, or the Marketing Mix

In the traditional marketing environment, companies know that some factors will motivate customers to buy their products. Often referred as the *marketing mix*, these factors are products, price, place (location), and promotion, also known as "the Four *P*s." (There are several versions of marketing mixes including a variety of *P* words.)

By aligning these four elements in different ways, companies develop the ability to reach multiple target markets. They successfully *promote products* that customers will find at the right *price*—based on a competitive market value—in an accessible *place*.

In a social marketing approach, however, professionals listen to the needs of the target audience and build their marketing strategy from there. In addition to considering the "Four *P*s," the traditional elements of a marketing mix, a social marketing approach includes aligning the following: publics, partnerships, policies, and purse strings. Let us take a closer look at these elements in the library environment.

Product Choices

What are the products and services you are "selling" (offering, in this case)?

Make an extensive list of all the materials and services in your library according to the following categories (some examples are provided):

- Tangible, physical materials: books, DVDs, CDs, and so on.
- Services: library loans, classes, Internet access, interlibrary loans, and so on.
- Practices: improving literacy levels, acquiring or improving English knowledge, researching job opportunities, improving health literacy, improving employment and computer skills, and so on.
- Intangible ideas: equal access to information; opportunities for acculturation and/or knowledge to make an easier transition into life in the United States; advancement in literacy and education; expansion of ideas, experiences, and interests; keeping history, traditions, and roots alive; right and freedom of information; freedom of speech; etc. (To complete these intangible ideas, see the chapter 1 sidebar, "Ten Reasons for Multicultural Library Services," and also Worksheet 2.1, "Your Mission and Vision.")

It is important that you spell out as many of these ideas as possible because you will base part of your promotional strategies on these intangible ideas. Remember that in order to have a viable service, your customers must perceive it as a good solution to their problems.

When it comes to deciding the purchase of tangible, physical materials, however, librarians are bombarded with sales pitches from editorial distributors and publishing houses that want to sell their products, regardless. Exercise caution when purchasing materials for your Latino patrons. Publishers and distributors usually follow national trends—because their profit is in the numbers—but what they sell you might not fit your local audience's needs. If your collection budget is limited, it would be a waste to buy materials appropriate for the Los Angeles Latino population when you are located in a small town in Pennsylvania. Some library materials do not get utilized because they are inappropriate, and libraries do not always have the financial ability to replace them for something that would more accurately target their local community's needs.

Product Choices with a Twist

The following guidelines are related to language matters when purchasing collections for the Latino customer. Pay attention to your organization's mission, the results of your demographics analysis, your community needs assessment, and your market segments in order to make quality decisions about acquiring Spanish materials. It's not as daunting as it may seem—here are some suggestions:

Fiction

1. **Once you have defined your local audience's background,** try to select material written by native writers from their country or countries of origin, especially if you are building a fiction collection in Spanish. If your audience has immigrated recently, then materials from the same country of origin written in Spanish will be more enticing. Some publishing companies, such as Random House, import books in Spanish from Spain, Mexico, Colombia, Venezuela, Chile, and Argentina.[6] Simon & Schuster's Atria imprint publishes books written by Latinos in English as well as in Spanish.

2. **If your local audience has been established in the area for a long time,** try American Latino authors both in English and Spanish if translated versions are available. Try to advertise them together as publishers have found success when launching both versions simultaneously.

   A wealth of literature from the Chicano (Mexican American) movement, the Nuyorican (New York Puerto Rican) movement, and many other Latin American authors are either published in Spanish, English, or both.

3. **When acquiring materials translated into Spanish,** choose those translated by a native speaker of a Latin American country. Try to group the materials geographically or regionally: South Americans will feel more at ease when reading translations done by professional translators from Argentina, Uruguay, and Chile. People from the Caribbean might identify with translators from Cuba, Dominican Republic, or Puerto Rico, not because they are from those countries but because they likely are more familiar with the language differences and similarities in that region. Translators from Venezuela, Colombia, and Ecuador, although South Americans, might be familiar with Central American regionalisms and expressions. It's a stretch, but it can work. You can try to find translators' background information directly from the publishers or Google them, as some might have professional Web sites. Check also the American Translators Association (ATA) Web site to see if these translators are included in their membership list.[7]

4. **Your last option is getting materials written and/or translated in Spain or in the United States.** The reason U.S. translations are suggested as the last choice is that until recently, the quality of domestic translations was poor—not because there are no good translators in the United States, but because, among other factors, publishing companies were "penny wise" and sometimes did not hire the services of top-quality translators. Also, the translation industry is not regulated, and many states do not require a translator's license or certification, which permits abuses. Now that larger companies are tapping into the market, more accurate and appropriate language adaptations are available. Look for those companies that can afford good, professional translators. Also, look for niche companies that specialize in the Latino or Spanish-speaking market.[8]

Nonfiction

Nonfiction books and reference materials are usually written in standard Spanish. Except for some specific publications—which might use words more accepted in the Iberian

Peninsula—the use of standard Spanish should allow all people to read these publications. Standard Spanish is well understood in the Spanish-speaking world especially in reference and other nonfiction materials.

Pay Attention to Your External Competition

At the 2006 BookExpo America (BEA) held in Washington, DC, the Spanish Pavilion housed 40 to 45 Latin American and Spanish publishers. The "Latino Publishing 2.0: Where the Market is Headed" seminar sponsored by *Críticas* magazine[9] discussed the growth and concentration of Spanish-speaking markets.[10] Most publishing companies agreed that the Spanish-speaking market could not be ignored as sales have increased significantly in recent years. However, the biggest trend is not the library market but the retail market.[11] Publishing companies are jumping on the bandwagon, and so should you.

Here are some tips from the publishing industry that you can incorporate into your collection development plans:

Trends

- The Latino market seems to look for self-help and spiritual materials (printed and audiovisuals), school subjects, test preparation materials, popular materials from countries of origin, audiovisuals, medical information, American best sellers translated into Spanish, movie tie-ins, and titles written by or including celebrities (for example, Scholastics' collection *Lee y serás*, launched in 2006, focuses on Latin American figures for Latino children living in the United States).
- Other publishers are translating financial best sellers and career-oriented and career advice materials, but also look for material published in English and Spanish simultaneously.
- Search drugstores, supermarkets, and mass merchandisers for well-known authors and hot topics in Spanish.
- Diversify your purchases with mass-market books and a variety of paperback formats, including pocket size and larger imprints.
- Favorite audiovisual materials are ESL courses and those covering pregnancy, parenting, and health-related issues.
- Purchase Spanish-language films for the whole family produced abroad or in the United States with famous movie and TV actors (such as Antonio Banderas, Penélope Cruz, Salma Hayek, Gael García Bernal, Javier Bardem, Jimmy Smits, Jennifer Lopez, John Leguizamo, and George Lopez). Display posters alongside the audiovisual collections.
- Research the most important film era in each country. Mexico, for instance, is currently experiencing a film boom and is exporting good films to the United States and so are other Latin American countries as well.[12]

Suppliers

- Ask for personalized service. Do not accept generated lists from distributors and publishers; instead, ask them to research your community's particular needs.
- Attend international book fairs such as those in Guadalajara, Mexico (November–December); Madrid, Spain (October); Buenos Aires, Argentina (April–May); Bogotá, Colombia (August); Santo Domingo, Dominican Republic (April–May); Santiago, Chile (October–November); Miami, Florida (November); Lima, Peru (July–August); and Puerto Rico (October), among others. You can

cover a lot of ground by checking book fairs from your customers' countries of origin (and have fun while traveling!). If you are unable to attend, I suggest obtaining promotional materials, such as an exhibitor's guide, from such book fairs; these might be available on a Web site established to promote each fair.

Finally, remember that your selection is the result of your organization's conscious decision about the way it wants to serve the local community. Are you using your Spanish-language collection to attract your target community to library services? Are you trying to provide your Latino residents with the materials they need and enjoy? Are you setting the path for their acculturation process? All these questions have to be answered *before* starting your selection, and in your answers you will find guidelines to buy materials that will become part of your Spanish collection.

Collecting Spanish-language Material

Finally yet importantly, it is worth noting that once you begin collecting Spanish-language material, purchasing additional materials needs to be a regular part of your buying cycle. You want your Spanish-speaking patrons to know you are serious about meeting their needs with attractive materials in good condition, not just buying materials when your organization has some extra money.

Take the time to develop a comprehensive listing of all services offered in Spanish, and keep it at the Reference Desk and on the library's Web site. You can also include a summary of this listing in your promotional campaigns. Update the listings regularly so dates and times are accurate. Find out what other resource guides exist in your community, and include your Spanish services.

Include a short survey in all your translated materials with questions such as: Did you find the book (or CD or DVD, etc.) you were looking for? What did you like most about your experience at the library? Did you encounter any problems or concerns during your visit? Why did you come to the library? In addition, asking for referrals of other potential patrons can be part of the survey, which will provide a continuous source of information and feedback. An incentive, such as an entry to a monthly prize drawing for a Spanish best seller or DVD, can be offered for returning the survey—but only if your bylaws allow such practices. Your library can make it convenient for patrons to return the survey by placing boxes at the circulation desk, at the reference desk, by the computer lab, or even outside in the lobby with a display calling attention to the survey. You can also use a mailer that patrons can take home and fill out at their convenience, although the logistics of this strategy would be more expensive.

Price

Your price has no competition because library services are generally free to the public. However, although people love the concept of free, in some cultures there is also the belief that "You get what you pay for," or "What is cheap turns out to be expensive," as translated from the Spanish saying *"Lo barato sale caro."*

Do not assume that because your services are free, Latinos will pour into your library. Your free services also have to be useful and convenient, and materials must be current, making it worth the effort to go to the library instead of stopping at the local video store or going online to look for information.

Price also refers to what the consumer must do in order to get a product or service. The effort might not be monetary. In this case, we talk about *cost* rather than price. The perceived value of the offering needs to be higher than the actual cost, otherwise it is unlikely the products or services will be adopted or requested. For example, ESL and computer classes have proven to be a great way to attract Latinos into public libraries. However, if the classes are too crowded, if they have many different levels, or if your class schedule does not fit your potential patrons' schedules, the offering will be dismissed.

Latinos might consider the following issues as *cost* when deciding use of library services:

- Having to make time out of their busy schedules (with children, work, seasonal schedules, or time spent with the family)
- Sacrificing available time spent at church
- Lacking transportation (car or public); library far from home or work
- Lacking child care for at-home mom with small children
- Overlapping library activities with other leisure activities (entertainment, sports, friends, or family reunions)
- Monetary cost to participate (extra cost for transportation, or food if the activity takes place after work, for instance)
- Discomfort, embarrassment, being unfamiliar with the library environment (neighborhood, building, or library system)
- Not knowing other people in the library, class, or activity (formality in social interaction)
- Lacking the ability or skills related to the activity at hand
- Lacking the motivation or social pressure from influential people in their lives (friends, spouse, children, employers, colleagues, etc.)

These issues will need to be evaluated and addressed as part of your outreach strategies. For instance, issues such as transportation, child care, or extra monetary cost can be thought of as part of your activity's expense and included in your funding request. Others, such as schedules, can be addressed with careful planning and knowledge of the potential customers' work and leisure timetables. Lastly, most of these issues must be addressed in your promotional efforts, which we discuss in chapter 8.

Place (Distribution or Location)

How accessible is the location of your library? What physical, emotional, or cultural barriers must your customer overcome in order to access your products and services?

Usually, the logistics of a library are simple: the customer comes to your facility. Although some library systems have home delivery, bookmobiles, and satellite outposts, most of your patrons regularly travel to your facility in order to find the products they are looking for. Moreover, most regular patrons were first brought to the library by their parents or grandparents, making the use of library services a long tradition in U.S. culture.

For your Latino community, however, your facility's location is a big factor. If your library is centrally located downtown or in an urban setting, many Latinos will walk or ride their bicycles, take public transportation, drive their cars, or arrange a ride with a friend or family member—not every family has two or more cars. Thus, weather conditions and transportation availability will likely affect the traffic of your Latino customers.

When libraries are located in city outskirts or in wooded areas with hills and winding roads, they are more difficult to reach for those without a car. This type of location opens a whole new discussion on how to bring the library to your patrons.

Whatever your library's location, consider the methods of commercial services that might have similar problems reaching customers, not so much because of location issues but because their competitors found new ways of distributing their products. Video stores, a hot business trend in the 1980s, have had to find new ways to deliver their products in recent years because of competition with on-demand satellite, cable television, and the Internet. To keep their customers motivated, they had to offer more than convenient brick-and-mortar locations and a broad selection of products—some techniques used have been incentives through promotions, home delivery, and no late fees. Companies are also selling collections and used videos and DVDs for people who prefer to collect movies, something to think about in terms of educated Latinos who like to own their materials. In this case, an incentive would be to request a book for review at the library—even maybe offer a librarian's review—and a service to purchase the book through the library to ensure the book or material will fit the patron's needs. Some members of your CLO or Latino Advisory Board might offer to review some materials, or you might find reviews on specialized Web sites such as *Criticas Spanish Language Authors and Book Reviews.*[13]

So, how do you bring the library to your customers who do not have transportation access to your facility? Consider the following ideas.

Media Drop-Off Boxes Located in Latino Neighborhoods

If the Latino population is concentrated in a particular part of town, as they often are, set up a drop-off station, accompanied by large bilingual signs, colorfully painted, where patrons can return books, CDs, videos, and other borrowed materials. This convenience will not only save patrons a trip, it also will provide your library with a visible presence right where they live.

You can work with your town officers for permission to set up drop boxes on streets or in other readily accessible public locations. You can also work with community partners to install drop boxes within their facilities—for example, a health clinic, a social services agency, a company with a large number of Latino employees, and so on. Ask permission to set up a drop-off box in a visible place where its use will not distract the organization's personnel. Arrange pick-up days two or three times per week.

When setting up drop-off stations, label Spanish books and videos with a phrase such as, "*Puede devolver este libro en los buzones situados en* [state locations of drop-off boxes]. *¡Gracias!* "This book/video can be returned at [state locations of drop-off boxes]. Thank you!"

Tell *all* of your patrons about the drop-off boxes, and encourage them to use this convenience so that your investment is more cost effective. Try the program for a certain amount of time, and then evaluate the results. The drop-box idea might be fundable by a corporation, a foundation, or an individual supporter with a particular interest in literacy—you might reduce your expense by securing such funding; the box could even provide a donor's recognition opportunity ("This drop-off station is made possible through the generous support of Mr. and Mrs. XYZ").

Deposit Collections

A different approach was used in Colorado's Lake County Public Library (Chickering-Moller 2001, pp. 51–52) as reported in their project outline and evaluation. They placed 150 inexpensive paperback books (in Spanish, English, and bilingual), for readers from preschool age through adult, at three nonprofit agencies during the project year. Each book carried a bookplate in Spanish with library locations and phone numbers and a label saying: "Welcome to the library. Please return this book to any one of the community libraries." Books were placed in plastic crates and distributed to the Catholic church, public health office, and community day care center.

The project assumed books might not be returned to the library. Staff members of hosting agencies were not asked to facilitate the project. Results indicated the church location and the day care center worked the best, while the public health office personnel, unaware of the project, moved the crate to an inaccessible location.

Temporary Library Card

Another way of bringing the library to the community is to hand out temporary library cards designed to introduce patrons to your library and entice them to apply for a real card. Without getting fancy, come up with a simple design printed on card stock (see Figure 6.1). Leave blanks for basic information such as name, address, and phone number so the potential customer can fill it in and bring it to the library for entry into your patron database.

Hand out these temporary cards in as many locations and on as many occasions as possible (such as strategic partners, market channels, and community leaders). Before or after Spanish mass or ESL or computer classes at community colleges, to children at public schools or at parent-teacher conferences, and at other market channels you have identified for your endeavor. Reach your audience with a promotional slogan, if you have one (and if not, we will work on one in chapter 8). Be sure to indicate that personal information is confidential, and specify what other documents they need to bring in order to verify their address. Include, if at all possible, a phone number with the legend "*Se habla espanol*" (Spanish spoken).

Little Haven City Public Library

123 First Lane

Little Haven City, NJ 12345

Nombre _____

Dirección _____

Teléfono _____

Si presenta esta tarjeta temporaria en su biblioteca pública
local, puede solicitar su membrecía permanente.
¡BIENVENIDO!

FIGURE 6.1   A Simple Design of a Temporary Library Card

Participating in your community partners' events will also give you the opportunity to sign up patrons and their families and advertise your free services. Network with your local hospital, health agencies, parade committees, local Latino Chamber of Commerce, church festivals, and celebrations and reach the local Latino community. If you have an available budget, offer magnets, bookmarks, or pens with bilingual information about your local library and/or your programs for Latino outreach. Even a coupon to borrow a free video, music CD, or educational CD-ROM or to enter a drawing to win promotional posters might do the trick.

Bookmobile

Bookmobiles are often successful in reaching families who live in distant areas, but the logistics can be complicated and expensive. Nevertheless, think about your resources and your community partners. Community partners might provide buses or vans to carry a small but enticing collection of Spanish and bilingual material and stop in front of the church after Spanish mass or on Saturdays and Sundays in the Latino neighborhood. Have plenty of library card applications and temporary library cards with you. Display big banners along the sides of the bus or van indicating the purpose of the bookmobile. Advertise bookmobile services with a picture of it on flyers distributed to children in schools; they will identify your vehicle and will lead parents to visit. An amplifier with some lively music might catch their attention even more. You do not have to offer this service on a continuous basis, but it may be a way of opening the door to your public library. The wonderful story of the Biblioburro, a Colombian ambulant library that reaches far outlying regions, is a great example of the power of willingness.[14]

Spanish-language Hotline

Establish a telephone hotline in Spanish, including a prompt for people who want to leave a question in Spanish, and have your Spanish-speaking personnel call them back with an answer within 24 hours. Ask callers to leave their name and phone number, and instruct your staff member to offer a free library card if they provide their complete information over the phone after they have answered their question. This is best at the end of the call because it is important to build rapport first. Promote the Spanish hotline in the local Spanish media, church, and community partners' bulletin boards.

Write a short pitch script for staff to use on the phone so they will feel comfortable and know what to say. Introductions and greetings are also important. Be aware of formalities and how to address people by their Spanish names. Although our U.S. society practices less formality, we need to recognize that not all people feel at ease having others address them by first name unless they are well acquainted, so in this case it's better to err on the side of formality.

Facilities and Location

Keep your signage multilingual so patrons can find their own way as much as possible, although as a last resort use graphic multicultural signage. Spanish Web sites and online catalogues are also useful tools.

Because online catalogues are hard to find in Spanish, keeping a card catalogue for Spanish and bilingual materials might be a good idea (this might be hard as many card catalogues disappeared a long time ago!). You can also run a printout of your Spanish collection and keep it close to the collection. Vertical racks for magazines and display shelves are visually enticing, as well. Use planograms (diagrams for book placement) and dual-language displays for marketing your Spanish books, and exhibit them together with their counterparts in English. Make it easy to find, make it fun!

Promotion

Creating promotional strategies consists of the integrated use of advertising, public relations, promotions, media, personal success stories, and promotional events to generate and sustain demand for your products and services. As already discussed, convincing messages geared to the Latino community need to accomplish the following:

- Highlight benefits your products and services will bring to their lives, and shore up disadvantages
- Emphasize and create awareness of library services
- Offer more appealing alternatives to usual behaviors, limiting beliefs, and habits through incentives, recognition, and rewards
- Inspire your Latino target audience to act
- Work closely with Hispanic media to advertise your offerings in locally read magazines and newspapers. It will generate positive buzz and word-of-mouth advertising about new books and services. If you have a more substantial budget, try some cross-promotion with local television and radio stations.
- Generate free publicity through press releases to local Hispanic media announcing newsworthy public programs and significant new services of special interest to the Latino audience. For example, story time featuring your new collection of Latino children's stories or film reviews for your Latino Movie Night.

Promotional strategies include creating appropriate and culturally effective messages and selecting media and communication channels that reach your Latino audience and other publics. You will also select appropriate media and communication channels, which involves defining which media to use, determining the timing for the promotion, and deciding who will deliver the message. Chapter 8 is dedicated to helping you develop practical ideas for promotional strategies you can use in addition to the ones you already have in place.

Publics (Empowering Your Latino Community)

Customers like to believe a company or organization's goal is to help them—not just take their money! For instance, people trust business owners who have experience in that business. As an example, a golf celebrity opens a golf store and advises his customers on merchandise and technique. Companies that represent their customers' interests, find out their customers' cultural preferences, and mirror their demographics internally and externally rapidly succeed in a new business environment.

Your target market—your local Latino customers—will be attracted to the fact that your services meet the needs and goals of their community because they are community-oriented individuals. Commitment and persistence are two very important factors in building credibility with your new Latino patrons, but knowledge and understanding of their needs and preferences are important, as well.

However, the term *publics* also refers to other groups involved in the strategic effort—people who influence your target market (family, relatives, spouses, friends, employers, colleagues, teachers, health care providers, government officers, and more) as we saw previously in this chapter when we discussed identifying your competition. Publics are also other members of your community, your library community, and your community at large; they are those who are involved in decisions about your library and your community—such as agencies that make decisions about budget and government officials who write, approve, and/or enforce legislation that might affect you or the Latino community you serve. Finally, also included in your publics are the *gatekeepers*, those who influence and control the content and delivery of media to your main Latino target audience, such as Latino newspapers, radio, TV, market channels, strategic partners, and so forth.

Influencing your Latino customers requires several strategic points of attack; one is directly to your target customers and the others are to these influencers. You will need to include them in your promotional efforts—to be discussed in chapter 8. To trigger your memory, see Worksheet 6.8.

Make a detailed list with contact information of all these allies whom you will partner with at different times in your marketing efforts, especially those policymakers and gatekeepers—media owners and producers and those who handle your information to the community—whose input you need to develop positive social pressure to encourage Latinos into action.

Partnerships

Changing social and cultural behaviors is often so complex that you will need other organizations' involvement to be effective. Strategic partnerships were extensively covered in chapter 3, but remember that you need to prioritize and define which organizations have similar goals to yours, which ones could become market channels for promotional purposes, and which others will work with you on a project basis. You will find specific tools and guidelines to work with your strategic partners in promotional efforts later in chapter 8.

Policy

Social marketing can help motivate change in individual behavior, but this change is difficult to sustain when the general and local environment ignores these efforts in the end. A social marketing approach to library outreach needs to be complemented with policy changes, media advocacy, and the support of the community at large. The benefits of outreach to the Latino community were discussed in chapter 1. The scope of this book—mostly to help librarians tackle outreach efforts in a practical way—does not allow extensive reflections on general or local policy. However, one way of influencing policies is to develop awareness about cultural factors in the choice of a profession or career and the shared responsibility of governmental agencies and the educational community. In a way, they are also gatekeepers that help create an attractive atmosphere toward the profession.

In the following you will find a list of initiatives, institutions, and organizations that have developed or participated in developing policies for Latino librarianship. Check them frequently to know their current and future plans. Remember to include these organizations, their policies, and their activities in your SWOT's external opportunities and threats related to promoting library jobs and educational opportunities for people interested in working with Latino populations, which is a vital element of positioning your library's resources. Subscribe to e-mail listservs for important policies, decisions, and issues in most of these organizations. Your Outreach Planning and Programming subcommittee will play an instrumental role in this research together with your human resources department.

If possible, become a member of those organizations that advocate for diversity in the workplace or in educational opportunities. You do not have to be Latino or speak Spanish to belong to REFORMA, the National Association to Promote Library and Information Services to Latinos and the Spanish-speaking—an affiliate of the ALA,[15] and/or EMIERT, the ALA's Ethnic and Multicultural Information Exchange Round Table.[16] You just have to share their values for your profession.

1. Initiative on Educational Excellence for Hispanic Americans (October 12, 2001): Signed by President George W. Bush creating the President's Advisory Commission on Educational Excellence for Hispanic Americans[17]
2. The National Library of Education (NLE): The federal government's primary resource center for education information provides collections and information services to the public, the education community, and other government agencies on current and historical programs, activities, and publications of the U.S. Department of Education; also offers federal education policy and education research and statistics[18]
3. The American Library Association (ALA);[19] its chapters, committees, discussion groups, and divisions; the Association for Library and Information Science Education (ALISE);[20] the International Federation of Library Associations and Institutions (IFLA);[21] state professional associations; and regional library cooperatives and consortiums, unions, and other local professional associations
4. State libraries; institutional and academic, school, and public libraries; friends of libraries and other associations, and institutions and philanthropic organizations interested in library development and success
5. Colleges and universities, community colleges, and all educational nonprofit and government organizations interested in diversity or the Latino community
6. The Hispanic Association of Colleges and Universities (HACU), representing more than 450 colleges and universities committed to Hispanic higher-education success in the United States, Puerto Rico, Latin America, Spain, and Portugal[22]

In addition, you can consult an excellent work, "Breaking through the Linguistic Barrier," where Sonia Ramírez Wohlmuth looks in depth at educational and librarianship opportunities for students who wish to serve Latino populations (Ramírez Wohlmuth 2000).

Purse Strings

Funding is always a hard call for libraries, not only for outreach efforts but merely to sustain day-to-day operations. Some sources come from government grants, donors, or foundations, but these types of funding are usually one-time events. Chapter 1 explored the need for a more sustainable funding effort, not only to provide products and services that serve Latino community needs but also to professionalize outreach efforts. By bringing together all the elements you need to consider, this book gives you the justification to research and obtain the necessary funding for your outreach strategy. Once you finalize your written plan, you have a document to show when you knock on doors for additional funding. Funding organizations need to see your plan in black and white, and the extent of your research will give you enough information to prove your point.

In closing this chapter, remember that your Latino customers are not going to pour in the door the first time you call. They might show up once for a program and then disappear for months, or they might come once in a while until they become familiar with the facility and your employees. They might also bring a friend, who might recommend someone else, and that someone might become a regular member. Even acculturated and highly educated Latinos might not be regular users of libraries.[23] You will attract these customers by building credibility within the community, empowering them to use your services and including them as a part of the library family with persistent programming and effective promotional strategies, two topics discussed in the following chapters.

Notes

1. SWOT strategy adapted from Bangs (1998).
2. W. Kandel and J. Cromartie, "Hispanics Find a Home in Rural America," *Amber Waves: The Economics of Food, Farming, Natural Resources, and Rural America,* U.S. Department of Agriculture Economic Research Service, February 2003, http://www.ers.usda.gov/AmberWaves/Feb03/Findings/HispanicsFind.htm (accessed January 11, 2010).

   In 1995, states with the largest share of the nation's Caucasians were California, New York, Texas, Pennsylvania, and Florida. Among these five states, only Texas and Florida are projected to have a larger share of the nation's white population in 2025 (compared to almost no change for California and decreases for New York and Pennsylvania). U.S. Census Bureau, "Population Projections for States by Age, Sex, Race, and Hispanic Origin: 1995 to 2025—Race and Hispanic Origin Distribution," October 1996, http://www.census.gov/population/www/projections/ppl47.html#hl-race (accessed January 11, 2010). The 2000 to 2006 projections have been superseded by estimates that are available at U.S. Census Bureau, "Population Estimates," http://www.census.gov/popest/estimates.php (accessed January 11, 2010).
3. WebJunction Spanish Outreach Program, Yolanda Cuesta, "SLO Workshop Materials Community Leader Interview Guide," October 6, 2006, http://www.webjunction.org/slo-workshop-materials/-/articles/content/439382?_OCLC_ARTICLES_getContentFromWJ=true (accessed January 11, 2010).
4. General degrees of acculturation, according to Terry J. Soto (2006), fall into the following categories: "unacculturated: 10 years or less; bicultural: 10–20 years; acculturated: 20+ years of residence in the U.S."
5. These assumptions are based on observations and surveys conducted by different marketing sources on several industries. You can also check the "Spanish Language Outreach Program Round 1 Focus Group Report" by Janet Salm, May 30, 2007, for additional information and to find focus groups questionnaires in English and Spanish that you can apply to your local Latino community at http://www.webjunction.org/slo-overview-and-reports/articles/content/448291?_OCLC_ARTICLES_ getContentFromWJ=true (accessed January 11, 2010).
6. Carmen Spina, "Random House Launches New Spanish Division," *Críticas,* May 15, 2006, http://www.criticasmagazine.com/article/CA6332341.html (accessed January 11, 2010).
7. Membership in the American Translators Association is not required to be a good translator. Moreover, many states do not require certification for translators and interpreters. However, belonging to a reputable professional association and having passed their examination is an indicator of professional status.
8. For additional information, see "Spanish-Language Publishing" in SpanishTranslation.com, May, 27, 2010, http://spanish-translation-blog.spanishtranslation.us/spanish-language-publishing-2010-05-27.html (accessed July 31, 2010).
9. BookExpo America, the biggest English-language review source for Spanish-language books, audio books, and videos for Spanish-speakers, was suspended at the time of writing this publication.
10. Aída Bardales, "Publishers Exhibit Plans for Spanish-Speaking Market," *Críticas,* June 15, 2006, http://www.criticasmagazine.com/article/CA6345642.html?industryid=48431 (accessed January 11, 2010).

11. Judith Rosen, "The Future of Hispanic Publishing," *Críticas,* May 15, 2006, http://www.criticas magazine.com/article/CA6332573.html (accessed January 11, 2010).

12. For a list of the top Latino movies, see "Top Ten Most Provocative Latino Films" and "Latino Films about Immigration" at LatinoStories.com, http://latinostories.com/Top_Ten_Lists/top_ten_latino_films_for_the_cla.htm (accessed July 31, 2010).

13. "Críticas Archives of Reviews of Spanish-language Titles for Adults and Children Available," LibraryJournal.com, June 11, 2009, http://www.libraryjournal.com/csp/cms/sites/LJ/Search/index.csp?search=criticas (accessed July 31, 2010).

14. Please see these pages published in the *New York Times* http://www.nytimes.com/2008/10/20/world/americas/20burro.html?_r=1 (accessed February 15, 2010). You can also watch this moving story at World Focus, http://worldfocus.org/blog/2009/09/14/biblioburro-a-donkey-library-visits-colombian-children/7240/ (accessed February 15, 2010).

15. See REFORMA's Web page at http://www.reforma.org (accessed January 11, 2010).

16. Find the EMIERT Web page at http://www.ala.org/ala/mgrps/rts/emiert/aboutemiert/aboutemiert.cfm (accessed January 11, 2010).

17. Find additional information at White House Initiative on Educational Excellence for Hispanic Americans, http://www.yic.gov/wwa/index.html (accessed January 11, 2010).

18. For additional information, see "The National Library of Education (NLE)," U.S. Department of Education, http://ies.ed.gov/ncee/projects/nat_ed_library.asp (accessed January 11, 2010).

19. The main page for the ALA is available at http://ala.org (accessed January 11, 2010).

20. The main page for ALISE is http://www.alise.org (accessed January 11, 2010).

21. The main page for IFLA is http://www.ifla.org (accessed January 11, 2010).

22. The main page for the Hispanic Association of Colleges and Universities is available at http://www.hacu.net/hacu (accessed January 11, 2010).

23. WebJunction Library Services, "Latinos and Perception of Public Libraries Report," conducted by the Tomas Rivera Policy Institute, http://www.webjunction.org/latino-perceptions/articles/content/10860971?_OCLC_ARTICLES_getContentFromWJ=true (accessed January 11, 2010).

WORKSHEET 6.1   Your Library's Internal Strengths and Weaknesses

Goal: Make a realistic inventory of your organization's internal resources.

Mission/Charter Statement	Internal Factor	Strength	Weakness
Provide and assure access to quality information, education, and recreational resources and learning opportunities	1. Collections: Adult Teens Children Seniors	Good start for adults (How good? What kind of Spanish-language or special-interest materials are there?)	Need to improve children's and teens' materials; no specific materials for seniors
	2. Additional services		Have not added new services in two years
Attract the local Latino communities	3. Latino membership	Some Latino library patrons (unknown number)	Need to increase and expand membership
Create, outreach, and promote culturally appropriate programs and services	4. Programs and services	Some experience with Día de los Niños/ Día de los Libros and Hispanic Heritage Month events in the past	High attendance, but lack of continuity in use of library services
	5. Outreach efforts	CLO in place	Sporadic programs, especially for children
	6. Promotional efforts	We work with one local Latino newspaper (Add more?)	Need to increase alternative and direct promotional methods

 From *¡Hola, amigos! A Plan for Latino Outreach* by Susana G. Baumann. Santa Barbara, CA: Libraries Unlimited. Copyright © 2011.

Mission/Charter Statement	Internal Factor	Strength	Weakness
Respond to their changing educational, cultural, and recreational needs and interests due to their different backgrounds and generational gaps	7. Demographics	Extensive demographics and cultural research in the local Latino community	Need to define better market segments by tracking demographic changes (not done in the past)
Commit to growing funding	8. Funding	Small but regular budget for collections	Not enough budget to increase programming
Develop internal and external resources including dedicated personnel	9. Customer service	Two bilingual part-time employees	Need two more? Some resistance to learn Spanish
	10. Personnel development	New LSTA grant for training	More bilingual and bicultural training needed
	11. Community partnerships	Two partnerships in place, some potential Latino Advisory Board members	Need to increase partnership opportunities
Develop appropriate technologies	12. Technology	WebJunction Spanish Outreach Program resources, also received donation of four computers three years ago	Lack of budget to buy enough computers jeopardizes program implementation

From ¡Hola, amigos! A Plan for Latino Outreach by Susana G. Baumann. Santa Barbara, CA: Libraries Unlimited. Copyright © 2011.

Mission/Charter Statement	Internal Factor	Strength	Weakness
Provide and assure access	13. Location	Bookmobile	Far from Latino neighborhood
	14. Facility	The inside is welcoming, with a clear and flexible layout	The outside is dull and unfriendly or unknown to other cultures
Help integrate this vibrant and diverse population	15. Reputation or credibility	New Latino trustee receptive to outreach effort	Low awareness; work with community leaders

NOTES

_____

_____

_____

_____

_____

_____

_____

 From *¡Hola, amigos! A Plan for Latino Outreach* by Susana G. Baumann. Santa Barbara, CA: Libraries Unlimited. Copyright © 2011.

Goal: Make a realistic inventory of your organization's external factors.

External Factor	Opportunity	Threat
1. Latino Advisory Board	Help to network and become library advocates	
2. Prospective members	Help define market segments	
3. Competition		Google Spanish library; local video stores expanding into Latino neighborhood
4. Legislation		Immigration law in Congress?
5. Economic environment	High rates of unemployment (offer employment information)	
6. ALA action	Support from Office of Diversity and round table discussions	
7. State Library		Possible budget cuts for next year
8. State Association	Diversity included as a conference topic	
9. REFORMA	Sources for collection development and hiring opportunities	We need to participate more and enroll our CLO members
10. Regional library cooperatives or consortiums	Training available to our employees	Budget cuts for next year (how would that affect us?)
11. Other		

From *¡Hola, amigos! A Plan for Latino Outreach* by Susana G. Baumann. Santa Barbara, CA: Libraries Unlimited. Copyright © 2011.

WORKSHEET 6.3 Long- and Short-Term Marketing Goals and Strategies

Goal: Determine concrete goals, assign responsibilities, and define schedules.

Three-Year Plan Long-Term Goals:	
What	1. Increase awareness of library services among the local Latino community.
	2. Increase number of cardholders.
	3. Select, prioritize, and address the most pressing informational needs in the local Latino community.
	4. Create appropriate and enticing activities for the whole Latino family.
How much	Awareness: Reach at least 30 percent of the Latino population in the community.
	Cardholders: Increase up to 3 percent of present cardholders. (If you presently have 100 Latino cardholders that would mean adding 30 additional cardholders each year. If your Latino membership is currently low, work with a low percentage of the community at large.)
	Prioritize three needs according to yearly needs assessment.
	Organize two family events and two bilingual programs for Latino children annually. Look for additional opportunities that might arise.
Who	Accomplish these goals through the Promotion and Advertising subcommittee, the Latino trustee (who also serves on the LAB), current Latino members, local media, market channels, and community strategic partners.
	Campaign will be supervised by the outreach director with the oversight and support of the CLO chair. (Remember, these roles might be one person.)
When	Three-year plan starts next month.

First Year: Short-Term Goal (first goal: Increase awareness of library services)	
What	Increase awareness through low-budget promotional strategies.
How much	Start with 10 percent of the Latino community at large and develop efforts progressively throughout the three years.
Who	Accomplish this goal through the Promotion and Advertising subcommittee, the Latino trustee (who also serves on the LAB), current Latino members, local media, market channels, and community strategic partners.
When	This will take place during the first month of each quarter in the current fiscal year (four times/year).

 From ¡Hola, amigos! A Plan for Latino Outreach by Susana G. Baumann. Santa Barbara, CA: Libraries Unlimited. Copyright © 2011.

First Year: Short-Term Goal (second goal: Increase number of cardholders)	
What	Increase number of Latino cardholders.
How much	Start by 3 percent of current Latino cardholders and develop efforts progressively through three years
Who	Accomplish this goal through the Promotion and Advertising subcommittee, the Latino trustee (who also serves on the LAB), and current Latino and general cardholders.
When	This will take place all through the year with an additional two-week mini-campaign during Hispanic Heritage Month.

NOTES

_____

_____

_____

_____

_____

_____

_____

WORKSHEET 6.4   Assess and Prioritize Needs

Goal: Define reasons to prioritize a need detected in your local Latino community.

1. What is the need your CLO and your organization will address?

2. What are the angles you could take or resources you could use in addressing this need?

3. How did you find out about this need, and what other sources did you use to confirm it?

4. Are segments of your local Latino population readier to receive the information related to this need? Are there segments for whom the consequences related to this issue are more severe?

5. What are the main ways in which the issue could be addressed?
   - Providing information
   - Providing a service/class/activity
   - Providing a location or facility
   - Expanding your local geographic area
   - Making connections with strategic partners
   - Other _____

6. What are the most common or most serious consequences the Latino community confronts regarding this issue?

7. What are the community's limiting beliefs and cultural behaviors related to this issue?

8. Are other organizations addressing the same issue? How can you collaborate/partner with them?

9. How can you afford to implement solutions—classes, events, locations, etc.—related to this issue? Do you have the funding, personnel, information, facility, and materials needed? If not, what action is required?

10. What are the expected results if your organization pursues this issue? What are the benefits for the Latino community, for segments of the community, and for the community at large?

 From *¡Hola, amigos! A Plan for Latino Outreach* by Susana G. Baumann. Santa Barbara, CA: Libraries Unlimited. Copyright © 2011.

Goal: Research and understand limiting beliefs, barriers, and established behaviors that prevent Latino customers from using library services.

My target group is: The Latino community at large in Little Haven City.			
What you want to promote	**Competing behaviors**	**Opposing messages/ messengers**	**Obstacles and limiting beliefs**
Literacy	Low literacy levels	Radio and television	I don't need to read more/better to do what I do.
Reading habits	Going out or partying, staying home with family	Friends	Reading habits are: Boring/hard/difficult Not necessary Good for children, not adults Good for females, not for males
Reading to their children	Playing sports or shopping	Spouse, children	I have no time. My children prefer something else (TV, games). My spouse wants me to take the children out of the house!
Computer literacy (at the library)	Staying home and resting	Family	Lack of typing skills Lack of English skills Not having a computer at home Not needed for work No transportation
Learning English	Speaking Spanish at work and at home	Family, employer, friends TV in Spanish News in Spanish	I don't need to learn English to work, communicate, or be informed. I have no time or transportation.

NOTES

_____

_____

_____

_____

My target group is: Latino and Latino American teens from different backgrounds who speak fluent English (immigrants and first generation born in the United States) but have difficulties with reading skills*

What you want to promote	Competing behaviors	Opposing messages/ messengers	Obstacles and limiting beliefs
Improve reading habits (reading skills *and* the inclination for reading)	It's vacation time! Going out or partying Staying home with family Playing sports Shopping Reading magazines, watching videos, playing video games Hanging out with friends Going to church	Radio and television Friends Family messages (parents do not read or do not read in English) Video games Working during the summer (to help support the family)	I don't need to read more/better to do what I do. College is not for me. I prefer something else (TV, games, hanging out). Reading habits are boring/hard/difficult. Reading is not necessary for physical work. I have no transportation.

*The distinction of Latino or Latino American teens compared to other immigrant teens or American teens might look discriminatory—why not include them in a more generic group? However, there might be different cultural issues you need to confront, for instance, between Latinos and youth of different nationalities. Reading material and activities might address those issues. These and other factors need to be considered at the preparation stage and will depend on the activity goals.

NOTES

_____

_____

_____

_____

_____

_____

WORKSHEET 6.6A Positioning Activities, Programs, or Services You Plan to Promote (Example 1)

Goal: Research and understand the benefits Latino customers expect from library services.

My target group is: Spanish-speaking immigrants looking for better employment opportunities

Product your library promotes	Perceived personal benefits	Fewer barriers/ obstacles/cost	Social pressure (influencers)
Learning English to improve employment opportunities	I can increase work opportunities and earn a better salary. I can help and communicate with my children. I can keep Spanish at home, be proud of my heritage, and pass it on to my children. I can (eventually) become a citizen of this country.	ESL classes are free at the library. They offer classes at different levels. They (also) offer classes through community partners that are closer to my house/work. Classes are scheduled around my work schedules. Classes address my needs (work, family, etc.).	I can "get ahead" of the **new immigration law!** I can communicate with **government officials, police, doctors,** and my **children's teachers.** I can become a role model for **my children** and **other immigrants** like me. My **employers** might provide better advancement opportunities.

NOTES

_____

_____

_____

_____

_____

WORKSHEET 6.6B Positioning Activities or Services You Plan to Promote (Example 2)

My target group is: Latino and Latino American teens from different backgrounds who speak fluent English (immigrants and first generation born in the United States) but have difficulties with reading skills			
Product your library promotes	**Perceived personal benefits**	**Fewer barriers/ obstacles/cost**	**Social pressure (influencers)**
Latino Teen Summer Club (For later promotional purposes, this *theme* is more appealing than promoting a reading summer session for Latino teens)	A place where I can go with my friends. I am free to choose activities and readings. I participate in additional activities related to reading (organize and participate in skits, do reading plays, post what I do on the Internet, etc.). I receive some sort of cool incentive if I finish the summer program. I meet new friends and we hang out at the library after the activity or do other things in town. I have a social activity apart from my family and can do something different in the summer.	The librarians are friendly and welcoming. They have a fantastic program that makes reading easy and not boring at all! The schedule is cool because it is after my working hours. If I miss one session, I can come during the week and catch up with a tutor. I can bring friends who want to participate. The library organized a carpool with some parents/volunteers so we all have transportation. We can play video games after the session and learn other computer activities.	I make **my parents** happy while I have fun. I will be in better shape for school next year. **My favorite teacher/ counselor** recommended this program. I receive new information about educational opportunities (for instance, I did not know I could get in a **community college** for a two-year degree before going to college!). Maybe **college** is an option for me after all, and I'll get a **better job** and **employment** opportunities.

NOTES

_____

_____

_____

_____

 From *¡Hola, amigos! A Plan for Latino Outreach* by Susana G. Baumann. Santa Barbara, CA: Libraries Unlimited. Copyright © 2011.

WORKSHEET 6.7 Positioning Statement

Goal: The positioning statement determines the aspects of your activity or program that are customer centered, grounded in actual accomplishments and relationships that make your place, products, and services unique for a particular audience. The positioning statement is the base, or concept, of your promotional campaign.

Your target audience: Latino and Latino American teens from different backgrounds who speak fluent English (immigrants and first generation born in the United States) but have difficulties with reading skills

The service name or category: Latino Teen Summer Club

Their problems, wants, and needs: Improve reading habits (reading skills *and* the inclination for reading)

A key benefit: A place where teens can go with friends, choose activities and readings, participate in additional activities related to reading (organize and participate in skits, do reading plays, post on the Internet, etc.), receive incentives, meet new friends, and have a social activity apart from their family

The key differentiation: Librarians are friendly and welcoming, they have a fantastic program that makes reading easy and not boring at all, the schedule is after working hours, tutoring is available, friends can participate, additional activities are offered, and logistics are solved

NOTES

WORKSHEET 6.8   Latino Customers' Influencers Memory Jogger

Goal: Get other publics or influencers to aid you in promoting library services when targeting a specific market segment.

1. State level: policy makers, immigration enforcement, employment, labor agencies, etc.

2. Town/city level: administrators, law enforcement, school administrators, teachers, etc.

3. Neighborhood: community organizers, social work agencies, clinics and hospitals, etc.

4. Other library cardholders: current members, Friends of the Library, stakeholders, etc.

5. Family environment: family, spouse, children, relatives, friends, colleagues, co-workers, etc.

6. Community leaders (from chapter 3)

7. Business and organizations (market channels) (from chapter 3)

8. Strategic partners (from chapter 3)

9. Media outlets: local and regional newspapers, magazines, radio, and television

NOTES

_____

_____

_____

_____

_____

From *¡Hola, amigos! A Plan for Latino Outreach* by Susana G. Baumann. Santa Barbara, CA: Libraries Unlimited. Copyright © 2011.

Chapter 7

Planning and Implementing Your Outreach Activities

Overview

"To get [Latino] parents' attention is a challenge," says Judith Rodriguez from the Connecting Libraries and Schools Project at the New York Public Library. "If the parents are not highly motivated, they will not go to the library to hear a library talk about reading" (Rodriguez 2000, p. 42).

Just as Rodriguez affirms, once you have created the best conditions to attract Latino patrons, your challenge is to bring them in and keep them coming into your library to use your services. Going out and finding customers is important, especially when they are not aware of your services or materials or are not familiar with the concept of your institution, but keeping them entails enduring commitment and persistent work.

Your goal is to create long-term credibility within the Latino community, have them trust your institution to represent their needs and wants, and make them feel at home every time they go for services. In addition, your outreach activities will help expand services in your area as well as increase awareness of what your target community is all about. Outreach activities involve developing ideas to attract specific groups of Latinos, to continue generating interest, and to ensure service continuity.

This chapter focuses on defining strategies for action and generating incentives to set in motion specific behaviors you want from your market. While general promotion of library services—see chapter 8—improves the library's image among Latinos, entices Latinos into the library and contributes to an educational experience for the community as a whole, outreach activities target specific market groups. Outreach activities are a call for action!

Understanding this difference is extremely important in outreach efforts. You might organize an activity with a good outcome, you may even be able to give out new library cards, but if you stop there, your new target audience might vanish! Why? Because people get busy with their lives!

Customers need constant motivation. Consider that there may be no real change in their belief system about library services with just one event; more importantly, they have not internalized the benefits of changing their old habits. In other words, your Latino customers might respond to a high stimulus—a fun event with good food—but then go back to their homes and their old ways.

Remember, people are creatures of habit. You can change habits by developing a persistent educational campaign while enticing your different target markets into activities specifically designed to fit their likes and needs. If the effort needed to break habitual behaviors is high, then the predisposition or readiness of your Latino customers toward your services is low. The effort required from you will be continuously high—and frustrating—if your efforts are sporadic, without an overall plan, direction, or evaluation of results. However, as you continue to sustain and target your efforts in an appropriate, planned way, your market's predisposition will increase and your efforts will diminish.

You also need to base your outreach activities on the ideas you developed in your vision and mission statement (chapter 2). If you talked about "lifelong learning opportunities for a diverse and changing population" (Queens Library Mission Statement), then you cannot offer just one or two activities every two or three years! If you talked about "books and a variety of other formats," then you need to make sure your collections are varied and in good standing. And if you talked about meeting "the informational, educational, cultural, and recreational needs and interest" of your local Latino community, then you better make sure you are totally immersed in the needs and wants of your current or potential Latino customers and ready to offer a variety of activities, services, and materials to fit that promise.

At the end of this chapter, you will find a series of possible topics, activities, and programs offered by libraries around the country and some other ideas and suggestions for services. Not all of these offerings will apply to your audience, so only try them if they seem to fit after you have done your market analysis and needs assessment. Resist the temptation of cutting corners; it will cost you money and effort and will be a frustrating experience for you and your staff.

Let us start by looking at specific target markets and prioritizing their needs and your resources.

Market Segments

> Your motto: Market segmentation, market segmentation, market segmentation!

In our Little Haven City list of potential needs (chapter 6), we talked about Latino families whose children need help with homework and after-school activities. Spanish-speaking mothers and Latino teenagers, for instance, have the same concern about homework help, however, the way mothers need to be addressed is different from the way teens will receive your message. Their views, concerns, and decision-making processes are different, and you need to make sure the message each one receives is the appropriate one to help them change behaviors.

Who belongs to a market segment? Chapter 4 discusses small groups of people who share variables, such as language ability, age, and country of origin or gender. These individuals can be grouped and defined as a market segment according to certain characteristics. In each market segment, a variable might take the lead to define the segment as in the following examples:

- When discussing Latinos of different religions, nationalities of origin, age, or gender, we make *ethnicity* the leading variable.
- With Latino seniors of all races, religions, and nationalities of origin, we make *ethnicity* and *age* the leading variables.
- In regards to Latino women of all races, nationalities of origin, and ages, we make *ethnicity* and *gender* the leading variables.

Each segment might have other common variables:

- Latino men, Catholic, married, who were born in the United States
- Latino seniors, of Mexican origin, retired, who were born in the United States
- Latino women, of Puerto Rican origin, students, who were born in the United States

Now you found a secondary common variable, "born in the United States," that ties all three subsegments together. However, does the fact that these three groups share the variable "born in the United States" make them a consistent monolithic segment? Certainly not, unless specific aspects are being targeted for that particular characteristic. Do they speak English? Are they familiar with the library system? Are or have they been part of the workforce? The answers to these questions will direct you to the type of materials and services you need to promote.

However, even if these individuals have similarities—they are all familiar with the library system, for instance—there still will be differences in the way they carry their backgrounds—how they handle information, their reading habits, and the way they will respond to different stimulus. You need to be specific about the characteristics of each segment to define *your goals* and create the desired strategies.

What do you want them to do? What changes in this group's behavior do you need to encourage to attract them into specific materials or services? For instance, in the aforementioned example, the goal might be to provide health literacy to Latinos, introduce them to the benefits of health prevention and nutrition, and help them lower their health risks. Then you need to find out how each segment uses the health care system, which of the three segments is more ready or is more willing to take action, and which one will need more incentive to change its behaviors.

In the library setting, you might consider *language ability* a common variable if your goal is increasing the local Latino population's English literacy by offering an ESL class at your library. However, you will need to know other characteristics of each segment. From the case scenario developed in chapter 4, we know that over 60 percent of the population needs English instruction. However, what is the level of readiness of each group? What is their level of literacy in Spanish? What logistics do you need for each group to participate in your class? What is each group's level of interest or motivation in learning English? With these results, you will then plan and implement your outreach strategy, devise your service or activity, and create promotional strategies to motivate change.

The more you segment your market, the easier it is to find common ground and target it more specifically. For instance, if you look at levels of education, you might find out that in your local population, most Spanish-dominant individuals share the variable "less than elementary or elementary level of education" (as seen on the example in Worksheet 7.1), which will raise a concern that these individuals may not have enough literacy in Spanish to learn a second language. Therefore, you focus on the second group, "less than high school or high school level of education," and you might make an educational milestone a requirement to enter the class or require a short placement test (this is just a hypothetical suggestion).[1]

It might sound unfair or discriminatory, but you need to use your resources in the most time- and cost-effective way possible. Community colleges and universities require placement tests for these reasons. Also, you do not want to create false expectations about the learning possibilities of all individuals. ESL classes with participants at different levels of literacy can end in frustration, disappointment, and desertion. You wasted your resources, your class is discredited, and your Latino patrons are not coming back for a second round. It also does not mean you will abandon your first group. It means you will prepare your resources adequately to approach the needs of that particular group.

Within your target segment, you might want to add another variable, such as gender, and gear your class to stay-at-home mothers who are ready to join the workforce again or males working locally in a specific industry. Your market segment is now reduced; however, you might be able to prepare very specific logistics for the class and conduct very specific promotional strategies to that particular group based on strong factors that will motivate the group to change their behavior.

When There Is More Than One Target Segment

Another important notion is that of market segment overlaps. This concept is important because we might think we have a lot in common with certain people in our lives, such as colleagues or friends. We perceive the societal segments we belong to, such as library employees or Caucasians or Americans, as monolithic. On the other hand, we share dimensions such as Catholic, parents, or sports fans with people we consider out of our segment or social bubble. Those overlaps are the ones marketers use to extend their strategies across different social groups and capitalize efforts targeting those groups for specific needs.

A clear example would be an activity such as an ESL class that targets market segments defined by language ability—for instance, Spanish-speaking patrons and speakers of other languages. You can look at the variables they have in common that would provide you with information for planning that service—levels of education, time of residence in the United States, and literacy levels—and plan the class for all of them. However, your promotional strategies would be different if you are targeting, for instance, Spanish-, Russian-, and Chinese-speaking populations because besides language differences, their lifestyles, levels of readiness, and motivation to take the class might be different.

You can also think of other variables Latinos share with *you* in order to better understand their needs: Are they parents? Do they love their families and children? Are their children in a public school just like yours? Are they Christian? Do they share your values about a society that prioritizes freedom and equality? Are they hard-working people just as you are?

Thinking about these variables that you and your Latino patrons have in common will help you bridge the cultural gap more than any training or workshop you could attend and will allow you to build personal relationships with your local Latino families. As discussed in chapter 1, this understanding will build the bridge that provides them with the opportunity to become well-integrated members of this society and its language and culture.

Your Market Segments' Priorities

By now, having done your market research, you already know how many prospects are in your market, and you have defined specific groups within your Latino market following the guidelines in chapter 4 and the criteria we described in the previous sections. Now it is time to establish priorities and make a decision about which groups within that population you are able to target first. Families with children or teens, recent immigrant workers, or established business and professional people are all part of your plan. However, you need to determine your target markets and arrange them in a sequence of time and effort defined by your target markets' levels of readiness and your resources (SWOTs).

For instance, in your Latino market mix you might have some Mexican families who have been established in the area for a while and send their children to local schools. You can target these families through their teenage children, who probably speak English well and are familiar with library services (because they have seen libraries in school or because they have participated in guided tours to the local public library). They may be more motivated to use the library and may influence their family to use it or bring home information about other activities related to their parents or adult relatives.

Your strategies do not have to target just one segment. Teenager and youth activities will generate parenting involvement—signing for their library card, authorizing an activity, or regarding school issues (homework help), in which case teachers or counselors (their influencers) might be involved. You can work with simple diagrams, such as Figure 7.1, to develop your priorities.

You can extend the diagram to another degree of influence if your purpose is to involve other members of the community in this effort (see Figure 7.2). In this case, you think of the influencers of the influencers and also try to work with them.

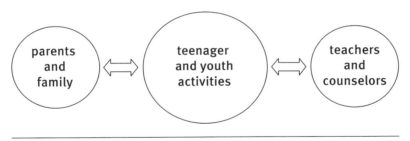

FIGURE 7.1   **Target Markets' Influencers**

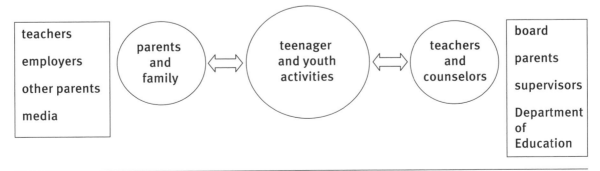

FIGURE 7.2   **Expanded Target Markets' Influencers**

You can use these tools to address different Latino market segments at different times of year, following school schedules, seasonal work, or other factors that might affect their involvement. Check your market analysis for guidance—it will pay off now.

Some groups will be easier to find than others, and some will be larger than others. As you go through possible materials and services to attract Latino clientele, you will find that some activities will be more costly than others, some will require less logistics, and some simply will not work with *your* Latino base. Some will not be appropriate for the segment you are trying to reach. Use your educated guess, and run ideas by your CLO and your LAB; pretesting strategies will give you a better chance to find the one that does work.

Never leave the decision in the customer's hands to contact you for services. Your odds of having Latino customers take the initiative about library services are low, so you need to be proactive and motivate them to take action.

Creating Incentives

In the general market, business owners are confronted every day with the uncertainty of who will buy from them until they establish a number of repeat customers from whom they learn buying habits. Once you establish a Latino customer base, you will also be able to learn what their needs are and what they are looking for—this information will help you make strategic decisions about what services you need to offer and how you should advertise them. In the meantime, however, you might want to try another approach that adds a little to the perspective of your Latino community needs assessment.

Coke, Anybody?

Marketing is not a science and, most of the time, is like navigating a plane. You have a route and need to keep your plane on course, but rarely are you perfectly on target. You are guesstimating with some accuracy and taking moderate risks. You need some a priori information to know that the service or services you have in mind will be well received; in actuality, however, many products on the market are imposed on us. Let us see how this strategy works.

Do you like to drink soda? Is there a real *need* for soda? Do sodas have nutritional value or some component essential to your health? You know the answers to all these questions. However, the soda market is one of the largest markets in the world! (For instance, Mexico is the world's number two consumer of soda after the United States with an average of 155 liters per capita consumed annually.)

How do soda companies assess the need of the markets to drink their product? They build on real needs, which are people's drinking habits and cravings for sugar—that is, cultural habits (Korzenny and Korzenny 2005); they develop a product that is presented to the market with particular physical and image characteristics. The process works like this:

Assess the need → redefine the need → create the incentive → change habits

Based on *real needs*—drinking/craving sugar—marketing *redefines the consumer's needs* and *creates incentives* that will *change habits* in the consumer.

Would you drink water with sugar? Most people would not, but they would drink lemonade, orange drinks, root beers, colas, and more. With well-formulated taste that appeals to a broad part of the population (hence the importance of marketing promotions and pre-testing products), companies offer cold, refreshing, bubbly, and sweet sodas. In addition, marketers build an attractive image of the product that relates the product to your personal characteristics, habits, or concerns—that is, they create an *appeal* for the product. For instance, Coke advertises over 700 low- and no-calorie beverages in their portfolio. They also announced that by the end of 2008, they plan to include Guideline Daily Amount (GDA) nutrition labeling on all their European packaging. And as a part of their branding campaign, the company and foundation spent $6 million to support active, healthy lifestyle programs in 2007. As you can see, they intentionally create an image that appeals to health and credibility among their consumers.

So how can you create *appeal* for your library materials and services? People are creatures of habit, and they get into a routine of doing or not doing things a certain way. It will take some incentives to break Latinos' behaviors related to library services.

An Outreach Strategy Is a Benefit-Oriented Strategy

If you observe product advertising on television, you probably notice that some ads are selling a benefit rather than the actual product features. For instance, cars sell safety or prestige, deodorizers sell relaxation or a cozy home, and baby products sell happy babies and tireless mothers.

This important shift in advertising is the result of the realization that if marketers concentrate on advertising products, customers might try a product once and then try another product from a different brand with similar features or characteristics. However, if marketers can build a strong relationship with the customer's emotional response to their product, based on their needs and concerns, by offering benefits and incentives that make their product unique, then they have won that customer for life. Korzenny and Korzenny (2005, pp. 11–12) maintain that "marketing is a work of love," and organizations need to establish strong relationships with Latino customers and must find out about their preferences, needs, and expectations in order to help them make reasonable behavioral changes based on the beneficial aspects of taking that action.

First, let us talk about incentives and benefits related to concerns. Is there anything more difficult than selling water in a bottle when you can open the faucet and have a drink? Yet companies are selling millions of bottles of water! They base their promotional efforts on certain emotional responses:

- **Fear**: The health risk of drinking contaminated water
- **Image**: The benefit of drinking more water to lose weight
- **Health**: The daily hydration needs
- **Stress and time constraints**: The convenience of carrying a little bottle in your bag
- **Social expectation**: Acting or looking like the celebrity on the commercial

All these ideas relate more to the consumer's concerns and emotional responses than with the product of water.

In our Little Haven City case scenario (chapter 6), we detected that recent immigrants in the Latino community need help with homework and after-school programs for their children. However, they do not come to the library for that help. The local school is overwhelmed with Spanish-speaking children of all ages who need extra help. You have a grant or online program that can help lessen the need. Why do Latino mothers not come to you for help? They might not know about the program, or they might be concerned about some of the issues we mentioned—confidential information, communication with your staff, transportation, work schedules, and so forth. Why do Latino teens not come for help? They might have similar concerns in addition to their own, such as lack of familiarity with the library, shyness, not having a computer at home, and so on. In order to reach your goals, you need to redefine the need, create incentives, and work on changing habits to overcome their inertia.

Developing your strategy with a positioning statement every time you plan to offer a material or service was discussed in chapter 6, and the case scenario is applied to the following example:

Your target audience: Little Haven City recent Latino immigrant families with children in school whose parents lack English language skills; mothers of children 9 to 12 years old and children will be addressed as two separate groups
The service name or category: Online homework help
Their problems, wants, and needs: Help with homework and after-school activities
A key benefit: Help for your child in free 20-minute sessions from a live online tutor
The key differentiation: Accessed from home, school, and even the library and available in English and Spanish for students in 4th to 12th grades

As you already know the service you are offering—online homework help—you are aiming now to change your customers' view of this service in response to their assessed needs and wants by presenting the service under a different light. Therefore, you also need to define the following:

1. The desired behavior you want to trigger
2. The concerns and emotional responses you want to address
3. Depending on the type of outreach activity, you might want to add an incentive—a promotional item, an idea, or a practice that will sustain your campaign

Examples of incentives include the following:

- Promotional products such as free handouts, storybooks, magazines or textbooks, promotional DVDs or CDs (some music publishing companies might donate or sell at cents per unit), premiums, and gifts (bookmarks, T-shirts, coffee mugs, etc.).
- Promotional ideas include promotional coupons or gift certificates from strategic partners, a recognition award, games, and contests (a trivia contest for a prize).
- Promotional practices consist of offering an extra service (help downloading and burning CDs from the Internet), a product or service demonstration (staff who help them learn the online homework help program), or a special activity to motivate your customers to engage in your offering (an employment fair after a résumé-writing class).

Our example of online homework help might target "Latino children in middle public schools" more specifically. Their grades might be dragging because they lack that extra help. The desired behavior you want to trigger in this group is that they take advantage of online homework help at home or at the library, as some might not have computers at home. Rethink the service in terms of the concerns and emotional responses you want to address. For instance, you can address these potential concerns of Latino children:

> The Los Angeles County Library System has an excellent video on their Web site targeting teenagers for live online homework help. All influencers are portrayed, including teachers, peers, and other young people in the community. The video is sponsored by strategic partners in the community. The video not only acts as a promotional tool but also as an implementation tool that shows how to use the online program. However, it would be interesting to know how they advertise the site among teenagers of different backgrounds and their rate of success with this program. To see the video visit http://www.colapublib.org/children/tutor/index.html (accessed January 10, 2010).

- **Fear**: Going to summer school or repeating the course
- **Image:** Looking inept in front of peers or not up to the task
- **Family:** Making parents upset or looking as uncooperative in front of extended family
- **Stress and time constraints:** Homework taking too much time and not being able to enjoy other activities outside school
- **Social expectation:** Looking and feeling like an outsider or foreigner

A promotional item, idea, practice, or object for this particular offering might be providing a promotional DVD with music they can enjoy, a coupon to the ice-cream parlor, or similar incentives just for learning to access the online homework-help program at the library.

You also will use these ideas later on in your promotional materials. However, these steps are part of positioning and implementing your service because some tasks need to be thought out and planned. Who is going to teach these teenagers how to access the online homework help? Is it someone at the library? Are you going to pair them with more advanced students or students who already use the online program? Is there going to be a schedule to get trained? Do they have to register or just show up? What type of incentives are you offering? Who is going to donate or cooperate with the incentives?

You might not be able to respond to all the needs and wants of your Latino customers, or you might be able to do it at a future time. However, this approach does not promote tangibles as much as a specific change of behavior—feeling better about themselves, achieving success, and contributing to their family's goals—and improves their perception toward those library materials, services, or activities that present a solution to their problems.

Worksheet 7.2 includes all aspects we discussed in this section. We have applied the same concepts to the example we developed in chapter 6 for the Latino Teen Summer Club. You will find a blank version in chapter 10.

Consider another example. Suppose you detected a need for learning English in your Latino community; however, because of busy working schedules, most workers in a certain location are unable to attend your ESL classes, which you already have in place or have the budget to conduct. Attending ESL classes after a long day of work—especially physical work—is hard for workers who might have literacy issues in Spanish or who have not been in school for a long time. In addition, learning English might not be attractive to some immigrants who have limiting beliefs—it's not necessary, it's not for me, and so on. Therefore, the old habits kick in—go home, rest, and stay with family—instead of coming to the library to take the class. An incentive to your outreach activity will trigger a change in behavior, something concrete they can look forward to—for instance, organizing a job fair with local employers at the end of the course for participants or providing work contacts with potential employers who sponsor the class.

This outreach activity involves a few benefits for you, for them, and for the community at large. You get to bring them in the door and promote additional services, they get to learn something specific that will enhance their lives and the lives of their families, and you get to work with community partners and influencers who benefit from workers who are more qualified and help improve the economic dynamic in your area. If the outreach activity is successful, local employers might become a potential source of funding for similar courses in the future. They might even offer their location to sponsor the class at a more convenient time for their workers—for instance, after a work shift. It is a win-win situation!

In summary, you redefine your service or activity by emphasizing your target community's perspective on the benefits, incentives, and results. Let us now see how you can implement your outreach strategy, a crucial step as all the elements of your plan will come together.

Implementing Your Outreach Strategy

The implementation phase covers all preparatory activities, follows up the activity development, sets up and follows up the promotional plan, and evaluates the strategy. An implementation plan includes the following:

- Defining your outreach activity
- Planning internal procedures
- Planning promotional materials and public relations strategies
- Putting monitoring and evaluation methods in place

The first two topics are covered in this chapter and the last two in chapter 8, "Promoting Your Library," and chapter 9, "Evaluating Results and Procedures."

Your Outreach Activities

You now are familiar with your target segments—you understand who they are, what they need, and how to approach them. How do you decide what materials/services to offer them? Go back to your list of wants and needs in chapter 6 and select and run ideas by your CLO and LAB.

Some programming ideas might be directly related to literacy; others may be informational, in sync with participation in community events or cultural celebrations. Whatever programs you choose for your target market, be sure to put them in context, verify the benefits your target segment will perceive, define a desired behavior change, and position the product in relation to old behaviors, your hardest competition.

Once you have chosen a service or activity that might fit your market segment's profile, follow the procedures we spoke about in chapter 6 and this chapter. It is recommended that you fill out worksheets 6.5 and 6.6, and worksheets 7.1 and 7.2 for each activity. It may sound like a lot of work, but you will get used to thinking through these ideas for each activity. Do not forget to include your CLO and LAB members, other staff potentially involved in the outreach strategy, or even current Latino cardholders.

You can also consider the ideas discussed in the next section, which might help you define specific outreach materials, services, and activities for the Latino community. Examples are from library programming around the country and even abroad, and the suggestions might enrich your activities or present them from another perspective. These outreach activities are organized by age and topic of interest specifically to your local Latino community but also to the library and your community at large. Please note that some of these activities might not be current; however, they still offer good ideas.

In pursuing attractive outreach strategies for your Latino patrons, you can generate interest with workshops, events, and ongoing activities. Some of the following activities need the input of community partners, and in some instances your library might merely act as an event coordinator or facilitator, offering your facilities, informational materials, and/or refreshments. Remember your goal: welcome the participants, and present a table with information to promote library services, bilingual library applications, brochures, and all the other "weapons" you can afford!

Topics and Activities

Latino Adults and Seniors

1. **Activities that will increase educational and literacy opportunities (for high school or vocational school degrees [GEDs], adult education classes, and community colleges and universities in your area):** Many libraries have been successful with computer classes. Offer assistance in Spanish, English, or a combination of both if you already include computer classes in your regular services.

   - Hector Marino, the Coordinator of Technical and Computer Services at Des Plaines Public Library in Des Plaines, Illinois, developed and conducted an Internet Basics class for Spanish-speakers and created additional classes on topics such as how to buy computers, using e-mail, using files/folders, searching the Internet, and using electronic resources. So did several other libraries around the country. All the classes were taught in Spanish. See WebJunction, "Spanish-Language Computer Classes for Patrons," http://www.webjunction.org/spanish-comput ers/-/articles/content/434071?printable=true (accessed January 21, 2010).
   - Elena Lara, the Hispanic Outreach Coordinator of the Round Lake Area Library (Illinois), is managing a successful computer workshop program in Spanish. "We offer basic workshops, which include an introduction to computers, learning to use a mouse, basic internet, MS Word, and E-mail." She believes word-of-mouth and working with partnerships are very important. She shares information with organizations like ChildServ, Mano a Mano, and various ESL programs and participates as an exhibitor at local and county events. "I make a point to inform them about all the services the library offers. During class, I pass out handouts in Spanish and try to get to hands-on experience as quickly as possible. I also incorporate English into the sessions. I feel it is important that they learn English computer vocabulary words since English is the most common language they will see on the screen."[2]

2. **Language acquisition and language literacy, both in English and Spanish, and how to acquire and keep bilingual skills in adult education:** Offering ESL classes at the library or collaborating with other agencies who offer the classes introduces immigrants to library services. Design ESL classes that are more specific to the needs of your Latino demographics, such as English for Specific Purposes.[3] Many libraries now start conversational bilingual classes to practice English and Spanish conversation.

  - The *Intercambio* program at Colorado Mountain College pairs Latinos with Americans to practice conversational skills. See http://www.coloradomtn.edu/cms/One. aspx?portalId=2935482&pageId=3447568 (accessed January 21, 2010).
  - The English Language Institute of Michigan University offers "The Migrant Worker and Outreach Education Program," which revolves around a service-learning course the English Language Institute (ELI) offers to students at the University of Michigan in the spring and summer terms about migrant farm workers' sociocultural background and how to teach them ESL. The Institute works with community organizations and agencies on the Southeast Michigan Migrant Resource Council. See http://www.lsa.umich.edu/eli/instruction/workers (accessed January 21, 2010).
  - Many regional organizations develop literacy programs in English and Spanish for different regions in the United States. Check with the National Council of La Raza (NCLR) for guidance and opportunities at http://www.nclr.org/ (accessed January 21, 2010). You can also coordinate activities with local community colleges and adult education programs such as Literacy Volunteers of America, which has state and local chapters in almost every state, at http://www.proliteracy. org/ (accessed January 21, 2010).
  - Two programs offered by Miami-Dade Public Library System are *Conexiones*, a service for people confined at home or with transportation problems that provides books by mail, and *Libros Parlantes,* which lends books and magazines on tape. See the library's Spanish offerings at http://www.mdpls.org/miespanol/sp_servi ces/sp_services.asp (accessed January 21, 2010).

3. **Information about local housing, transportation, utilities, local schools, and other survival skills in your community:** Additional subjects such as consumer and legal rights, rights in the workplace, discrimination and harassment policies, and worker's health protection might be totally new to your migrant workers and their families, who come from countries where such legislation is virtually nonexistent or not enforced.

  - Queens Library offers "Coping Skills," a series of "free lectures and workshops in the most widely spoken immigrant languages of Queens on topics essential to new immigrants' acculturation, such as citizenship and job training information, advice on helping children learn, and information on available social services." See http://www.queenslibrary.org/?page_nm=NAP+-+Programs (accessed January 21, 2010).

4. **Where to find employment and U.S. work requirements, immigration status and documentation, and citizenship classes, as well as retirement options and information about Social Security:** Finding a better job is often a good idea, but

few immigrants or young Latinos know how to go about it. Offering programs on interviewing skills, dress codes, or writing a résumé might work for your audience, as well. Consider including training on cultural sensitivity and how employers expect interviewees to act.

- Collaborate with organizations such as Dress for Success[4] in developing training for women. See http://www.dressforsuccess.org/whoweare.aspx (accessed January 21, 2010).
- Although not all Latinos or even all immigrants will qualify for immigration, your audience might qualify for special government plans, refugee plans, or the visa lottery (see http://travel.state.gov/visa/immigrants/types/types_1322.html; accessed January 21, 2010). Find out their situation before offering these services.
- Information about Social Security options, retirement, and disability are offered in Spanish at the Federal level. Organize an informational session with local agents and/or professionals, or just offer help navigating the site at http://www.ssa.gov/espanol/.

5. **Tax and financial education; how to start a new business and/or develop a small business; individual and business taxes:** Learning how to fill out a tax form or where to get a TIN (Tax Identification Number) are matters of interest in new immigrant communities. Financial education about topics like opening bank accounts, credit reports and scores, or obtaining credit is of great interest to Latinos.

- Contact your local banks and coordinate activities with them. They might even become a nontraditional funding source. For an informative discussion about this topic, see John Brinsley, "Two Differing Opinions on Banks' Outreach to Latinos," *Los Angeles Business Journal,* 1999, http://www.thefreelibrary.com/_/print/PrintArticle.aspx?id=56742993 (accessed January 21, 2010).
- Other financial issues, such as those related to landlord-tenants rights, first-time buyers, and mortgage loans, might also interest local real estate and mortgage brokers, who might be willing to conduct a workshop at your library.
- Information about insurance, financial planning, and saving for retirement might also appeal to your Latino community and could draw strategic partners to your organization.
- Queens Library offers "Financial Literacy Series" in Spanish, a series of workshops for Spanish speakers to help them "learn how to secure their financial future with good budgeting, credit management, and investment." See their New Americans Program offerings at http://www.queenslibrary.org/?page_nm=NAP+-+Programs.
- Denver Public Library offers a series of workshops in Spanish called "Your Life . . . Personal Financial Intelligence—*Inteligencia financiera personal*" directed to the whole family. Topics are related to budgeting, savings, opening a bank account and other financial services, credit history, college financing, buying a new car, and more. See http://espanol.denverlibrary.org/servicios/clases.html#busqueda.

6. **Family and children's needs (parenting, grandparenting, early childhood, teens, and senior citizens):** Of great concern to Latinos are family topics and how to deal with school teachers and counselors, school applications, and resources related to parents, grandparents, and more.

- Queens Library offers a workshop in Spanish called "Parent Teacher Conferences: Getting Involved in Your Child's Education." In this workshop, Spanish-speaking parents and students learn "about the importance of parent-teacher conferences; parents' rights to translation and interpretation services; how their immigration status may affect their children's education; and important vocabulary for interacting with teachers." See http://www.queenslibrary.org/?page_nm=NAP+-+ Programs.
- The State of Colorado Initiative Grant supported the Conejos County Library in teaching parents how to read effectively to their children. Day care workers' training, home-care licensing, and parenting skills might appeal to Latino mothers of young children (Chickering-Moller 2001, p. 29).
- Pima County Public Library, Arizona, offered "Stay and Play, Parent Connection / *Conexión de Padres, Grupo de Juego*," a bilingual play-based parenting group that "gives parents the opportunity to learn through interaction how to promote positive cognitive and emotional development" to their children ages 0–5 years. Pima County Public Library also has an excellent educational page about "Story Time—*La Hora del Cuento*," where Latino parents can understand the importance of reading and playing with their children and choose from several options explained by the library. See http://www.library.pima.gov/espanol/servicios/ cuentos.php#que (accessed January 21, 2010).
- Connecting Libraries and School Projects (CLASP) is an initiative of the New York Public Library initially funded by the DeWitt Wallace–Reader's Digest Fund, a library-school partnership that links schools serving students in kindergarten through 12th grade. It included parent workshops, an outreach effort to attract Spanish-speaking parents to use library services. You can find an excellent description of the program in "Parent's Workshops" (Rodriguez 2000, pp. 41–44).
- Family Language Kits, a project from the Family Literacy Advisory Group (FLAG), was funded by the Hamilton Community Foundation in partnership with the Community Action Program for Children, the Hamilton-Wentworth Regional Public Health Department, the Hamilton Public Library, and Stelco, Inc., in Hamilton, Ontario, Canada. See their Web sites: Hamilton Public Library, http://www.myhamilton.ca/myhamilton; and Hamilton Public Library, "Family Language Kits," http://www.myhamilton.ca/NR/rdonlyres/3A0EC539-9199- 43E9-B317-522A84607C2F/0/FamilyLanguageKitsReportSept05.pdf (accessed January 21, 2010).

7. **Health-related matters such as health disparities; health resources in your community; health access availability for children, adults, seniors, and caregivers; and nutrition, diet, and physical activity:** Your local hospital is a good resource for information on nutrition, pre- and neonatal care, and child care. Diabetes, high blood pressure, and nutrition issues are fairly prevalent in the Latino community. Work with a hospital or health care center to develop a good product/service to change behaviors and acquire information at your library, which will probably be a less intimidating environment than the hospital.

- Pima County Public Library (PCPL), Arizona, offered "Sexual Education for Parents—*Educación Sexual para Padres*," a 90-minute event about their teenagers' reality. The workshop provided information about adolescent development and a brief introduction to their teenage children's romantic lives, in person, through

MySpace, other social network sites, and text messaging. The PCPL site also has a well-organized Spanish page that addresses health concerns in Spanish and offers several useful resources at http://www.library.pima.gov/espanol/buscar/salud.php (accessed January 21, 2010).

- Ocean County Library, New Jersey, has compiled a bilingual "Immigrant Resource Directory" with updated information about agencies and health care facilities that assist immigrants in the library's coverage area. See http://theoceancountylibrary.org/espanol/ImmigrantResourceDirectory.pdf (accessed January 21, 2010).

8. **Mental, emotional, and spiritual concerns such as self-help, women's issues (domestic violence, teen pregnancy), alcohol and drug addiction, depression, and other mental issues related to immigration (loss of identity, family separation):** The most common causes of mental disease and drug addiction in the Latino community are lack of information and access to services. Between 60 and 75 percent of Latinos abandon their mental health treatment after the first session. The causes of this desertion are cultural and language barriers, and economic and social distress. Latin American youth suffer mental illnesses related to anxiety, depression, and the use of narcotics associated with emotional and cultural problems and generational conflicts with their parents, since in many cases the parents speak one language and they speak another.

- *La Administración de Salud Mental y Abuso de Sustancias* / The Substance Abuse and Mental Health Services Administration (SAMHSA) believes in life in the community for everyone and is focused on building resilience and facilitating recovery for people with or at risk for mental or substance use disorders. The Spanish site also has a 24-hour suicide assistance hotline *en español* at 888-628-9454. Access their site at http://www.samhsa.gov/espanol/ (accessed January 21, 2010).
- The United States Department of Health offers information in Spanish at http://www.healthfinder.gov/espanol/ (accessed January 21, 2010).
- The Centers for Disease Control and Prevention provides information in Spanish at http://www.cdc.gov/spanish/ (accessed January 21, 2010).
- Hispanic American Health at the National Library of Medicine can be found at http://www.nlm.nih.gov/medlineplus/spanish/hispanicamericanhealth.html (accessed January 21, 2010).
- The National Women's Health Information Center provides health information for women at http://www.womenshealth.gov (accessed January 21, 2010).
- Check with your state and local government and your area hospitals and ask them to include a reciprocal link to your Spanish Web site. It will also increase your organization's exposure on the Internet.[5]

9. **Increasing circulation and usage of specific materials (such as new items or services); information related to your Spanish Collection and Latino-related materials in English and in Spanish; a special collection, subscription, document, or archive acquired or received by the library related to Latinos or the general public:** Inform the community about bilingual and new English materials as many Latino households share several generations and a bilingual experience. Also, keep them updated about new services for Latinos or for the general public, such as photocopying, notary public, fax, e-mail, and so forth, or the cancellation of some services.

- Hennepin County Library, Minnetonka, Minnesota, developed a successful program of deposit collections to learning centers serving new Americans and dedicated staff and resources to support the program. They circulated boxes of materials instead of single items and included large-print, regular-print, and learning center materials including audiotapes for learning English, citizenship information, GED information, resources for teaching ESL, slower-paced audiobooks, and nonfiction books. See http://www.hclib.org/NewImmigrants (accessed January 21, 2010).
- Some libraries provide uncatalogued paperback novels and religious books to Spanish-speaking patrons who are not yet library members to encourage them to join and build trust on confidentiality issues (referred to as *libros de cortesía, courtesy books*).
- Hamilton Public Library, Ontario, Canada, has created over 100 dual-language kits in 15 different languages to promote reading, language development, and library use. FLAG is a family literacy initiative designed to reach new immigrant families and break down language and cultural barriers. See their "Family Language Kits," http://www.myhamilton.ca/NR/rdonlyres/3A0EC539-9199-43E9-B317-522A84607C2F/0/FamilyLanguageKitsReportSept05.pdf (accessed January 21, 2010).

10. **Generate cultural awareness, empowerment, and integration of the Latino community to your local cultural heritage:** The importance of holidays and religious celebrations in Latin America cannot be underestimated. Target your market segments with different events, and develop awareness about their cultural preferences. As mentioned before, it would be useful to have a calendar of Latino holidays related to your local population—if you have several groups of different nationalities, find out what holidays they celebrate. Not everybody celebrates Cinco de Mayo! They also want to celebrate national American holidays and learn about U.S. traditions and history.

- Pima County Public Library, Arizona, offered "Card Making for All Ages!—*Creación de Tarjetas de Felicitación*," where participants could create their own holiday cards at this workshop for all ages. The same library offered a Halloween party, a free family event where they decorated Mexican Sugar Skulls in celebration of Day of the Dead/*Día de los Muertos* at the Sugar Skull Workshop/*Taller de Calaveras de Azúcar*. See their community resources at http://www.library.pima.gov/community (accessed January 21, 2010).

11. **Members of the Latino community who have shown some sort of achievement, locally and/or nationally:** Remember that these celebrations have to be meaningful to your local community. South Americans might think a celebration of Chavez refers to Hugo Chavez (President of Venezuela) or Julio Cesar Chavez (boxer) and not Cesar Chavez, the Mexican activist (famous for his saying "You are never strong enough that you don't need help").

- Many libraries around the country also celebrate Hispanic Heritage Month with activities and events. Please look at the following Web sites for ideas and contact information about the success of the events and the demographic information of the populations they serve.

- Los Angeles County Library, California, "Celebrate National Hispanic Heritage Month," 2009, http://www.colapublib.org/hispanic (accessed January 21, 2010).
- Nova Southeastern University, Florida, "Celebrate Hispanic Heritage Month with Series of FREE Events at Nova Southeastern University," 2009, http://www.nova.edu/cwis/pubaffairs/news/july-sept2009/hispanic_heritage_month.html (accessed January 21, 2010).
- Springfield City Library, Massachusetts, "Hispanic Heritage" resources and recommended readings, http://www.springfieldlibrary.org/hispanic/hispanicheritage.html (accessed January 21, 2010).

- In 2008, EBSCO Publishing partnered with Arte Público Press to provide a new digital collection of a comprehensive bibliography of more than 17,000 books and pamphlets produced by Latinos in the United States until 1960. See http://www.latinoteca.com (accessed January 21, 2010).

12. **Members of the Latino community who participate in local, national, and international recreational and sports activities, such as figures in baseball, boxing, soccer, tennis, and even golf:** Invite local or national Latino artists and writers to give a guest lecture or educational program. They are looking for publicity, too! Ask them to become your library sponsor. Partnerships with local poets, writers, painters, crafters, or musicians can generate a constant source of programming and excitement around your library. Local Mexican crafters can build very creative piñatas or favors for wedding and *quinceañeras*. Young people may have local bands, do photography, write poetry, or have interesting hobbies they would like to share with others. Bringing them into the library will bring their families and community group as well.

- Since 2000, the Miami-Dade Public Library System has exchanged the historical and cultural highlights of a foreign country through their literature, folklore, and art. This outstanding library exchange program has already visited countries in the Caribbean and South America, among others.

You can also develop empowerment and leadership skills by creating opportunities for participation in activities, demonstrating a craft or ability, addressing parenting or community issues with community facilitators, inviting community members to become part of the Latino Advisory Board or the Friends of the Library, and other ways your CLO would find suitable.

As you can see, you can find plenty of topics or themes to organize special events and outreach activities. Some topics might be more related to your everyday affairs; some might be a little far from the ordinary. However, most of these are topics of concern in the Latino community—for recent immigrants and for long-timers equally. Do not tackle all these topics at once. Like cough syrup, awareness and new information need to be administered in small doses!

Starting a Latino Club

Not all Latinos might be familiar with public libraries in the United States, but they are familiar with the concept of belonging to an association, sports club, cooperative, or other community organizations that are popular in Latin America. Belonging to a circle, association, or club makes people feel special. Why not use the same concept to start a

Latino Club at your local library? You need not restrict membership to Latinos; other patrons might be interested in practicing their Spanish and discovering new Latino videos or magazines. In addition, recruiting for your Latino Club will provide you with more data about the community, and it will give your staff a wonderful opportunity to practice their Spanish!

Your first impulse as a librarian might be to focus on reading (i.e., a Latino Book Club). However, in the beginning this might discourage people who are not great readers, who might come along for a social event, or who are just curious. Maybe check with your LAB for ideas about the focus of the club. It might be watching a movie, discussing or bringing community leaders to inform them about a topic of concern, or presentations by local artists, as previously discussed.

The Latino Club might have one session a month for a specific purpose—for example, every first Thursday for a movie or another type of entertainment and every second Thursday for a discussion of community issues so you give members ample choices. You can make the activities seasonal according to your market research of your patrons' schedules and work activities.

You can suggest literacy activities within the Latino Club and ask members about their interests, but do not set the reading idea a priori. Empower them to make their own decisions and offer the materials, facilities, and resources you have in your library.

What incentives would members of the Latino Club receive? Maybe an e-mail blast notification of new releases, priority reservation of Spanish materials and DVDs, participation at events, or access to a hotline in Spanish. You may be thinking that you already offer all these services! However, you should present these services to your Latino Club in a unique way. Introducing these services as a very special package for Latino Club members increases the appeal. Include these ideas in a well-designed promotional package and see what happens! You can include informational material about your library's mission and advocacy. If you can stretch your budget a little, make a special library card with a different design that alludes to the Latino Club. Use simple software such as Microsoft Publisher or download free graphic design software from safe sites such as cnet.com (http://download.cnet.com/windows/graphic-design-software) or freeserifsoftware (http://www.freeserifsoftware.com). You could also start an institutional group page on Facebook, MySpace, or other social media sites. Look for images that might appeal to them, and perhaps let members choose from a selection of images. Remember, this is also a way to collect information and become aware of their preferences.

Consider also giving out awards to club members. For example, the Best Reader of the Month, Best Library Advocate of the Month, or any other incentives your organization might offer. Publicize these awards in your local column in the Spanish newspaper, on the local radio station, or even on TV local stations—before and after they are awarded.

Once you have a few members, encourage and empower Latino Club members to start their own committees to define the club's activities and suggest program ideas and materials for the library. They may wish to start their own conversation classes in Spanish for English speakers and talk about their own problems and concerns. Ask them to become library advocates in their community. Help them become the protagonists of their own lives!

Latino Youth

In addition to activities for adults in which children and teens can participate, the following ideas are more specific to the needs of teens.

1. **Activities to create and increase educational and literacy skills (from middle school to high school or vocational school degrees), promote after-school activities, and develop special skills in culturally integrated and bilingual programs:** These are the events and activities for which the most information is available because children's and teens' activities abound in libraries. A few that seem to have special appeal to Latino families and library personnel are included here:

   * Computer classes work great for teenagers when they find some specific interest outside their school academics. San Antonio Public Library has a virtual library for its Young Adult section. The program, began in 1997, was funded by Microsoft and the American Library Association, MCI WorldCom, and a local foundation (truly some outside-the-box funding). Teenagers were encouraged to build their own Web sites and even had a short summer program where they learned to create their own short videos. In addition, the program encourages them to play video games and read good books or watch movies. See http://www.youthwired. sat.lib.tx.us (accessed January 21, 2010) or the library's MySpace page for teens, http://www.myspace.com/210teenlibrary (accessed January 21, 2010).
   * Talk to your local school system to start bilingual drama classes for teenagers— this could perhaps become a strategic partnership opportunity, as well—and offer to share space with the local drama class for bilingual plays that will enhance both cultures. In addition, teens can research the library for plays, authors, and more.
   * A literary contest, perhaps in collaboration with a local publisher or printing press, honors first-time writers who have written short stories that might qualify for publishing or self-publishing on the Internet. Graphic novels, short stories, or poems written by teenagers might be especially attractive to this population.
   * With the same approach, students can be encouraged to write and illustrate books for younger students, or Spanish-speaking teenagers can read and record short stories for Spanish-language students and other members of the library who are interested in Spanish conversation. Reward their efforts with posters, coupons, and gift certificates donated by some of your local stores or community strategic partners.
   * As part of the Latino Club or Latino Teen Club, ask high school students to submit pieces or articles for a bilingual library newsletter, and distribute it to families in the area.
   * San Antonio Public Library sponsored a Hispanic Cultural Love-In during the summer of 1996. Local Latino artists, writers, and actors were invited to participate.
   * Redwood City Library, California, had a session called "Making Chilean Rainsticks" where children made ceremonial musical instruments used to invoke the rain spirits. Children were instructed by teachers from Art in Action; see their Web site at http://www.artinaction.org (accessed January 21, 2010).
   * The purpose of the Teen Library Council at the Idaho Public Library is to "give teens an opportunity to give to their community through the library by sharing their views and insights on popular teen culture and the needs of teens in Bonneville County." See http://www.ifpl.org/teen/index.asp?p=Council (accessed January 21, 2010).
   * Pikes Peak Library District in Colorado Springs sponsored a series of skits developed by teens based on well-known fairy tales in English, Spanish, or

CELEBRITY PROMOTIONAL PRODUCTS

The ALA store promotes celebrities who support literacy and libraries through the ALA's Celebrity READ Posters.

George Lopez is the official spokesperson for the ALA's Smartest Card Campaign, which encourages everyone to acquire and use a library card. In addition, he and his wife lead the George & Ann Lopez-Richie Alarcon CARE Foundation, which is dedicated to providing community and arts resources for education. Lopez has received the Manny Mota Foundation Community Spirit Award for his charity work and was named honorary mayor of Los Angeles because of his efforts helping earthquake victims in El Salvador and Guatemala. Harvard University presented him with Artist of the Year and Humanitarian Awards. *Time* magazine named Lopez as one of the 25 Most Influential Hispanics in America. A supporter of the National Kidney Foundation, George Lopez, one of today's top comedians, is the co-creator, writer, producer, and star of the popular family TV show *George Lopez,* the fourth Latino sitcom in television history. He has also published his autobiography, *Why You Crying?*[6]

bilingual versions. The library holds a Youth Advisory Council and a great "Teens Zone" on their Web site. See http://ppld. org/Teens/index.php (accessed January 21, 2010).

- Partner with local banks and law enforcement personnel to hold an information fair at the local high school to provide information to senior Latino students about becoming a library member, opening a bank account, managing credit, getting a driver's license, or safe driving practices.
- A Latino Teens Club—the same concept as the adult Latino Club but for teens and pre-teens—might offer a series of Latino or Spanish movies at the local library on Friday or Saturday nights. Ask local stores and community partners to provide incentives such as popcorn and snacks.
- Hosting a series of improvisation sessions or workshops that address the pressure and anxiety generated by the acculturation process, new school environment, new friends, and differences between both cultures with teen participation coordinated by local social workers and school counselors can be a positive experience. Teens need to be heard and un-derstood in their struggle for acculturation.
- Additional topics of interest for further teen programming could be a Salsa dance contest; an introduction to or discussion of Latino music and musicians, sports, low-riders and muscle cars or car mechanics; or a program for younger teen girls on planning a *quinceañera.*[7]

Latino Children

Suggested topics for preschool and early school-aged children are often related to storytelling and initiating children into the reading world abundant in the library environment.[8] However, you need to consider some cultural barriers that might affect your activities. Latino families generally prefer to keep their young children at home until they go to school; many times, they skip the preparation years for language and learning skills acquisition. Many Latino moms stay at home with their young children, both mother and child are not exposed to the English language. Public libraries can be the link between these years and kindergarten by involving parents or, at least, mothers.

Helping Latino parents understand that storytelling is part of their parenting skills is instrumental for beginning the education process. They know that education and English-language skills are very important parts of their lives that will allow them and their children to get better jobs and opportunities, but sometimes they are reluctant to take time out of their schedules or they have limiting beliefs about their literacy ability in front of other people.

It might be hard for an immigrant family to understand the importance of storytelling or a puppet program when they need a job or health care. However, children need to be exposed to written and spoken language in order to acquire a broader vocabulary and activate their thinking ability. You will need to address these issues in your promotional materials.

1. **Culturally integrated and bilingual programs that encourage and stimulate the thinking process in the early stages of childhood development to set the base for future intellectual maturity are broadly offered all around the country:**

   * *El día de los niños / El día de los libros* (Children's Day/Book Day) is a celebration of children, families, and reading held annually on April 30. Sponsored by the Association for Library Service for Children (ALSC) and REFORMA, the English event started in 1952 followed in 1996 by the Spanish event when nationally acclaimed children's book author Pat Mora proposed linking both celebrations. See ALA, "About Día," http://ala.org/ala/mgrps/divs/alsc/initiatives/diadelosni nos/aboutdia/aboutdia.cfm (accessed January 21, 2010).

   * Medical clinics in Saint Luis Valley, Colorado, participated in a program sponsored by the American Academy of Pediatrics called "Reach Out and Read." In addition to taking care of children's physical needs, physicians hand out free books for parents to read to their children. See http://www.reachoutandread.org/index. aspx (accessed January 21, 2010).

   * The Aurora Public Library in Illinois worked in conjunction with the Visiting Nurse Association for similar programs.

   * Born to Read / *Nací para leer* is an ALA/ALSC-sponsored-program to help expectant mothers and new parents "become aware that reading to a baby from birth is critical to every baby's growth and well being." Several libraries around the country participate in this program. See ALSC, "Born to Read," http://www. ala.org/ala/mgrps/divs/alsc/initiatives/borntoread/index.cfm (Accessed January 21, 2010).

   * Under the same title "Born to Read," the Naperville Community Unit School District 203 in Illinois distributes bags of books and materials to infants through pediatricians and community organizations. Bags in English or Spanish include information and books. The Spanish bag also contains a survey and incentives to fill it out. See http://www.naperville203.org/community/BorntoRead.asp (accessed January 21, 2010).

   * The University City Regional Library, one of the five regional branches in the Public Library of Charlotte and Mecklenburg County, North Carolina, organized an annual storytelling festival for children in third, fourth, and fifth grades. The site offers information and multicultural stories as suggested resources. See North Carolina Library Association, "Governors' Village Storytelling Festival," http:// www.nclaonline.org/css/summer2001/ChapbookStorytelling.htm (accessed January 21, 2010).

   * Establishing a routine for your storytelling time is important for kids because they learn through repetition. A librarian from the Miami-Dade Public Library System, Florida, uses a counting song with children participating; reads a story

related to their lives, rhymes and riddles, and oral folk tales; and uses puppets that other librarians can duplicate. Puppets and dolls represent different ethnicities and skin color. See Miami-Dade Public Library Spanish Web site for additional information at http://www.mdpls.org/miespanol/sp_services/sp_services.asp (accessed January 21, 2010).

- *Cuentos y Más* is a one-of-a-kind program that promotes reading among children while having fun through Arlington Virginia Network (AVN) Comcast Cable Channel 25 or Verizon FIOS Channel 40 as storyteller Mariela Aguilar and special guests perform bilingual stories and more for children ages four through eight. The program also enables viewers to practice English and Spanish in a fun and interactive way. *Cuentos y Más* is an AVN production brought to you by Arlington Public Library. See http://arlington.granicus.com/ViewPublisher.php?view_id=13 (accessed February 5, 2010)
- *Chiles*, or Children & Libraries en Español, is a site "dedicated to bringing together children's librarians who serve Spanish-speaking youth but who do not speak Spanish themselves." The site is a resource for best practices, ideas, inspiration, and language as well as a community to share ideas and resources. See http://www.chil-es.org/joomla/ (accessed February 6, 2010).

Getting Referrals

In addition to your programming and outreach efforts, keep in mind that your best prospects are people who are already motivated enough to contact you. You need to create stimulus to generate that type of behavior. Some of the ways you can interest people are included here:

1. **Include** your Spanish hotline number in every ad, flyer, or pamphlet; on your Web site; in your community newsletter (if you have one); and on all other giveaways. Encourage people to call you; when they do, be sure to take down their information, making certain—if necessary—to reassure patrons about the confidentiality of the information you collect.
2. **Offer** a free evaluation or free information about a subject important to your community. For instance, "Do you know how and where to get your tax ID number? At your local library, we can help you! Call today." Make your message simple and effective, communicating only one subject at a time. If you do not have Spanish-speaking personnel at all times, leave a message on your hotline explaining briefly: "Are you interested in finding out how and where you can get you tax ID number? Please leave your name and phone number, and a Spanish-speaking person will return your call within 24–48 hours." Customize the message according to your available resources.
3. **Provide** a guest book so people can sign in with their name and contact information every time they participate in an event or just visit the library. Include a column for comments or requests.
4. **Organize** a contest so people send you their personal information. Whatever it is, publicize widely and for a long time, or organize a monthly response so people get used to seeing it. Talk to the media in your community about this project.
5. **Set up a booth** at community fairs, events, and after Sunday (or Saturday) mass. Gather all the forms you have translated into Spanish, part of your paperback col-

lection, some videos or DVDs, and a small TV/VCR to show Latino movies at the fair. Fill out applications or hand out temporary cards, and let people know the materials can be returned at the local library.

> As the publisher of a bilingual newspaper, we once organized a contest with phrases from several different Latin American countries and asked the public to recognize the slang's country of origin. The template was: "If I say . . . , I'm from . . . " We offered a pair of tickets to a local concert or sports event to be raffled among participants every month; we got the prize from an exchange of advertising (you might be able to get something similar from your strategic partners). It was a huge success, and those who participated were later contacted to subscribe to the newspaper.

6. **Create a regular schedule of activities** that can be associated with your library. These activities can promote library cards while targeting specific markets. If Latinos find these activities regularly at the library, they will continue to come and use other library services you promote at their events. These activities can also be considered outreach—for instance, organizing a Spanish Movie Club, Latino Rock 'n Roll Club, Latino Comics Club, Bilingual Cartoon Designers Club, Bilingual Readers Club, Bilingual Story Times, and more.

   You can provide a moderator from your own staff who speaks Spanish or have leaders of their own community coordinate the events. In any case, be sure to provide the appropriate library materials for each session so they see what's available. Always get the participants' information for your database.

7. **Use your regular membership for referrals.** Do any of your Latino members benefit from your services already, and are they willing to bring a buddy to the library and introduce him or her to your services? Do any of your long-time or recent American members know a Latino person who could benefit from library services the way they do? Maybe Latinos work for them at home or in their business. Maybe they see Latino patients at the hospital or doctors office or send their children to the same day care center.

   Organizing a promotional campaign through your members' word-of-mouth has certain advantages. It can be done easily, might require low logistics, and will have third-party credibility right from the start—they trust the person who will bring them to the library.

   A brochure explaining the campaign and its purpose can be handed out each time a person checks out or returns books. Invite them to browse the new Spanish collection—especially if they are interested in learning Spanish—and share services with their Latino friends, relatives, employees, or co-workers. Include a temporary library card so they can help them fill it out, and maybe they will bring their friend or relative with them next time around.

   Many times, people are motivated by recognition, and giving a Member of the Month reward to the person who offered more referrals, with a name and picture on the library's wall, might be a good way to say thank you.

8. **Encourage young members to bring a Latino friend from school.** Following the same concept, you can use your strategic partners by reaching out to public schools and enticing children to bring their friends from school. Elementary, middle, or high school, make sure you organize a good activity at the time they show up. Once you have attracted children and teens to membership, they will have to bring their parents or guardians to get their library card. Always include the phrase *"Para más*

información, llame a su biblioteca pública local" (For more information, contact your local public library) in all your promotional materials, and provide your contact information. Advertise your initiatives through your community partners, regular members, and other market channels.

Hopefully, all these ideas can expand or improve the ones you have already tried and can offer new opportunities to reach out to your local Latinos. As said before, your decisions regarding collection development, outreach activities, and the role your organization gives to this outreach plan are conscious decisions about the way your library intends to serve the Latino members of your community.

Many programs and activities can be found and exchanged with other libraries around the country. However, keep in mind that not all of them will apply to your community. The guidelines in this chapter and the previous ones should help you minimize the risk of falling flat with a community activity, program, or event. Once you have come up with the best idea or ideas that address your community's priorities, it is time to set up some guidelines for program or activity implementation.

Planning Internal Logistics

Hopefully your CLO has been as involved in planning your activity, event, or program as you are—which means you have a CLO! However, other people in your library as well as your community might not be as aware of the program or all the details. Therefore, your next two steps are to define the logistics of your event and make everybody aware of the program details.

The following basic checklist will help keep your actions on track. Feel free to add tasks or other details to it or use the ones you need for each specific event.

Planning Activities or Events Logistics Checklist

1. Initiate and develop the idea.
2. Define necessary resources.
3. Decide the setting.
4. Prepare a detailed budget.
5. Participate in the writing and administering of grant applications.
6. Make budget recommendations.
7. Develop a timeline chart.

Participant Organizations

1. Select and invite strategic partners.
2. Develop and negotiate contracts with strategic partners.
3. Coordinate communications.

Event Implementation and Execution

1. Handle scheduling and coordinate activities.
2. Make sure you have all materials to be distributed.
3. Look for internal and external help.
4. Give instructions to staff setting up.

5. Develop and maintain data files on participating organizations.
6. Maintain records and prepare reports.
7. Try to anticipate constraints and obstacles.

Promotional Activities

1. Plan and coordinate promotional activities.
2. Inform all affected agencies.
3. Develop and produce event calendars.
4. Define promotional items.

In chapter 10 you will find Worksheet 7.3, which reproduces in detail the same activity or event logistics checklist to help you with planning purposes. In addition, use your internal communication process (chapter 2) to communicate with your internal staff about the details of the event. For those directly involved, make sure you communicate the following:

Event Planning Communication Procedures

1. **Use your internal communication process.** Ensure all your library staff is aware of and informed about the event, program, or activity. Even if people are not directly involved in the activity, they might have to answer a phone call or respond to a question from a potential participant in the event. If your event is in Spanish for Spanish-speaking patrons, make sure to create enough posters for the public to see and Spanish *cheat cards* for your staff to use.
2. **Go over each collaborators role.** Ensure everybody knows the procedures inside out. If necessary, gather your staff in a short meeting to give insight into the event or campaign and provide clear written information about each person's role. Include a copy of the timeline chart.
3. **Inform your support staff**—such as your telephone receptionists or circulation desk clerks—about the event or activity. If possible, delineate an outline of possible questions and answers that might arise.
4. **Clarify your plan and expectations with strategic partners**, especially if their participation is instrumental for the success of the event, if the event takes place at their location, or if you need their cooperation to distribute materials. Listen to their concerns and address them right away.
5. **Name a media contact person**—or maybe two for backup—and make them aware of potential calls from the media, photo shooting opportunities, or additional information about the event.
6. **Get ready for your public's reactions**—such as phone calls from patrons, organizations, or agencies that might disagree with your activity or campaign. If possible, designate a spokesperson from your organization who can respond to these inquiries to make sure the message is consistent and prepared.

Worksheet 7.4, which develops these procedures in detail, can be found in chapter 10. These are important steps to keep in mind; you need all the help you can get and do not want a mishap on the public relations end of your event or activity to create problems at the event or campaign. Be careful with media calls as some writers might feature misquotes or comments from an unprepared member of your staff. Good communication with your staff is as important as clear communication with your strategic partners.

Chapter 8 expands on types of promotional materials and media contacts. For now, your last step in implementing your program, event, or activity is to monitor its implementation.

To help you track the success of your program, you need to ask the following questions:

- Are all the people, elements, and parts of the program in place?
- Do all the materials and resources have the quality you envisioned?
- Is the library staff ready and enthusiastic about the program?
- Did we cover all possible media and distribution channels?
- Are all strategic partners in agreement and in sync with the implementation of the program?
- Are our spokespeople ready to address community comments and concerns?
- Are we on budget and on time?
- Are all promotional materials distributed?

These same questions are presented in Worksheet 7.5 in chapter 10. Keep asking yourself—and your CLO—all these questions until all answers are a sound YES! In the meantime, continue to look for possible solutions to prevent or address problems. Preregistration was more than you expected and you are afraid of not having enough printed materials? Make some phone calls to your strategic partners to see if someone can help print some extras. Your press releases are not running on time? Ask your contact person to double follow up on your media outlets. You think you might have a last-minute cancellation of your speaker or presenting artist? Plan a library activity that will entice your Latino audience (a library tour, storytelling for adults, or a game activity). Are you afraid you might run out of refreshments or food? Have a backup donation just in case.

In any case, guidelines to evaluate your strategy are provided in chapter 9, which presents tools and procedures to decide whether your program—but most importantly, your outreach strategy—really worked. Before we get there, however, let us now turn to chapter 8 to see how to promote these wonderful activities you are planning to offer!

Notes

1. There are several short free language placement tests online that you can research and use for your purpose, such as the one offered by World-English.org, which provides you with quick results and defines different levels: http://www.world-english.org/test.htm (accessed July 31, 2010).
2. Rebecca Paul, *Round Lake Area Library—Ahead of the Outreach Curve,* WebJunction Spanish Outreach Program, http://www.webjunction.org/spanish-computers/articles/content/439391 (accessed January 21, 2010).
3. For additional information on English for Specific Purposes, see the following sites: "English for Specific Purposes," http://www.rong-chang.com/esp.htm; and ESP World, "English for Specific Purposes World Online Journal for Teachers," http://esp-world.info/contents.htm (accessed February 15, 2010).
4. Dress for Success Worldwide is an international nonprofit organization dedicated to improving the lives of women located in 78 cities across the United States, Canada, the United Kingdom, and New Zealand.
5. Google has a way to rate Web pages called PageRank, which compares all the other pages on the Internet. "A hyperlink to a page counts as a vote of support. The PageRank of a page is defined recursively and depends on the number and PageRank metric of all pages that link to it ('incoming

links'). A page that is linked to many pages with high PageRank receives a high rank itself. If there are no links to a web page there is no support for that page." Wikipedia, "PageRank," http://en.wikipedia.org/wiki/PageRank#Description (accessed January 21, 2010).

6. For additional information about ALA Celebrities READ posters, see the ALA store at http://www.alastore.ala.org/ (accessed January 21, 2010). For additional information about George Lopez and other celebrities who participate in community campaigns and charity efforts, see Look to the Stars, http://www.looktothestars.org/ (accessed January 21, 2010).

7. *Quinceañera* is a traditional Latin American coming-of-age ceremony held on a girl's fifteenth birthday.

8. One source that provides very specific guidelines on how to organize any type of program for Latino teens and children is the book *Library Services to Youth of Hispanic Heritage* (Immroth and de la Peña McCook 2000), a manual with very detailed information about resources, session planning, and activities.

WORKSHEET 7.1   Variables Comparison to Address Market Segment Needs

Goal: Determine overlapping segments that require similar services.

Variable	Specifics	Group 1 Size: 550 people	Group 2 Size: 350 people	Group 3 Size: 150 people	Group 4 Size: 75 people
Language ability	English dominant	5	23	12	3
	Bilingual	25	26	25	27
	Spanish dominant	70	51	63	70
Levels of education	Less than elementary or elementary	60	45	64	74
	Less than high school or high school	40	35	35	25
	Some college or Four-year college +		20		

NOTES

_____

_____

_____

_____

_____

Variables are expressed in percentages.

 From *¡Hola, amigos! A Plan for Latino Outreach* by Susana G. Baumann. Santa Barbara, CA: Libraries Unlimited. Copyright © 2011.

WORKSHEET 7.2 Positioning Statement with Incentives

Goal: In addition to defining all the aspects of your activity or program that are customer centered, grounded in actual accomplishments and relationships that make your place, products, and services unique for a particular audience, you also need to address the emotional concerns your target audience might have regarding this specific activity.

Your target audience: Latino and Latino American teens from different backgrounds who speak fluent English (immigrants and first generation born in the United States) but have difficulties with reading skills

The service name or category: Latino Teen Summer Club

Their problems, wants, and needs: Improve reading habits (reading skills *and* the inclination for reading)

A key benefit: A place where teens can go with friends, choose activities and readings, participate in additional activities related to reading (organize and participate in skits, do reading plays, post on the Internet, etc.), receive incentives, meet new friends, and have a social activity apart from their family

The key differentiation: Librarians are friendly and welcoming, they have a fantastic program that makes reading easy and not boring at all, the schedule is after working hours, tutoring is available, friends can participate, additional activities are offered, and logistics are solved

The concerns and emotional responses you want to address:

> **Fear:** Avoid failing the subject and going to summer school
>
> **Image:** Look like a winner, feel like a winner!
>
> **Family:** Surprise parents with improved reading skills
>
> **Stress and time constraints:** Savvy students get better grades with less stress because they get the help they need
>
> **Social expectation:** Enjoy summer activities with friends while having fun at the library

The library will provide promotional items, ideas, or practice: A promotional music DVD for those who register, and a coupon to the ice-cream parlor for those who finish the summer session

From *¡Hola, amigos! A Plan for Latino Outreach* by Susana G. Baumann. Santa Barbara, CA: Libraries Unlimited. Copyright © 2011.

Chapter 8

Promoting Your Library

Overview

Your next step into this outreach plan is to devise promotional strategies to attract customers and bring them into your store. Your store is not only your library in terms of your physical facility—many Latino customers might already be using your services— but also your system, your technology, your information, and, in a broader sense, your community and your society. My society, you might ask?

In a society where the sum of minorities is becoming the majority of the population—Hispanics, African Americans, Asians, and Native Americans will comprise over 45 percent of the population by 2050—expanding equity of access and ensuring equity of service constitute two of libraries' foremost challenges for the 21st century. "The United States is experiencing a cultural renaissance that no one could have predicted 20 years ago . . . Although some in the United States may still think that this country can remain isolated and powerful on its own, reality contradicts this belief. Quite simply, the forces that propel this cross-cultural phenomenon of U.S. Hispanization are too strong" (Korzenny and Korzenny 2005, pp. 302–3).

In this chapter we discuss the different promotional strategies necessary to build a steady and loyal Latino clientele. In chapters 6 and 7, we anticipated the need for creating compelling messages that would highlight the benefits your Latino customers perceive when they make using the library one of their habitual behaviors. In a social marketing approach, the ultimate goal is to help people improve their quality of life; therefore, the customer rather than the products needs to be at the center of the library's promotional strategy. We also discussed the incentives, recognitions, and social pressure that will make your community take action. We covered the importance of being in touch with clients' needs, keeping services consistent, improving offerings, and maintaining steady and friendly customer service. Now, you need to persistently promote all these efforts, without which all the other hard work you have done so far will be in vain.

This chapter describes *general promotional strategies* for your library services, which in marketing equate to branding efforts, and *specific promotional strategies,* which relate to your outreach programming efforts. General strategies, or branding, will work with most Latino customer base and will include educating your Latino community about your library, its resources, its organizational culture, and its commitment to deliver quality services as a community-oriented organization. Specific strategies are addressed to motivate different Latino market segments to take action, as discussed in chapter 7. Every time you plan a program, activity, or service, or to celebrate their cultural heritage and empower your Latino community, you must develop a specific promotional mini-campaign for that specific offering. These mini-campaigns are parallel to ongoing general promotional strategies. In this chapter, you will find tools you can apply at both levels.

Also discussed are the benefits of working with a communications model based on social marketing strategies. Communications models are necessary to make sure your customers are ready and motivated to take action and use your services. In following this model, we will discuss the advantages and disadvantages of using various tactics and media in the library environment. Finally, ideas and recommendations on how to develop creative messages with culturally appropriate content and images are presented.

Letting your Latino customers know about all the wonderful materials, services, and information that await them at the library is instrumental in creating the bridge to access and, therefore, to your success. Promoting your library services to Latinos means to let them know that you care. Your Spanish collection might be extensive or small, but if it is in sync with their wants, if the information you provide talks to their needs, and if library activities reflect their dreams, traditions, and hopes, you show that you care about them and their well-being.

Marketing Strategies versus Promotional Strategies

> Finding customers is the single most difficult marketing activity for small–medium businesses.

Before getting into the heart of promoting your library, let us consider the differences between marketing and promotion. Because promotional efforts are such a big—and the most visible—part of a marketing plan, we often think of marketing in terms of advertising and sales. However, a marketing plan is a bigger, more comprehensive task. It is made up of the set of tasks necessary to build a business, as we discussed in previous chapters, while promotion—or advertising, a term more used in a commercial setting—is one of those tasks that is used to communicate those features, benefits, and advantages, and encourage your potential customers to take action.

Table 8.1 shows the essential elements of a marketing plan compared with the essential elements of a promotional campaign.

TABLE 8.1   A Marketing Plan versus a Promotional Campaign

Marketing Plan	Promotional Campaign
Define your organization's mission	Establish the identity of your brand or products
Conduct a market analysis	Identify your target audience and influencers
Assess external resources	Establish your campaign objectives
Assess internal resources	Create an image or theme
Position your library	Develop your message
Promote your library	Select and implement a media plan
Manage and evaluate your plan	Evaluate results and procedures

As you can see, the marketing plan and the promotional campaign's steps are related and could not exist without each other. By defining your organization's mission—and vision—you are able to establish the identity that best represents your organization and the ideas you want to promote to build a positive customer perception of the library and its services. Is your organization one that goes all the way when it comes to Latino services? Have you established your organization among Latinos in the community as a friendly, welcoming organization that cares about their needs and wants? Does your organization have a more conservative image that needs to be upgraded a little?

Conducting a market analysis gives you a thorough knowledge of the Latino community you serve. A complete and detailed profile of who's who in your local community will allow you to target specific market segments—smaller groups—with appropriate promotional strategies and, consequently, obtain better results. Lastly, you cannot establish your promotional objectives and develop a promotional message if you have not positioned your library in the community, as discussed in chapter 6.

Promotional activity occurs toward the end of the marketing planning process and cannot be seen as a stand-alone series of activities with little or no relation to the organization's goals, purpose, and markets. Promotional strategies and tactics will constitute the main aspects of your promotional efforts, and you need to work at two different levels—general and specific—in order to achieve results.

General and Specific Promotional Strategies

No matter how good or well presented your materials or services are, how much the customer needs them, or how much cheaper—for free!—you can offer them compared to your competition, if customers do not know about them, then your materials and services won't sell.

Because of a lack of tradition in library services—remember, even some Latinos born and raised in the United States do not use libraries as frequently as Anglo Americans (Flores and Pachon 2008)—you need to develop promotional strategies to attract and sustain your Latino patrons. Promotional strategies will define *what* you want to promote, for instance, if some local segments have never used the library, make your potential Latino patrons aware of the services you provide. If they are already using some of those services, expand their knowledge about additional offerings. But most importantly, promotional strategies need to encourage them to take action.

General promotional strategies or branding efforts will let them know who you are, what you stand for as an institution, and what you are doing to improve services for them, welcome them to your facility, and make their whole library experience a user-friendly one. These branding efforts include public relations campaigns, speaking engagements, press releases, and word-of-mouth, to name a few.

Your general promotional strategies or branding efforts could also include advocacy campaigns to generate annual membership and increase general circulation and usage of materials and services. These strategies should be planned and implemented on a continuous basis.

On the other hand, keeping your potential or current Latino library users engaged through yearly outreach programs, activities, and services at the library requires planning and developing *specific promotional strategies* or mini-campaigns. These activities should also generate cultural awareness about the community you serve, both from Latinos to the English-speaking community and from them to Latinos; empower your Latino community members; and help them integrate to your local cultural heritage—by celebrating, for instance, Hispanic Heritage Month, other holidays, and important dates and historic figures that contributed to the world's and our country's history.

All these initiatives—persistent general promotional and recurring specific promotional strategies—should prompt Latinos to get going! Learn to develop continuous tools and strategies to handhold them through the process, and motivate them to use library services.

In summary:

Your general promotional strategies or branding efforts should accomplish the following:

- Develop education and awareness about your organization and library services
- Generate annual membership
- Encourage involvement with the library
- Increase circulation and usage of materials in general

Your specific promotional strategies or mini-campaigns should accomplish these goals:

- Promote outreach programs, activities, and services
- Increase circulation and usage of specific materials (such as new items or services)
- Advocate for the library by increasing membership at a specific time of year (a mini-campaign)
- Generate cultural awareness, empowerment, and integration of the Latino community's cultural traditions to your library and your local cultural heritage—for instance, Hispanic Heritage Month

It generates a feeling of frustration when your staff plans and implements an activity and nobody shows up! Been there? Many factors might be affecting Latinos' response to your promotional efforts, but with consistency and persistence, a well-used budget, and a smart promotional plan, you will certainly see increasing results.

Long- and Short-Term Promotional Goals

In addition to promotional strategies at two different levels—branding and mini-campaigns—your CLO needs to define timetables. These are the suggested guidelines to handle your course of action:

- Long-term promotional strategies will be defined every three years with annual adjustments (following your three-year marketing plan). They include your general promotional strategies.
- Short-term promotional strategies will be defined yearly and on a campaign basis and adjusted quarterly (following your outreach programming and activities). They will include specific promotional strategies.
- Implementation and schedules will be defined on each campaign basis.
- Pre- and post-campaign evaluation will be conducted on a campaign basis, at the end of each year and at the end of the three-year plan.

In addition to establishing timetables and defining your promotional goals, the CLO should allocate time and money to the following tasks:

- Develop and produce promotional materials
- Develop distribution lists for potential membership
- Organize mailings (writing, stuffing, delivering, etc.)
- Organize open houses and improve the friendliness of your facility's image
- Campaign through the Internet and the library Web site
- Request and track referrals
- Follow up on all these efforts

Doing your own promotion has its downside, and it is not always the best strategy because you have to wear many hats. However, the reality of the library environment is that you hardly have a budget for promotion at all, so the idea is to make the best out of the resources you have. In the next section, you will find tools to evaluate each effort to make sure your advertising/promotion dollars can run longer and deeper into the Latino community.

Your Promotional Tactics and Budget

Promotional tactics determine *how* you promote your activity to the target audience you want to reach and their influencers—the people your target audience trusts—and which media is appropriate to reach those audiences. In other words, tactics are the way and the means through which you communicate with your target audience and publics or the way and the means through which they learn about your offerings.

In the library environment, where pennies and dimes count, low-budget tactics are appropriate—and probably not new to you—but let us analyze the advantages and disadvantages of each one when targeting Latinos. For the purpose of this work, I have divided tactics in two groups: free tactics, which refers to free or low-cost tactics, and paid tactics, which includes tactics with a cost for materials or third-party labor.

Free Tactics

1. Publicity
2. Word-of-mouth
3. Public relations
4. Public service announcements (PSAs)
5. Personal networking
6. Popular and social media

Publicity

This tactic gives you a lot of exposure with a small budget and a moderate to persistent effort. Publicity is inexpensive and works most of the time.

- **Press releases:** Spanish or bilingual newspapers and other Latino media will often spread your press releases and keep the information updated for the community (most multicultural or ethnic media are community-oriented media). Send them as many press releases as you can so you have a constant presence in their pages. Pitch also to local newspapers, newsletters, and small community college radio stations; even if they are English-speaking, listeners might "roll the ball" with Latinos they know.
- **Weekly column:** Build a monthly or weekly column in local media answering questions from readers (real questions or some you come up with), and always offer additional information on that particular subject at your library or through your Spanish hotline. Invite readers to contact you directly at the library through mail or e-mail. Explain that questions must be in writing so you can print and answer them without misinterpretations.
- **Local radio and TV:** News releases to local radio and TV stations can be great ways to advertise your services and programs. Hosting events, participating in a local radio talk show, or giving a spotlight at the local TV station can generate responses. Announce it to your Latino Club members, and bring some with you. Even if they do not speak on air, their families, neighbors, and relatives will be delighted to see them on the screen and will be your best advertisers!

Word-of-Mouth

We encourage word-of-mouth in the Latino community. The Anglo American market does not rely on this type of communication; therefore, the use of word-of-mouth with those customers is not as wide as in the Latino market. However, word-of-mouth cannot be a passive strategy, nor should it be your only strategy. Advantages of this strategy are the following:

- It is inexpensive compared to other strategies (however, it requires planning and budget).
- It relies on third-party credibility (a friend, a relative, or a neighbor).
- It is delivered face-to-face (people pay attention to what you have to say).
- People believe it is not professionally designed to manipulate the customer.

The message delivered by word-of-mouth is a good, true, and credible story about Latino patrons or library users—something they talk about and repeat over and over because it gives them credibility or a sense of belonging, makes them look or feel good, or gives them some type of incentive or emotional reward. It has to be based on a real-life story, and it also has to be a success story, such as someone who has already used your services and, as a result, has accomplished something—acquiring citizenship is an example. Other examples are stories about how helpful members of your staff are to the Latino community, especially if they are bilingual, about a teacher who is getting ready to conduct an ESL class, and so forth.

When using word-of-mouth advertising, remember that your message cannot be boring—it has to have some life to it! A word-of-mouth campaign, like any other form of advertising, needs to be planned, and a strong emotional message needs to be delivered. Also, be aware of negative messages around the library. Customers tell negative stories three times more frequently than positive ones!

Mark Hughes (2005), in his work *Buzzmarketing: Get People to Talk about Your Stuff,* gives great insight into the world of word-of-mouth advertising; he talks about the different ways you can motivate people to start a conversation with funny and outrageous examples of word-of-mouth campaigns.

Public Relations

If your library belongs to a large system, you probably have an office of public service, outreach, or marketing. These are the people who have the media contacts in your community and know how to communicate with them. In conjunction with your CLO, present them with your promotional strategy or campaign, and they will help you decide how, who, and when to contact each media. Bring your own ideas, stories, and articles; propose your own spokespersons; pitch celebrities in your area; and get them to commit to your effort, letting them know that you are knowledgeable about the market and its behaviors. Also invite the Latino media to become part of your community partners or even your LAB; they are great allies to work with!

Public Service Announcements (PSAs)

Public libraries can make public service announcements on public television or radio. Keep these channels in mind when organizing your campaigns. Free seconds of fame might be all you can afford in the local news. Get out from behind the shelves and secure your spotlight in the community!

Personal Networking

Personal networking is a wonderful tool if you have the ability, disposition, and confidence to talk to anyone, any time. If you are a people person and passionate about outreach, you can be the designated networker for your CLO! Small business owners base most of their small promotional budget on this type of advertising because nobody can talk more enthusiastically and convincingly about an idea or concept than its owner, right? Small business owners know they *are* their business. Their image, the way they conduct and present themselves, and the way they talk about their materials and services tells everybody else a lot about how they conduct their business and how credible and reliable they are. So, if you are a natural, go for it. Inform yourself about the promotional campaign at task, and do it with passion. However, even the most passionate advocate can get burned out without the proper support. Overall, personal networking, like word-of-mouth, has to be professionally planned (and trained for).

To apply these strategies, keep in mind the cultural intricacies of the Latino community you are trying to target and the high level of stimulus you need to overcome their inertia. You can also network by requesting or verifying information about your local Latino community or by calling leaders in your area, telling them about your library efforts and eventually engaging them into your efforts.

Popular and Social Media

Imagine how wonderful it would be to have high school teens composing a hip-hop or rap song about their local library and singing it at different school events with parents in attendance! Alternatively, hold a contest for a bilingual *fotonovela* or cartoons about teens' and children's library services that you can use for your promotional campaigns! On the other hand, ask elementary or middle school students to bring their drawings about bilingual story time for you to put in a little booklet or display together for parents to see! Creating a character to represent your Latino campaign, a jingle on the local radio, or any other pop culture idea elicits audience participation, and your audience will bring ideas to you about their cultural preferences. Do not discard this powerful tool!

A special word regarding social media and Web site translation, two powerful online tools that most libraries forget—only a few libraries around the country have their Web sites completely translated into Spanish.[1] Although Latinos are lagging behind in the digital gap—a growing 56 percent of Latinos use the Internet, according to a study conducted by the Pew Hispanic Center (Livingston, Parker, and Fox 2009)—you can access and create interesting bilingual or Spanish groups related to library activities in Spanish portals and on regular social media, including Internet forums, weblogs, social blogs, wikis, podcasts, pictures, and videos. Some of these technologies are more popular than others, including blogs, picture sharing, vlogs, wall postings, e-mail, instant messaging, music sharing, crowdsourcing, and voice over IP (VoIP). Examples of applications, to name a few, are Google and Yahoo! groups (reference, social networking), Wikipedia (reference), MySpace (social networking), Facebook (social networking), MouthShut.com, yelp.com (material reviews), Youmeo (social network aggregation), Last.fm (personal music), YouTube (social networking and video sharing), Avatars United (social networking), Second Life (virtual reality), Flickr (photo sharing), and Twitter (social networking and microblogging). Talk to your techie about the possibilities within your system. Check out the Latino/Hispanic videos at YouTube—there are plenty and they are very popular among Latinos. Several free downloaders (software allowing you to download your video on the Internet) are offered—just Google it—and you can post your library-made video about Latinos in your community and the use of your library. Make it fun, make it funny, or make it the way you want, but make it![2]

Remember, none of these strategies can be applied alone. Your successful promotional strategies will result from the best mix of some of these strategies at different times according to budgetary constraints, a good sense of opportunity, and a judicial use of resources.

Paid Tactics

Certainly more costly advertising tactics might work better for you if you belong to a large system in a large city. The larger the system, the larger the budget—although not always—but you can try to make use of these advertising tactics by getting help from your outside resources:

1. Printed material
2. Paid advertising
3. Promotional items

Printed Materials

Printed materials may be your main promotional effort if your budget is restricted (or almost nonexistent). To be successful with your printed materials campaign, keep in mind the characteristics of the target market (low levels of literacy in some cases). Brochures, flyers, posters, calendars, even a newsletter are great promotional tools. Including pictures of and comments about past events and posting them on your Web site is a great, inexpensive way to reach your Latino customers, especially if your Web site is translated into Spanish and they visit it frequently.

> A short story about printed materials: A Mexican woman I knew once showed up at my house very upset, almost in tears. The school had given her notice that the bus was not stopping to pick her little girls up any more because they had been late to the bus stop several times. The situation was difficult because she had no transportation, and taking the girls to school and picking them up every day conflicted with her and her husband's work schedule. I asked her if the school has sent her a note at the beginning of the school year letting her know about this policy. She responded, "Well, I guess so, they sent me all those flyers but it was too much to read so I threw them away!"

Paid Advertising

Includes ads in television, radio, Internet, magazines, newspapers, direct mailings, and telemarketing. The media channels for paid advertising are usually costly, and you will have to work with a creative agency to develop your campaign. Magazines and newspapers usually offer ad design for an extra cost. Remember to take advantage of your nonprofit status and go through your powerful strategic partners to request help. Tax-exempt funding could be enticing to corporations and other businesses in your community. Also, use your local community colleges and universities to help in the task of generating complex campaigns for your library, or request pro-bono services with local advertising agencies—especially Hispanic agencies. Knocking on doors might open them—but they won't open if you do not knock!

Promotional Items

It would be great to have an ample yearly budget that allowed for the purchase of promotional items, such as magnets and baseball hats or T-shirts. But if you don't have it, don't be discouraged. Wait for an opportunity when your more powerful community partners can provide the funds. For instance, perhaps your strategic partner can donate T-shirts and, in exchange, put their logo or slogan on the T-shirts as your campaign's sponsor. By working with sponsors, you cooperate with your strategic partners' efforts and get your name out there. Also, ALA Graphics—the American Library Association store—has excellent promotional items, and you can request some customized items, such as bookmarks and posters, for a particular campaign.

Furthermore, if some of your CLO members or staff have graphic design software and skills, you can also print your own bookmarks, stickers for children, lapel buttons, posters, and more. Invite your Latino patrons, children, or families to come to the library and pose for a poster. Use it as a reward for referrals. Give Latinos the opportunity to become the real stars of their community!

These concepts have been summarized on Table 8.2 for quick reference. Some of these tactics might not be allowed by your system's policies. Find out the limitations, and try to negotiate with your board for temporary or specific policies for your Latino campaign. In these times of tight budgets and limited funding, a temporary exemption that shows success might become a permanent policy in the future!

It would be ideal to have a qualified professional in house to deal with your promotional, advertising, and public service efforts. However, you might have to assign responsibilities to a CLO subcommittee for the implementation of your promotional strategies, overseen by your outreach director or CLO chair, who might be, all in all, the same person!

TABLE 8.2 Advantages and Disadvantages of Tactics Targeting Latino Customers

Tactic	Medium	Advantages and Disadvantages
Free Tactics		
1. Word-of-mouth	A true, successful story that includes third-party credibility	Widely accepted in the Latino community, needs planning with a strong emotional message
2. Publicity	Press releases, weekly columns in local newspapers, radio and TV	Local, good if targeted to the Spanish/bilingual media or mainstream in areas of long-established population
3. Public relations	Identify your relevant publics; conduct media interviews; provide speakers at conferences, events, fairs, trade shows	Invite your publics to become part of your community partners or even your LAB
4. Public service announcements (PSAs)	Public television and radio, community boards, and local government announcements	Should be done often; partner with local government, local media, and companies that serve Latinos
5. Personal networking	Talk to Latinos with enthusiasm and convincingly about your library, learn techniques, build a success story	Personal, one-on-one, targeted; overcome language barrier with tools (cheat cards, games, Spanglish!)
6. Popular and social media	Use all online resources, especially Latino portals, online social networks, blogs, newsletters, as well as library-made songs and videos, contests, bilingual cartoons, *fotonovelas* about the library, displayed drawings, etc.	"I love my Library" (an advocacy initiative of ALA—www.ilovelibraries.org) shows a successful experience. These tactics empower the community, especially youngsters.
Paid Tactics		
1. Printed materials	Brochures, flyers, posters, calendars, even a bilingual newsletter	Direct, inexpensive; use visuals and colors, and post them on your bilingual Web site and social media
2. Paid advertising	Ads in television, radio, Internet, magazines, newspapers, direct mailings, telemarketing	Costly, impersonal, massive, will need long-running campaigns; effective in large cities and large systems
3. Promotional items	Budget promotional items or make your own: posters, cards, coupons, bookmarks, T-shirts, and more	Very successful as incentives; seek your more powerful community partners for donations or funding

Starting a Promotional Campaign

Where to start? In order to help you easily tackle this task, answer in detail the seven questions in Worksheet 8.1 every time you need to start a promotional campaign. Answering these questions will define every aspect of your promotional campaign.

Your strategy defines *what* needs to be promoted (either the branding task or the mini-campaign at hand), the target audience and additional publics, and the objectives to be attained. The strategy is contained in the first three questions. Your tactics determine *how* the message is going to be communicated to the target audience—in other words, how they learn about your brand or your program, activity or service. Questions 4, 5, and 6 define your tactics. Finally, question 7 helps you evaluate results and procedures of your promotional campaigns.

We will discuss in the next sections how to start a promotional campaign for both a branding effort and a promotional mini-campaign.

Creating an Organizational Brand

What is branding, and what do we use it for? In chapter 6, we discussed the need to position your organization as a unique response to Latinos' problems and needs. We analyzed your competition and the potential obstacles, barriers, and limiting beliefs Latinos might have related to library services and determined responses to those concerns through benefits and positive social pressure. As a result, we came up with a positioning statement example based on a customer-centered approach, espousing values Latinos cherish as a community, grounded in actual accomplishments and relationships, and defining your organization as a unique place for serving a particular target audience. You will have to define your own based on the goals and values of your library strategy.

Branding is a marketing strategy that persuades your prospects to see you not as the best but as the only organization that provides a solution to their problem. The objectives of a good brand include delivering a clear message of who your organization is and what it stands for, validating your credibility among your target audience, making a rational and emotional connection with your target audience, and developing customer loyalty. Now is the time to create a promotional strategy to communicate your brand to your Latino customers.

General promotional strategies or branding efforts will include developing education and awareness about your organization and its services. The following topics are recommended to be included in branding efforts:

1. Your library's mission statement and/or diversity statement
2. The existence of a CLO
3. The existence of a LAB and how they can participate
4. Your location and hours of operation
5. Free services your library offers
6. Requirements to become a library member
7. Ways they can borrow and reserve materials
8. Guidelines for using the Internet and online databases
9. Your Spanish Web site and how to use it—if you have one—and other social media networking
10. Library materials available for the Spanish-speaking community
11. Library materials available for Latino families, teens, and children
12. Other available resources including educational, health, and social information
13. Why the library charges fines for unreturned materials and fees for damaged materials

14. Who are the Friends of the Library and how anybody can volunteer for the library
15. How they can trust the library with confidential personal information
16. Any other matters related to library logistics that they need to know

Do not try to promote *all* these elements at the same time. Combine the ones that make sense to increase understanding of your message. For instance, if you want to let your Latino community know that your library is concerned about their well-being, you can advertise items 1, 2, and 3. When you are trying to convey the know-how of your library, you might combine 4, 6, 7, and 8. Any combination that makes sense for you and your CLO will work as long as you keep it short and on target. Do not try to explain too many aspects of becoming a library member at the same time.

Avoid long brochures or flyers with crowded text and small fonts. Remember that the attention span of a low-literate individual might be short, and you may need several promotional pieces to communicate the message. You can target individuals who are more educated with the same promotional campaign. A simple message with clear content is effective at all levels.

Let us see what a general promotional strategy might entail. Following our example from chapter 6, we defined the following elements:

Defining Branding Goals

Develop a yearly awareness campaign for three consecutive years. The first year will focus on awareness of the organization's mission statement and its friendly outlook to build strong relationships with the Latino community. The second year will focus on how the library responds to the local Latino community's needs and preferences—following a Latino community assessment—with appropriate programs and services. The third year will focus on how the library can increase and sustain past programs and services and expand materials and collections to serve the local Latino community. You can choose your own strategy based on your organizational goals, the stage of your library's marketing plan, and the decisions of your CLO.

Our first-year short-term goal was to increase awareness of library services through low-budget promotional strategies. Strategies and tactics for this purpose need to be developed.

Branding Strategy

1. Describe your branding effort (What are we trying to promote?) Explain the main purpose of this campaign and the benefits it will generate to your target audience. The brand needs to be related to the mission or charter statement, and it will describe your purpose and goals as described in chapter 2. It ultimately can be expressed in a slogan or motto for your Latino campaign that can be related to the general slogan of your library.

2. Identify your target audience and influencers (Whom are we trying to reach?) Define the specific Latino audience you are trying to reach. In this case, it is the Latino community at large and their influencers. We suggested a memory jogger list in Worksheet 6.8.

3. Establish your campaign objectives (What are we trying to achieve?) In promoting your organization's brand, you need to be specific about what you want to accomplish. Do you want them to know what your organizational values are? Promote the ideas in your mission or charter statement regarding your Latino customers. Do you want them to know how you deliver that promise? Promote your SWOT's strengths and the solutions you propose to your weaknesses. Do you want them to know what you provide that others cannot? Promote what is unique in your organization and how you position yourself in the community, what strategic partners you work with, and how you plan to achieve your goals to serve the Latino community. Finally, make an emotional appeal to your target audience by engaging them in your goals.

Branding Tactics

4. Create an image or theme (How do we communicate it?) Creating a theme for your promotional campaign is not describing your services but rather involves portraying your organization in a way that is relevant to your target audience. Your potential customers should easily spot the theme because it speaks to them. The campaign theme sets the direction for all advertisements and communication pieces. It can also be a logo, a motto, a slogan, or any strong idea later translated into a recognizable image, color or colors, and/or words that link your message to all aspects of a campaign: from flyers and printed materials to Web sites, library displays, and stationary. Sometimes it can be a well-designed character or cartoon that is meaningful to your Latino community and to the library environment, but please check the cultural implications of a character with your Latino community leaders and even research it on the Internet before you implement this type of tactic.

Your general theme—logo or slogan—needs to create an emotional bond with your potential customers. For instance, New Jersey's Ocean County Library's branding slogan is "Connecting People . . . Building Communities." New York's Queens Library's slogan is "Enrich your Life." We chose *"Ayuda a tu biblioteca a ayudar a tu comunidad"* ("Help Your Library Help Your Community") for our Little Haven City Public Library plan for Latino outreach. The tagline is reminiscent of an old Christian aphorism in Spanish, *"Ayúdate que Yo te ayudaré"* (Help yourself so I can help you). An accompanying cartoon character personifying helpfulness will show up in every message to help (a similar idea to the old Microsoft Office help paper clip). Make it culturally relevant and *simpático!* Repetition will identify your organization, and every effort you implement will be recognized by the coherence of the theme. Ideally, the theme of your Latino branding campaign will be tied to your library's brand features.[3]

5. Develop your message (How do we say it?) Creating messages is one of the most interesting phases of the communication process. In this phase, the content and theme determined in previous steps are creatively turned into appealing and thought-provoking phrases. You define a message strategy by developing a creative brief. The following sections will expand on how to develop a creative brief and how you can use it for your campaigns. You will also find a blank form for a creative brief in chapter 10.

6. Select and implement a media plan (How do we deliver it?) This is one of the trickiest steps in the promotional campaign. No matter how good your products or your messages, if the target audience does not hear about them, they don't exist. Each step of the communication process has its own appropriate media tactic, and we will analyze the advantages and disadvantages of each one. Developing a media plan and campaign implementation will help you decide the best way to execute your campaign in your specific situation. You will be able to complete these forms in chapter 10 as well.

Worksheet 8.2 at the end of this chapter exemplifies a year's general promotional tactics with the ideas previously described. See chapter 10 for a blank version of this worksheet.

For the first year, we use low-budget, culturally appropriate promotional tactics for the Latino community focusing on success stories at the library; our tactics will focus on publicity (press releases, and articles in local newspapers), word-of-mouth, monthly PSAs, and printed materials.

Although the topics of the press releases are library related, they should be presented with the Latino customer in mind. Talking about the changing demographics of your area, the idea of a library serving the needs of the different groups in the community, the contributions of the Latino community to the economy, and other arguments we discussed in chapter 2 are good elements to build these press releases. The four additional human-interest stories can be included as third-party credibility. Try to combine the elements the best way possible. Remember that the stories' focal point is not materials and services or your library. The protagonist role—the spotlight—is on your Latino customer. In a customer-centered approach, materials and services are a solution to their problems: the most important messages are the success stories and the benefits these protagonists received—or will receive—from your organization. Prepare similar tactics for each year of your three-year plan focusing on different topics and issues that relate to your branding strategies.

Lastly, not everything can be expressed through printed materials. Personal contact is important for this community, and although it might be hard to get Latinos to participate, once you have them, it might be easier to promote your services by including information in activities they participate in or value. Offer anytime guided tours of the library as a way for patrons to meet friendly bilingual staff and become acquainted with everything that is there for them. Also, take advantage of ideas from other libraries around the country—for instance, the "Parents' Workshops" at the New York Public Library that Judith Rodríguez (2000, p. 43) describes so eloquently: "Now we do reading aloud, storytelling, flannel board stories, or origami stories and book talks, no more than four minutes each. Many times we get the parents to volunteer a story or song. We talk about the library services and rules in between activities and books presentations. The conversation is in simple language—their own language."

Evaluating Results

7. Evaluate results and procedures (How did we do?) The last step in your promotional campaign is related to an evaluation of your promotional effort. This is not the evaluation of your marketing plan (chapter 9) but the assessment of what went well and what when wrong in terms of communicating your ideas to your target audience at this particular stage. It includes evaluating your message and procedures before the campaign, your results after the campaign, and customer satisfaction. The evaluation process includes several steps, and even if it looks like additional tasks you cannot really afford, what you really cannot afford is to lose your funding, discourage your staff, and not even make a dent in your target audience's knowledge about library services because of repeated mistakes.

The evaluation phase is, then, a learning stage where you can see your target audience's reactions to your promotional efforts and become aware of the necessary adjustments to cater more specifically to their needs and preferences. It also requires a customer-centered approach. Set some benchmarks before and after your campaign. For instance, you can evaluate and compare tactics before choosing your strategy. After the campaign, you can evaluate soft and hard data, such as responses from strategic partners, media, your community, your employees, and other publics—soft data—before even evaluating the response from the

Latino community—your ultimate target market. You will find tools and guidelines to evaluate both your branding and mini-campaigns toward the end of this chapter.

The Arizona Department of Education Division of Educational Services & Resources Adult Education Services created a complete booklet in English designed for instructors to teach students how to use the library, revised in March 2008. The booklet was adapted from an undated Tucson-Pima Public Library book authored by Mary Konstanki (the original version was also in Spanish). The booklet can give you a better idea of what was included in the original curriculum to plan your own branding campaign. State of Arizona Department of Education, "Becoming Library Literate," http://www.azed.gov/Adult-Ed/Documents/Resources/BecomingLibraryLiterate.pdf (accessed January 21, 2010).

Running a Promotional Mini-Campaign

In addition to your general promotional strategies, you also need to keep your Latino audience engaged in library activities and encourage them to use your services. To activate your Latino community, you need to promote primarily the outreach programs, activities, and services that respond to their needs and wants as discussed in chapter 7.

Your CLO will define promotional mini-campaign strategies and tactics for each program or activity. These promotional efforts are not complete until you find a way to encourage your customers to take action. How do you motivate your potential customer to choose you over the competition (their old habits)?

In a social marketing promotional mini-campaign, the product you are promoting is not the program, activity, or service you offer but the *behavior* you want your potential customers to adopt because you offer a unique solution to their problems or a way to improve their lives. It might sound a bit strange at the beginning, but think in terms of the intangible ideas we discussed in chapter 2 and also in chapter 6, especially about benefits and ways to overcome barriers and obstacles.

A customer-centered approach promotes *benefits* that help people *change habits* (such as trusting an experienced librarian to find free credible information instead of unlikely word-of-mouth resources outside the library); *acquire knowledge* (acquiring literacy skills in a friendly environment with flexible schedules); *adopt a practice* (borrowing free books or DVDs on a regular basis instead of buying or renting them); or *use a service* provided by the library (using Internet access at the library when your target audience does not have computers at home).

As also discussed in chapter 6, the product needs to be dressed up to become enticing and attractive to your audience. Following the seven questions of a promotional campaign, here are guidelines to start a promotional mini-campaign and the main areas in which you need to define specific strategies and tactics.

Mini-campaign Strategy

1. Describe your product (What are we trying to promote?) Establish the *behavior* you want to change related to this mini-campaign. Explain the main purpose of this campaign as described in your positioning statement (Worksheet 7.2.). Then choose a campaign focus positioning the key benefits your target audience will encounter at such an event and why their participation is relevant to them and other influencers. From your campaign positioning statement, extract those key benefits and features that make your offering unique to become the promotional mini-campaign's central points. Look at our Latino Teen Summer Club example: the benefits were summarized in Worksheet 7.2.

2. Identify your target audience and influencers (Whom are we trying to reach?) Define the specific segment you are trying to reach within your Latino audience. Try to be very specific about who you are targeting, as defined in chapters 3 and 7. You also need to address your other publics or influencers, people in your community your target audience trusts or are influenced by: in the Latino teens example, these influencers are their parents and relatives, schoolteachers and counselors, their peers, and other people they look up to in the community. For other target audiences, refer to the memory jogger list in Worksheet 6.8.

3. Establish campaign objectives (What are we trying to achieve?) Define measurable objectives. A simple acronym used to set objectives is called SMART objectives.[4] SMART stands for Specific, Measurable, Achievable, Realistic, and Time:

Specific: Objectives should specify what you want to accomplish through your promotion, such as increased membership in certain Latino segments (specify which ones), increased Internet use (determine how often), reaching a new geographic location or segments (specify which ones), or attracting a certain population to participate in a specific activity (determine how many people). The change can be quantitative or qualitative.

Measurable: You should be able to measure your results in order to evaluate whether you are meeting your objectives or not. This can be tricky as it might be difficult at the beginning to reconcile your wants with your resources. Use a 10/10 guideline (target 10% of your Latino market or market segment using 10% of your resources for promotional efforts). For instance, if you have a $2,000 grant for an activity designed to attract 500 Latino families, dedicate at least $200 to promotional strategies to target at least 50 families. You may ask what happens with the rest. The reality is that you cannot do much with $200, so it is better to target a smaller group with your best effort. Use free tactics for the rest with little expectation. Your best bet is to be successful this one time so participants will do your job for you. Then adjust accordingly as you acquire more experience in the type of response you receive. Start with baby steps. The bigger the numbers, the larger the effort!

Achievable: What do you want your target audience and your publics to do because of your promotional efforts? Are those goals achievable and attainable with the target audience's present level of readiness? What type of effort is needed to get them to a successful result? Check again with your primary and secondary data, run your mini-campaign objectives by your Latino Advisory Board and your community leaders, and take a calculated risk. They have experience about how the community responds, what and where local Latinos should be targeted, and what incentives they need to take action.

Realistic: Can you realistically achieve the objectives with the resources you have in the proposed time? Again, check your target/resource ratio. Make a list of all tasks that need to be accomplished before—preparation tasks—and during—implementation tasks—your promotional campaign. Do not forget to include the manpower factor into the equation. Funding is needed, but people are instrumental!

Time: When do you want to achieve the set promotional objectives? Start from the time you would launch your service or activity and work backward towards the present, establishing timelines. Again, set your goals realistically. Also, be moderate in your estimation. Excitement at the beginning of a campaign can set you out of perspective. Compare with other campaigns you have run in the past for benchmarks or similar campaigns for other groups—other minorities, groups with special needs, and so forth. Check seasonal work schedules, school schedules, and holidays. Do not overlap with other activities, and provide additional services—if possible—to facilitate the activity.

At first, you will have to make use of more resources, more time, and more effort to target fewer patrons. However, once you have established a loyal customer base, they will help you bring in others by spreading the word. Your efforts and resources then should be able to be scaled back or will at least be more balanced with results.

Mini-campaign Tactics

4. Create an image or theme (How do we communicate it?) As discussed in general promotional strategies, creating a theme portrays your activity or service with an original idea or presents the activity in a new way. It should be easily spotted by your targeted audience because it is relevant to their needs and a solution to their problems. The campaign theme—a logo, a motto, a slogan, or any strong idea later translated into a recognizable image, color or colors, and/or words—is central to all your communication pieces including flyers and printed materials, Web sites, videos, and library displays. If you have a well-designed character or cartoon for your branding efforts that is meaningful to your Latino community and to the library environment, this is the time to put it to work.

If you established a general theme—logo or slogan—for your three-year branding effort, now is the time to use it in your specific promotional mini-campaign. You can use a tagline related to your program and add the branding slogan. Your tagline has to be the link between the branding effort and the specific mini-campaign. For instance, the tagline *"Cómo ser un super héroe en tu biblioteca"* (Be a superhero at your library) used for a tutoring program of advanced Latino teens helping disadvantage students could work in the library followed by *"Ayuda a tu biblioteca a ayudar a tu comunidad"* (Help your library help your community).

5. Develop a message (How do we say it?) Your mini-campaign message defines all the elements you want your target audience to know about your program or activity and the behavior you want them to perform as a result of the message. In a specific promotional mini-campaign, the central message is a direct call for action. Rational and emotional components will address your target audience's different levels of readiness related to your program or activity. In the next sections, we will discuss a communication model that brings the target audience through the process of making such decisions to end in an action. As mentioned, we will define also a message strategy by developing a creative brief.

6. Select and implement a media plan (How do we deliver it?) As said, no matter how enticing your programs or activities are, how well your message is crafted, or how appealing your images are, they are not enough if they don't reach their audience. Each step of the communication process has its own appropriate media tactic. A media plan and campaign implementation will help you execute your campaign successfully. Look at Table 8.2. to define which tactics are appropriate for the task at hand. Later in this chapter we discuss a media plan implementation.

Evaluating Results

7. Evaluate results and procedures (How do we evaluate results?) Mostly, advertising campaigns in traditional marketing are assessed by their results: people who buy the product, people who show up at the event, and so on. However, in social marketing, you are monitoring and evaluating people's change of behavior. So evaluation of your promotional effort has more to do with what you can learn about your target audience than with the results themselves. Although results are also important, they might take time. Do not get discouraged if your first mini-campaign does not bring in outrageous results. It may take several attempts before your target audience makes the necessary changes in their lives to use your services. Evaluating promotional efforts is covered toward the end of this chapter.

These seven questions for a promotional effort should be answered every time, whether you are planning for your long-term strategy, your yearly strategy, or a promotional mini-campaign for an event or activity. But before you decide on your strategy, find out if everybody is ready for your promotional efforts. In chapter 10 you will find a blank version of Worksheet 8.2 that you can use for any promotional campaign and short- or long-term goals.

A Communication Model: Awareness, Acceptance, Action

Your local Latino audience has different levels of readiness toward the use of library services. Some people might not know services exist, some might know but do not use them, and some might want to use them but can't. To use your services, they need to change their routines or belief system or just find the time in their lives.

In order to work effectively with any audience, either to produce effective promotional campaigns and/or to create behavioral changes, a social marketer needs to be familiar with theories and research in behavioral change[5] and communication models.

A communications model is simply a procedure that helps you understand customer behavior and establish a productive way of communicating with them. Companies survey and analyze customers' behavior constantly in order to be successful at promoting their products, and that data helps develop these models or procedures.

For instance, if we say, "Maria decided to go to the library for ESL classes," what class is Maria taking? Maybe none, because making a decision is *not* attending or even registering for a class. When you decide to buy something—a car, a house, even a new suit or a pair of shoes—there is a lot happening from the moment you make the decision to the moment you actually purchase the product: the larger the purchase, the more complicated the process. In addition, do you remember the time when you were exhilarated about signing that contract for a new house, the sellers accepted your offer, and then you started to have second thoughts about the house? That is common human behavior, and companies know that all these changes in customers' feelings might modify the course of an action. They work on special communication models to keep customers motivated until the end of their decision-making process.

In traditional marketing, the first goal when a product is launched is to grab the customer's attention. Then they have to keep the customer interested in the product, create a desire or momentum to acquire the product, and finally push the customer to buy. The purchase is usually based on an emotional response to the promotional stimulus.

Several communication models in the marketing industry help companies develop successful promotional strategies.[6] Based on these models, I created one for the library environment targeting Latinos, but you can use a similar model for other groups in your community.

For the library environment, the AAA model works well. It includes three stages in the communication process: Awareness, Acceptance, and Action. These stages are based on social marketing guidelines.

At first, you need to not only grab your Latino customer's attention but also develop *awareness* about the ideas you want to promote. Awareness implies knowledge gained by means of information, so there is an educational component the customer needs to learn. In this case, Maria needs to be made aware of the benefits the class will bring to her life—she might already know this but may need to be reminded. She also needs to be informed about the benefits of taking this class at the library—maybe because it is free, has an advanced level she needs, is addressed to mothers with children, or is in a more convenient location close to her job. She will also learn that the class is developed for people like her—people with specific needs, such as a particular job or activity, or who need help with their children or applying for citizenship. Knowing about the presence of a bilingual teacher—if that is the case—and any other feature that will make her feel interested and confident at the same time will provide extra assurance to her decision. As you see, when you promote benefits, you try to make it really personal!

Once the customer is knowledgeable about the ideas you recommend and feels comfortable with them, he or she reaches the stage of favorable reception or even approval of the promoted idea. The customer might have evaluated other choices and has decided that what you offer is favorable to his liking or need. This is the stage of *acceptance*. Maria might have researched or asked her friends and relatives about the class, found out that the library is closer than other classes offered in the area, and liked the idea that the classes at the library are free or suited for her learning level. She might have heard from her friends who took that class in the past—third-party credibility or word-of-mouth—or may be thinking of registering with a friend who is also interested in the class. All these factors have a strong influence on her decision.

Thirdly, although the customer might have accepted your idea as the best choice, he or she still might not be ready to take *action*. The customer might be waiting for additional information, maybe plans to act later, or has a particular obstacle that impedes his or her decision. Finding out what is stopping Maria from taking action and solving the issue is the final task in the communication process. Maybe Maria cannot take the class because she has small children at home, or she feels inadequate because she does not have great literacy skills in Spanish, or maybe her final issue is lack of transportation and she is counting on a friend to give her a ride. Even if the customer has made a favorable decision and decided to accept your offer, you need to help him or her overcome those final obstacles—if you can. If your organization has been successful with its strategy then the target customer should take action.

Do not always assume you need to take all your Latino customers through all these stages. Current Latino customers might be aware of library services and have some knowledge and information about how the library works; however, they might need additional information—for instance, on how to use the interlibrary loan system, how to access a database, or how to request the purchase of a specific material. They might not know about your CLO and its activity, or they may know about the Latino Advisory Board but are timid about being a part of it. They might be professionals who know the library well but are hesitant to offer a workshop or activity related to their professional skills or other related topics to the community at large because the opportunity has not been offered. The possibilities are endless! These are customers with different levels of readiness to respond to your promotional efforts, and you need to find out who they are. You can find this information through community leaders, ethnographic interviews, patrons' surveys, and informal interviews, as discussed in previous chapters.

"The communicator must . . . identify the stage that characterizes most of the target audience and develop a communications message or campaign that will move them to the next stage. Rarely can one message move the audience through all three stages" (Kotler and Fox 1985, p. 371). You will have to find a cost-effective tactic that will help you move your Latino customers from one stage to another. Also, remember that people act on impulse, so create an emotional response to your advertising and capitalize on that impulse, resulting in your customer taking action. This is why you need effective messages that touch Latinos deep inside!

Lastly, you will need to determine who to reach and when. With a short budget you want to reach out first to those customers who are readier than others, as we previously discussed, which will require less advertising effort and frequency. Someone who already participated at past events, friends and family of current patrons or library members, parents of Latino children in the Head Start[7] program or the local public schools, or people who will hear a message channeled by a strategic partner—these are your readiest customers, so always try these tactics with them first. In Table 8.3 you will find a summary of different tactics that can be used at different stages of the communication model.

Tactics that can help you disseminate information, such as publicity (press releases, articles, and weekly columns), word-of-mouth campaigns, personal networking, and social media can provide more extensive and detailed information at the time when you need to

TABLE 8.3   Appropriate Tactics According to Communication Stage

Stage of Awareness Goal: To provide information and educate your target audience and influencers	**Free tactics**: Press releases, a weekly column, a public relations or a word-of-mouth campaign (speakers, events, fairs, tradeshows, etc.), personal networking, online social media, and library-made videos
	Paid tactics: Direct massive mailing, other printed materials, radio and television spots with an educational message, professionally made videos
	Incentives: A prize contest to call attention to the event, short videos about the activity or demo of the practice you offer, "bring your friend" or "tell a friend" and other introductory tactics
Stage of Acceptance Goal: To reaffirm options and benefits	**Free tactics**: Interviews on local radio or television discussing the initiative and the benefits to your audience; additional press releases with updated information or new developments; additional PR activities such as panel discussions and participation at community events; videos or pictures stating benefits of the activity; pictures or library videos of similar past events; pictures of the facility or your staff who are involved in the activity or are frontline personnel; a social media page—preferably bilingual—to post additional information and answer questions/collect information from potential customers with links to Spanish portals and main search engines
	Paid tactics: A follow-up direct mail letter to potential or targeted customers; distribution of calendars, newsletters, and/or cartoons about previous successes or benefits of this activity or event; third-party credibility (participants, people in the community, or celebrities supporting the program) in videos, radio, or TV spots
	Incentives: Interactive request for contact information—such as a photo gallery or a game on your Web site or social media page, a subscription to a library newsletter or a library *fotonovela*, or a trivia contest related to cultural issues or what is going on at the library, all requiring free registration

(Continued)

TABLE 8.3 *(Continued)*

Stage of Action Goal: To encourage the customer to take action	**Free tactics**: Flyers, public service announcements in the local media (on local radio and TV), or an event calendar reminding them to take action. "Pitch" your target audience at this time with last-minute potential obstacles: "Register now, seating is limited." "Is lack of transportation preventing you from attending this event? Call us, we provide rides from point A to point B." "Please preregister your child for FREE child activities at the time of your class." "Not enough time to go home before class? Snacks and refreshments are on us."
	Paid tactics: A direct mail reminder card, a brochure with a registration form insert, a phone call to entice potential registration, or a massive e-mail with a registration deadline if you have their contact information
	Incentives: A gift to register—free materials for the class; a chance to win a flash drive or a CD or DVD related to the activity; bookmarks; children's story books; a coupon for a local strategic partner's product, activity, or event; and other tangible incentives

educate your potential customer about the promotional task at hand. Also, incentives that will catch Latinos' attention related to that awareness should be offered.

In the stage of acceptance, tactics that will help your customers compare your option with other choices, discuss advantages and disadvantages, and show the uniqueness of your offer are appropriate. It is also appropriate at this stage to present third-party credibility or success stories to create enthusiasm and momentum for your offer. Also, activities to follow-up the awareness stage are necessary to keep the customer engaged in your promotional effort, such as mailers, calendars, and "save the date" pieces.

Finally, the action stage requires a series of short but very effective communication pieces that will motivate your target audience to make a decision based on an emotional response. This is when your cultural images and concepts play a huge role. Incentives are also important at this stage (but do not get confused with incentives offered for your customers to complete the activity). Incentives at this stage encourage Latinos to register, attend, request the information he or she needs, and use your facilities. At the session, class, or any other activity or program, you can also offer incentives—the most common incentives offered are food and/or free materials.

You need to determine what stage of the communication model your target audience is and choose the appropriate tactic to ensure they get the information they need at their level of readiness. Low-cost tactics are abundant and effective once you get to use them frequently. And remember, there is more in the world of communications than flyers!

Building a Media Plan

After taking advantage of all the choices we just analyzed, your best option is to put together a media plan that includes a mix of free and paid media coverage. You could start with a kick-off event inviting all local media if you are planning branding efforts, if this is your first time targeting this community, or if the nature of the event justifies a special launching affair. Consider the extent of your campaign depending on your organization's size and area of coverage. If you cover a large area such as a big city, you might have to narrow down your options to keep your campaign focused and work by neighborhood or city sections.

Your CLO's task is to build a media contact list that includes updated information about each media outlet and gatekeepers. Find out who covers your topic, their frequency, and their printing or airing schedule. You can consult media directories—however, if they are in print, they might be updated only once a year—or work with news organizations.[8] Worksheet 8.3 will help you build your contact media list. Chapter 10 includes a blank copy.

You can build a spreadsheet (i.e., an Excel file) with these same data or just a word processing document to keep on your computer. You can also use any database that would allow you to build letters and do mail merges, such as Outlook Business Manager. You can also use Microsoft Access, FileMaker, or IBM Lotus Approach. Another alternative is MyDatabase, a part of Elibrium's MySoftware line that lets you create flat-file databases from scratch. The program provides templates for common business and personal applications and imports data from several other databases, including Access, ACT, and Outlook. You can also make copies of the blank forms provided in this book. In any case, follow these guidelines:

1. Start a publicity file with folders for each media, contact information, press release templates, and a calendar that will follow your programming so you can send press releases and PSAs with enough time—but not too much—to be published. Follow your target publications' deadlines.
2. Write down ideas, keep publicity pieces, and browse magazines and newspapers to get ideas on how big companies spending thousands of dollars reach out to the Latino market. Cut articles and keep them in your file for future reference.
3. Make a commitment to promote a newsworthy event within the Latino community at least once a week/month even if it is *not* directly addressed to the target audience. It is important to remember to keep press releases short; identify the organization or individual sending the release, including a contact name and phone number of the person who can respond to their inquiry; and the release's date—clarify if it is for immediate use or for release at a later date.
4. Keep Latinos in the loop for other events—they might be willing to participate, or it will at least make them feel included. Use bilingual press releases, newsletters, and other appropriate pieces.[9]
5. Designate two persons in your CLO—one for backup—to be the contact for all media relations and to respond to inquiries from the media for more information or photo shoot opportunities.

During the campaign, prepare your staff to contact the designated CLO members to respond to reactions from the public at large, other members of the community, government agents, and others who might call the library with positive or negative reactions. CLO members should be trained and prepared to respond to questions and comments about your campaigns. We will expand on this topic later in this chapter.

Timing and Scheduling Your Promotional Efforts

A brief word about timing your promotional strategies and campaigns: As previously suggested, your CLO members need to work with your PR, outreach, or marketing staff in order to plan your efforts and not overlap with other activities. There are two questions to ask related to timing:

1. When is your target audience most likely to be reached? In marketing jargon, these opportunities are called *openings*. In other words, these are the occasions your target audience is more *open* to hear and receive your message. Look at yearly schedules as well as daily schedules. What months, weeks, days, and hours are better to launch and sustain your campaign? Find out what other activities and events in the community might distract your market or interfere with your campaign. For instance, starting December 8—Virgin of Guadalupe's Day—and continuing into the holiday season, many people in the Mexican community will be very much engaged in the celebrations of their religious beliefs, thus taking their attention away from library services—unless those services are related to the holiday season.

2. When will your target audience be more predisposed to listen and participate? Discovering the time of highest predisposition can boost your campaign. Do you want to promote a class on learning Internet and e-mailing? Try before the holiday season so participants can send e-cards and greetings to their friends and relatives. Do you want to promote a workshop on taxes and how to get a tax ID? Try January, February, or March—just before the April 15 deadline. Timing is important because your customers are concerned with that particular issue at that particular time (see Worksheet 8.4).

In addition, follow the guidelines we discussed earlier in this chapter about the advantages and disadvantages of selected media. You will be able to identify additional information and define your media contacts on Worksheet 8.2 more precisely. You will find blank copies of all these worksheets in chapter 10.

Once you have defined your media tactics, including scheduling and timing, it is time to develop messages that will directly and effectively reach out to your Latino customers.

Creating Effective Messages

Spending a fabulous amount of money on creative advertising is not always necessary, but keep in mind that you need to know your audience's inclinations and weak spots and make them prominent in your promotional materials.

For instance, there is a cultural weak spot for witty and funny in the Latino community. Latinos speak with idioms and sayings, double entendres and jokes; they like to have the last word in a sharp conversation, make other people laugh, or get emotional.

Multicultural advertisers know that if they grasp that peculiarity of Latinos in their message and images, they are sure to get the target market's attention. Of course, the message should also connect the product with the potential customer in a rational way so it triggers a response or action. In other words, the potential customer needs to be knowledgeable about and connect with the offering.

To create these cultural connections to your event, materials, or services, you need to understand what makes sense to your target audience—as explained in chapter 5. Your biggest pitfalls are to believe that your Latino customers will react to the same stimulus as the general market and that all Latinos will react to the same cultural stimulus. However, you have done your homework by now, so you should have pretty good knowledge of the market you are targeting, the segments within that market, and their needs and wants. Now you just need to know what makes Latinos shake! For that, you have your Latino Advisory Board, your community leaders, and your current Latino patrons; they can help you brainstorm for ideas.

Creating effective messages involves accurately defining message content and images, implementing your promotional tactic efficiently, and selecting the right medium or means of communication and the right time to use it.

If you are going to create a word-of-mouth campaign, advertise on TV, or anything in between, you need to develop a creative brief to make sure your message is clear. The creative brief is a tool advertising agencies use for promotional strategy development. The creative brief provides direction for message design and the selection of advertising tactics (Kotler, Roberto, and Lee 2002, pp. 264–66). Creative brief ideas have been adapted for your specific needs.

The Creative Brief

> Working without a written brief is a waste of time and money.

A creative brief is like a road map. A great brief—a short page addressed to a team of creative people—leads to imaginative and persuasive messages. Through a creative brief, you are asking your team to translate your ideas into words and images that will persuade your target audience to change their relationship with a brand, product, or service—your library and your offerings. So think in terms of "I'm trying to explain briefly what ideas I want the creative team to convey"—although, in the end, you might be the one wearing the creative hat, too.

The intention in developing a creative brief is to help you clarify your ideas, be more precise, and keep your focus on the message you want to deliver and not rumble about other ideas that are not the center of your campaign. Think of a funnel: you have done a lot of research; you have plenty of information about your target audience, its behaviors, and its beliefs; and you know what makes them press on, but now you need to filter that information to deliver just a few strong ideas that will make them tick!

A creative brief also is used to address your other publics and influencers. Some of the information will be the same; however, the way you address your target audience or their influencers will change according to who they are. For instance, in our Latino Teen Summer Club, a creative brief to help you create a message addressed to the targeted Latino teens will be different from the one addressed to their parents or the one for counselors in certain aspects such as key message or tone of the communication piece.

To start your creative brief, you need to be precise in explaining the benefits of your products or services, how and in what ways your potential Latino customers' lives will improve by using those services, and how you can motivate them to take action. Here are some questions to start a creative brief:

1. Who is the market segment target audience for this particular message?
2. What benefits does this event, material, or service offer to this particular audience?
3. How does this event, material, or service deliver those benefits—advantages, special features and augmented products, details such as schedules, and customer services or skilled personnel?
4. Why is choosing this event, material, or service better than choosing those offered— or not offered—in the area? Are there similar ones offered?

5. What is the biggest cost, effort, competing behavior, or limiting belief Latino patrons need to overcome to take action?
6. How do Latinos feel about this event, material, or service?
7. What language should be used to talk about this event, material, or service? (Think not only in terms of Spanish or English but also literacy levels, acculturation, generational gap, etc.)

You already worked on almost all these answers in previous chapters, so it should be easy to develop a creative brief at this stage. These answers give you a very specific image of your target audience that you will focus on for the rest of your campaign. Now look at the common elements of a creative brief on Worksheet 8.5.[10]

Let us see in more detail what each of these creative brief sections entails.

Campaign Background

Campaign background is a description of the problems/needs that you detected in the community and that motivated you to carry out this effort. State briefly how the branding effort—or program, activity, or service —that is the focus of this campaign will address those problems. Add why choosing your services is better for them than choosing others offered—or not offered—in the area. These elements will become your campaign background.

Target Audience

This is a description of your target audience as discussed earlier, including demographics and geographic profiles. In addition to your primary segment, you need to target one or more additional groups: their influencers and media gatekeepers (chapter 6). For instance, a primary target group would be "Puerto Rican mothers of children two to six years old"; their influencers would be extended family, teachers and caregivers of their children, and employers; their media gatekeepers would be those making decisions about the type of information published in the media that these mothers use or trust.

- Include demographic and geographical description (including national origin, age range, gender, occupation, location, etc.).
- Create a description of the target audience's habits relating to the specific service or activity you are promoting. (Have they participated in a similar activity in the past? Have they used the service at the library? In what ways and for what purpose?)
- List the number of targeted families or individuals in your area.
- Who are the influencers of this particular segment? Are they aware of this service or activity at the library?
- Who are the media gatekeepers of this particular segment? How do they reach this particular segment (frequency, medium, etc.)? (Go to your Worksheet 8.3 and select the appropriate ones from there.)
- Who else might have an influence on this particular segment?

Campaign Statement

Your campaign statement is the single paragraph that summarizes your branding focus or the nature of the activity, program, or service; how the customers will benefit from its features; and how you will communicate these benefits to the targeted audience. It is *not* the tagline or slogan of the campaign. For instance, in chapter 6 we came up with a positioning statement: "All members of local Latino families find enjoyable free activities and useful information for the advancement of their lives in the United States at the local library, a safe, enjoyable, and welcoming place where staff is bilingual and customer friendly." You can use a similar idea for your campaign statement if you are working on a branding campaign, or you can find other ideas in chapters 1, 2 and 6. Next add the communication piece:

> Under the campaign theme *Help Your Library Help Your Community,* the Little Haven City Public Library will launch a branding campaign to address the needs of all members of local Latino families through library services. This campaign will be conducted over a three-year period using low-cost effective promotional strategies. The main objective of the campaign is to create awareness among Latino customers and entice them to use free activities and useful information they can find for the advancement of their lives in the United States at the local public library, a safe, enjoyable, and welcoming place where staff is bilingual and customer friendly.

You will have to come up with a specific campaign statement for every campaign. Keep all sequential statements consistent. Also, keep the ideas close to Latinos' hearts: family values, safety, and a friendly environment, or other ideas you discuss with your CLO and LAB.

Remember that if you choose to work on other issues, then your wording will be different, or if you decide to target a different market segment, then "All members of local Latino families" should be replaced by a description of that segment.

An example for a specific mini-campaign statement could read: "Little Haven City Public Library, in the belief that stable communities contribute to growing and productive communities, and concerned with the situation of Little Haven City Latino homeowners who might be in economic distress or facing foreclosure, will promote two informative sessions with [what you offer—printed information, one-on-one free consultation with an expert, or referrals] in English and Spanish at the [nearby or specific branch location] to help them make informed decisions about their particular situation."

Notice that these statements are grounded in reality, position the customer at the center of the message, and are based on actual actions, activities, and building relationships. These statements make your place, products, and services unique for that particular market. When defining your campaign statement, look for those same characteristics: customer centered, grounded in reality and/or accomplishments, based on building relationships, and positioning the identity of your library.

Key Message

The key message is a brief statement that summarizes what you want them *to do* after they hear, watch, or experience this piece of communication. Again, note that the key message should not be confused with the slogan, tagline, or headline. Start your key message by saying, "*I want them to . . .*" so you do not get confused with the tagline.

Example 1: I want them to visit our library, call an 800 number Spanish hotline, and request additional information to find out what we have to offer Latino families. I want them to find out how to become cardholders and use our services. I want them to tour the library. I want them to see the children's activities we have to offer.

Example 2: I want Latino homeowners to request additional information on our Spanish hotline, attend and participate in an event [in what form, shape, or fashion] and receive information, sign up for a referral to a local Hispanic agency or local government agencies, and so forth. (All these will be according to the program you have planned for outreach.)

Example 3: If you are addressing their influencers, define the actions you want them to take: support and help in some way with your campaign; talk to their Latino neighbors, friends, and acquaintances or provide referrals about the campaign at hand; provide information to that particular target segment, especially if the influencers are media people; or distribute information or promotional materials about the campaign among Latinos in their area of influence—employees, students, customers, and so on.

Be precise with your descriptions; this level of detail will trigger ideas on how to define a message that has to do with your objectives and how to generate the action you want. You can work on three aspects of the message:

What you want them to know: You want to convey facts and information to motivate them to act. For instance, libraries offer free services to Latino families despite their level of literacy, immigration status, or lack of knowledge of library services. Libraries are in sync with the needs of their community and provide important information and activities for all family members. Libraries are institutions that help Spanish-speaking patrons build their English language skills, the most important factor in their chances for success. Libraries collaborate with other local agencies and support institutions, including housing agencies, workforce and business development agencies, health providers, and schools by providing accurate and reliable information. Libraries also encourage civic engagement by addressing the immigrant's experience in the community at large.[11] Add your own ideas about what you want them to know about libraries. These are just examples. DO NOT work on all these ideas at the same time. Choose one that is appropriate for the stage of the campaign at hand.

What you want them to believe (and trust): This brings up emotional issues or limiting beliefs and the reason to respond. Libraries are community-oriented organizations that really help people. Libraries can be trusted. Libraries do not discriminate. They welcome all members of the community regardless of their nationality or immigration status. Libraries help Latinos achieve their goals and dreams. Libraries share Latinos beliefs for the right to free information and free speech. Add your own!

What you want them to do: These are specific actions to fulfill your communication objective. For instance, "Talk to our bilingual staff on Thursdays and Sundays," "Call a phone number for additional information," or "Come to an open house." Other desired actions are as follows: listen to us, get involved, help your friends and family, think about your actions, make a resolution, open your mind, open your eyes, open your heart, teach, mentor, bring referrals, talk to your Latino friends and acquaintances, and so on. Think of other examples we have talked about, or add new ones.

Identified Behaviors, Limiting Beliefs, and Opposing Messages/Cost

This statement describes how your target audience sees, thinks, and feels about performing the desired behavior. Does the event, material, or service appeal to your customers among other products or services offered by the competition—in this case, their old habits and limiting beliefs about libraries or the activity you promote? Knowing about the culture and its values becomes imperative in order to push their buttons (in a good way!).

In a branding campaign, for instance, this might refer to the expectations that encouraged the immigrants to migrate to the United States in the hope of making a better life for their families (positive elements), the fact that you understand the difficulties they encounter because of their inability to communicate well in English, the lack of places to go for reliable or accurate help, and other obstacles/barriers we have discussed and that you would like to address:

- Proximity to your facility and potential transportation issues
- Reasons they do not use library services (lack of time or busy schedules, lack of knowledge of library services, low levels of literacy, and so forth)
- Competing behaviors of opposing messages or messengers for your target audience

You might also want to address previous attempts to advertise library services and the results or the image this target market or segment has of this program or service if the image is negative or detrimental. Do not try to avoid obstacles; instead, confront them. Latinos will trust those organizations that recognize their past limitations and show a willingness to correct them; empower the community to help you correct those mistakes by requesting their participation.

Key Benefits/Consequences

This statement refers to benefits you want them to see and consider and/or the consequences of not taking the proposed action. Benefits might be presented as positive (what they get) or negative (what they miss) elements in your message. They can refer to factual statements or emotional responses to problems.

Examples of positive elements: Materials and services at the library are provided at no cost because all people in the community pay their taxes to fund libraries. Helpful and friendly staff speaks Spanish.

Example of negative elements: Missing fun activities for my children at the library delays their language acquisition and socialization skills and may cause poor performance in school.

They might consider other key benefits, as well:

- Libraries in the United States are different and really care about people.
- I trust library staff because they are helpful and some speak Spanish; they can guide me through complicated information because they have lots of experience.
- They also have good activities for my children.
- All services are offered at no cost; however, they are updated and provide current information.
- Many of the helpful staff speaks Spanish, so I can ask them any questions I might have.
- I owe it to my family.
- I am a better parent by doing so.

Again, do not try to convey all these benefits in one shot. Just prioritize a few for your campaign. Keep it simple!

Support Statement/Third-Party Credibility

The support statement essentially refers to testimonials and endorsements, a description with real stories—from Latinos in your community or community leaders and influencers (perhaps local Latino leaders or celebrities)—related to using the library or participating in the type of activity, program, or service you are promoting. Successful stories can involve someone who learned English at your ESL classes, who became a citizen by attending citizenship classes at your facility, or who acquired computer literacy. They can also refer to moms who learned English by sharing bilingual story times with their children. All these stories will support your promise to provide benefits.

Spanish-speaking staff can tell their success stories helping customers, or community leaders can recommend your services by telling their personal struggle of inclusion and how the library helped them achieve their goals. They can explain the reasons they participated and how it worked for them despite the obstacles they encountered. An appropriate voice to communicate such a story would be your established Latino trustee, whose family has been in this area for generations and who is advocating for the library and the community. In other words, they explain how the benefits outweigh the obstacles; if they did it, your potential customers can, too. Sometimes these reasons become the message, but do not get ahead of the game yet. You still need all the other information on the brief!

Tone/Language

What tone do you want the creative team to take, both visually and in copy? Do you want it casual or formal? Is it technical or for the layman? Humorous or dramatic? Do you prefer a first-person message—more personal—or a third-person ad—more authoritative? I recommend you use cultural communication styles in a tone and manner that is consistent with the brand positioning of your library. Your tone also depends on the service or activity you are promoting and if you are addressing your target audience or their influencers.

If you are promoting your facility, make it inviting and familial; promoting your CLO or LAB should convey the idea that "they are people like you"; if promoting services for young people or teenagers, the tone might be casual and humorous unless you are talking about "serious" stuff. If your promotional piece is in Spanish, remember to use *tú* for younger segments—teens and young adults—and *usted* for adults, seniors, or setting up a more authoritative, reflective environment. Remember that messages must be vivid, personal, and concrete. The following are six cultural communication styles with particular tones that work with the Latino market:

The fantastic: Triggering emotional response and relating to magical realism, regional legends, and cultural beliefs; the tone is grandiose, spiritual, magical, or out there

The familiar: Daily life stories of people whom Latinos might identify with or the familiarity of the everyday life—family, school, work, and so forth; the tone is cozy, loving, caring, humorous, and tender

The heroic: The uniqueness or leadership of Latino customers, community leaders, people in your community who act on behalf of other people, or everyday heroes; the tone is formal and consummate, one of expertise and reliability

The dramatic: Conflict, struggle, loss, or pain to which you offer a solution; the tone is dedicated, sad with a moral at the end, or a lesson to be learned (at the library)

The moral: Explains what is the right thing to do for themselves, their families, and their communities; the tone is almost imperative, showing an obligation or correct choice

The humorous: The witty, savvy cultural jokes and sayings in the Latino community; the tone is casual, vibrant, and musical

Another concern that might come up at this point is if your communication should be in more than one language. You may decide on a bilingual or monolingual campaign at this point. The decision is related to your target markets and demographics, age and generation, and the focus of your campaign. In addition, if the campaign is Spanish only, for instance, your creative team should know that wording and expressions as well as visuals should be appropriate for a Spanish-speaking target audience and should take into account all the cultural elements we have discussed. Unfortunately, a bilingual branding campaign *cannot* be a Spanish translation of the English branding campaign that targets your general Anglo American audience. Moreover, your English branding campaign targeting bilingual and/or English-speaking Latinos cannot be the same as your general Anglo American audience. It has to be designed and thought through in English and in Spanish to target your Latino constituents. Here are five blunders marketers make when creating bilingual promotional pieces:[12]

Mistake 1: Simply translating the piece. Language is more than words. Meaning, perceptions, and cultural references are hard to convey in a translation, so most specialized advertising agencies trans-create the message or start from scratch. Keep in mind, however, that the core message needs to be consistent.

Mistake 2: Always writing the English copy first. Sometimes it is better to start with the Spanish copy because it expands more than in English—Spanish expands up to 20 percent from English copy. In advertising, though, a slogan or tagline might have a completely different wording. For instance, we might say "*un sapo de otro pozo*" (a frog from another pit), which would be the equivalent to "a fish from another pond." Although the copy extent is similar and could be easily translated (*un pez de otro estanque*), the intonation, modulation, and connotation of both copies is different in English than in Spanish.[13]

Mistake 3: Making the same key appeal message in both languages. Everyone's hot buttons are not the same. While the concept of free might be appealing for Anglo Americans, some Latinos might distrust that concept (thinking you might want something in return). Once again, bilingual marketing is about appealing to the receptivity of two different audiences.

Mistake 4: Translating phrases or ideas without considering different cultural uses of the same word. The Parker Pen company sold a ballpoint in Mexico with the copy, "It won't leak in your pocket and embarrass you." The word embarrass (*embarazar*) has two meanings in Spanish—make you uncomfortable and make you pregnant. The first is more commonly used in Spain while the second is widely used in Mexico and other Latin American countries. The campaign was really embarrassing!

Mistake 5: Make sure you know what you are doing. You can plan the message, but you need to bring in people who understand both languages and cultures and have experience addressing them. Several pairs of eyes from different Latino nationalities will also give you input about the accuracy of the translation. If you have discrepancies, think in terms of your target audience and who they are.

Although Spanglish might be seen as inappropriate by some, it is the way most Latinos speak, going back and forth from one language to the other! An English copy with a Spanish word or expression here and there will certainly catch people's attention if you craft it carefully. Politicians know this very well!

Creative Considerations

Is there anything else your creative people should know? The creative brief takes a little bit of work because at this point you have gathered so much information that it is hard to summarize it in just a couple of pages. However, this effort will pay off in the effectiveness of the campaign as you will be able to concentrate on what is important in your message. Talk about schedules and creative rounds with your creative team, and set deadlines and bench-

BRAINSTORMING SESSIONS

Some brainstorming sessions are not as productive as they could be because of lack of planning, inexperience, or poor leadership. Here are some guidelines to effectively conduct your creative brainstorming session.

- Make copies of the creative brief. Distribute it to participants, and post it for all to see during the session.
- Include your CLO and, if possible, your Latino Advisory Board and volunteer co-workers. Split larger groups into teams if necessary, and mix people with different professional perspectives.
- Give them some background on your campaign, and answer all questions that might arise at that time to make sure they understand the concept. Review the campaign statement with participants.
- Explain the rules of the brainstorming session:
    - No negativity.
    - Add to ideas.
    - Say it rather than censor it.
    - Encourage the unconventional.
    - Build on the ideas of others.

Capture all ideas as they flow from the group. Write them down—have two or three people take notes at the session—or make lists on a flip chart. Post the posters around the room so everybody can see them during the session and evaluate the ideas. You can also use this technique to do basic drawings to plan images, combinations of text and images, video clip shoots, cartoon stories, and much more.

Then, evaluate the ideas, selecting the best—even if it is not your preference. Your selection criterion should incorporate the following:

- The wording and images that best reflect the intention expressed in your campaign statement
- The idea that is most culturally appropriate for your specific campaign target audience
- The idea that reflects all elements summarized in your creative brief

Now, go ahead and assign the next steps to implement the idea.

marks, especially related to pretesting copy with your CLO and LAB members. Also, talk about the message's timeliness for your target audience and their influencers. You might want to target both at the same time or one or the other in advance, according to opening opportunities and the benefits timing will provide for delivering the message in an effective way.

Now you are ready to fill out your creative brief (see Worksheet 8.5 in chapter 10). Fill out separate worksheets for your target audience and their influencers. And remember, keep it brief!

How to Generate Creative Thinking

As stated before, your creative brief is a road map to help your creative people understand what you are trying to communicate. If you are lucky enough to have a budget that allows for a creative team, you will just have to wait and see what they come up with. If you do not have this type of budget, it is time to take off the hat you are wearing—whatever it is—and put on your creative cap or bonnet (it has to be colorful, too!). Although there are no guaranteed formulas to generate creative ideas, these guidelines might help. First, your message should be the following:

- Relevant and meaningful
- Original, or stating the message in a new way
- Noticed

With this in mind, start a brainstorming session (generally 10–30 minutes) to create ideas for your campaign.

Here are some questions you can ask during the brainstorming session:

1. Expectations: What does your target audience expect to hear? What would be unexpected? In what unusual ways can you present the facts?

2. Emotional response: Which emotions do you want to trigger? Which ones are appropriate for this message? What feelings do you want to portray with your message?
3. Words: Can you think of words you can play with that can make sense (especially in Spanish) or sound smart? A double entendre, a popular saying, or a common phrase?
4. Image of your offering: If your message were a cartoon, what type of character would it be? What would the character say? What would its voice sound like? Formal, informal, a child, an adult, serious, humorous, informative?
5. Ask "What ifs?" What if libraries were not free? What if most people did not know how to read? What if we all spoke the same language? Answer these questions in as many ways as you can!

You will also need to come up with questions that are specific to your campaign objectives, especially if it is a mini-promotional campaign that publicizes a specific program or activity.

Language used in communications will also affect how your target audience comprehends and processes ideas. Some suggested guidelines on language use are detailed here:

1. Personalize your message: Use *you* (*tú* or *usted*?).

   - Example: "You can improve your life" instead of "Latinos can improve their lives."

2. Emphasize immediacy: Use present tense and words that feel closer to your target audience.

   - Example: "*Your* local public library is *here* to serve *your* needs" rather than "Local public libraries serve the needs of their Latino populations."

3. Start off with a question that has a *yes* for an answer.

   - Example: Do you think there are no bilingual librarians at your local library? Do you think finding a Spanish dictionary is impossible in (name of your town)?

4. Write at the reading level of your target audience. Minimize technical jargon; keep the number of multisyllabic words to a minimum.[14]

   - Example: "Learning basic computer skills will help you and your family get things done" instead of "Learn Microsoft Office 2007, the essential software suite that provides tools, templates, and more to facilitate you and your family accomplishing everyday activities."

Remember to keep your promotional materials focused on a small number of related topics, and prioritize two or three points to emphasize. We talked about this issue in this chapter in terms of topics for general strategies. Most importantly, remember that you have a great weapon in the use of culturally appropriate and effective images.

What Images Do for You

> Visually dominated advertising provides the customer with a perception of greater familiarity with the product.
>
> —Elizabeth C. Hirschman, 1986

A picture is worth a thousand words . . . if it is the right picture. Pictures help people identify and remember messages, quickly grasp the content of the message, and even perceive hidden or subliminal meanings in the message. Pictures seem to be better at communicating certain concepts and ideas, such as space and size of objects and situations, in providing instructions or directions, in becoming familiar with an object or situation before encountering it, and in providing additional information and support to a verbal or written message (Najjar 1998).

In the age of the Internet, transmitting devices, and television, we are a society dominated by visual and hearing stimuli.[15] Using visuals is extremely important when people do not speak English as a primary language, have low literacy levels in English—or even in Spanish or any other language—or have special learning needs. Graphics, pictures, animations, cartoons, comic strips, representations, and illustrations are just some of the visual tools we can use to better convey messages to these audiences and support or even substitute the written word.

Questions frequently arise about the value of images: Do they need to reflect the Latino community? Is using this or that image offensive? Which ones have a better impact in conveying the message? There seems to be an extended idea—even in sophisticated advertising—that if you are talking to Latinos—who represent 19 different countries—you need to show brown people in your pictures—or if talking to people as diverse as Chinese, Filipino, Indian, Vietnamese, Korean, Japanese, Cambodian/Khmer, Pakistani Americans, and others whose national origin is from the Asian continent you must portray Asian-looking people, and so on.

FIGURE 8.1 How can you help an overwhelmed Latino student pass her exams? Trigger the emotion and offer a way out!

This idea derives from common knowledge in advertising that your company and your message need to reflect the market you target. However, not only is this impossible with the diversity involved, for instance, in both the Latino and the Asian communities, but also this is a simplistic and linear interpretation of the idea. So here are some guidelines in terms of the appropriate selection of images:

1. Know your target audience: Who is your most dominant target audience? Are they Dominicans, Mexicans, Salvadorians, or Colombians? Each has their own traditions in imagery and cultural perceptions of objects and people. For example, *sombreros* and hot peppers are not representatives of all Latinos! Only certain parts of Mexico use the round *sombreros*, and certainly Dominicans do not! Avoid images that are specific to a region or a nationality if you have a mixed audience.

2. Use appropriate but unexpected images: Is your message about people? Do you absolutely need to use people on your message? Are there other ways to illustrate the message?
   Examine the ideas you came up with in your creative brief. If you did your homework, you will have plenty of concepts to work with—benefits, features, and emotions you want to convey or trigger. Show your potential Latino customers your knowledge about their cultural preferences. Remember that promoting your library services to Latinos means letting them know you care. For example, including a tango dancer in a library advertisement directed to Argentineans might be nice, but including a picture of the Argentine National Public Library in your message will not only surprise your audience because it is unexpected, but it will also tell them you took the time to find an educational image that speaks to their culture and background.

3. Avoid stereotypes: Stereotypes are constantly portrayed in the media. Stereotypes are not good or bad per se as long as you understand their implications. We spoke about the difference between stereotypes and archetypes in chapter 5. Latinos are family oriented, so lots of TV ads show a happy-go-lucky "Latino" family doing something. Would you say all Americans love to eat hot dogs? Or that they are all cold and dis-

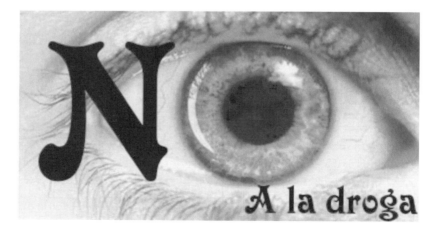

FIGURE 8.2 (Translation: "No to drugs.") The image of a body part may represent any nationality and still address the issue you need to talk about.

FIGURE 8.3 The main entrance of the National Library of the Argentine Republic in Buenos Aires. An unexpected image can recall memories and nostalgia.

tant individuals? Use a stereotype in a positive, archetypical way to *connect* your idea to your target audience. Also, put to work your politically correct sensors, but do not overdue it! Present images that solve problems: If your message has been carefully crafted, you do not need to portray your target audience.

A picture of hands on a computer keyboard, a cartoon character, a symbolic animal or bird, or another creative idea can do the trick. Also, pictures that translate emotions are appropriate, even if those portrayed do not look "Latino." (And, by the way, how *do* Latinos look?)

4. Pretest your message—text and image—before you deliver it, especially if you are producing ads with a motto, slogan, logo, or image for the main promotional campaign of your library services. It is easier to retrieve a bad message from a small campaign, but yearly efforts must certainly be tested before spending all your money and investing your energy into it!

Most importantly, try to get out of *flyer fever*. Flyers are a great tool, but they are not appropriate for all stages of the communication process. As we discussed, there are an array of low-cost tactics you can use to introduce awareness of your campaign and encourage acceptance of your offering. Because they are easy to distribute, use flyers toward the end of your campaign as a reminder of the five *W*s (who, what, where, why, and when) and a strong call to a specific action: Call! Register! Come! Visit! Also, remember to include catchy phrases pertaining to last-minute potential obstacles or barriers for your Latino customers: transportation, baby-sitting, or tight scheduling issues that need to be addressed and, if possible, solved. Also, try different flyer formats that might be more attractive. Just using a landscape layout or a half-page format can make the flyer stand out.

FIGURE 8.4 Your computer does not respond to your commands? Picture the universal frustration of dealing with technology and offer a solution!

If you're only able to print in black and white, use gradients and screens to give your design interesting dynamics. A textured color stock can add color and attention. A flecked stock can also help lines and screens look better.[16] Once you are happy with your promotional message and materials, you need to know if your Latino customer will be, too. Additional ideas about pretesting your message are presented in the next section.

Pretest Your Campaign

Pretesting your promotional materials will help you verify that your message will have the impact you are looking for and generate the action you anticipate within the appropriate cultural message. It will also help you prevent pitfalls and correct them before hundreds of dollars go to waste. Follow these easy steps:

Step 1: Check the Message

Because you and your CLO have been working on the task for a long time and have followed a process, you have become *blind* to possible errors in wording and lack of clarity in your message—this happens even to professionals! You might see your message clearly, but a casual viewer who did not follow the same process might not have the same understanding and perception of the message.

- Check that the message is in sync with your target audience's level of readiness (remember AAA: awareness, acceptance, action).
- Check level of readability—according to the SMOG Readability Formula[17]—and/or comprehension.

- Check precision in the words—especially if you are using Spanish; look for typos, false cognates, and any other unintended grammatical implications or cultural uses.
- If your message has been crafted in English for your bilingual population, make sure the wording and images are still culturally appropriate. Even English promotional materials need to appeal to the recipient's culture and maintain consistency with the message.
- If slang is used, check that is appropriate and not offensive.
- Several sets of fresh eyes—both English and Spanish volunteer copyeditors—will minimize potentially costly or catastrophic mistakes.
- Ask for possible additional interpretations of the message: Are the main points clear? Is all the information needed present in the material?
- Check if the tester can recall the message after one or two viewings.
- If it is an audio message, check for correct pronunciation of words, and confirm that regional accents—especially in Spanish—are softened or neutralized.

Step 2: Check the Images

If your image is distracting, culturally inappropriate, or offensive, the message will be lost. Also, if the image is stronger than the message, your target audience will not remember the message.

- Do these images best fit the message? Do they fit your target audience's and/or your publics' needs and preferences?
- If you are using symbols and pictographs, confirm that they are either universal or culturally appropriate and not offensive.
- Is the piece overwhelmingly dense in text? Is the text/picture ratio in the right balance (approximately 40% text to 60% image in printed materials, although the lower the level of readability, the larger the percentage of images)?
- Are there details that distract the viewer from the message? Do the people's expressions fit the message? Are there unwanted objects in the picture? If the message has audio, is the music too loud or unrelated to the tone of the message?
- Are these stereotypical images? Are they used in a positive way? Are they humorous/funny or humorous/offensive?
- Are the colors and shapes appropriate for the message? Do they anticipate what the message says so viewers are curious and eager to read the message?
- Are materials attractive, and do they stand out from the crowd?

If you are unsure about any of these elements, check with your LAB and current Latino patrons. An image that is acceptable in one country might not be in another.

Step 3: Check the Approach

Evaluate the strategy, tone, and communication style of your message.

- Is the approach appropriate for this stage of your communication process (AAA) and your target audience or publics?
- If you are working on awareness, do the message and tactic provide enough information to your Latino target audience or publics? If your goal is acceptance, do you give enough arguments and third-party credibility to encourage your Latino audience

to make an informed decision? If you are working on the action stage, are you enticing them to follow through and take the action you propose?

Keep in mind that a good advertising strategy requires you to be open to new thinking: if the concept is communicated clearly and uses the right tone and manner, even if it is not your favorite result, your personal preferences need to be set aside. It is not *your message;* it is the best message you are aiming at!

In the end, if you encounter problems in any of these areas, review each step of the promotional materials development process to find out what went wrong. Include the comments from the people who pretested the materials to improve effectiveness, and redefine as needed.

Implementing Your Promotional Campaign

Though a lot of planning goes into a promotional mini-campaign, the implementation phase is the backbone of the whole effort. Now that you are excited about your flyers, videos, and press releases, you imagine your target audience flocking through your doors. For this to happen, you need to make sure all the information gets to your potential customers.

The implementation phase, as with other steps of the promotional campaign, needs to follow each stage of the AAA communication model. Each stage will need its own external distribution plan and internal execution plan.

External distribution plan: Plan for the dissemination of materials according to the stage of the communication process. You will determine who is helping you in the distribution process according to your promotional mix.

Internal execution plan: This plan includes briefing your staff about the promotional effort, preparing them for performing the necessary tasks—answering phones, providing additional information, talking to the media—and defining the logistics of your promotional effort.

Do not confuse the promotional internal execution plan with the actual execution of your event or service—which also entails preparation and logistics, as discussed in chapter 7. You are now ready to execute your promotional campaign—that is, telling your target audience, and the world, about your offering.

External Distribution Plan

To ensure correct distribution of your promotional materials, you need to gather as much help as possible. Just a few flyers will not do the trick! You need to recruit strategic partners, community leaders, market channels, and even other branches in your library system to help distribute your promotional materials. You already determined the media outlets timing, and scheduling for your press releases and articles, your public service announcements, and all other media-related tasks (you can use Worksheet 8.4). Now it is time to organize your other promotional activities, including your word-of-mouth and public speaking campaigns, personal networking and social media, and all paid advertising tactics—radio and TV advertisements, printed materials, paid public relations campaigns, direct mail, and more.

Let us say you are in the awareness stage and have selected the following tactics mix:

Free Tactics

1. Publicity: Press releases/PSAs in local Spanish and mainstream radio station
2. Public relations: A word-of-mouth and speakers campaign (events, fairs, trade-shows, etc.)
3. A social media page published by the library in a popular online social media (such as Facebook or MySpace) with the addition of an incentive to generate leads

Paid Tactics

1. Printed materials: Educational brochures and posters to be distributed at those events and through strategic partners

Incentives

1. An incentive such as a promotional item—a bookmark, a music download, etc.—in an online social media page offered to encourage those interested in participating to request additional information so you receive potential customers' information

We covered media timing and scheduling in this chapter (worksheets 8.3 and 8.4), so here are some guidelines to help you determine how to proceed with the rest of your tactics:

1. A word-of-mouth and speakers campaign: How are you going to disseminate the message? What events are you going to participate in? Who will be the speakers at each of these events? You should already have selected your staff, community leaders, board members, or celebrities in your creative brief. Now you need names—contact them or their agents, negotiate contracts, and so forth. Create talking points to help the speakers disseminate the information according to your creative brief and campaign message.
2. Define who hosts your online social media page—your library's Web site, Facebook, YouTube, MySpace, or another site—according to your target audience's preferences. If you need help from a creative agency, research those that might offer pro bono help. If it is an in-house task, brief your Webmaster with his or her responsibilities. Find out the best ways to advertise your social media page: cross-reference the information in your printed materials, through your strategic partners, in your weekly column, and so forth.
3. Printed materials: Estimate the potential demand of educational brochures, flyers, and posters, and define points of distribution through your organization's branches or strategic partners. Do strategic partners need to be brought on board to encourage them to help? Brief your partners and their staff with the necessary information to ensure the correct distribution of materials. Have moderate expectations, and do not assume everybody understands what to do. In addition, if you are planning to run ads—or you have enough budget to do so—prepare enough art work copies for each media outlet to avoid running short (things can get confusing during campaigns, and some media outlets might request your promotional materials several times).
4. Incentives: Define the details of the incentive, where to place the information, deadlines, prizes and promotional items or activities, and so on.

Cross-referencing your media is extremely important. You can spread the word by just including a slogan, catchy phrase, or blurb in your e-mail signature, your stationary, or any other material that represents your organization. Most successful campaigns cross-reference multiple communication pieces with phrases like "see our ad in such and such magazine." Include your site or social media page in as many Internet search engines as possible for your target audience or influencers to see.

Worksheet 8.6 is an example of an external distribution plan. You will find a blank version of this worksheet in chapter 10.

Internal Execution Plan

If you and a small team of people have been working on this promotional mini-campaign, now is the time to engage the rest of your colleagues in what you are planning to do and recruit them into the effort. Among the tasks you need to accomplish in order to carry out your campaign, you will need to prepare the planned promotional materials for distribution, inform the personnel that will collaborate in this effort as well as all other staff in your library about the promotional effort, confirm your strategic partners participation and also establish a solid relationship with the media you are working with so that the promotional effort runs smoothly through the whole campaign.

You will find in Worksheet 8.7 is a description of the steps you will follow to achieve this task. Worksheets 8.7.1, 8.7.2, 8.7.3, and 8.7.4 in chapter 10 will provide more detailed information on how to handle this process.

Monitoring Your Progress

Monitoring your mini-campaign implementation and execution will help ensure success. Following are some recommendations to help you catch problems and adjust your course:

- Monitor all stages of your effort, and make sure all people involved are on task and on time.
- Make sure the quality of the information conveyed is in sync with your goals.
- Keep your staff and your strategic partners involved and excited!
- Address potential problems, and adjust the course of your promotion if necessary.
- Monitor the reaction of your target audience in order to make necessary changes to your mini-campaign. Are more materials needed? Is the information clear? Is further action needed? Have you detected unintended results (not enough response, people confused about the schedule or where the class is being held, and so forth)?

Tracking these issues can prevent potential damage to your campaign and improve your target audience's response. Monitoring the campaign will also pay off when you evaluate your promotional efforts.

Evaluating Your Promotional Efforts

In the library environment, evaluating your promotional campaign will guarantee that efforts and funds do not go to waste and that your organization learns from each evaluation to improve outreach efforts. Like aiming for a target, the more precise you make your shots, the better your chances to be successful.

Evaluating a promotional campaign is more than just counting how many people show up. Table 8.4 outlines a simple evaluation process.

TABLE 8.4 Evaluation Process for Promotional Campaigns

Evaluate before the campaign	Evaluate after the campaign	Monitor customer response
Evaluate your tactics and message	Evaluate soft data results	One-on-one interviews
		Questionnaires
Evaluate your market channels		Focus groups
		Response cards
		Online surveys
		Event attendance
Evaluate customer predisposition	Evaluate hard data results	Response to activities
		Customer complaints
		General comments
		Use of Spanish hotline

Evaluate Tactics before the Campaign

In the case scenario presented in chapter 5, one of your main goals was to generate Latino library membership. Here are three examples of low-cost tactic to promote your services to the Latino community at large. First, we will pre-evaluate these tactics by comparing the efficiency of each market channel or display location used for our promotional effort. Then we will look at the advantages and disadvantages of using each tactic in those market channels and the related cost versus efficacy of the distribution. Finally, we compare customer predisposition to absorb the information in each market channel or location.

For our example, we selected the following tactics:

A flyer in Spanish: Create a flyer that includes brief descriptions of library services, address and telephone numbers including a hotline phone number *en español*, and a coupon they can use to borrow a graphic novel.[18]

A video crate: Put together crates filled with empty DVD boxes with a bookplate in Spanish that invites people to pick up the materials at the public library for free. Include your library's address and phone number and the legend *Hablamos español* (We speak Spanish). Make sure to include new releases in Spanish or movies[19] that will appeal to your largest market segments. For instance, if your largest segment is first- or second-generation young workers of Mexican origin, look for movies and DVDs that are popular in Mexico, such as Mexican bands and musical groups, popular characters (such as *Cantinflas* and *El Chavo del Ocho*), comedians, and Mexican film classics. If you are targeting a mainly Puerto Rican community long established in the United States, try DVDs both in English and Spanish of salsa musical bands and stories of Puerto Rican artists and their lives and struggles in this country. Include movies, comedies, or TV seasons addressed to Latina women, especially young women. Place the crates in different locations Latinos visit, such as doctors offices, Hispanic agencies, local Latino markets, and so on.

A small Spanish magazine display: Display a few Spanish magazines, newspapers, or graphic novels on simple shelves or in a visible location with a Spanish bookplate stating to return the materials to any of the local public libraries, where other issues and titles can be found. Include the library address and phone number and the legend *Hablamos español* (We speak Spanish). Again, place these displays in places Latinos go frequently.

Here are three ways to pre-evaluate your mini-campaign tactics to promote an activity, material or service.

1. Pre-evaluate the performance of each tactic comparing the real cost of the tactic—how much you spend in printing flyers, how much would the video boxes cost to be replaced in case they are not returned, and how much you paid for the magazines. Then evaluate the labor time necessary to produce the materials and distribute those materials, and if any additional elements are needed, such as a small display. Finally, guesstimate the cost in terms of loss of materials. You can use low, medium, and high variables with intermediate combinations (low/medium or medium/high), or you can scale from 1–5 to compare selected tactics (see Worksheet 8.8).
2. Pre-evaluate the effectiveness of selected market channels or locations where media is placed (see Worksheet 8.9). For example, places where Latino adults and teenagers go for services, where they might spend a considerable amount of time (doctors offices and hospital), or where they become a temporary captive audience (public transportation). Use the evaluation scale ++ for very positive placement, + positive placement, and − for inconvenient or placement with obstacles. You can choose other evaluation scales, but always include your comments. Remember, a negative evaluation is not a reason for discarding the strategy, just food for thought on how that problem can be solved (or not).
3. Worksheet 8.10 contains observations about customers' predisposition at the selected location, how they might feel when they are at that location, the level of motivation needed at that location because of any distractions, and competition with other messages at the same location. Again, you can use a High to Low scale or measure with a 1–5 estimation.

Now compare and make notes of results for each tactic. For instance, a tactic that might come up as less costly—such as printed flyers—might require intensive distribution efforts, which translates into additional staff dedication. If you are short-handed, then this tactic might not work for you at this time.

You might come up with negative observations about a location you thought was appropriate for the campaign, or confirm that the cost/effort of a tactic was appropriate for your resources.

Every time you adopt a new strategy, analyze these and any other aspects you feel will affect the campaign. This will reduce your risk and help your campaign succeed. Again, consider every negative aspect but do not simply discard the strategy. Maybe there are negative aspects you consider acceptable, such as the fact that Spanish magazines might get lost or graphic novels might not be returned. These factors become a part of your equation and your budget. Maybe it is worthwhile to try each different strategy at least once instead of repeating the same strategies over and over (and expecting different results!). Once the locations and the strategies become familiar to you—you created relationships with your strategic partners and market channels, you have a better idea of what it takes for each campaign based on past results, and so forth—your need to verify each step will decrease because you will be able to foresee results.

You will find blank templates of these worksheets in chapter 10 so you can fill them out with your list of market channels. Even if you don't use all of them, they might provide new ideas to keep in mind when organizing your distribution campaign.

Make a quick decision on how you believe these market channels will perform. This is an a priori evaluation. Take your five best choices and start with your plan. After you evaluate your results, you may find that some of these tactics were not the best choice. Keep the ones that worked and move on to the next five tactics on your list for future promotional efforts. You might find out that the ones you discarded first are the ones that work the best. Whatever works to bring your Latino customers to your store, that is the strategy you need.

Evaluate Results after the Campaign

In traditional marketing, a customer chooses a brand product because there is a conscious—or sometimes emotional—decision-making process that places value on the choice. In other words, I buy this particular car because it has high ratings of safety (a tangible value), because it denotes prestige (intangible value), or because it is economic (price). These three elements play different roles in the customer's decision at different times and with different products or services.

In the social marketing environment, however, tangibles are almost nonexistent—you are dealing with ideas and behaviors—so intangible values become the focus of the decision. Your potential patrons evaluate the benefits or solution of a particular event, service, or material in terms of its price—or, as we said, to overcome its cost. In other words, we focus on showing Latino customers that the intangibles are a solution to their problems or a benefit to gain while we help them overcome the cost of performing the desired action. We expect the promotional campaign will help change the perceived value of the event, material, or service and will encourage them to take action!

However, this decision-making process occurs in your Latino customers' heads. How do you evaluate changes in value perception? Ultimately, if they change their behavior, we know the campaign has been successful. Nevertheless, we also need to consider the stages of readiness related to the communication model (AAA: acceptance, awareness, or action) to evaluate the process in your customers' minds. For instance, if we are promoting awareness, we need to evaluate that the information has reached the audience and that they have received and understood it. Not every stage will produce the same results.

Look for soft data that will help you know if your promotional pieces at any stage are on track. Here are some guidelines:

1. If you set your incentives appropriately at each stage of the communication model, you will be able to monitor the activity of your promotional efforts collecting responses for that particular incentive.
2. You can also evaluate your public's knowledge of and the scope of the campaign by asking your staff, your strategic partners, community leaders, trustees or board members, and other organizations and market channels when, where, and what they saw outside the library about this particular campaign, including frequency, content, and comments about it. To help you evaluate, you need to make them aware of the campaign—starting dates, frequency, channels or outlets, and so forth—and ask them to keep their eyes and ears open. Also, prepare your staff to receive and respond to comments, responses, and even nasty or inappropriate gripes about the campaign.
3. Encourage your influencers and gatekeepers to give you feedback on the campaign as it is running—feedback from the media could be especially useful.
4. Finally, evaluate results with hard data. If your customers are ready to take action, then evaluate your customers' attendance or participation at the promoted event or

activity or their response to the desired action, such as class registration, increasing circulation of the Spanish collection, or any other activity you are promoting.

If results are not what you expected, work with all the feedback you can collect, including from your current Latino cardholders, the CLO, and your LAB. Check your strategy, your message, and your images. Also monitor the frequency and performance of your news outlets and channels and make sure they are honoring their end of the contract. Ask your gatekeepers what you can do next time to increase newsworthy interest in your promotional pieces.

A Reality Check

In Worksheet 8.8 "Cost Comparison of Selected Tactics," you compared different low-cost tactics. In Worksheet 8.11 you are evaluating the actual procedure used for distribution and its results—for example, how many flyers you rendered—or how many video boxes, or how many Spanish magazines, depending on which course of action you chose—and how many promotional rounds you actually needed to achieve your goals.

You should also verify the cost and compare it with the cost you forecasted at the beginning of your promotional efforts—a reality check. Cost includes cost of goods including wasted materials as well as labor cost—that is, how many times you sent personnel, how many participated, and for how long. By evaluating these procedures, you are estimating the *reach* of your campaign (e.g., if you printed 1,000 flyers in a two-month period for the hospital, you can guesstimate that at least 70% of your flyers were actually read, passed along, or taken home while 30% were wasted, not read, or put away by the hospital's personnel). How do you guesstimate this turnaround?

Here are some statistics from the marketing field: According to Alan Sharpe, a Business2-Business direct mail guru,[20] you can reach an average of 70 percent inquires in direct mail (including direct mail lists already qualified as a target market). Of that 70 percent, only 20 percent will be qualified to buy your product (qualified means the customer is interested, can make a decision, has the money, *and* is ready to buy).

However, from that 20 percent of qualified buyers, some people will not be interested in your services, some will not know about your services or might be planning to go away, some will lose the flyer before reaching their home, and some will use the flyer for another purpose—such as writing a note or telephone number on its back—or any other contingency. Optimistic response rates do not go beyond a 1 to 2 percent return. In other words, for your 1,000-flyer campaign, the number of people who would really respond to your offering would be around 10 to 20 people. Yes, the numbers are pretty low, but consider what you do with your own junk mail. Do you throw it away without opening it? Do you open only certain mail? What criteria do you use? Do you open direct mail promotions when you are looking for something that matches the offer? These are strong reasons why your message needs to be attractive, easy to read, and requiring some action, as discussed in this chapter.

In addition, you can never rely on just one strategy; you need to develop several consistent promotional efforts throughout the year. It is important to know your target market well, who they are, and what makes them rock. Finally, evaluation skills come, in part, with experience, and over time you will learn to see which of your efforts pay off better in the long run.

Comparing Procedures with Outcomes

Why is it important to evaluate procedures when you can evaluate outcomes? Because procedures are instrumental in defining and adjusting your promotional efforts. Let us suppose you have determined that the Latino population in your area is around 10,000 individuals, and you set your goal of increasing your number of cardholders by 3 percent in three years, which means 300 new cardholders a year. If at the end of your campaign's first period you have only registered 100 new cardholders, look for the cause of this gap. Go back and review the following:

1. Your reach and frequency, which includes your distribution channels (market channels, strategic partners, and media)
2. Your message
3. Your target market

If your flyers do not move, your temporary cards are not coming back, or your radio spots are not doing the job (remember to check if the radio station audience is being audited),[21] you need to re-evaluate your reach through the distribution channels you chose, which involves your promotional effort procedures. Maybe your strategic partners are not doing what they promised, maybe they do not have the infrastructure to help you accomplish your campaign (e.g., the location they gave you is not appropriate or there is low traffic), or maybe they did not inform their personnel about the campaign and someone threw the flyers away!

If you determine that your reach and frequency were adequate—at an estimated 5,000 to 7,000 radio listeners a week, 1,000 flyers and 1,000 temporary cards rendered, press releases in four to six media outlets, 100 courtesy Spanish magazines circulating every three months, or whatever your planned amounts were according to your target markets—then the next step is to look at your message.

Maybe the message was not clear enough, maybe it did not convey a call for action, or perhaps its image was unappealing. Go back to your SWOTs and start from there, adjusting and trying a different idea. Get the help of your CLO or a Latino focus group—ask them to criticize your message and make suggestions.

If you determine that your reach and frequency are working fine and that your message is sound and enticing, then you need to go one step further back: you need to check if you have enough information about your target market segment and if there are additional limiting beliefs you did not consider in your first round or changes in your market segment such as people moving at the end of the season or other demographic changes in your area.

Remember, if you chose a mass distribution channel such as radio or television, evaluation of your reach will need similar features—that is, it will have to be massive. Let us say you are broadcasting in a regional or cable television system reaching tens of thousands of viewers. In such a case, the evaluation of your reach cannot be based on a random phone survey of 10 Latino families. If your library system has 10 or more branches, the combination of massive campaigns and local evaluation might work very well. Each branch can evaluate its area of service. However, always remember to start small and build on!

Customer Response

Even if your results are or exceed what you expected, you still need to monitor customer response so you will know what goes on in your Latino customers' heads at every stage of the communication process. Table 8.5 displays methods used to monitor customer response.

When you plan these evaluations, check with your current Latino patrons to consider cultural intricacies even when designing a simple survey or asking for general comments. For instance, American marketers are used to measuring everything with numbers or amounts (different types of scales), which might present an interpretation problem for your Latino patrons. Remember, some will agree just to be polite or might have difficulties with the difference between "I agree" or "I strongly agree." Korzenny and Korzenny make a sound analysis of the cultural bias surrounding evaluation design (2005, pp. 221–230); they recommend, among others, the use of the "Little Faces Scale" method (*Las Caritas*), which seems to work with Latino customers (2005, p. 228).

Latinos are usually very cooperative in community affairs and will be willing to talk to you. For most part, phone surveys seem to generate cooperation among Latinos.[22] Your advantage is that you are the local library, not a telemarketer, and they likely respect your organization. How do you select your random sample? You can buy marketing lists—the price will depend on the degree of refinement and accuracy and the number of people included in the list, generally from a few hundred dollars to several thousand—request help from strategic partners, or just go to the phone book and look for Latino surnames in your city or zip code, although this criterion is somehow limited as many Latinos might carry European or Asian surnames and Latino women might be married to Anglo Americans or people of other nationalities.

If your organization serves a small town, contact information may be harder to find; Latinos might be spread out or living in rural areas. Call your strategic partners—such as the local school system or utilities companies—and see if they can include your survey in their direct mailings. If you live in a large city, you will have to set criteria by neighborhood, or *barrio,* and work your way through. Keep in mind that with the phone approach, you will need bilingual callers in the interviewee's language of preference.

In summary, know when your resources match the market opportunity, and be sure you can afford your promotional strategy. You might come up with a very creative promotional

TABLE 8.5 Monitor Customer Response

One-on-one interviews	Personal interviews to evaluate promotional efforts; can be formal—planned questionnaires—or informal
Focus groups	Same concept but a planned interview of 6 to 10 people
Questionnaires	Telephone and direct mail questionnaires
Response cards	Direct mail or distribution through market channels, usually offering an incentive to return the card
Printed and online surveys	At service location and online through the library Web site or other social media page
Event attendance	Signature book, sign-in list, and short surveys to attendants or participants
Response to activities	Physical box at your location or online virtual box
Customer complaints	Book of complaints and dedicated phone lines or online links
General comments	Letters to the editor or columnist if you have a column, direct letters to your organization, comments on your blogs, or verbal comments to your customer service staff
Use of Spanish hotline	A dedicated line for concerns, suggestions, compliments, and complaints in Spanish

strategy that would potentially bring many customers to your door right away, but if you cannot afford it, it is not the right strategy for your library at this time.

With these tools, you can feel confident in starting your promotional campaigns, improving the activities you have already organized with few results, or simply applying some of these concepts to better evaluate your campaigns.

Guidelines to help examine your marketing plan's outcomes as well as procedures are included in the next chapter. Measuring and evaluating the good efforts you made throughout your outreach and promotional strategies will help you adjust your modus operandi, try new alternatives, and discover solutions for challenges or obstacles you found over the course of your actions.

Notes

1. To view a complete list of libraries with Spanish Web sites go to REFORMA, "U.S. Public Library Websites with Information in Spanish," http://www.reforma.org/spanishwebsites.htm (accessed January 21, 2010).
2. Watch this video to see how Queens Library (New York) promotes its library (in this case to attract potential diverse employees): http://www.youtube.com/watch?v=E48IJQkYLvc&NR=1.
3. The ALA's "@ your library slogans" is a list of library slogans you can use in your own library for different programs and activities. See http://www.ala.org/ala/issuesadvocacy/advocacy/publicaware ness/campaign@yourlibrary/prtools/yourlibrary.cfm (accessed February 6, 2010).
4. Adapted from Learn Marketing.net, http://www.learnmarketing.net (accessed January 21, 2010).
5. Please find a summary of theories of behavior change in Weinreich (2005), chapter 10.
6. For additional information about marketing communication models, see Duncan and Moriarity (1998).
7. Head Start is a national program that promotes school readiness by enhancing the social and cognitive development of children through the provision of educational, health, nutritional, social, and other services to enrolled children and families.
8. Associated Press has a bureau in every state. See their Web site at http://www.ap.org/pages/con tact/contact_pr.html. You can email United Press International for news tips or a press release at news-tips@upi.com. Reuters requires press release submissions via PR Newswire, Business Wire, GlobeNewswire, marketwire, or their list of locations at http://www.thomsonreuters.com/about/ locations (accessed January 21, 2010).
9. For a wonderfully designed bilingual library newsletter that includes all programs offered to the community, please see the work of Elena Lara in the Round Lake Area Public Library Newsletter at http://www.rlapl.org/docs/20101212NewsWinterSpring.pdf (accessed February 17, 2010).
10. The example is adapted from the prototype that appears in Kotler, Roberto, and Lee (2002, pp. 265–66), which is designed for social marketing promotional strategies.
11. Adapted from Norman Oder, "ULC Report Details How Libraries Serve Immigrants," *Library Journal,* February 21, 2008, http://www.libraryjournal.com/article/CA6534210.html (accessed January 21, 2010).
12. Adapted from Dean Rieck, "5 Big Bilingual Copy Mistakes Direct Marketers Make (and How to Avoid Them)," http://www.targetmarketingmag.com/article/5-big-bilingual-copy-mistakes-direct-marketers-make-and-how-avoid-them-402976_1.html (accessed January 21, 2010).
13. For aphorism and saying correspondence, see the site *El Refranero Multilingüe,* a research project of the Centro Virtual Cervantes (CVC). The site offers translation and equivalency of Spanish aphorisms in more than 10 other languages, including English. http://cvc.cervantes.es/lengua/refra nero/Default.aspx (accessed February 15, 2010).

14. "G Harry McLaughlin created the SMOG Readability Formula in 1969 through an article, *SMOG Grading—A New Readability Formula* in the *Journal of Reading*. SMOG Readability Formula estimates the years of education a person needs to understand a piece of writing. McLaughlin created this formula as an improvement over other readability formulas. You may come across SMOG as an acronym for Simple Measure of Gobbledygook, but it's widely believed the title is a nod to Robert Gunning's FOG Index." From ReadabilityFormulas.com, "The SMOG Readability Formula," http://www.readabilityformulas.com/smog-readability-formula.php (accessed February 6, 2010). "The SMOG formula is a recommended and tested method for grading the readability of written materials. The method is quick, simple to use and particularly useful for shorter materials, e.g., a study's information pamphlet or consent form." Hunter College Institutional Review Board, "SMOG Readability Formula," http://www.hunter.cuny.edu/irb/smog_readability_formula.htm (accessed February 6, 2010).

15. Visual and hearing stimuli are dominant compared to the stimulation of other basic human senses such as touch, taste, and smell.

16. Please see the All Graphic Design News blog for interesting ideas for your next flyer project: http://www.allgraphicdesign.com/graphicsblog/2007/11/cool-flyers-posters-leaflets-great-flyer-design-inspiration (accessed February 6, 2010).

17. See Note 14.

18. For general advice on how to start a graphic novel collection and concerns about graphic novel content and how to respond to them, see the article "Graphic Novels: Suggestions for Librarians" prepared by the National Coalition Against Censorship, the American Library Association, and the Comic Book Legal Defense Fund, 2006, at http://www.ncac.org/graphicnovels.cfm (accessed February 6, 2010).

19. For a useful introduction on how to start and maintain your video collection, see Kaneko (2003).

20. Alan Sharpe is a fundraising practitioner, author, trainer, and speaker. Through his books, handbooks, and workshops, Alan helps not-for-profit organizations worldwide acquire more donors, raise more funds, and build stronger relationships. See Alan Sharpe, CFRE, http://www.raisersharpe.com/ (accessed July 31, 2010).

21. For more information about rating audits, see the Media Rating Council, a federal organization that ensures the establishment and administration of minimum standards for rating operations; the accreditation of rating services on the basis of information submitted by such services; and the auditing, through independent CPA firms, of the activities of the rating services. See http://www.mediaratingcouncil.org/ (accessed February 7, 2010).

22. See Korzenny and Korzenny (2005, p. 241). According to these authors, some markets are more cooperative than others, depending on level of acculturation and time in the United States.

WORKSHEET 8.1   Starting a Promotional Campaign

Goal: Answering these seven questions will help you define the general plan of your promotional campaign. You will work on details in the following worksheets.

1. Establish the identity of your brand or products	What are we trying to promote?
2. Identify your target audience and influencers	Whom are we trying to reach?
3. Establish campaign objectives	What are we trying to achieve?
4. Create an image or theme	How do we communicate it?
5. Develop your message	How do we say it?
6. Select and implement a media plan	How do we deliver it?
7. Evaluate results and procedures	How are we going to evaluate?

NOTES

_____

_____

_____

_____

_____

From *¡Hola, amigos! A Plan for Latino Outreach* by Susana G. Baumann. Santa Barbara, CA: Libraries Unlimited. Copyright © 2011. **261**

WORKSHEET 8.2   Planning Promotional Tactics (Branding Example)

Goal: Develop a yearly <u>awareness</u> campaign for three consecutive years. This campaign will concentrate on branding efforts through low-cost promotional strategies.

First-Year Short-Term Branding Campaign for Little Haven City Public Library

Campaign promotional goals: The first year will focus on awareness of the organization's mission statement and its friendly outlook to build strong relationships with the Latino community.

Tactic	Plan
Publicity Press releases	Prepare four press releases to be published quarterly in local media during first year: Topic 1: Share the library's vision and mission. Topic 2: Discuss the requirements to become a member. Topic 3: Discuss why Latinos need library services. Topic 4: Encourage Latinos to become a part of the library community. Include social media information about library Web site (see the following).
Articles (press release format) in local mainstream and Latino newspapers and radio **Word-of-mouth** **Public relations** (panels, talk shows, etc.)	Prepare four success stories to be presented as word-of-mouth, delivered in public speaking scenarios, and published in local Latino and mainstream newspapers and radio. Success stories: 1. Latino trustee: How and why he or she joined the Board or the LAB 2. A Latino cardholder: Why he or she joined the library and how it has helped him or her 3. Bilingual children's librarian: How she helps children and their families 4. A community strategic partner or Friend of the Library who works with the library in outreach to Latinos
PSAs	Write public service announcements about an invitation to attend meetings and become a member of the Latino Advisory Board (LAB). Include social media information.
Personal networking and social media	Create a Little Haven City Public Library fan page on Facebook posting the same four stories and four discussions presented in the press releases over time. Allow fans to comment and provide interactive activities such as suggestions, ideas, submission of stories and pictures, and so forth.
Paid tactics **Printed materials**	Design and print brochures with brief summaries of success stories and the protagonists' pictures (one for each) using information on the press releases and success stories. Include social media information. Call to meet with the LAB members: Design and print flyers with an invitation to participate or become a member; include meetings' time and location.

 From *¡Hola, amigos! A Plan for Latino Outreach* by Susana G. Baumann. Santa Barbara, CA: Libraries Unlimited. Copyright © 2011.

WORKSHEET 8.3   Media Outlets Contact List

Goal: Develop a media contacts file to plan and execute timely media promotional efforts.

Publications:

Publication	Frequency	Contact person	E-mail address	Phone/Fax	Submission deadline
Latinos Unidos	Weekly	M. Garcia, news editor	mg@latun.com	000-111-2222	Thursdays 4 p.m.
		J. Perez, public service	jp@latun.com	000-111-3333	Thursdays 4 p.m.

Brief description of the publication: Spanish newspaper covering Little Haven City and four surrounding counties
Circulation: 15,000 weekly
Distribution: Street, stores, churches, public libraries, other businesses
Price: Free

Broadcast outlets:

Local radio/TV stations	Program/ Frequency	Contact/ Producer	E-mail address	Phone/Fax	Submission deadline
WBCC	Images/ Imágenes Tuesdays 10–11 a.m.	Pete Clark, prod. mgr.	pete@wbcc.org	000-111-4444 000-111-5555	Two weeks before broadcast

Brief description of broadcast outlet: Local talk show about Latino topics in Little Haven City
Cumulative audience: Between 2,000 and 4,500 listeners/half hour
Planning schedule: Three to four months in advance

WORKSHEET 8.4 Media Outlets Timing and Scheduling

Goal: Schedule the right timing for your promotional effort. The opening has to meet the right need at the right time.

Name of event/activity/campaign to be promoted: *Help Your Library Help Your Community*

Stage of campaign: Awareness (see communication model in this chapter)

Publicity/media tactic selected: Articles in local Latino and mainstream newspapers

Format: Press release

Implementation	Distribution	Topic	Schedule
Prepare four success stories to be published in local Latino and mainstream newspapers	To be published approx. once every three months in the following local newspapers: - Latinos Unidos - La Prensa - Reporte Hispano - Little Haven Daily News	1. Latino trustee: How and why he/she joined the Board or the LAB	August/September when LAB resumes activity and before Hispanic Heritage Month
		2. A Latino cardholder: Why he/she joined the library and how it has helped him/her	October/November right before offering citizenship classes (or an ESL class) and when customers go back to their regular yearly activities (work, school, etc.)
		3. Bilingual children's librarian: How she helps children and their families	March/April before Día de los Niños/ Día de los Libros and when mothers are looking for spring break activities.
		4. A community strategic partner who works with the library in literacy efforts	May/June before a community event or summer reading programs when mothers are looking for children's summer activities.

Purpose of media attention: Awareness campaign about library services for Latinos

Newsworthy information: Extensive outreach to Latinos to encourage use of library services/positive stories of real people in the community using the library. (Include some demographic data and characteristics of the local Latino population. Describe the needs of local Latinos and the leadership role the library can play in the community.)

Type of coverage: (sections that cover this type of news; for each media outlet's contact information, go to worksheet 8.2.)

☐ News

☑ Feature

☐ Editorial

☐ Entertainment

☑ Public Service

WORKSHEET 8.5   The Creative Brief (Summary)

Goal: Summarize all aspects of your promotional campaign in one or two pages. Topics that will differ in each creative brief (either if addressed to your target segment or to influencers) are marked with an *.

1. Campaign Background

Problem or need detected in your Latino community that motivated the campaign. (Selected from chapter 6 information on needs assessments and consulted with strategic partners and community leaders chapter 3)

2. Target Audiences and Publics/Influencers*

Who do you want to reach with your communication? Be specific. If addressing other publics or influencers, complete a separate worksheet. (Chapters 4, 5, and 6)

3. Campaign Statement

Description of the campaign focus for the activity or event. (Chapter 6 and 7 worksheets)

4. Key Message*

What your target audience—or other publics/influencers—is expected to do after they hear, watch, or experience this piece of communication. (What do you want them to know, believe, or do?)(Worksheet 7.2)

5. Identified Behaviors, Limiting Beliefs, and Opposing Messages/Cost

How are you going to address behaviors, cultural practices, pressures, and misinformation that stand between your target audience and the desired objectives? (Worksheet 6.5)

6. Key Benefits/Consequences

Benefits your target audience will experience upon taking action and/or consequences for not taking action. (Worksheet 6.6)

7. Support Statements/Third-Party Credibility*

Third parties talk about the reasons why the key benefit outweighs the obstacles and why what you are promoting is beneficial. These reasons often become messages. (Check with community leaders and research other organizations with similar offerings.)

8. Tone/Language*

What feeling should your communication have? Should it be authoritative, light, or emotional? Is it a monolingual or bilingual piece of communication? The tone will also change if the creative brief is addressing your target audience or other publics or influencers.

9. Creative Considerations*

Define the production schedule of your promotional message and campaign at this time for both your target audience and your other publics and influencers.

WORKSHEET 8.6 External Distribution Plan

Goal: Recruit strategic partners, community leaders, market channels, and even other branches in your library system to help distribute your promotional materials.

Stage of campaign: Awareness

Name of campaign: To provide information and educate the local Latino community and other publics about *Help Your Library Help Your Community*

Strategic partners:					
Name of strategic partner (community leader, market channel)	**Distribution frequency**	**Contact person**	**E-mail address**	**Phone/ Fax**	**Delivery deadline**
Hispanic Professional Association (brochures and flyers, news spot on organization's newsletter)	Monthly meetings/ Quarterly newsletter	Juan Guevara	Guevara@new horizons. org	800-123-7654	Monday before meeting/Three weeks before publication

Speaking engagement at community events:					
Name of event	**Frequency**	**Contact person/ Producer**	**E-mail address**	**Phone/ Fax**	**Registration deadline**
Little Haven City Health Fair	Two-day weekend once a year in May	Stan Less, producer	sless@abc.org	800-111-6666 888-111-7777	Speaker's registration and booth: Two months to two weeks before event

Brief description of event: Health care organizations and health care providers offer free health awareness literacy and educational screenings, along with other vendors and community participants

Attendance: 50,000 people/day average

Location: Santa Ana Park, close to the Latino neighborhood in town

Speaker(s) for this opening: CLO chair and Latino trustee

Incentive:

1. Start a Latino Outreach Facebook fan page to encourage Latinos to request additional information about library services by [launching date]. Follow theme and message of campaign and other creative decisions in creative brief.

2. Instruct Webmaster with direction and content of page, incentives, and all other necessary details.

3. Offer to provide a printable library poster or bookmark to those who register their personal contact information (follow your library's guidelines for incentives).

4. Include the Facebook page information in all other promotional materials and outlets.

NOTES

_____

_____

_____

_____

_____

_____

_____

WORKSHEET 8.7   Internal Execution Plan (Summary)

Goal: Make sure you have all promotional materials in place, and engage and recruit the rest of your colleagues in your planning effort.

Materials Readiness (see worksheet 8.7.1 in chapter 10)

1. Written materials (press releases, columns, articles, PSAs, radio and TV spots): Determine who is writing the piece. Make sure the information is in sync with the stage of the communication process and the basics of your creative brief. Tell the writer(s) your expectations. Make sure there is copyediting and spell-checking of each piece. Determine who is responsible for the delivery and follow-up of the pieces to the appropriate media contact.

2. A word-of-mouth campaign or personal networking: If the participants are part of your staff, make sure they are available for the programmed dates, determine who is participating at each event, and make sure they can correctly convey the information. Also, determine who is going to be at each appearance. Take care of the event logistics.

3. Printed materials: What brochures posters, and other pieces need to be made and distributed at events and through strategic partners? Define the quality and quantity of the materials. Make sure you have enough copies, and track them through each stage of the communication process. Determine who is responsible for distributing and monitoring inventory at each point in the distribution process and with each strategic partner.

4. An online social media page including library-made videos: Determine who will design, launch, and update the page; track responses to the information; follow up and monitor; make necessary adjustments; and respond to potential questions from your target audience and your other publics.

5. Prepare the logistics of any other tactic (promotional items, popular media, and so forth) by contacting vendors and contributors, checking and replacing inventory, making sure the materials are ready and on budget.

Personnel Readiness (see worksheet 8.7.2 in chapter 10)

1. Brief your staff, colleagues, and volunteers at the library about the goals of the campaign and their expected role in it—even if it is just to answer the phones and connect the caller with the right spokesperson.

2. If you need extra hands, ask around for volunteers, and inform them precisely what needs to be done.

3. Use co-workers' resources in media, the target audience, or the publics. They might know people who know people who can make a difference in your program.

4. Receptionists or spokespersons will need a telephone protocol to help them with key answers to questions your target audience or publics might have.

5. Define a person or two who will speak to the media to expand on key ideas about the event, material, or service or the target audience and their needs. Media love statistics, how your organization is addressing a community problem, your approach to solving it, and possible reactions or objections to your program. Remember your information needs to be entertaining, enticing and newsworthy!

 From *¡Hola, amigos! A Plan for Latino Outreach* by Susana G. Baumann. Santa Barbara, CA: Libraries Unlimited. Copyright © 2011.

6. Prepare your spokespersons to address possible reactions of your target audience, your publics, and community members at large. It is impossible to make everybody happy!

Strategic Partners Follow-Up (see worksheet 8.7.3 in chapter 10)

1. Secure the contact information of person who is the liaison at your strategic partner or market channel. Do not assume they know what to do!

2. Make contact in the previous weeks to ensure they remember their commitment. Remind them about their task or role in the activity at hand (material distribution, speaker participation, word-of-mouth, and so forth.)

3. Keep track of materials sent, date and additional instructions. Follow up to make sure your liaison received the information (materials, advertising pieces, or other).

4. Follow up if they need additional materials for replacement, or additional information for participation.

Media Follow-Up (see worksheet 8.7.4 in chapter 10)

1. Keep track of all written pieces (articles, columns and press releases, radio and TV spots) you sent, and the contact information of your media liaison.

2. Include the name and format of the event you are promoting (very important in case you are promoting several activities, programs or services at the same time).

3. Keep track of dates sent, and publication dates. Verify if the pieces was published or aired. If it was, send an email or make a call to say thanks and acknowledge them. If it did not, contact your liaison and ask if they need additional information or to reschedule the information.

4. Remind them of the launch or event day and time so they can participate and report the offering.

WORKSHEET 8.8   Cost Comparison of Selected Tactics

Goal: Here are three ways to evaluate your tactics to promote library services. First, evaluate the cost in terms of money and labor of tactics that might be used for your promotional effort.

Variables	Tactic 1	Tactic 2	Tactic 3
Low-cost tactics	Flyers with coupon	Crate w/ video boxes	"Courtesy" Spanish magazines
Cost of tactic ($)	Low (without the cost of lost material)	Medium	Medium / high
Effort from your staff to prepare campaign	Medium (design of message, printing, copying, etc.)	Low	Low
Distribution frequency	High, probably weekly for a period of time	Low, probably monthly	Low/medium, probably bi-weekly if magazines are not returned
Display expense and material replacement	Low	Low (No materials are lost, only the boxes)	High (Consider the cost of lost and not returned magazines)

NOTES

_____

_____

_____

_____

_____

WORKSHEET 8.9 Comparison of Selected Locations' Effectiveness

Goal: Pre-evaluate how effective each market channel or distribution location will be according to your knowledge of each one.

Selected market channels or locations	Flyers	Crate with empty video and DVD boxes	Spanish magazines, newspapers, and graphic novels
Latino grocery store	++ will accept the flyers – might not pay attention	+ will accept the crate – might get lost in clutter	– competition with other products for sale
High school	+ teens will bring home – might not pay attention	++ teens will bring boxes home – might be lost	– might get lost or not returned unless placed in school library or other supervised room
Public transportation	++ captive audience + can take home for information	+ captive audience – no space	– might get lost or not returned – no space
Hospital	+ high traffic – might not pay attention in a stressful situation	+ waiting halls/time – might be put aside by personnel	+ waiting halls/time – competition with other magazines

NOTES

_____

_____

_____

_____

_____

WORKSHEET 8.10   Comparison of Customer Predisposition at Different Locations

Goal: Pre-evaluate how you think people might act at these different locations. You will confirm your predictions after the campaign, once you evaluate how people responded to the stimulus.

Selected market channel or location	Customer predisposition	Motivation needed	Competition with other messages	Cost	Amount of advertising needed
Latino grocery store	High (people are looking for items to buy)	Medium (materials need to be attractive)	Medium (there might be similar items for sale); must indicate FREE!	Low (except if the store requests a fee)	High (to focus people's attention on something different!)
High school	Low/medium (teens are usually less motivated to read unless . . .)	High (same reason)	High (school boards, notices, etc.); good location necessary!	Low (free)	High (get their attention with a good spot or display!)
Public transportation	High (captive audience, bored but maybe tired)	Medium to low (too shy to take materials)	Medium/low (depends on many factors)	Low (bus line will not request a fee?)	Medium (captive audience has time to look over or read)
Hospital	Low (distracted with other issues)	High (distracted with other issues)	Low (maybe some magazines in waiting room?); depends on location	Low (hospital will not request a fee?)	Medium (depends on location; ER has long wait!)

 From *¡Hola, amigos! A Plan for Latino Outreach* by Susana G. Baumann. Santa Barbara, CA: Libraries Unlimited. Copyright © 2011.

WORKSHEET 8.11   Evaluation of Promotional Tactics' Procedures

Goal: Compare cost of procedure (distribution rounds, picking up returns, lost materials) with outcomes.

Selected market channels	Selected media		
	Flyers	**Crate with empty video boxes**	**Spanish (courtesy) magazines display**
Latino grocery store	Printed: 1,000 Distribution rounds: 3	Crates: 5 Boxes: 20 in each (100) Distribution rounds: 2	Distributed: 100 Distribution rounds: 3
	First round: 350 Patrons who showed with flyer: 30 Unused: 30 Taken/Lost: 290	First round: 50 Returned to library: 6 Unused: 42 Taken/Lost: 2	First round: 35 Returned to library: 10 Unused: 17 Taken/Lost: 8
	Second round: 350 Patrons who showed with flyer: 50 Unused: 150 Taken/Lost: 150	Second round: 50 Returned to library: 12 Unused: 30 Taken/Lost: 8	Second round: 35 Returned to library: 10 Unused: 7 Taken/Lost: 18
	Third round: 300 Patrons who showed with flyer: 10 Unused: 190 Taken/Lost: 100		Third round: 30 Returned to library: 5 Unused: 24 Taken/Lost: 1
Totals	Printed: 1,000 Patrons who showed with flyer: 90 Unused: 370 Taken/Lost: 540	Boxes: 100 Retuned to library: 18 Unused: 72 Taken/Lost: 10	Distributed: 100 Returned to library: 25 Unused: 48 Taken/Lost: 27

From *¡Hola, amigos! A Plan for Latino Outreach* by Susana G. Baumann. Santa Barbara, CA: Libraries Unlimited. Copyright © 2011. **273**

Chapter 9

Evaluating Results and Procedures

Overview

In business, evaluating your marketing plan's results and procedures is important to minimize mistakes and customer dissatisfaction and to increase sales and profits. However, in the case of library services, evaluating results and procedures goes beyond these business goals.

Author Arlene Dávila sustains that it is important to know the way people engage with certain products "not in order to ascertain the authenticity of these representations or to draw decisive conclusions about their effect on consumers . . . but [to understand] how people's discussions of media texts are enmeshed in wider social issues so that Hispanic marketing may be experienced either as a medium of marginalization or as a repository of language and tradition" (Dávila 2001, p. 182).

Assessing the progress and growth of your organization over time is a vital part of your Plan for Latino Outreach because it allows you to reexamine your own goals, mission, and vision in relation to the Latino community participation in and expectations from the library environment, as well as from other diverse populations you serve. The purpose of evaluation focuses on your organization's internal and external results and will ultimately determine if your role as an organization is really relevant in your community.

It also helps you adjust your course of action, redefine strategic goals, collect additional or missing information, try new alternatives, find solutions for challenges or obstacles, reassess your internal and external resources, and find new ways to comply with current legislation.

In order to evaluate your plan, you will ask yourself these four simple questions (adapted from Kotler, Roberto, and Lee 2002, p. 327):

- What are we evaluating?
- How are we evaluating it?

- When do we evaluate it?
- How do we use those conclusions?

Once you have answered these questions simply and fully, you will be able to plan your next outreach stage. A major pitfall most organizations fall into is to fail to realistically balance their efforts against their results and to apply those improved conclusions to their marketing efforts. Consequently, they keep repeating the same mistakes over and over.

This chapter helps you develop criteria and tools to carry out your marketing plan's evaluation. Although we are discussing this topic in the last chapter, setting up evaluation criteria should be considered at the time of planning and followed all along. Also included in this chapter are concluding considerations about making ethical decisions at every step of your outreach process. We will discuss how you can be loyal to your organization and your professional goals within an environment of respect for different ideas and approaches.

What Are You Evaluating?

Because evaluation focuses on your organization's performance, you must examine outcomes as well as procedures. *Outcomes* are evaluated in relation to *internal or external goals,* while *procedures* assess *activity* (what was done) and *implementation/execution* (who did it and how it was done) (see Figure 9.1).

Use the following indicators to acknowledge outcome measures based on the goals your organization set at different levels for the duration of the whole marketing plan (adapted from Kotler, Roberto, and Lee 2002, p. 327):

1. **Indicators related to your organization's diversity goals in Latino outreach,** which include your organization's purpose to market services to Latinos, action(s) carried out to achieve that purpose, and how your organization showed commitment to that purpose (chapter 2). These indicators will show at four different levels:

   - Collections, materials, and services
   - Customer service and outreach efforts
   - Funding
   - Facility

2. **Indicators related to strategic partnership participation,** which include assessing the number and nature of strategic partnerships achieved during the marketing plan duration, the sustainability of strategic partnerships throughout the plan, and the response from market channels, influencers, and media

FIGURE 9.1 The Evaluation Process

3. **Indicators related to general goals of promoting library services to the Latino community,** which include changes of behavior in the target audience, services awareness and knowledge, changes in Latino customers' beliefs about your organization, campaign awareness, response to the campaign, customer satisfaction, and unintended outcomes

4. **Indicators related to the specific goals of each outreach activity targeting a specific market segment,** which include specific benefits received by each Latino market segment, desired behaviors/actions to be triggered, awareness and knowledge of the specific service or product, response to the mini-campaigns, customer satisfaction, and unintended outcomes

You will also need to plan the evaluation of these indicators according to the short- and long-term goals you defined yearly, quarterly, or for a specific campaign, which will define the frequency of your evaluation:

1. Post-promotional mini-campaign evaluation is conducted *immediately* after the campaign as seen in chapter 8.
2. Short-term goals of marketing/outreach strategies and promotional/advertising efforts are evaluated quarterly.
3. Long-term goals of marketing/outreach strategies are evaluated at the end of each year, which will add up to support the final three-year marketing plan evaluation.

In general, these are your evaluation goals. Keep in mind to add up the results: your promotional mini-campaigns will show high-peak outcomes during certain times of the year; quarterly, you will report how participation continued or was supported by your organization's branding efforts; finally, long-term goals will be evaluated as a result of adding up these results plus the outcomes of your branding efforts in the three-year effort. Let us see how these indicators work.

The How-To: Indicators

Internal Outcome Indicators

Outcome indicators related to diversity goals in your mission statement are reflected in changes in internal policies and infrastructure. In addition to the outreach efforts targeting Latinos, all levels of your organization should be committed to the new short- and long-term strategic goals. Internal outcomes manifest and can be measured in the following:

- Collections, materials, and services: Refocusing and expansion of the Spanish and bilingual collections, improved and more appropriate services targeting the Latino community, and diverse and frequent programming and outreach activities
- Customer service and outreach efforts: New bilingual hires on a permanent budget, increased staff participation at diversity and cultural competency training, personnel involvement in outreach activities and the CLO, personnel efforts to recruit LAB members, and hiring of professional outreach staff
- Funding: Increase and use of funding and/or inclusion plan in permanent budget—no soft money—to support outreach and promotional efforts, collection development, and hiring necessary personnel

- Facility: Space and image changes of the facility to accommodate Latino patrons—from bilingual signage to culturally appropriate and Latino-friendly displays—and efforts to take the library outside the walls

Over time, you will continue to keep track of new initiatives, feeding back the process with new outcomes.

External Outcome Indicators

You will be able to evaluate your external outcomes of promoting general library services or branding and outreach efforts to the Latino community in three different areas: comparing your measurable goals you set at the beginning of the plan with outcomes, changes in behavior of your potential customers, and results of your promotional efforts as discussed in chapter 8.

Numbers and Amounts

Indicators can be measured mostly in percentages or numbers by comparing goals to outcomes. For instance, in our case scenario for a promotional campaign for general library services, we set the goal of increasing Latino membership by 3 percent in a calendar year. We also could have set a number—for instance, to add 300 Latino cardholders in three years—especially in a highly populated area. At the end of that period, your outcome should show an increase in Latino membership plus or minus that amount.

Indicators in Your Communication Stages

As we discussed before, these indicators can be seen mostly in the community's awareness of library facts. These indicators will follow the AAA communication model. You cannot use the same indicator for an awareness stage (where you are checking knowledge and information about the library) as for the action stage, when you need to see active participation.

For instance, the awareness stage will be based around statements such as "There is a Spanish-speaking librarian every Monday and Thursday at the library," or "Spanish newspapers and magazines are distributed for free at the library," or even precise information about classes and activities such as time of year, type of activity, continuity, and content of classes. In order to succeed in these outcomes, you need to convey that type of information in your campaign in order to evaluate specific results.

The acceptance stage will show indicators reflected in a change in your Latino patrons' beliefs about your organization and services, including attitudes, opinions, and limiting beliefs about themselves. You know there is a change in attitude, for instance, when asking for contact information does not trigger suspicion or distrust regarding confidentiality issues. Opinions related to the library and the Latino community might be evident in statements such as, "The library has friendly and bilingual customer service that I can speak to," "The library is a welcoming space for Latinos because it is easy to find your way around," "The library has updated and useful materials and services my family and I can use," or comments about other activities they might consider appropriate. Evaluating a change in limiting beliefs involves tracking such statements and summarizing them.

Finally, in the action stage, indicators will be measured in increased participation at ESL, conversation, or computer classes; increased attendance at activities and events; or patrons taking advantage of all materials and services the library has to offer. A final evaluation level—which falls out of your control or ability to measure results—will show in improved levels of literacy in the community, improved job and educational opportunities, increased income levels, more stable communities, and an easier acculturation process for Latino immigrants including a broader acceptance from the hosting culture.

The Extent of Your Promotional Campaigns

Another area of evaluation is which elements from the contents of your campaigns were noticed and how they were noticed. In chapter 8, we discussed efforts at two promotional levels and provided procedures to evaluate results from your promotional campaigns.

In addition, results might keep showing up after the campaigns are over. For instance, if you have set up a hotline for Spanish inquiries about a specific mini-campaign, calls to the number should be easy to track during the campaign, but you also should track the continuity of those calls after the campaign is over. People might keep that number in mind to request information about additional services. Responses from your library employees and the frequency of the calls at certain times of the day, month, and year should also be tracked as they will help you discover reasons your Latino patrons called frequently and the appropriate times to have a live responder. Topics of the patrons' questions and inquiries are also valuable in terms of defining materials and services the community wants or needs.

If you channeled your campaign incentives through your translated Web site, a game through mass media (e.g., newspaper or radio), questions in a column you publish in local newspapers or newsletters, or any of the other promotional ideas discussed in chapter 8, you will measure the number and content of responses to understand your reach and presence in the Latino community. Be sure to keep an orderly method of tracking these responses. But remember to keep track of responses beyond the promotional efforts—such as members bringing their Latino friends and relatives to the library after the campaigns have ended if at all possible.

Other tactics may also include measuring an increase in current cardholders without recent activity who started using the library again, the number of temporary cards returned but not turned into permanent cards, or the number of courtesy magazines or books returned or exchanged without turning into new cardholders—that is, unintended results of all those actions you encouraged while promoting general library services. Maybe these patrons were not ready at that time, but you can contact them again in the future.

You can also evaluate the responses you obtained through strategic partners' and market channels' promotional efforts, such as those we described at the hospital, the high school, and on public transportation in chapter 8. Or you can survey your publics and influencers, media gatekeepers, and members of your Latino Advisory Board and library community.

Lastly, you need to keep track of negative unintended results—negative responses not promoted during a campaign that might make you decide to rethink your process. Negative unintended results are usually—and hopefully, in your case—the consequences of pitfalls in promotional materials, such as reactions from the public to cultural issues and/or incorrect or incomplete messages; they can also be related to political and biased reactions to your organization and its resources. Unintended results may be positive, as well, such as unexpected referrals, new programming ideas Latino patrons bring to you, or new strategic partnerships that reach out to you. Note any surprises, positive or negative, and evaluate why you are getting these results in order to re-present the promotional campaign.

Worksheet 9.1 includes a summary of how to evaluate outcomes according to these indicators and also suggests techniques to keep track of outcomes. A blank version can be found in chapter 10.

Evaluating Changes in Your Organization's Procedures

Procedures assess the activity you carried out during the marketing plan (what was done) and the implementation/execution of that activity (who did it and how was done). For instance, procedures indicators related to diversity goals in your mission statement show up in changes in internal policies and infrastructure. In addition to outreach activities to Latinos, all levels of your organization demonstrate commitment to the new strategic goals and the way business is conducted.

You can evaluate procedures changes when your organization takes action in the following areas:

- Collections, materials, and services: Develops a Plan for Latino Outreach for a certain number of years, advocates for external changes in policies and legislation, and revises internal policies to guarantee equal access to library services
- Customer service and outreach efforts: Establishes and implements new hiring policies, offers increased diversity and cultural competency training; encourages and rewards personnel involvement in outreach activities, community events, and the CLO; and creates a career path toward professionalizing outreach staff
- Funding: Pursues additional permanent funding for expansion of the Spanish collection, appropriate services for the Latino community, and promotional efforts; allocates funding for CLO's projects; requests additional grants and subsidies
- Facility: Refocuses and changes protocols and procedures to serve the Latino community according to their needs; translates applications and other forms, Web sites, and brochures and materials on how to use library services; determines new telephone protocols and Spanish hotlines; relocates collections and displays for friendlier use, and so on

Procedures evaluation also assesses the activity that was generated to promote library services in general (branding) as well as the specific outreach efforts targeting each market segment, how they were implemented, and by whom, as explained in chapter 8.

Additional Ideas for Evaluation

In addition to your outcomes and procedures, your promotional efforts will generate increased additional usage of library services among other unintended patrons. For instance, you can also measure outcomes by monitoring activity with these methods:

1. Keeping track of regular library activity (such as borrowers of the Spanish collection, attendance at activities or classes, personal inquires, calls to a Spanish hotline, or regular Latino members using library services)
2. Keeping track of new cardholders brought in by referrals
3. Keeping track of participation at outreach activities and follow-up (number of participants, number of leads with personal contact information you were able to gather from the outreach activity for telephone or direct mail follow-up)
4. Keeping track of revolving users and why they rotate

Your library might already be keeping track of some of these actions on a regular basis. Follow established procedures, and add an item or two to track your Latino activity.

Timing of Your Evaluation

Monitoring activity is necessary to aid your evaluation process but monitoring your promotional efforts—as discussed in chapter 8—provides the flesh of your evaluation process and can help you quickly detect any pitfalls. Checking your efforts by taking notes, making observations, and flagging elements at regular times is instrumental to discover the progress of your activity and prevent disaster. There are four times during your marketing strategy when evaluation is necessary:

1. Prior to defining your marketing goals and strategies
2. During the promotional campaign
3. After the promotional campaign
4. A post-evaluation of your marketing strategy

Prior to Defining Your Marketing Goals and Strategies

Inventory the focus of your strategy and make it the baseline parameter to which you will compare outcomes. Then, evaluate if it is a realistic goal. You researched a total Latino population of 10,000 people and your strategy goal was to increase by 300 members. Your baseline parameter is to increase 100 members a year. How many Latino members do you have now? If you have 100 cardholders, duplicating what you already have (getting 100 more cardholders) with promotional efforts on your part seems to be realistic. However, if you only have 10 current members, 90 new members implies an effort of 10 times your current base, which is probably unrealistic.

You also need to measure the extent of your numbers compared to your resources. How much funding do you have? What staff is going to participate in this strategy? Do you need to train this staff, or have they already participated in similar experiences? If they did, what was the result of the former effort? Did you evaluate those results and learn from that experience?

During Your Promotional Campaign

During the process, you are tracking the implementation of the campaign, such as procedures and timetables, and making notes of any problems. The purpose is to be able to make changes if necessary and possible during the campaign and to track changes over time. You can do it during the campaign flow—weekly, biweekly, monthly, or quarterly—according to your schedule. Do not wait until the end of the campaign to make notes of problems; you can add this information to your baseline parameters in a defined period of time.

After Your Promotional Campaign

Evaluate the topics discussed in detail in chapter 8—outcomes, procedures, and timetables—according to net results (how many, how often, which ones, who did it, and how it was done). Evaluate resulting cost, time, and human efforts. This is the balance of your promotional campaign and is similar to closing the books at the end of the year.

Post-Evaluation of Marketing Strategy

The post-evaluation includes a comparison of your outcomes and procedures with the strategic goals you set up at the beginning of the campaign. It includes a comparison of cost, time, and effort related to your forecast (what you actually accomplished compared with what you planned to do). Short-term goals (one year) should be evaluated within the period of planning, while it is advisable that long-term goals (three years) are measured three times during the terms of the marketing plan, as results need to accumulate.

Your post-evaluation will include responding to some simple questions according to the goals you set at the beginning of your outreach plan (see Worksheet 9.2). Although the questions seem simple, the level of detail in your answers will depend on the level of your tracking during the implementation phase of your activities and promotional campaigns. If you kept good tracking records, just summarize those results in a report format and attach all tracking elements to the report.

How to Use Evaluation Outcomes

In chapter 1 you learned that your Plan for Latino Outreach would help you to accomplish a number of goals:

1. Prioritize decisions to help you focus your Latino outreach activities and maximize your resources: Once you evaluate your results, you will have a better idea of the promotional efforts and outreach activities that work with your local Latinos and can discard those that do not work, consequently maximizing your resources.
2. Collect important information regarding the community you serve: Evaluate whether the information you collected was appropriate and useful to your strategic goals, and collect and adjust information that is still missing.
3. Link and partner with other community organizations to develop a team approach: You will be able to assess your strategic partnerships and market channels and continue to work with those that respond to your needs and you to theirs—a true idea of partnership.
4. Foresee and pass up blockages and barriers that are obstacles to performing your services efficiently: With an increased and accurate knowledge of cultural and language barriers to your services, you can evaluate which of the services you are promoting are generating a response and which need to be discarded so you can create a smoother, more relaxing encounter with your Latino patrons.
5. Expand your organization's horizons and your employees' perspectives: Evaluation of procedures, which includes activities (what was done) and implementation/execution (who did it and how it was done), contributes to create a culturally competent organization and personnel.
6. Assess progress and growth of your organization over time: You will know how to improve services, attract and sustain Latino cardholders to your library community, and set goals that are more realistic in order to continue targeting this community. You will also increase your organization's level of relevance in your community.
7. Find new funding resources and tap deeper into the old ones: You will collect the information needed to fulfill grant expectations and secure funding in the future, in addition to creating new funding policies and strategies.

8. Comply with national and state goals for underserved markets in an efficient, orderly way: You will gain consensus among stakeholders, prove why Latinos need to be included in library efforts, and document how they respond to your efforts over time.

Apply the questions in Worksheet 9.2 to each of these topics. Discuss your findings with members of your CLO, and set up a format for disclosing your evaluations. End-of-campaign reports, end-of-year reports, and end-of-marketing-plan reports would be appropriate. Also, decide who should receive the information and determine the timing of the report. Internally, discuss evaluation findings with your trustees, management, personnel, and volunteers; externally, with community leaders, strategic partners, market channels, the media, the Latino population, and the population at large. Write a newsworthy summary of the reports and send them to the media with whom you worked for publication. In chapter 10 you will find Worksheet 9.3, a template for an end-of-campaign report. This worksheet can be used for several purposes, just like the other worksheets in this chapter, for instance, ass a template for an end-of-branding campaign, an end-of-promotional mini-campaign, an end-of-yearly marketing campaign, and so forth.

Looking for Challenges in the Evaluation Process

Most campaigns and marketing strategies have pitfalls and drawbacks. Some are easily seen by the public—you don't want that happening to you—and many are just behind the scenes. Evaluations mostly show challenges related to the following issues (Kotler, Roberto, and Lee 2002, p. 335):

1. **Your expectations were unrealistic:** You set your goals too high, you did not research your market enough, and you were too enthusiastic overall!

   • What to do: Regroup, start small, and develop with time.

2. **Your resources turned out to be insufficient:** Your initial assessment of resources was insufficient, resources changed midstream, or the tactic simply was not developed the way you planned. Do not be too hard on yourself.

   • What to do: Correct, adjust, and try again.

3. **You relied on a single approach:** This is usually a very risky decision, as discussed throughout this book.

   • What to do: You need to develop a plan and multiply efforts in several different venues.

4. **You asked the wrong questions:** This challenge directly involves the multicultural nature of your Latino market, and you will gain experience with time and homework.

   • What to do: Just keep doing it! Get help from current Latino patrons, your LAB, and other leaders in the community.

5. **You had technical problems:** Who has not had a technical problem? Your Spanish database is too hard for your Latino customers to search on, your computer lab is too small for the response you had in your campaign, your flyers were not printed on time, or the newspaper printed the wrong telephone number.

- What to do: Make adjustments and keep going! Use all tools you have—and that have been provided in this book—to help you implement and execute your plan.

6. **You found resistance in staff or participants:** The human factor, the human factor!

   - What to do: Increase training and participation, open your discussion about the results, and build more knowledge about the reasons it is important to serve this market. Finally, keep in mind that some people will and some people won't!

7. **You failed to evaluate procedures and results or monitor during, before, and after your efforts:** The lack of evaluation makes it impossible to compare results.

   - What to do: Set up an evaluation plan and stick to it! It is better to do some evaluation than nothing at all. Avoid repeating the same mistakes over and over.

The plan requires commitment and involvement, and you will have to follow every step carefully. Your organization's commitment to this endeavor is instrumental in giving you time, resources, and some funding to pursue your goals. Evaluation is essential to seek additional funding, to recruit additional strategic partners, and to create enthusiasm among your target Latino audience, your publics, and your co-workers at the library.

Making Ethical Decisions

The introductory framework of this book, as presented in chapter 1, is based on equity of service, equity of access, the changing role of libraries as community leaders, and the need to reach out to diverse communities that lack knowledge and experience in using library services.

All through this book, there are goals, strategies, and tactics following those criteria. Along the way you have hopefully found insights and useful tips to facilitate your work and improve access to library services for Latinos or other diverse groups in your area.

Your commitment to goals of equity and diversity is evident in your obtaining and reading this book. However, let's face it—not everybody will agree with or pursue these recommendations with the same commitment or enthusiasm. When making decisions about a course of action, you are also making ethical decisions about those same issues; you will choose some goals, strategies, or tactics over others. We spoke about the human factor as a challenge; however, you may also find challenges in your decision-making process.

First, be certain that your motives are clear and that there is no conflict of interest between your proposition of changing behaviors in the Latino community and your organization's or your strategic partners' agendas—such as favoring certain vendors, suppliers, or funding sources.

The intrinsic idea behind making ethical decisions rests on the fact that society as a whole needs to benefit, not just a part of it. The following ideas are guidelines for your reflection as you and your organization discuss the ethical framework of your Plan for Latino Outreach.

Making ethical decisions at every step of the way might become a challenge, especially when there are disagreements about how (or whether!) to approach your Plan for Latino Outreach.

When Kotler, Roberto, and Lee (2002, p. 393) make their observations about ethical decisions, they mention that by using social marketing principles, we are influencing the behavior of individuals, groups, or society in a way we believe is beneficial for them. However, the selection of one approach over another might be a detriment to others, and these disagreements can take months to settle. For instance, an effort to attract Latino customers might be seen as detrimental to other minorities or groups in your community. Set a timed framework for discussion on the matter, and then move on. If there are different opinions, try the approach that has the larger consensus with the promise that you will try other approaches if results do not meet expectations.

In your marketing efforts, you might find that promoting a certain change in behavior could conflict with other desired behaviors or trigger undesired outcomes. For instance, you promote free ESL classes at the library or with a strategic partner like a church, but because these classes are free Latinos do not pursue other venues for learning more advanced English, such as community colleges, because they are paid options. Can you find a way to work with other educational institutions to reduce competition? Perhaps offering your classes at different times or making your classes the introductory class that leads into the community college's classes might create an unexplored path that would benefit your Latino patrons and the college's students.

In collecting information, are you infringing on confidentiality, bringing up issues of trust and deception, or creating possibilities for information abuse? How are benefits explained without making false promises or creating false expectations? How do you prioritize the social equity factor from members who use library services the most versus members who need them the most? Are you prioritizing one part of the population over another, even within the Latino community itself? Do the messages you create carry accurate information? Are there gray areas you need to avoid? How are you deciding what is appropriate and what is not in your marketing strategies? Are you making the best effort possible within your resources? These are other questions that need honest answers.

Another ethical situation you may wish to discuss has to do with the acculturation process. All along, this book has explicitly reinforced the idea that libraries are one of the most instrumental paths for immigrants' acculturation. If some immigrants, for any number of reasons, oppose acculturation—and there might be some criticism in any efforts to get their families to do so—be aware that you might experience some expression of resistance from members of the Latino community as well as the community at large.

This book's goal has been to provide useful ideas, tools, and procedures. Now the job is all yours. Enthusiasm is a good place to start, but your efforts do not end there. Overall, there has to be conviction in your ideas, persistence in your actions, and the deepest belief that your accomplishments will help enhance the life of Latinos in the United States.

WORKSHEET 9.1   Summary of Indicators to Evaluate Outcomes

Goal: Compare goals set at the beginning of your comparison period-three year marketing campaign, short-term goals, or long-term goals-with outcomes.

1. Numbers and amounts

What you are measuring: Changes of behavior in Latino patrons, mostly measured in percentages and numbers, comparing goals to outcomes

Changes detected: Number of inquiries; percentage of response; increase in use of services, circulation of collections, or cardholders—measured by response to promotional tactics and incentives

Tracking mechanisms: Tracking sheets, activity reports, activity logs, circulation and registration tracking systems

2. Indicators in your communication stages

What you are measuring: Latinos' awareness of library facts, change in your Latino patrons' beliefs or opinions about your organization and services (attitudes, opinions, and limiting beliefs), and increased participation in programs and activities and other library services (different stages of communication process)

Changes detected: Statements and informal comments in the community; comments to staff; thank you letters; response to activities, events, and services; public opinion; media and blogs unsolicited articles; referrals; responses to awareness-building activities (newspaper or newsletter columns, Web site games or interactive activities, donation of Spanish materials to the library, etc.); and anecdotal comments

Tracking mechanisms: Surveys and questionnaires (telephone or in-person informal interviews), tracking files for informal comments and letters, clipping services, sign-in book or complaint book, suggestions box, "mystery" patrons interacting with other patrons

3. The extent of your promotional campaigns

What you are measuring: What was noticed and how it was noticed; number and content of inquiries to understand your reach and presence in the Latino community

Changes detected: Promotional campaign and incentive responses; number, timing, and nature of inquiries; feedback from publics and influencers

Tracking mechanisms: Distribution lists, tracking logs and sheets, media tracking logs, and surveys

 From *¡Hola, amigos! A Plan for Latino Outreach* by Susana G. Baumann. Santa Barbara, CA: Libraries Unlimited. Copyright © 2011.

WORKSHEET 9.2   Post-Evaluation Questionnaire

Goal: The level of detail in your post-evaluation questionnaire will depend on the level of your tracking during the implementation phase of your activities and promotional campaigns.

	Yes	No

1. Did you do everything you planned to do?
   If not, why?
 	
   How can you solve or improve this next time?
	❏	❏

2. Did you complete the activities on time?
   If not, why?
 	
   How can you solve or improve this next time?
	❏	❏

3. How do your goals compare to outcomes related to time, money, efforts, materials, staff participation, organization chart participation, or anything else you wanted to measure? How can you solve or improve this next time for each category?		

4. Did you achieve the outcomes you expected?
   If not, why?
 	
   How can you solve or improve this next time?
	❏	❏

Chapter 10

Your Plan for Latino Outreach

PLAN FOR LATINO OUTREACH [COVER]

[number of years]-Year Plan
[Organization's name]
[Location]

About Us [Brief history of the organization]

_____

_____

_____

Purpose [The need for a Latino outreach plan]

_____

_____

_____

Contributors

_____

_____

_____

[date]

CONTENTS

Changing the Outreach Outlook

WORKSHEET 1.1   Benefits and Challenges of Latino Outreach

Goal: To develop awareness among staff regarding the benefits and challenges of providing services to Latinos.

Instructions: You and your staff will reflect on the benefits this effort will bring to your organization, to your local Latino community, and to library staff according to the ideas developed in chapter 1. Be specific, and try to bring up details from your local situation. With your group, brainstorm ideas related to these topics (some ideas are offered). Then follow the instructions provided.

A. Make a list of benefits to your organization, to the Latino community, and to your staff:

YOUR ORGANIZATION

Makes the institution relevant in the community

How? Can you give examples? How can you measure being relevant?

_____

_____

_____

Reinforces libraries' service role.

What is the main service role of libraries, and how can they validate that role by reaching out to Latinos?

_____

_____

_____

Increases circulation and funding.

How does increasing membership among the Latino community benefit funding in your local library? Give specific scenarios of what areas of circulation or other services will bring additional funding, and approximate the magnitude. Think of alternative, nontraditional sources of income that might address Latinos' specific needs.

_____

_____

_____

Forces institutions to upgrade logistics.

What logistics have changed in your local library due to the need to serve populations with language and cultural barriers? What can be changed or improved?

_____

_____

_____

Presents new challenges to developing business.

What are these challenges? Think of staff, facility, accessibility, collections, customer service, schedules, etc.

_____

_____

_____

Empowers Latinos and provides them with leadership opportunities.

How can the library empower the Latino community to its own benefit? Think in terms of advocacy, constituency, Friends of the Library, etc.

_____

_____

_____

Strengthens the foundation of democracy

How can libraries support the foundation of democracy and promote it through the Latino community in a way that will affect the community at large?

_____

_____

_____

Creates new advocates for library services

How can you motivate Latinos to become advocates for library services and act for your benefit?

_____

_____

_____

Assures the future of libraries!

How can Latinos sustain not only the continuation of library services but also their expansion and improvement? Think in terms of current services you can expand and future services you can offer.

_____

_____

_____

Your own ideas

_____

_____

_____

From ¡Hola, amigos! A Plan for Latino Outreach by Susana G. Baumann. Santa Barbara, CA: Libraries Unlimited. Copyright © 2011.

Increases their educational opportunities.

Where does your Latino community stand in terms of education? How can your institution help increase educational opportunities and become a friendly learning environment for Latinos?

_____

_____

_____

Increases their employment opportunities.

What are the main sources of employment for Latinos in your local community, and how can the library help them find better jobs and improved opportunities? What has been done? What can be done?

_____

_____

_____

Provides access to information vital for survival.

Considering that immigration requires a learning process of navigating a new culture, a new system, and new customs and values, how can the library provide information to improve civic and survival skills? What specific information do Latinos need to be a part of your community?

_____

_____

_____

Provides access to free recreational materials.

Is recreation an important part of an individual's life? Is it different for Latinos?

_____

_____

_____

Offers acculturation opportunities.

Finding a new identity in a new culture and a new country can be difficult. How can the library help Latinos integrate into the fabric of society—in this case, your local community? Is your community welcoming and open to immigrants? Is it beneficial to your local community that Latinos establish their own enclaves and closed neighborhoods?

_____

_____

_____

Expands their socialization opportunities.

Socialization of individuals in a new environment can become a challenge when there are language and cultural barriers. How can the library provide opportunities for socialization in this context?

_____

_____

_____

Empowers their social, political, and economic development.

How is it beneficial to Latinos (and your community at large) that they get integrated and become an active part of its civic development? How does it create opportunities for social, political, and economic responsibility?

_____

_____

_____

Presents them with an opportunity to "belong"

Being cast out of a society or group can generate individual discontent, anomie, resentment, and even criminal behavior. How can the library help create a sense of belonging for Latinos living in your community? What added benefits can result from this acculturation or assimilation process?

_____

_____

_____

STAFF/YOU

(AS STAFF, SUPERVISOR, DIRECTOR, BOARD MEMBER, LIBRARY VOLUNTEER OR ADVOCATE, ETC.)

Creates opportunities for advocacy.

How can library staff become advocates for the Latino community? What would be the goals and philosophy of such advocacy? What actions should be taken to develop advocates in your library community?

_____

_____

_____

Professionalizes and systematizes outreach activities.

How can your organization create opportunities to professionalize outreach activities? In addition to funding, which is the last step, what previous steps must you take to lay the foundation to professionalize these activities?

_____

_____

_____

Strengthens diversity in the workforce.

How diverse is your workforce? How can your organization diversify its staff despite the difficulties implicit in hiring Latino or Spanish-speaking librarians? What organizations in your community can aid this effort? What other libraries have a model workforce, and how can you benefit from their experience?

_____

_____

_____

Increases professional and personal growth and expands horizons.

How can your staff grow professionally and personally by working with and for the Latino community? What changes result from an awareness of cultural differences? How can your organization offer opportunities for awareness of Latino culture, especially your local Latino culture?

_____

_____

_____

Challenges staff's own comfort zone.

How can your organization provide opportunities to help people expand their horizons and share experiences with each other? How can your staff exchange best practices in serving the Latino community with other libraries ahead of the game? How can you create enough enthusiasm and commitment to get your staff out of their comfort zone?

_____

_____

_____

Develops career choices and personal choices.

Who on your staff is a people person? Who has shown leadership and enthusiasm for outreach activities? How can the organization support these members of your staff to help them achieve their potential and eventually become pros?

_____

_____

_____

Provides recognition for a job well done.

What specific rewards can you establish to encourage and motivate your staff to participate in Latino outreach? Is it recognition or compensation? If you can't compensate them at this point, what sort of recognition does your staff value the most?

_____

_____

_____

Outlines accountability and "service pressure."

How can your organization develop incentives to make people aware of their responsibility to serve all members of your community, including Latinos and people who speak other languages?

What efforts have been made, and what was the result? How can you improve? How can you enforce existing guidelines or refresh them to obtain results?

_____

_____

_____

Contributes to our libraries' future and our means of employment!

What is at stake if libraries do not expand their services to all members of their community? How can you stand out in such a tight competitive market so that Latinos choose you over other organizations as their main source of information?

_____

_____

_____

Your own ideas:

_____

_____

_____

B. Choose two benefits to the library, to the Latino community, and to staff/you that particularly interested you!

Benefits to the library

_____

1. _____

2. _____

Benefits to the Latino community

_____

3. _____

4. _____

Benefits to staff/you

_____

5. _____

6. _____

Describe briefly why those interested you:

_____

_____

_____

C. Now think of a list of challenges. Develop a "contrast list." A contrast list reflects your ideas of how challenges can be solved.

CHALLENGE: **SOLUTION:**

Community members' complaints   Look at benefits that local Latinos bring
                                       to our area

Some resistance from staff   Increase diversity training opportunities

_____   _____

_____   _____

_____   _____

_____   _____

 From *¡Hola, amigos! A Plan for Latino Outreach* by Susana G. Baumann. Santa Barbara, CA: Libraries Unlimited. Copyright © 2011.

Your Organization's Vision

WORKSHEET 2.1   Your Mission and Vision

Goal: Analyzing your organization's vision and mission statements can bring into discussion how you and your co-workers understand diversity and outreach goals.

Instructions: Examine both your organization's mission statement and vision statement as they relate to the institution's commitment to diversity, and consider ideas to expand that content and make it more explicit and inclusive if necessary.

A. Look at your library's mission and vision statements and the institution's strategic plan. Do they include specific references to offering inclusive services or serving a broad community? Do they mention terms such as "diverse," "diversity," "underserved populations," "disadvantaged," "cultural competency," "equality of access," "immigrants," "non-English-speaking populations," or other such terms? These are common key-words, but the statement could express the same idea in other ways.

Your organization's current mission statement/vision/diversity goals:

B. Look at your library's vision or diversity statement and "fish" for values described. Not all libraries have a vision or diversity statement—if yours doesn't, the planning process provides an opportune time to develop one.

C. Answer the following questions:

1. What are the diversity purposes of your organization, and how are they expressed?

2. What actions is your organization taking in order to achieve these purposes?

 From *¡Hola, amigos! A Plan for Latino Outreach* by Susana G. Baumann. Santa Barbara, CA: Libraries Unlimited. Copyright © 2011.

3. How does your organization show commitment to these purposes?

4. What ideas would you like to add or change in your mission statement?

5. What new actions should be taken to increase support of diversity purposes?

6. Is the mission statement customer focused and concerned with the diversity in your community?

7. What new goals or pursuits—expressed in a charter statement—could be added or expanded to the present ones?

8. Who will be supporting these new goals?

GROUP DISCUSSION 1: Setting Goals

Instructions: To help you conduct an orderly discussion for the previous worksheet and keep track of your activity and participation, use this discussion form:

Setting new goals regarding the Latino population:

Who participated in this discussion?

Management: (includes your trustees, directors, branch managers, and supervisors)

Staff: (includes your personnel, interns, advocates, and volunteers)

1. Your current goals and policies regarding the Latino population:

   Are your goals and policies in writing? Are they efficiently publicized among all members of your organization?

2. Defining new goals:

   What needs to be done in order to set new goals? Who should participate in the process of setting new diversity goals and policies? Should these goals be expressed in your mission statement or a new charter statement?

3. Time commitment to this Latino outreach plan:

   Think of the total length of your plan and possible phases (for instance, a three-year plan will probably have three phases, one per year, with goals for each one, such as a first phase of market analysis and community needs assessment, a second of positioning the library and its resources, and a third of promotion and outreach). Be realistic with your resources and time constraints, including staff dedicated to this effort. For now, defining your time commitment is just part of setting goals, not a definite pledge.

Discussion report: (add pages as needed)

 From *¡Hola, amigos! A Plan for Latino Outreach* by Susana G. Baumann. Santa Barbara, CA: Libraries Unlimited. Copyright © 2011.

WORKSHEET 2.2   Committee for Latino Outreach (CLO) Board Members

Goal: Encourage co-workers and colleagues to become active members of your Plan for Latino Outreach in a balanced and productive team.

Instructions: Think of co-workers who might be good candidates to serve as members of your CLO, and consider the role or roles each might play. In this worksheet, give the reasons you think each individual might be interested and/or what skills they could bring to the position. It will give you a better idea of your potential CLO's strengths and weaknesses. Include other co-workers, members of management, and any other people who might be interested in starting this effort.

For the position of _____

Name _____

Current position _____ Location _____

Personal or professional interest _____

Qualification for this particular position _____

Availability _____

(Duplicate as needed. Define additional positions and subcommittees according to your needs.)

GROUP DISCUSSION 2:   Defining Participation

Instructions: These are guidelines for interviewing potential candidates for your CLO and how to think of potential candidates in terms of their interest, talents, and skills.

Participants in this discussion:

1. Personal and professional interest of participants in the Latino community.

_____

_____

2. What is the candidate's commitment to joining this outreach effort?

_____

_____

3. What is the candidate's interest in advocacy efforts and her or his view on professionalizing outreach in the library environment?

_____

_____

4. Does she or he have any knowledge of the local Latino community?

_____

_____

5. Is the candidate familiar with the organization's vision and mission? (If necessary for this discussion, go back to the ideas on Worksheet 2.1. Some participants might not have participated in that previous discussion, especially if you are trying to incorporate new members. Review the goals with them, and add necessary changes.)

_____

_____

6. Is the candidate familiar with the responsibilities of a CLO member? (See ideas developed in chapter 2)

_____

_____

 From *¡Hola, amigos! A Plan for Latino Outreach* by Susana G. Baumann. Santa Barbara, CA: Libraries Unlimited. Copyright © 2011.

7. Does he or she have knowledge of local contacts and Latino community leaders? (Suggest the candidate make a list of the people he or she knows in the community without leaving anybody out. They need not be Latinos or working only with Latinos.)

Organization	Name of contact person	Best way to be reached

8. According to this previous discussion, what type of position would the candidate be comfortable with?

_____

_____

(At this point in the discussion, you can go back to your notes on Worksheet 2.2 to show them your perception of their skills and talents and compare notes with the results of the group discussion.)

From ¡Hola, amigos! A Plan for Latino Outreach by Susana G. Baumann. Santa Barbara, CA: Libraries Unlimited. Copyright © 2011.

GROUP DISCUSSION 3:   Other Roles to be Considered

Who is going to be involved in defining the plan (other than members of the CLO—think in terms of decision makers)?

_____

_____

Who is going to provide support and resources to the plan?

_____

_____

Who makes the budget decisions?

_____

_____

What are the roles of the board members and library director/branch managers in this effort?

_____

_____

Also, think of guidelines for the following:

- Criteria for rotation of officers
- Accountability
- Volunteer and advocacy opportunities

Discussion report: (add pages as needed)

WORKSHEET 2.2.1   CLO Foundational Members

Instructions: Now you are ready to define your foundational members and officially launch your CLO. Do not be concerned if you do not have all your members yet. That will come with time and your current CLO members' efforts at generating enthusiasm!

Chairperson/President

Name _____

Position _____ Location _____

Secretary/Vice Chair

Name _____

Position _____ Location _____

Treasurer/Administrator

Name _____

Position _____ Location _____

Market Research Subcommittee

Name _____

Position _____ Location _____

Strategic Partners Subcommittee

Name _____

Position _____ Location _____

Funding Subcommittee

Name _____

Position _____ Location _____

Internal Resources (personnel, collections, facility)

Name _____

Position _____ Location _____

Planning and Programming Subcommittee

Name _____

Position _____ Location _____

Promotional Strategies Subcommittee

Name _____

Position _____ Location _____

Define additional subcommittees according to your needs:

_____

_____

_____

_____

WORKSHEET 2.3 Latino State of Affairs

Goal: Review your organization's capabilities and intentions regarding the local Latino community.

Instructions: Discuss and answer these questions with other CLO members:

1. How many Latino customers does your library presently serve (estimated), and what fraction of the local Latino community do they represent? Do you need to attract more members of this community, or do you just want to sustain the numbers you already serve?

_____

_____

_____

2. What geographical area does your organization serve? Do you need to expand your geographic reach?

_____

_____

_____

3. Who are your present Latino customers?

Individuals _____

Institutions _____

Businesses _____

Other _____

4. Who are your potential Latino customers?

Individuals _____

Institutions _____

Businesses _____

Other _____

5. What products and services does your library currently offer to the Latino community?

Collections _____

Literacy _____

Services _____

Technology _____

Programs and Events _____

Other _____

6. Which products or services would you like (or see the need) to create, expand, or improve?

Collections _____

Literacy _____

Services _____

Technology _____

Programs and Events _____

Other _____

7. What is unique in your organization that will attract Latino customers to your products and services? Describe facts and values (for instance, "free services" is a fact; "staff commitment to work with Latino customers" is a value).

Facts:

_____

_____

_____

Values:

_____

_____

_____

 From *¡Hola, amigos! A Plan for Latino Outreach* by Susana G. Baumann. Santa Barbara, CA: Libraries Unlimited. Copyright © 2011.

WORKSHEET 2.4   Your CLO's Charter

Goal: Define your service purpose and the goals to be achieved through this Plan for Latino Outreach.

Instructions: Discuss and answer these questions with other CLO members:

1. What are the service purposes of your CLO to the Latino community? (Some action words you can use include provide, expand, increase, create, foster, promote, assure. offer, make available, empower, celebrate, etc.) (Include ideas from Worksheet 1.1.)

_____

_____

_____

_____

_____

2. Who are the recipients of these efforts in your Latino community? (Include answers from Worksheet 2.3 questions 1 through 4.)

_____

_____

_____

_____

_____

3. What actions do you propose the CLO undertake in order to fulfill your purposes? (Trigger words include create, attract, outreach, develop, recruit, advocate, improve, expand, etc.: and answers from Worksheet 2.3 questions 5 and 6.)

_____

_____

_____

_____

_____

4. How does your organization show its commitment to those purposes? (Commitment of time, personnel, technology, collections, facilities, funding, etc.: Include facts and values from Worksheet 2.3 question 7.)

_____

_____

_____

_____

_____

5. Summarize these ideas in a paragraph or two. Do not be too concerned about creating the perfect statement as you will probably revise it down the road.

Charter Statement

_____

_____

_____

_____

_____

WORKSHEET 2.5   Creating an Internal Communication Process

Goal: These ideas will help you encourage and inspire your colleagues and co-workers to build a communication process and support your outreach plan.

Instructions: You can promote the following actions in your communication process:

1. Share an activity or success story related to customer service to Latino community members:

   These stories need to be specific in their topic. They should talk about an experience of inclusion and diversity and its positive impact or influence on a patron, a staff member, and/or the organization.

   How are you going to develop or collect these stories?

   _____

   _____

2. Submit a review of a new Spanish or bilingual printed material or DVD in the library's collection

   You can involve other people in this task, such as your reference librarians, the person who is in charge of collection development, members of your CLO, interns and volunteers, and current Latino patrons. Set a calendar, and keep adding reviews that you can eventually publish on your Spanish Web site. You can also create a community wiki where members of your community can post reviews of their favorite materials. If time constrains are a problem, research online for similar information and share with your staff.

   Briefly explain the criteria to accomplish this task:

   _____

   _____

3. Post questions (and answers) regarding Latino cultural issues.

   The purpose of this action is to develop awareness and generate enthusiasm and interest in Latino cultural issues. Do not emphasize (only) food or customs but also cultural behaviors and beliefs.

   Describe briefly how you can set up this activity:

   _____

   _____

4. Report operational or materials needs and suggest solutions or activities to fulfill those needs.

   Keep track of operational or material needs, from bilingual dictionaries to making it easier to use your facility (signs, location of materials, etc.). Keep short surveys (three to five questions max) at the front desk that

Latinos and other patrons can fill out so that you can know their needs and wants. (See the following Sample Service Tracking Survey.)

Describe an idea or two about this action and who will be responsible for implementing it:

_____

_____

5. Announce opportunities for staff diversity training and/or Spanish-language classes (internally or in the community):

Management wants solutions, not problems! Front-liners usually know what the problems are and can provide practical solutions that management might—or might not—implement. Give everybody a chance to do what they do best.

Describe who might be able to help you in this task, and provide guidelines to get it done:

_____

_____

6. Research and share ideas for activities and services other libraries offer to Latinos:

Constantly research what other libraries are doing for Latinos. Do not reinvent the wheel! Library Web sites and programs such as WebJunction Spanish Language Outreach have a wealth of information that you can apply to your local community if there is a good demographic match.

What other libraries/organizations will you research?

_____

_____

7. Report CLO activities and invite staff to participate

Always publicize and generate enthusiasm about CLO activities so people see your effort is working. Publicize the phases of your plan, discussions and meetings, findings, help from other organizations, and so forth. Also, keep asking for inclusion and participation, even if co-workers just provide information or a hand every now and then. Do not expect the same type of commitment from everybody, but everybody can add to the effort. And don't forget to always recognize them publicly.

Please briefly describe an instrument or tool—such as a newsletter, a weekly memo, or another piece of communication—you will use to publicize your accomplishments:

_____

_____

SAMPLE SERVICE TRACKING SURVEY

[Greeting section]

Hola! Le agradecemos su visita. Por favor, ayúdenos a ofrecerle un mejor servicio.

Hello! Thanks for your visit. Please help us serve you better.

[About the interviewee]

*Por favor, díganos cuál es su país de origen*_____

Please, tell us your country of origin_____

Y su edad _____

And your age _____

[About the service]

Usted buscaba . . . (Por favor, marque el que corresponde)

Did you look for   (Please circle)

Un libro?	A book?
Un video?	A video?
Un CD/DVD de música?	A music CD/DVD?
Una revista?	A magazine?

O tal vez buscaba . . .

(or maybe you were looking for)

Un libro para niños?	A children's book?
Información de servicios comunitarios?	Community services information?
Otra cosa _____	Other _____

Lo buscaba . . .   en inglés   en español   bilingüe?   (Por favor, marque el que corresponde)

You were looking for materials . . .   in English   in Spanish   bilingual?   (Please circle)

Encontró lo que buscaba?   *Sí   No*

Si no lo encontró, ¿puede describir en detalle el material que buscaba así podemos tratar de encontrárselo?

_____

Did you find it? Yes   No

If you did not find it, can you describe in detail what were you looking for so we can try to find it for you?

_____

[About your staff]

¿Quién le ayudó a buscar lo que quería?

Who helped you look for what you needed?

La persona del mostrador	Circulation desk person
El/la bibliotecario/a de referencias	Reference librarian
El/la bibliotecario/a de niños	Children's librarian
Otro empleado o nadie _____	Some other staff or no one _____

[About the communication process]

Prefiere hablar . . .   en español? en inglés? le da lo mismo?   (Por favor, marque lo que corresponda)

Do you prefer to speak in . . .   Spanish? English? either way?   (Please circle one)

¡Gracias por participar! ¡Tratamos de servirle lo mejor posible!

Thanks for your participation! We try hard to serve you the best we can!

Por favor, háganos sugerencias para ofrecerle un mejor servicio.

Please make any suggestions so we can offer you better services.

_____

_____

Assessing Strategic Partnership Opportunities

WORKSHEET 3.1 Researching Potential Strategic Partners

Goal: Research all potential organizations in your local community that might be involved or interested in targeting your local Latino community.

Instructions: Using a spreadsheet or database, make a list of businesses, organizations, or distributors that might become your potential strategic partners, community leaders, or market channels. Include contact information, addresses, and telephone numbers. Consider that Latinos shop, work, and play in almost every industry and activity, especially in largely populated areas where Latinos have lived for over 13 generations! Look at Yellow Pages and other sources in your community.

1. Where do Latinos in your community shop?

   Retail stores, jewelry stores, Latino markets and specialty stores, music stores, video stores, computer stores, supermarkets, car dealers, department stores, fast-food chains, utility companies, cellular phone stores

2. Where do Latinos in your community go for services?

   Doctors offices, hospitals, clinics, mechanics/auto repair shops, public transportation, laundry services

3. Where do Latinos in your community go for help?

   Churches (remember that not all Latinos are Roman Catholic, or even Christian) and faith-based organizations, schools, day care centers, Latino or Hispanic resource centers, government agencies

4. Where do Latinos in your community work?

   Construction companies, banks and co-ops, landscaping companies, schools and universities, hospitals and medical offices, farms, corporations, law firms, insurance agencies, hotels and restaurants, manufacturing facilities, cleaning services, janitorial and maintenance agencies, etc.

5. Where do Latinos in your community play or seek entertainment?

   Restaurants, fast-food restaurants, movie theaters, theaters, sporting events, comedy clubs, dance clubs, music venues, gyms and recreation centers, etc.

WORKSHEET 3.2 Assessing Strategic Partners

Goal: Assess potential strategic partners, market channels, and community leaders to aid you in your outreach efforts.

Instructions: Try to contact at least three people in each organization (if possible). You can fill out this data yourself or send it out to your potential candidates with a short letter explaining your outreach plan goals and your interest in their participation according to potential common goals.

Short letter sample:

Dear Mr./Ms. [Last Name],

Little Haven City Public Library is getting ready to reach out to Latinos in our area to attract them to library services. However, we cannot do this task alone. We need strategic partners and community leaders like you who know and are involved with this community to help us promote and support our efforts.

Our plan is designed to promote library services for three consecutive years starting this fall. We believe it would be valuable to work together at achieving a common purpose—to support and promote the advancement of the local Latino community—for which we will share responsibilities, resources, and competencies. We also understand that only mutually beneficial results create successful strategic partnerships.

We welcome your participation in this effort, so we encourage you to fill out the short form enclosed and mail it back at your earliest convenience. We will then follow up with a phone call to confirm the details of our understanding.

We look forward to working with you in the near future, and we thank you for your time.

Sincerely,

On a separate page, include the following information (these are suggestions; you can customize your own contact sheet).

Name of organization _____

Department: Public Relations, Community Relations, Human Resources, Diversity and Outreach, Diversity Committee, Community Services, Outreach Programming, Other (specify)

_____

First contact name: _____

Position: _____

Phone:_____ E-mail address: _____

Second contact name: _____

Position: _____

Phone:_____ E-mail address: _____

Third contact name: _____

Position: _____

Phone:_____ E-mail address: _____

Organization type (please describe briefly):

_____

_____

Summary of the organization's mission and goals:

_____

_____

Does the organization include social responsibility/diversity goals?

Summary:

_____

_____

What can you provide us that will support our plan/project/event/activity/campaign?

We can help with:

☐ Contact information   ☐ PR   ☐ Advertising/Word-of-mouth

☐ Credibility   ☐ In-kind donations   ☐ Publicity

 From *¡Hola, amigos! A Plan for Latino Outreach* by Susana G. Baumann. Santa Barbara, CA: Libraries Unlimited. Copyright © 2011.

We can provide contacts with chairs/executive directors/board members and officers of the following:

☐ Community groups or associations

☐ Businesses

☐ Foundations

☐ Faith-based organizations

☐ Business chambers

☐ Funding sources

☐ Nonprofit organizations

☐ Professional associations

☐ Business leaders

☐ Government agencies

☐ Natural leaders

We can provide the following resources:

☐ Funds/Fundraising

☐ Translators

☐ Interpreters

☐ Volunteers

☐ Focus groups

☐ Joint events

☐ Cross-information

☐ Resources

☐ Training/Teaching

☐ Grant writers

☐ Professional development

☐ Community assessment

☐ Collecting/Analyzing data

☐ Facilities

☐ Creative services

What can we offer you in exchange?

☐ Demographics and statistics

☐ Information

From ¡Hola, amigos! A Plan for Latino Outreach by Susana G. Baumann. Santa Barbara, CA: Libraries Unlimited. Copyright © 2011. **323**

☐ Cross-information

☐ Materials

☐ Bilingual materials

☐ Facilities

☐ Mutual promotional efforts

☐ Tax deduction

☐ Credibility

☐ Training/Teaching

☐ Other

(Add or subtract other ideas according to your possibilities and organizational guidelines.)

Comments:

_____

_____

(Add one page for each contact.)

GUIDE FOR CONDUCTING COMMUNITY LEADER INTERVIEWS

Author: Yolanda Cuesta, 2006, Cuesta Multicultural Consulting (Reprinted with permission)

Introduction

Community leader interviews are a very effective technique for learning about the Spanish-speaking community. The technique is personal and informative and begins the trust-building process that is essential for reaching this community. Local libraries are expected to partner and collaborate with community leaders.

Community Leader Interview Process

The major steps in conducting community leaders interviews are as follows:

- Identify community leaders (see these guidelines and Community Resources list in this section)

- Set up interviews (see Sample Process for Community Leader Interview in this section)

- Conduct interviews (see Sample Community Leader Interview in this section)

- Analyze/summarize information (see these guidelines)

- Set up follow-up interviews (see these guidelines)

See the following guidelines for conducting each step of the process.

Goals of the Community Leader Interviews

1. To gather information about the needs of the Spanish-speaking community in your community

2. To begin building relationships with community leaders within the Spanish-speaking community

3. To identify potential community partners and collaborators to help you increase access to public access computers by Spanish-speaking residents

Identifying Community Leaders

Use the following Community Resources list to help you begin identifying potential community agencies and groups to contact. Your goal is to identify community leaders who have knowledge of or experience working with the Spanish-speaking community.

The leaders you interview do not necessarily have to be Spanish-speaking themselves. They must, however, be knowledgeable about the needs and issues of the community. They might have gained their expertise by working for an agency that serves the community, or they may be community activists with a broad knowledge of community problems and issues.

From *¡Hola, amigos! A Plan for Latino Outreach* by Susana G. Baumann. Santa Barbara, CA: Libraries Unlimited. Copyright © 2011. **325**

Not all types of organizations on the Community Resource list may be represented in your community. You may already be familiar with some community leaders through the newspaper or other media coverage. Start with what and whom you know. Talk to other people in the library, in your church, or friends, neighbors, and so forth who may have a personal connection with a potential interviewee. It helps to be able to say that someone they know referred you to them.

Make a list of a minimum of five community leaders to interview. These are busy people, and your schedules and deadlines may not coincide.

Setting Up the Interview

The sample process provided is intended to be a checklist for you rather than a script. You are starting a personal relationship so be sure you are as comfortable and informal as possible. Practice what you want to say before you make the first call.

At the end of the interview, be sure to ask the interviewee for additional names of people you should contact. By now, the community leader knows you and what you are trying to accomplish. This can be invaluable in expanding your list of contacts. Be sure to always mention your contact's name if you follow up on their referral.

Conducting the Interview

Even though the community leader may offer to come to the library or your office, make it a point to conduct your interviews out in the community. You want to see them in their milieu, and you want others in the community to start seeing you out in the community. Face-to-face interviews are preferable to phone interviews.

The interview questions are intended as a guide. Be flexible and alert. The interview doesn't usually follow a simple pattern of questions. Often the leader will answer several of your questions at once. If so, when you get to a question the leader has already addressed, simply summarize what they said and ask if they have additional thoughts on the question.

Practice saying the questions out loud ahead of time. Rephrase them so you feel comfortable asking them.

Start by building rapport on a personal basis. The session should be informal and relaxing. Find out about the person, the organization, and key services and projects they provide before you start the interview questions.

If someone they know has referred you to them, be sure to mention this. Strive to make a personal connection immediately.

The focus of the interview questions is to identify community needs and issues. The purpose of the interviews is to get to know the community from an insider's perspective. The focus is not to get the community leader's perspective on what the library should be doing to serve the community. That will come later. At the interview, your role is to acknowledge and tap into the expertise of the community leader.

Take notes, but do not use a tape recorder. Feel free to take the time to write good notes. Ask the interviewee to repeat if you missed something or rephrase what you thought you heard. The interviewee wants to help you get it right.

If at all possible, end the interview by letting them know when you will be in touch again. Let them know that you will send them a copy of your findings, results, and so forth.

Summarizing the Interview

Review your notes immediately after the interview. Sit in your car or outside the interviewee's office, and be sure you can read what you wrote.

Transcribe and summarize your notes as soon as possible. Make a list of the needs and issues identified; highlight those that are repeated or mentioned more than once.

Set Up a Follow-Up Interview

The community leader interview process is the start of a relationship. As a minimum, plan to meet with the leader at least three times:

- The first meeting should be to conduct the interview and begin the relationship.

- The second meeting should be a personal follow-up with the results/findings of your interviews and to get the leader's input on your preliminary action plan.

- The third meeting should be to get the leader's help in marketing your activities and services to begin implementing your action plan.

Community Resources

Note: This list is not inclusive; selected examples are in parentheses.

You DO NOT need to contact every category on the list.

You DO need to tailor your list to your community.

You DO need to reach out to people not usually included.

- Youth service organizations (Big Brother/Sister, Boy Scouts, child abuse agencies, recreation programs, Girl Scouts, Jr. Achievement, Head Start, Even Start, child care associations, Association for the Education of Young Children, school age care, and enrichment programs)

- Women's centers/service organizations (battered women' shelters, YWCA, NOW)

- Refugee/immigrant centers/services (Catholic Social Services, refugee rights association)

- Religious organizations (church organizations, ministerial association)

- Senior centers/service organizations (Area Agency on Aging, elder abuse/care agencies, RSVP)

- Organizations of and for people with disabilities (Center on Deafness, Council for the Blind, health and human services agencies, Easter Seals, Goodwill, independent living centers, United Cerebral Palsy)

- Organizations serving the homeless (food closets, homeless assistance programs, Salvation Army)

- Organizations serving ex-offenders (Department of Corrections, Friends Outside)

- Technology experts (computer clubs, consultants, community colleges, Internet providers, universities)

- Organizations fighting discrimination (Anti-Defamation League, human rights groups, NAACP)

- Miscellaneous organizations (arts and cultural groups, athletic groups, censorship groups, historic preservation groups, local neighborhood groups, men's groups, veterans' groups, women's groups)

From *¡Hola, amigos! A Plan for Latino Outreach* by Susana G. Baumann. Santa Barbara, CA: Libraries Unlimited. Copyright © 2011. **327**

- Educational organizations (community colleges, multilingual programs, PTA/PTO, school boards, other libraries, private schools, home school organizations, higher education institutions/organizations)

- Government/political representatives (mayors, city councils, county supervisors, city/county fiscal offices, law enforcement, job training programs)

- Health organizations (American Cancer Society, American Heart Association, hospitals, public health nurses, early intervention programs, public health clinics)

- Legal organizations (ACLU, bar associations, legal aid, NAACP Legal Defense Fund)

- Ethnic organizations (Asian Resources Center, Hispanic centers, Inter-tribal Council, Urban League)

- Family services organizations (Social Services Department, Family Service Agency, Jewish Family Service)

- Media representatives (newspapers, radio, TV, ethnic media, local magazines and newsletters)

- Financial representatives (bankers, credit unions, financial planners, stockbrokers)

- Community services organizations/associations/clubs (AARP, AAUW (American Association of University Women), American Red Cross, B&PW (Business and Professional Women), Kiwanis, Lions, literacy organizations, Rotary Clubs, Soroptimists, United Way)

- Economic development organizations (economic development councils, real estate brokers)

- Businesses/chambers of commerce/visitors bureaus (major employers, minority business owners, small business owners; city, county, and ethnic chambers)

Sample Process for Community Leader Interview

Call to ask community leaders to participate in an interview.

Introduce yourself, and explain why you are calling. Ask if it is a convenient time to talk.

Sample explanation:

I am Rose Nelson, and I am with the Colorado State Library. I am calling to ask your help in identifying the needs of the Spanish-speaking community. Our goal is to [*state the purpose of your activity, event, promotional effort, or program*].

We want to learn more about the needs and problems of the Spanish-speaking community in Colorado and how they might be solved. We are conducting interviews with people like you who play an important role in helping the Spanish-speaking in Colorado.

We estimate the interview will take no longer than 30 minutes.

If you are willing to participate in an interview, I will send you a copy of the questions prior to the interview. Thank you for your time.

Send them a copy of the interview questions.

Meet with them or call them back at the scheduled time.

Ask the interview questions.

Thank the person for his/her time and explain how you will keep him/her informed about your progress.

Sample Community Leader Interview

Note: Start by building rapport on a personal level. The session should be informal and relaxing. Find out about the person, the organization, and the organization's key services and projects before you ask the following questions.

1. Tell me about the Spanish-speaking community in Colorado.

2. What are the major needs, issues, and problems facing the Spanish-speaking community in Colorado?

3. What kind of help do Spanish-speaking community members need to have a better life in Colorado?

4. What services are available to help the Spanish-speaking community? What are their strengths? What are their weaknesses? What else needs to be done?

5. Who else should we contact to help us identify the needs of the Spanish-speaking community in Colorado?

6. Is there anything else you would like to say about the Spanish-speaking community in Colorado?

7. What questions would you like to ask me?

Getting to Know Your Latino Patrons: Part I

WORSHEET 4.1   Demographic Variables in My Local Community (Community Profile)

Goal: Create a local Latino community profile to offer specific and targeted materials and services to the library's local Latino community.

Instructions: Fill out the information as best you can with the most predominant groups in your area. Add the necessary columns according to representative groups in your area. (Representative groups would be a percentage of your current Latino population. This percentage will have to be defined by your CLO by asking questions such as: Is 1 percent of a 10,000 population a representative group? What other populations do we serve with the same level of representation? Is this group in more need to be served even if the percentage is small?)

Variables	Specifics	Group 1 Size:	Group 2 Size:	Group 3 Size:	Group 4 Size:
Origin	Country Region				
Race	White Mixed Amerindian Afro-Indian Other				
Time in the United States	0–5 years 5–10 years 10–15 years over 15 years U.S. born second generation third or more generation				
Age	0–10 11–17 18–25 26–40 41–64 64+				
Occupation	Administrative/ Professional (skilled)				

Variables	Specifics	Group 1 Size:	Group 2 Size:	Group 3 Size:	Group 4 Size:
	Construction (OJT) Food/Farming (OJT) Production (OJT) Sales Other				
Income range	Less than $20,000 20,001 to 30,000 30,001 to 50,000 50,001+				
Socioeconomic status	Blue-collar White-collar Other (describe)				
Geographic mobility	Seasonal Settled Other (describe)				
Immigration status	Undocumented Temporary visa Legal immigrant/ Permanent resident Naturalized citizen U.S. born				
Age at immigration	0–10 11–17 18–25 26+				
Levels of education	Less than elementary Elementary Less than high school High school Some college Four-year college +				
Level of literacy	Illiterate Read and write				

 From *¡Hola, amigos! A Plan for Latino Outreach* by Susana G. Baumann. Santa Barbara, CA: Libraries Unlimited. Copyright © 2011.

Variables	Specifics	Group 1 Size:	Group 2 Size:	Group 3 Size:	Group 4 Size:
	Male Female				
Language ability	English dominant Bilingual Spanish dominant				
Gender	Male Female				
Family composition	Single Couple Couple w/ children Couple w/children and extended family (6+)				

Source of your information:

_____

_____

_____

From *¡Hola, amigos! A Plan for Latino Outreach* by Susana G. Baumann. Santa Barbara, CA: Libraries Unlimited. Copyright © 2011.

WORKSHEET 4.2   Country of Origin, Time in the United States, and Occupation Combined

Goal: The following worksheets (4.2 to 4.7) look at the interaction of several variables to understand your Latino market needs.

Instructions: Fill out these worksheets as best as you can according to your research and interviews with community leaders and current Latino patrons. You can combine any information in these worksheets or other you believe is important according to your objectives (for instance, gender, single-parent families, unemployed men or women, and so forth.) If you live in a large city, market segmentation is even more important. You will have to work with variables at a branch level and divide your city by your coverage area, the location of your Latino population (perhaps in neighborhoods or "*barrios*"), or place of work.

Variables	Specifics	Group 1 Size:	Group 2 Size:	Group 3 Size:	Group 4 Size:
Origin	Country Region				
Time of residence in the United States	0–5 years 5–10 years 10–15 years over 15 years U.S. born				
Occupation	Administrative/ Professional (skilled) Construction Food/Farming Production Sales Other				

Source of your information:

_____

_____

_____

 From *¡Hola, amigos! A Plan for Latino Outreach* by Susana G. Baumann. Santa Barbara, CA: Libraries Unlimited. Copyright © 2011.

WORKSHEET 4.3   Occupation, Time in the United States, Income, and Socioeconomic Status Combined

Variables	Specifics	Group 1 Size:	Group 2 Size:	Group 3 Size:	Group 4 Size:
Occupation	Administrative/ Professional (skilled) OTJ skill Other				
Time in the United States	Less than 5 More than 10 More than 20 Second generation Third generation Fourth generation				
Income range	Lower income (less than $20,000) Medium income (between $20,000 and $50,000) Higher income (more than $50,000)				
Socioeconomic status	Blue-collar White-collar Other				

Source of your information:

_____

_____

_____

From ¡Hola, amigos! A Plan for Latino Outreach by Susana G. Baumann. Santa Barbara, CA: Libraries Unlimited. Copyright © 2011.

WORKSHEET 4.4   Time in the United States, Occupation, and Levels of Education Combined

Variables	Specifics	Group 1 Size:	Group 2 Size:	Group 3 Size:	Group 4 Size:
Time in the United States	Less than 5 More than 10 More than 20 Second generation Third generation Fourth generation				
Occupation	White-collar Administrative / Professional (skilled) OTJ skill (describe) Other				
Levels of education	Less than elementary Elementary Less than high school High school Some college Four-year college +				

Source of your information:

_____

_____

_____

 From *¡Hola, amigos! A Plan for Latino Outreach* by Susana G. Baumann. Santa Barbara, CA: Libraries Unlimited. Copyright © 2011.

WORKSHEET 4.5 Time in the United States and Language Ability Combined

Variables	Specifics	Group 1 Size:	Group 2 Size:	Group 3 Size:	Group 4 Size:
Time in the United States	Less than 5 More than 10 More than 20 Second generation Third generation Fourth generation				
Language ability	English dominant Bilingual Spanish dominant Other				

Source of your information:

_____

_____

_____

WORKSHEET 4.6 Age and Immigration Status Combined

Variables	Specifics	Group 1 Size:	Group 2 Size:	Group 3 Size:	Group 4 Size:
Age	0–10 11–64 65+				
Immigration status	Undocumented Temporary visa Legal immigrant/Permanent resident Naturalized citizen US born				

Source of your information:

_____

_____

_____

 From *¡Hola, amigos! A Plan for Latino Outreach* by Susana G. Baumann. Santa Barbara, CA: Libraries Unlimited. Copyright © 2011.

WORKSHEET 4.7   Horizontal Comparison of Variables

Variables	Group 1 Size:	Group 2 Size:	Group 3 Size:	Group 4 Size:	Specifics:

From *¡Hola, amigos! A Plan for Latino Outreach* by Susana G. Baumann. Santa Barbara, CA: Libraries Unlimited. Copyright © 2011. **339**

Getting to Know Your Latino Patrons: Part II

WORKSHEET 5.1   A Template for an Ethnographic Interview

Goal: To help develop the interviewing skills of your library outreach staff.

Instructions: You can use this format while adapting the questions to several different topics.

Regarding your topic

To define your topic related to cultural behaviors and beliefs, go back to Table 5.1, "Cultural Dimensions in Latino Culture," in the individual and group levels. You can base your questions on this chapter's considerations at the cultural level.

Purpose of the interview

At the beginning of every interview, give a short explanation about the nature of the interview and the research you are trying to accomplish.

For example, "I would like you to share with me about [topic]." (For instance, people you know from other Latin American countries, family, work, health care information in the Latino community, and so forth. Give a generic topic so people do not feel it is too personal. You will get a little more personal as you build trust along the interview.)

"There are no right or wrong answers, and you may choose to share information with me if you want. I do want to learn about your experiences related to this topic so the library can come up with services that can help you and other Latinos in your community with the information they need."

Recording the interview

"I will write down some of your answers so I can recall and share with my colleagues at the library what you have said. I will not mention your name or any confidential information you share with me [if there are confidentiality issues]. I will also take notes, so if you feel there are important answers you want me to write down, please let me know and I will take notes of that particular issue." (You may ask permission to tape the interview if you see the interviewee is at ease with that method.)

Keep it simple

"I am not interested in technical language about the library or any other topic we talk about. I appreciate simple answers and your honest opinion in the language you use every day, in the way you might talk to a family member or a friend."

Looking at materials and images

"Along the way, I may ask you to look at [materials, brochures, or magazines if you brought any with you] and tell me what catches your attention on it." (If this is the case, you may bring magazines, pictures, library brochures, Latino newspapers, any other type of publication that might help you in interpreting their image and message preferences. You can bring pictures according to the topic of your choice—a picture of a family or a magazine or newspaper article that talks about the topic as an icebreaker. Printed material has great visual power, and they will understand the topic right away.)

Conclusion

"Finally, I will review my notes from the questions and ask any clarifying questions that were not already asked in the course of our conversation. Thanks so much for your time!"

Wrap up the interview

Review your notes out loud with the interviewee and ask any clarifying questions that were not already asked in the course of conversation or double check if you interpreted the answers correctly. Ask the interviewee if he or she has a specific statement to say about any particular question.

Thank the interviewee and state that you will get back to him or her when you have services or any other information regarding the specific topic of the interviewee. Do follow up with him or her!

Questions organized by type

Each interview pattern varies according to the kind of responses provided by the interviewee. The following questions are listed by type. I give you a description of the type of question, but you will have to come up with the actual questions.

Descriptive questions

These questions help you understand the experience of the interviewee related to the topic and a first approach to the topic. For instance, if the topic is family and family relationships, descriptive questions will include the following:

"Can you tell me about your family?" "Do you have children?" "Are you here alone or with your family?" "And who else is here with you?" "Do you have relatives in other cities or states?" "Do you have family back in [country of origin]?"

A personal preference that works: While conducting ethnographic interviews with Latinos and other populations, I always disclose something about my personal life related to the topic as part of the questions, such as the following: "You know, I also have two children but they are grownups now," or "I came in 1990, but I still have family back in Argentina." If you are not an immigrant, try to relate to the questions in other terms: "My grandparents were also from another country." Intertwining these comments with questions makes the interview more relaxed and friendly.

Grand tour questions

You can also phrase your questions in the following way:

"Can you tell me how is typical [week, day, Sunday, family celebration, holiday, day at work, doctor's visit] in your life?"

"Can you tell me about the last time you had [a family celebration, a holiday, a doctor's visit, a meeting with your children's schoolteacher] and what happened?"

Task-related questions

Ask them to look at some library material or other material you brought according to the topic of choice—a library application, a library brochure, a brochure from another organization, a family picture, a picture of a teacher with school children, a piece of health literacy, and so forth.

"Can you tell me what you see on this [piece] and what it brings to your attention, such as thoughts or experiences you had with [your visit at the library, the doctors office, your family reunion or celebration, a meeting at school or work, etc.]?"

Example questions

"Can you give me an example of what you are saying?"

Experience questions

"Can you tell me some story or anecdote about [your visit at the library, the doctors office, your family reunion or celebration, a meeting at school or work, etc.]?"

Direct language questions

"How would you describe [your visit at the library, the doctors office, your family reunion or celebration, a meeting at school or work, etc.]?"

Indirect language questions

"So, if you were telling a friend about an experience that you had [at the library, at the doctors office, at your family reunion or celebration, at a meeting at school or work, etc.], how would you describe it to them?"

Verification questions

"I have heard that other Latinos have different experiences when they [go to the doctor, celebrate a holiday, talk to their children's teachers, talk about . . . , raise their children, etc.] because they come from different countries. Have you also heard about differences or can you describe any differences from people you know—friends, neighbors, acquaintances, co-workers, and so forth?" (Again, try to disclose what you have heard, such as: "Mexicans like spicy food; do you? I like spicy food and did not know that not all Latinos like spicy food!")

Warning: You do not have to use all these type of questions, but these options allow you to structure your questions in such a way that your Latino interviewee will feel more at ease. You can try different approaches to see which one is more productive.

Adapted from *The Ethnographic Interview*, by James P. Spradley (Fort Worth, TX: Harcourt Brace Jovanovich College Publishers, 1979).

 From *¡Hola, amigos! A Plan for Latino Outreach* by Susana G. Baumann. Santa Barbara, CA: Libraries Unlimited. Copyright © 2011.

WORKSHEET 5.2   The Green Light, Red Light Method

Goal: Verify if your assumptions about your target market are correct.

Instructions: Use an educated guess and question every assumption you made in your target market segment's description. Cross-reference information with additional sources.

Green Light	Red Light	Action
Insert your assertion here as a question.	Stop: Insert your cultural suspicion about the topic.	Define the action you will take to verify the information.

Positioning Your Library
and Its Resources

WORKSHEET 6.1   Your Library's Internal Strengths and Weaknesses

Goal: Make a realistic inventory of your organization's internal resources.

Instructions: Organize a brainstorming session to complete the worksheet. Some of your CLO members, other co-workers, and supervisors might need to be involved to assess internal resources. Add necessary categories to your organization's structure. Complete the worksheet as best you can at this point. You will be able to come back to it when you find additional information.

Mission/Charter Statement	Internal Factor	Strength	Weakness
	1. Collections		
	2. Additional services		
	3. Latino membership		
	4. Programs and services		
	5. Outreach efforts		
	6. Promotional efforts		
	7. Demographics		

Mission/Charter Statement	Internal Factor	Strength	Weakness
	8. Funding		
	9. Customer service		
	10. Personnel development		
	11. Community partnerships		
	12. Technology		
	13. Location		
	14. Facility		
	15. Reputation or credibility		
	16. Other		

 From ¡Hola, amigos! A Plan for Latino Outreach by Susana G. Baumann. Santa Barbara, CA: Libraries Unlimited. Copyright © 2011.

WORKSHEET 6.2   Your Library's External Opportunities or Threats

Goal: Make a realistic inventory of your organization's external factors.

Instructions: Organize a brainstorming session to complete the worksheet. Some of your CLO members, other co-workers and supervisors might need to be involved to assess external factors. Add other factors you consider appropriate for your library. Complete the worksheet the best you can at this point. You will be able to come back to it when you find additional information.

External Factor	Opportunity	Threat
1. Latino Advisory Board		
2. Prospective members		
3. Competition		
4. Legislation		
5. Economic environment		
6. ALA action		
7. State Library		
8. State Association		
9. REFORMA		
10. Regional library cooperatives or consortiums		
11. Other		

From *¡Hola, amigos! A Plan for Latino Outreach* by Susana G. Baumann. Santa Barbara, CA: Libraries Unlimited. Copyright © 2011.

WORKSHEET 6.3 Long- and Short-Term Marketing Goals and Strategies

Goal: Determine concrete goals, assign responsibilities, and define schedules.

Instructions: This is your first approach to defining a marketing strategy. Choose related SWOT elements from worksheets 6.1 and 6.2 as discussed in chapter 6 to determine your goals, and describe them in detail when completing this worksheet. Use the same format when describing each of your short- and long-terms goals in your plan.

[Length of time] plan [long- or short-term] goal:	
What	
How much	
Who	
When	

 From *¡Hola, amigos! A Plan for Latino Outreach* by Susana G. Baumann. Santa Barbara, CA: Libraries Unlimited. Copyright © 2011.

WORKSHEET 6.4   Assess and Prioritize Needs

Goal: Define reasons to prioritize a need detected in your local Latino community.

Instructions: Answer these questions to understand and address the repercussions offering a service or organizing an activity might have internally and externally. These reasons are also justifications for pursuing funding, training your co-workers, and persuading strategic partners and other members of your community to collaborate in this effort.

In order to answer the following questions, follow the next steps:

Step 1: From the needs assessment list, choose two or three topics for which you have information readily available (this material should be bilingual and/or translated into Spanish and easily available through the library, through a strategic partner, or through your bilingual staff helping patrons find such information); also see if you need additional personnel, funding, facilities, or strategic partners.

Step 2: From your demographic research in chapter 4, choose the group that is easier to reach, is more open or ready to receive your information, or has a more pressing need for the information you are ready to provide.

Step 3: With the focus on your three-year plan goal, prioritize those needs according to your SWOTs.

Questions:

1. What is the need or problem your CLO and your organization will address?

2. What are the angles you could take or resources you could use in addressing this need or problem?

3. How did you find out about this need or problem, and what other sources did you use to confirm the need or problem?

4. Are segments of your local Latino population readier to receive the information related to this need or problem? Are there segments for whom the consequences related to this issue are more severe?

5. What are the main ways in which the issue could be addressed?

   Providing information

   Providing a service/class/activity

   Providing a location or facility

   Expanding your local geographic area

   Making connections with strategic partners

   Other _____

6. What are the most common or most serious consequences the Latino community confronts related to this issue?

7. What are the community's limiting beliefs and cultural behaviors related to this issue?

8. Are other organizations addressing the same issue? How can you collaborate/partner with them?

9. How can you afford to implement solutions—classes, events, locations, etc.—related to this issue? Do you have the funding, personnel, information, facility, and materials needed? If not, what action is required?

10. What are the expected results if your organization pursues this issue? What are the expected benefits for the Latino community, for segments of the community, and for the community at large?

 From *¡Hola, amigos! A Plan for Latino Outreach* by Susana G. Baumann. Santa Barbara, CA: Libraries Unlimited. Copyright © 2011.

WORKSHEET 6.5 Competing Behaviors in the Library Environment

Goal: Research and understand limiting beliefs, barriers, and established behaviors that prevent Latino customers from using library services.

Instructions:

1. Using the questionnaire provided in Worksheet 5.1, prepare an interview with no more than 15 questions, and interview potential customers in your target group.

2. Following the examples provided in chapter 6, summarize your findings and complete this table with their answers.

My target group is:			
What you want to promote	**Competing behaviors**	**Opposing messages/ messengers**	**Obstacles and limiting beliefs**
(Describe a service, activity, event, or new product you want to promote)	(From your ethnographic interviews, community leader interviews, and/ or comments from your Latino Advisory Board members)	(List all the people or situations that might negatively affect your Latino patrons related to this specific topic)	(List physical, skill-related, cultural, emotional, or psychological issues that might negatively affect their decision to use your service)

WORKSHEET 6.6   Positioning Activities, Programs, or Services
You Plan to Promote

Goal: Research and understand the benefits Latino customers expect from library services.

Instructions: Following the examples provided in chapter 6, summarize your interview findings and complete this table with their answers.

My target group is:			
Product the library promotes	**Perceived personal benefits**	**Fewer barriers/ obstacles/cost**	**Social pressure (influencers)**
(Explain the new behavior you want your target audience to adopt and how you plan to present it for later promotional purposes)	(From your ethnographic interviews, community leader interviews, and/ or comments from your Latino Advisory Board members)	(List all ideas you will promote among your target audience to overcome their barriers, obstacles, and limiting beliefs— from worksheet 6.5— when adopting this behavior)	(List all situations and people that might positively affect and influence your target audience's decision to adopt this behavior)

 From *¡Hola, amigos! A Plan for Latino Outreach* by Susana G. Baumann. Santa Barbara, CA: Libraries Unlimited. Copyright © 2011.

WORKSHEET 6.7 Positioning Statement

Goal: The positioning statement determines the aspects of your activity or program that are customer centered, grounded in actual accomplishments and relationships that make your place, products, and services unique for a particular audience. The positioning statement is the base, or concept, of your promotional campaign.

Instructions: Summarize the unique aspects of your activity or program that would appeal to your potential customers. Use comments from worksheets 6.4, 6.5, and 6.6.

Your target audience:

The service name or category:

Their problems, wants, and needs:

A key benefit:

The key differentiation:

WORKSHEET 6.8   Latino Customers' Influencers Memory Jogger

Goal: Get other publics or influencers to aid you in promoting library services when targeting a specific market segment.

Instructions: Make a list of all the people outside your organization who have an influence on your Latino customers at these different levels:

1. State level: policy makers, immigration enforcement, employment, labor agencies, etc.

2. Town/city level: administrators, law enforcement, school administrators, teachers, etc.

3. Neighborhood: community organizers, social work agencies, clinics and hospitals, etc.

4. Other library cardholders: current members, Friends of the Library, stakeholders, etc.

5. Family environment: family, spouse, children, relatives, friends, colleagues, co-workers, etc.

6. Community leaders (from chapter 3)

7. Business and organizations (market channels) (from chapter 3)

8. Strategic partners (from chapter 3)

9. Media outlets: local and regional newspapers, magazines, radio, and television

 From ¡Hola, amigos! A Plan for Latino Outreach by Susana G. Baumann. Santa Barbara, CA: Libraries Unlimited. Copyright © 2011.

Planning and Implementing Your Outreach Activities

WORKSHEET 7.1   Variables Comparison to Address Market Segment Needs

Goal: Determine overlapping segments that require similar services.

Instructions: Comparing the different groups in your community that need similar services will help you determine the scope of services, funding, and promotional efforts needed. Qualify the segments with an additional variable that makes each group as homogeneous as possible.

Variable	Specifics	Group 1 Size:	Group 2 Size:	Group 3 Size:	Group 4 Size:
First variable					
Second variable					

 From *¡Hola, amigos! A Plan for Latino Outreach* by Susana G. Baumann. Santa Barbara, CA: Libraries Unlimited. Copyright © 2011.

WORKSHEET 7.2   Positioning Statement with Incentives

Goal: In addition to defining all the aspects of your activity or program that are customer centered, grounded in actual accomplishments and relationships that make your place, products, and services unique for a particular audience, you also need to address the emotional concerns your target audience might have regarding this specific activity.

Instructions: Fill in those aspects of your program that can enhance the activity and address your target audience's specific concerns with solutions that are beneficial to them.

Your target audience:

The service name or category:

Their problems, wants, and needs:

A key benefit:

The key differentiation:

The concerns and emotional responses you want to address:

Fear:

Image:

Family:

Stress and time constraints:

Social expectations:

Other concerns:

The library will provide promotional items, ideas, or practice:

WORKSHEET 7.3   Planning Activities or Event Logistics Checklist

Goal: Define the logistics of your event, and make everybody aware of the program details.

Instructions: Define each step considered here (not all steps will apply for all programs). Feel free to add tasks or other details to each event's needs.

1. **Initiate and develop the idea** as discussed in chapters 6 and 7.

2. **Define necessary resources** to be used at the event or program (including funding you already planned on using for this particular purpose).

3. **Decide the setting** of the activity if needed or how the activity will be carried out. It could be your facility, a strategic partner location, a promotional campaign about library awareness through the media, and so on.

4. **Prepare a detailed budget** including materials, staff time, promotional items, and additions such as child care or transportation if needed. Define your vendors if necessary.

5. **Participate in the writing and administering of grant applications** to support the program if necessary.

6. **Make budget recommendations** relative to service and staffing levels, programming costs, and equipment and set-up staff needs.

7. **Develop a timeline chart** that will be distributed among all event collaborators (CLO, staff, strategic partners, and LAB).

Participant organizations:

1. **Select and invite** strategic partners related to the activity or event at hand.

2. **Develop and negotiate** contracts with strategic partners if appropriate, especially if they participate with funding, in-kind donations, and other money-related matters.

3. **Coordinate communications** relative to program logistics with strategic partners and make sure to have a clear procedure that will keep them informed of program development.

Event implementation and execution:

1. **Handle scheduling and coordinate activities** related to the event, including provision and rental of event equipment as needed (e.g., public address systems, risers, trash containers, tables, chairs, push carts, etc.).

2. **Make sure you have all materials** to be distributed at the event or plan the design and reproduction of library materials. Check if you need bilingual materials for your particular event.

3. **Look for internal and external help,** additional people who will participate at the event—from internal staff to help you welcome people to external performers, storytellers, or bus drivers if needed.

4. **Give instructions to staff setting up** for events. Attend event to ensure that all arrangements have been carried out and that other issues are dealt with appropriately.

 From *¡Hola, amigos! A Plan for Latino Outreach* by Susana G. Baumann. Santa Barbara, CA: Libraries Unlimited. Copyright © 2011.

5. **Develop and maintain data files** on participating organizations, news media, venue options, funding sources, and other related materials. Maintain files and insurance documents for street-use events.

6. **Maintain records and prepare reports** on event expenses, attendance, and other factors as requested.

7. **Try to anticipate constraints and obstacles** before a disaster can arise at the event (parking, weather, excess of attendees, or security and safety issues).

Promotional activities:

1. **Plan and coordinate promotional activities** and the development and dissemination of promotional materials for events including posters, display ads, news releases, flyers, and other public relations materials.

2. **Inform all** affected city, county, state, and national agencies of upcoming event.

3. **Develop and produce event calendars** for outdoor distribution and for distribution to strategic partners.

4. **Define promotional items,** research pricing and quality, decide quantity, and purchase.

WORKSHEET 7.4 Event Planning Communication Procedures

Goal: Make sure all people involved—internally and externally—are in sync and in contact with all details of the program or service.

Instructions: Follow each step of the communication procedures until you cover all event details. Feel free to add tasks or other details to each event's needs.

1. **Use your internal communication process.** Ensure all your library staff is aware of and informed about the event, program, or activity. Even if people are not directly involved in the activity, they might have to answer a phone call or respond to a question from a potential participant in the event. If your event is in Spanish for Spanish-speaking patrons, make sure to create enough posters for the public to see and cheat cards for your staff to use.

   What are you going to communicate?

   How are you going to communicate it?

   Who is receiving the information?

2. **Go over each collaborators role.** Ensure everybody knows the procedures inside out. If necessary, gather your staff in a short meeting to give insight into the event or campaign and provide clear written information about each person's role. Include a copy of the timeline chart.

   Participants:

   Role 1 description:

   Role 2 description:

3. **Inform your support staff**—such as your telephone receptionists or circulation desk clerks—about the event or activity. If possible, delineate an outline of possible questions and answers that might arise.

   What are you going to communicate?

   How are you going to communicate it?

   Who is receiving the information?

 From *¡Hola, amigos! A Plan for Latino Outreach* by Susana G. Baumann. Santa Barbara, CA: Libraries Unlimited. Copyright © 2011.

4. **Clarify your plan and expectations with strategic partners,** especially if their participation is instrumental for the success of the event, if the event takes place at their location, or if you need their cooperation to distribute materials. Listen to their concerns and address them promptly.

   Strategic partner contact person:

   What are you going to communicate?

   How are you going to communicate it?

5. **Name a media contact person**—or maybe two for backup—and make them aware of potential calls from the media, photo shooting opportunities, or additional information about the event.

   Internal media contact person 1:

   Internal media contact person 2 (backup):

6. **Get ready for your public's reactions**—such as phone calls from patrons, organizations, or agencies that might disagree with your activity or campaign. If possible, designate a spokesperson from your organization who can respond to these inquiries to make sure the message is consistent and prepared.

7. **What should staff know?** (name of event/activity/campaign, spokesperson's name and phone number, the message they should convey to callers)

From *¡Hola, amigos! A Plan for Latino Outreach* by Susana G. Baumann. Santa Barbara, CA: Libraries Unlimited. Copyright © 2011.

WORKSHEET 7.5 Monitor Implementation of Your Activity Checklist

Goal: Before launching your event, make sure you have control over all aspects of your program or service.

Instructions: To help you track the success of your program, you need to ask all these questions and adjust accordingly until all answers are YES! Use this form to make notes of missing details or reasons why the task or tasks have not been completed yet.

Are all the people, elements, and parts of the program in place?

Do all the materials and resources have the quality you envisioned?

Is all the library staff ready and enthusiastic about the program?

Did we cover all possible media and distribution channels?

Are all strategic partners in agreement and in sync with the implementation of the program?

Are our spokespeople ready to address community comments and concerns?

Are we on budget and on time?

Are all promotional materials distributed?

364 From ¡Hola, amigos! A Plan for Latino Outreach by Susana G. Baumann. Santa Barbara, CA: Libraries Unlimited. Copyright © 2011.

Promoting Your Library

WORKSHEET 8.1 Starting a Promotional Campaign

Goal: Answering these seven questions will help you define the general plan of your promotional campaign. You will work on details in the following worksheets.

Instructions: Discuss with your CLO your first ideas about this particular campaign according to the information you gathered in previous worksheets. You will work the details of these ideas and will give them shape at a later time.

1. Establish the identity of your brand or products	What are we trying to promote?
2. Identify your target audience and influencers	Whom are we trying to reach?
3. Establish campaign objectives	What are we trying to achieve?
4. Create an image or theme	How do we communicate it?
5. Develop your message	How do we say it?
6. Select and implement a media plan	How do we deliver it?
7. Evaluate results and procedures	How are we going to evaluate?

 From *¡Hola, amigos! A Plan for Latino Outreach* by Susana G. Baumann. Santa Barbara, CA: Libraries Unlimited. Copyright © 2011.

WORKSHEET 8.2   Planning Promotional Tactics

Goal: Develop a [type of campaign] for [amount of time, occasion, or time of year]. This campaign will concentrate on [type of campaign—branding or mini-campaign] through [type of tactics that will be used].

Instructions:

1. For branding efforts, follow each short-term marketing goal determined in chapter 6, worksheet 6.3, and decide appropriate promotional tactics as discussed in chapter 8 using this same format.

2. For mini-campaigns, complete this worksheet answering questions provided in the chapter 8 section entitled, "Starting a Promotional Campaign."

[Type of Campaign] for [Name of your library]	
Campaign promotional goals:	
Tactic	**Plan**
Word-of-mouth	
Publicity	
Public relations	
PSAs	
Personal networking	
Popular and social media	
Printed materials	
Paid advertising	
Promotional items	

From *¡Hola, amigos! A Plan for Latino Outreach* by Susana G. Baumann. Santa Barbara, CA: Libraries Unlimited. Copyright © 2011.

WORKSHEET 8.3   Media Outlets Contact List

Goal: Develop a media contacts file to plan and execute timely media promotional efforts.

Instructions: Complete this simple format for each local media that covers your area of service. A memory jogger list is provided. (You can also use a spreadsheet file.)

Publications:

Type of publication	Frequency	Contact person	E-mail address	Phone/Fax	Submission deadline
Newspaper Magazine Newsletter Journal Column Online publication Blog	Daily Weekly Monthly Quarterly				
Brief description of the publication: Circulation: Distribution: Price:					

Broadcast outlets:

Local radio/TV stations	Program/ Frequency	Contact person/ Producer	E-mail address	Phone/Fax	Submission deadline
Brief description of broadcast outlet: (relevant segments, public affairs programs, talk shows, etc.) Cumulative audience: Planning schedule:					

CLO member for media contact _____

Backup CLO member for media contact _____

 From *¡Hola, amigos! A Plan for Latino Outreach* by Susana G. Baumann. Santa Barbara, CA: Libraries Unlimited. Copyright © 2011.

WORKSHEET 8.4   Media Outlets Timing and Scheduling

Goal: Schedule the right timing for your promotional effort. The opening has to meet the right need at the right time.

Instructions : Complete this format for each media outlet in your promotional campaign plan (worksheets 8.2 and 8.3)

Name of event/activity/campaign to be promoted:

Stage of campaign:

Publicity/media tactic selected:

Format:

Implementation	Distribution	Topic	Schedule

Purpose of media attention:

Newsworthy information:

Type of coverage: (For each media outlet's contact information, go to Worksheet 8.3.)

☐ News

☐ Feature

☐ Editorial

☐ Entertainment

☐ Public Service

WORKSHEET 8.5   The Creative Brief (Summary)

Goal: Summarize all aspects of your promotional campaign in one or two pages.

Instructions: Following the guidelines given in chapter 8, develop one creative brief for each of your target segments or for each of their influencers. Topics that will differ in each creative brief are marked with an *.

1. Campaign Background

Problem or need detected in your Latino community that motivated the campaign. (Worksheet 6.4)

2. Target Audiences and Publics/Influencers*

Who do you want to reach with your communication? (Worksheet 7.2) Be specific. If addressing other publics or influencers, complete a separate worksheet. (Worksheet 6.6)

3. Campaign Statement

Description of the campaign focus for the activity or event. (Follow instructions in chapter 8 The Creative Brief.)

4. Key Message*

What your target audience—or other publics/influencers—is expected to do after they hear, watch, or experience this piece of communication. (What do you want them to know, believe, or do?) (Follow instructions in chapter 8 The Creative Brief)

 From *¡Hola, amigos! A Plan for Latino Outreach* by Susana G. Baumann. Santa Barbara, CA: Libraries Unlimited. Copyright © 2011.

5. Identified Behaviors, Limiting Beliefs, and Opposing Messages/Cost

How are you going to address behaviors, cultural practices, pressures, and misinformation that stand between your audience and the desired objectives? (Worksheets 6.5 and 6.6)

6. Key Benefits/Consequences

Benefits your target audience will experience upon taking action and/or consequences for not taking action. (Worksheet 6.6)

7. Support Statements/Third-Party Credibility*

Third parties talk about the reasons why the key benefit outweighs the obstacles and why what you are promoting is beneficial to your target audience. These reasons often become messages. (Check with community leaders and research other organizations with similar offerings.)

8. Tone/Language*

What feeling should your communication have? Should it be authoritative, light, or emotional? Is it a monolingual or bilingual piece of communication? The tone will also change if the creative brief is addressing your target audience or other publics or influencers.

9. Creative Considerations*

Define the production schedule of your promotional message and campaign at this time for both your target audience and your other publics and influencers.

WORKSHEET 8.6 External Distribution Plan

Goal: Recruit strategic partners, community leaders, market channels, and even other branches in your library system to help distribute your promotional materials.

Instructions: Determine an external distribution plan for *each stage* of the promotional campaign. Use this same format for all three stages.

Stage of campaign:					
Name of campaign:					
Strategic partners:					
Name of strategic partner (community leader, market channel)	**Distribution frequency**	**Contact person**	**E-mail address**	**Phone/Fax**	**Delivery deadline**

Speaking engagements at community events:					
Name of event	**Frequency**	**Contact person/ Producer**	**E-mail address**	**Phone/Fax**	**Registration deadline**

Brief description of event:
Attendance:
Location:
Speaker(s) for this opening:

Incentive:
(Describe all details of incentive attached to this stage of the promotional campaign.)

 From ¡Hola, amigos! A Plan for Latino Outreach by Susana G. Baumann. Santa Barbara, CA: Libraries Unlimited. Copyright © 2011.

WORKSHEET 8.7   Internal Execution Plan (Summary)

Goal: Make sure you have all promotional materials in place, and engage and recruit the rest of your colleagues in your planning effort.

Instructions: Use these worksheets for every stage of your campaigns.

Materials Readiness (worksheet 8.7.1)

1. Written materials (Press releases, columns, articles, PSAs, radio and TV spots): Determine who is writing the piece. Make sure the information is in sync with the stage of the communication process and the basics of your creative brief. Tell the writer(s) your expectations. Make sure there is copyediting and spellchecking of each piece. Determine who is responsible for the delivery and follow-up of the pieces to the appropriate media contact.

2. A word-of-mouth campaign or personal networking: If the participants are part of your staff, make sure they are available for the programmed dates, determine who is participating at each event, and make sure they can correctly convey the information. Also, determine who is going to be at each appearance. Take care of the event logistics.

3. Printed materials: What brochures posters, and other pieces need to be made and distributed at events and through strategic partners? Define the quality and quantity of the materials. Make sure you have enough copies, and track them through each stage of the communication process. Determine who is responsible for distributing and monitoring inventory at each point in the distribution process and with each strategic partner.

4. An online social media page including library-made videos: Determine who will design, launch, and update the page; track responses to the information; follow up and monitor; make necessary adjustments; and respond to potential questions from your target audience and your other publics.

5. Prepare the logistics of any other tactic (promotional items, popular media, and so forth) by contacting vendors and contributors, checking and replacing inventory, making sure the materials are ready and on budget.

Personnel Readiness (worksheet 8.7.2)

1. Brief your staff, colleagues, and volunteers at the library about the goals of the campaign and their expected role in it—even if it is just to answer the phones and connect the caller with the right spokesperson.

2. If you need extra hands, ask around for volunteers, and inform them precisely what needs to be done.

3. Use co-workers' resources in media, the target audience, or the publics. They might know people who know people who can make a difference in your program.

4. Receptionists or spokespersons will need a telephone protocol to help them with key answers to questions your target audience or publics might have.

5. Define a person or two who will speak to the media to expand on key ideas about the event, material, or service or the target audience and their needs. Media love statistics, how your organization is addressing a community problem, your approach to solving it, and possible reactions or objections to your program. Remember your information needs to be entertaining, enticing and newsworthy!

6. Prepare your spokespersons to address possible reactions of your target audience, your publics, and community members at large. It is impossible to make everybody happy!

Strategic Partners Follow-Up (worksheet 8.7.3)

1. Secure the contact information of person who is the liaison at your strategic partner or market channel. Do not assume they know what to do!

2. Make contact in the previous weeks to ensure they remember their commitment. Remind them about their task or role in the activity at hand (material distribution, speaker participation, word-of-mouth, and so forth.)

3. Keep track of materials sent, date and additional instructions. Follow up to make sure your liaison received the information (materials, advertising pieces, or other).

4. Follow up if they need additional materials for replacement, or additional information for participation.

Media Follow-Up (worksheet 8.7.4)

1. Keep track of all written pieces (articles, columns and press releases, radio and TV spots) you sent, and the contact information of your media liaison.

2. Include the name and format of the event you are promoting (very important in case you are promoting several activities, programs or services at the same time).

3. Keep track of dates sent, and publication dates. Verify if the pieces was published or aired. If it was, send an email or make a call to say thanks and acknowledge them. If it did not, contact your liaison and ask if they need additional information or to reschedule the information.

4. Remind them of the launch or event day and time so they can participate and report the offering.

WORKSHEET 8.7.1   Internal Execution Plan: Materials Readiness

Instructions: Define promotional materials needed and their general schedule. Each category will require a more detailed production description at a later time.

Type of material	Size	Quantity	Design/Artwork deadline	Printing/Launching deadline
Printed materials				
Art work				
In-house video				
Social media page				

(Add categories as needed.)

From *¡Hola, amigos! A Plan for Latino Outreach* by Susana G. Baumann. Santa Barbara, CA: Libraries Unlimited. Copyright © 2011.

WORKSHEET 8.7.2   Internal Execution Plan: Personnel Readiness

Instructions: Develop criteria to give directions to your staff according to regular procedures in your library.

Spokespersons: (names and availability)
Key talking points about your promotional campaign:
Phone protocol: (procedure for staff)
One-on-one protocol: (procedure for staff explaining additional information to customers)
Media protocol: (procedure to connect media with spokespersons)
Procedure to deal with unfavorable reactions to promotional campaign: (target audience, publics, and community at large)
Additional information for media reporters: (statistics, how your organization is addressing a community problem, your approach to solving it, and possible reactions or objections to your program)

 From *¡Hola, amigos! A Plan for Latino Outreach* by Susana G. Baumann. Santa Barbara, CA: Libraries Unlimited. Copyright © 2011.

WORKSHEET 8.7.3   Internal Execution Plan: Strategic Partners Follow-Up

Instructions: Keep track of your communications with strategic partners that participate in distribution of promotional materials. Do not assume that everybody knows what to do!

Strategic partner	Contact name/ Information	Type of material	Quantity	Sent date	Instructions sent	Follow-up/ Replacement date

WORKSHEET 8.7.4   Internal Execution Plan: Media Follow-Up

Keep track of media that help in your promotional efforts. Follow up with a phone call to confirm that materials were received.

Media outlet	Contact name/ Information	Event name/Type of material sent	Sent date	Follow-up date	Run from date to date	Publication or release date

 From *¡Hola, amigos! A Plan for Latino Outreach* by Susana G. Baumann. Santa Barbara, CA: Libraries Unlimited. Copyright © 2011.

WORKSHEET 8.8   Cost Comparison of Selected Tactics

Goal: Here are three ways to evaluate your tactics to promote library services. Remember that cost refers to both money and effort.

Instructions: Guesstimate the approximate labor and funds necessary for each tactic. Some tactics might be more labor intensive than others. Evaluate according to your resources and possibilities.

Variables	Tactic 1	Tactic 2	Tactic 3
Type of tactic			
Cost of tactic ($)			
Effort from your staff to prepare campaign			
Distribution frequency			
Display expense and material replacement			

From ¡Hola, amigos! A Plan for Latino Outreach by Susana G. Baumann. Santa Barbara, CA: Libraries Unlimited. Copyright © 2011.

WORKSHEET 8.9   Comparison of Selected Locations' Effectiveness

Instructions: Appraise approximately the way each location will perform in capturing the attention of potential customers.

Selected market channels or locations	Tactic 1	Tactic 2	Tactic 3

380 From *¡Hola, amigos! A Plan for Latino Outreach* by Susana G. Baumann. Santa Barbara, CA: Libraries Unlimited. Copyright © 2011.

WORKSHEET 8.10 Comparison of Customer Predisposition at Different Locations

Instructions: Guesstimate these five factors in the way people behave at these locations.

Selected market channel or location	Customer predisposition	Motivation needed	Competition with other messages	Cost	Amount of advertising needed

From ¡Hola, amigos! A Plan for Latino Outreach by Susana G. Baumann. Santa Barbara, CA: Libraries Unlimited. Copyright © 2011.

WORKSHEET 8.11   Evaluation of Promotional Tactics' Procedures

Goal: Compare cost of procedure (distribution rounds, picking up returns, lost materials) with successful outcomes.

Instructions: Make a detailed follow up of the labor involved in the promotional materials' distribution and the way customers responded at each tactic. By comparing these procedures, you can evaluate which one attracts more customers with less cost and labor. If you can, make notes of the reasons why each round had more or less successful outcomes.

Selected market channels	Selected media		
	Tactic	**Tactic**	**Tactic**
	Description: Distribution rounds:	Description: Distribution rounds:	Description: Distribution rounds:
	First round: Returned to library: Unused: Taken/Lost:	First round: Returned to library: Unused: Taken/Lost:	First round: Returned to library: Unused: Taken/Lost:
	Second round: Returned to library: Unused: Taken/Lost:	Second round: Returned to library: Unused: Taken/Lost:	Second round: Returned to library: Unused: Taken/Lost:
	Third round: Returned to library: Unused: Taken/Lost:	Second round: Returned to library: Unused: Taken/Lost:	Third round: Returned to library: Unused: Taken/Lost:
Totals	Total: Returned to library: Unused: Taken/Lost:	Total: Returned to library: Unused: Taken/Lost:	Total: Returned to library: Unused: Taken/Lost:

 From *¡Hola, amigos! A Plan for Latino Outreach* by Susana G. Baumann. Santa Barbara, CA: Libraries Unlimited. Copyright © 2011.

Evaluating Results
and Procedures

WORKSHEET 9.1 Summary of Indicators to Evaluate Outcomes

Goal: Compare goals set at the beginning of your comparison period—three-year marketing campaign goals, short-term goals, or long-term goals—with outcomes.

Instructions: Go back to your marketing strategic goals and check the changes found as a result of outcomes. Be precise in all details.

1. Numbers and amounts

What you are measuring:

Changes detected:

Tracking mechanisms:

2. Indicators in your communication stages

What you are measuring:

Changes detected:

Tracking mechanisms:

3. The extent of your promotional campaigns

What you are measuring:

Changes detected:

Tracking mechanisms:

 From *¡Hola, amigos! A Plan for Latino Outreach* by Susana G. Baumann. Santa Barbara, CA: Libraries Unlimited. Copyright © 2011.

WORKSHEET 9.2   Post-Evaluation Questionnaire

Goal: The level of detail in your post-evaluation questionnaire will depend on the level of your tracking during the implementation phase of your activities and promotional campaigns.

Instructions: Respond to these simple questions according to the goals you set at the beginning of your outreach plan. If you kept good tracking records, just summarize those results in a report format and attach all tracking elements to the report.

	Yes	No
1. Did you do everything you planned to do? If not, why? How can you solve or improve this next time?	❏	❏
2. Did you complete the activities on time? If not, why? How can you solve or improve this next time?	❏	❏
3. How do your goals compare to outcomes related to: Time: Money: Efforts: Materials: Staff participation: Organization chart participation: Anything else you want to measure: How can you solve or improve this next time for each category?		
4. Did you achieve the outcomes you expected? If not, why? How can you solve or improve this next time?	❏	❏

WORKSHEET 9.3   End of Marketing Campaign Report Template

Goal: Write your end-of-promotional campaign reports, end-of-year reports, and end-of-marketing-plan reports.

Instructions: This format would be appropriate for different types of reports. Complete the following information to be included in your report. You can vary the categories or redistribute the order according to your reporting needs:

1. Campaign strategic goal

2. Target market (or Market segment)

3. Campaign statement

4. Campaign background

5. Behavioral change/Desired actions

6. Report on promotional campaign

      Strategy

      Tactics

      PR/Media used

7. Strategic partners' participation

8. Outcomes evaluation

9. Procedures evaluation

10. Recommendations for future actions

 From *¡Hola, amigos! A Plan for Latino Outreach* by Susana G. Baumann. Santa Barbara, CA: Libraries Unlimited. Copyright © 2011.

Bibliography

Agar, M. 1996. *The Professional Stranger: An Informal Introduction to Ethnography*. New York: Academic Press.

Agustí, L. 2007. *Essential Guide to Spanish Reading: Librarian's Selections*. Coral Gables, FL: Trade Commission of Spain.

Ainslie, R. C. 2002. "The Plasticity of Culture and Psychodynamic and Psychosocial Processes in Latino Immigrant Families." In *Latinos: Remaking America,* ed. Marcelo Suarez-Orozco and Mariela Pa Lez. Berkeley, CA: University of California Press.

Alcalay, R., Alvarado, M., Balcazar, H., Newman, E., and Ortiz, G. 2000. "Evaluation of a Community-Based Latino Heart Disease Prevention Program in Metropolitan Washington, D.C." *International Quarterly of Community Health Education* 19 (3): 191–204.

Alire, C., and Archibeque, O. 1998. *Serving Latino Communities.* New York: Neal-Schuman Publishers.

Alire, C., and Ayala, J. 2007. *Serving Latino Communities,* 2nd ed. New York: Neal-Schuman Publishers.

Anuario Hispano Hispanic Yearbook: A Unique Resource and Referral Guide for and About Hispanic Americans. 2005/2006. McLean, VA: TIYM Publishing Company.

Argyle, Michael. 1988. *Bodily Communication,* 2nd ed. London: Methuen and Co. Ltd.

Arrendondo, P., Toporek, R., Brown, S., Jones, J., Locke, D. C., Sanchez, J., and Stadler, H. 1996. "Operationalization of the Multicultural Counseling Competencies." Alexandria, VA: Association for Multicultural Counseling and Development. http://www.tamu-commerce.edu/counseling/Faculty/salazar/OperationalizationOfTheMulticulturalCounselingCompetencies1996.pdf.

Arreola, D. D., ed. 2004. *Hispanic Spaces, Latino Places: Community and Cultural Diversity in Contemporary America.* Austin, TX: University of Texas Press.

Azeveda, K., and Ochoa Bogue, H. 2001. "Health and Occupational Risks of Latino Livings in Rural America." In *Health Issues in the Latino Community*, ed. M. Aguirre-Molina, C. W. Molina, and R. Zambrana, 327. San Francisco, CA: Jossey-Bass Publishers.

Bacon, D. 2008. *Illegal People: How Globalization Creates Migration and Criminalizes Immigrants.* Boston, MA: Beacon Press.

Bangs, Jr., D. H. 1998. *The Market Planning Guide.* Chicago, IL: Upstart Publishing Company.

Benítez, C. 2007. *Latinization: How Latino Culture is Transforming the U.S.* Ithaca, NY: Paramount Market Publishing.

Berger, P. L., and Luckmann, T. 1966. *The Social Construction of Reality: A Treatise in the Sociology of Knowledge.* Garden City, NY: Anchor Books.

Berry, J. W. 1998. "Acculturative Stress." In *Readings in Ethnic Psychology,* ed. P. Balls Organista, K. Chun, and G. Marin. New York: Routledge.

Birdwhistell, R. L. 1970. *Kinesics and Context: Essays on Body Motion Communication.* Philadelphia, PA: University of Pennsylvania Press.

Borda, J. 2007. *Salsa, Soul, and Spirit.* San Francisco, CA: Berrett-Koeheler Publishers.

Bourhis, R. Y., Moise, L. C., Perreault, S., and Senecal, S. 1997. "Towards an Interactive Acculturation Model: A Social Psychological Approach." *International Journal of Psychology* 32 (6): 369–86.

Brodie, M., Suro, R., Steffenson, A., Valdez, J., and Levin, R. 2002. "2002 National Survey of Latinos, Summary of Findings." Menlo Park, CA: Kaiser Family Foundation and Washington DC: Pew Hispanic Center. December. http://pewhispanic.org/files/reports/15.pdf.

Carrión, G. 1977. "Progress and Problems of Librarianship in Latin America with Emphasis on Mexico." Speech delivered at the Graduate School of Library Science, the University of Texas, Austin, TX.

Chapa, J. 2000. "Hispanic/Latino Ethnicity and Identifiers." In *Encyclopedia of the U.S. Census*, ed. Margo J. Anderson, 243–46. Washington, DC: CQ. http://www.latinamericanstudies.org/latinos/identifiers.htm.

Chavez, L. R. 2004. "A Glass Half Empty: Latina Reproduction and Public Discourse." *Human Organization* 63 (2). http://www.anthro.uci.edu/faculty_bios/chavez/Chavez-glass.pdf.

Chavez, L. R. 2008. *The Latino Threat: Constructing Immigrants, Citizens, and the Nation.* Palo Alto, CA: Stanford University Press.

Chávez Campomanes, M. T. 1969. "La biblioteca pública en México: su historia, su funcionamiento y organización y perspectivas para el futuro." *Boletín del Instituto de Investigaciones Bibliográficas* 1 (2): 31–38.

Chickering-Moller, S. 2001. *Library Service to Spanish-Speaking Patrons: A Practical Guide.* Santa Barbara, CA: Libraries Unlimited.

Chong, N. 2002. *The Latino Patient: A Cultural Guide for Health Care Providers.* Yarmouth, ME: Intercultural Press.

Chong, N., and Baez, F. 2005. *Latino Culture: A Dynamic Force in the Changing American Workplace.* Yarmouth, ME: Intercultural Press.

Cluff, E. D. 1991. "Libraries and Librarians in Mexico." *College and Research Libraries News* 52 (6): 370–71.

Coda Garrido, L. G. 2001. *El libro y las nuevas tecnologías.* México: Ediciones del Ermitaño.

Comsky, A. 2007. *"They Take Our Jobs!" and 20 Other Myths about Immigration.* Boston, MA: Beacon Press.

Cornelius, W. A. 2002. "Ambivalent Reception: Mass Public Responses to the New Latinos Immigration in the United States." In *Latinos Remaking America,* ed. M. M. Suárez-Orozco and M. M. Páez. Berkeley, CA: University of California Press.

Cuban, S. 2007. *Serving New Immigrant Communities in the Library.* Wesport, CT: Libraries Unlimited.

Dávila, A. 2001. *Latinos, Inc.: The Marketing and Making of a People.* Berkeley, CA: University of California Press.

Dávila, A. 2008. *Latino Spin: Public Image and the Whitewhasing of Race.* New York: New York University Press.

Davis, D.M., and Hall, T.D. 2007. "Diversity Counts." ALA Office for Research and Statistics, ALA Office for Diversity. Revised January. http://www.ala.org/ala/aboutala/offices/diversity/diversitycounts/diversitycounts_rev0.pdf.

Davis, M. 2007. *Magical Urbanism: Latinos Reinvent the U.S. City.* London: Verso.

de la Garza, R.O., and Fujia, L. 1999. "Explorations into Latinos Voluntarism." In *Nuevos Senderos: Reflections on Hispanics and Philanthropy,* 55–78. Houston, TX: Arte Público Press.

de la Garza, R.O., Desipio, L., Garcia, F.C., Garcia, J., and Falcon, A. 1992. *Latinos Voices: Mexican, Puerto Rican, and Cuban Perspectives on American Politics.* Boulder, CO: Westview Press.

Délgado, R., and Stefancic, J., eds. 1998. *The Latino/a Condition: A Critical Reader.* New York: New York University Press.

Duncan, T., and Moriarity, S.E. 1998. "A Communication-Based Marketing Model for Managing Relationships." *Journal of Marketing* 62 (1): 13.

Fetterman, D.M. 2009. *Ethnography: Step-by-Step (Applied Social Research Methods),* 3rd ed. Thousand Oaks, CA: Sage Publications.

Flores, E., and Pachon, H. 2008. "Latinos and Public Library Perceptions." Tomás Rivera Policy Institute and WebJunction Spanish Language Outreach, a project of the Bill and Melinda Gates Foundation and OCLC. September. http://www.webjunction.org/c/document_library/get_file?folderId=10860985&name=DLFE-2520003.pdf.

Foster, D. 2002. *The Global Etiquette Guide to Mexico and Latin America.* New York: John Wiley and Sons.

Fox, G. 1996. *Hispanic Nation: Culture, Politics, and the Constructing of Identity.* Tucson, AZ: University of Arizona Press.

Fox, S., and Livingston, G. 2007. "Latinos Online." Washington DC: Pew Hispanic Center, a Pew Research Center Project. March 3. http://pewhispanic.org/reports/report.php?ReportID=73.

Fraga, L.R., Garcia, J.A., Hero, R., Jones-Correa, M., Martinez-Ebers, V., and Segura, G.M. 2007. "Key Findings from the 2006 Latinos National Survey." The Woodrow Wilson International Center for Scholars. http://www.wilsoncenter.org/index.cfm?fuseaction=events.event_summary&event_id=201793.

Frauenglass, S., Routh, D.K., Pantin, H.M., and Mason, C.A. 1997. "Family Support Decreases Influence of Deviant Peers on Hispanic Adolescents' Substance Abuse." *Journal of Clinical Child Psychology* 26 (1): 15–23.

Fry, R. 2004. "Latino Youth Finishing College: The Role of Selective Pathways," June 23. Washington DC: Pew Hispanic Center, a Pew Research Center project. http://pewhispanic.org/files/reports/30.pdf.

Fry, R. 2005. "Recent Changes in the Entry of Hispanic and White Youth into College," November 1. Washington DC: Pew Hispanic Center, a Pew Research Center project. http://pewhispanic.org/reports/report.php?ReportID=56.

Fry, R. 2006 "Gender and Migration," July 5. Washington DC: Pew Hispanic Center, a Pew Research Center project. http://pewhispanic.org/files/reports/64.pdf.

Fry, R. 2009. "The Changing Pathway of Hispanic Youths into Adulthood," October 7. Washington DC: Pew Hispanic Center, a Pew Research Center project. http://pewhispanic.org/files/reports/114.pdf.

Fry, R., and Lowell, B. L. 2002. "Work or Study: Different Fortunes of U.S. Latino Generations," May 29. Washington DC: Pew Hispanic Center, a Pew Research Center project. http://pewhispanic.org/files/reports/9.pdf.

Fuch, Lawrence H. 1990. *The American Kaleidoscope: Race, Ethnicity, and the Civic Culture.* Indianapolis, IN: Wesleyan Publishing House.

Gans, H. J. 2004. "The American Kaleidoscope, Then and Now." In *Reinventing the Melting Pot: The New Immigrants and What it Means to be American,* ed. T. Jacoby, 33–46. New York: Basic Books.

Gastelum, S. 2006. "Inside Mexican Libraries." *Críticas,* June 15. http://www.criticasmagazine.com/article/CA6344733.html?nid=4113.

Gil, R. M., and Inoa Vazquez, C. 1996. *The Maria Paradox: How Latinas Can Merge Old World Traditions with New World Self-Esteem.* New York: Perigee Books.

Givens, D. B. 2008. *The Nonverbal Dictionary of Gestures, Signs, and Body Language Cues.* Spokane, WA: Center for Nonverbal Studies Press. http://members.aol.com/nonverbal2/diction1.htm.

Gleeson, S. 2005. "An Analysis of the Determinants of the Economic Integration of Immigrants: A Multi-Dimensional Approach." University of California–Berkeley. Paper presented at the 2005 Population Association of America annual meeting, Economic Integration of Immigrants session 142, Philadelphia, PA.

Gloor, L. B. 2006. "From the Melting Pot to the Tossed Salad Metaphor: Why Coercive Assimilation Lacks the Flavors Americans Crave." *HoHoNu, A Journal of Academic Writing* 4 (1). http://hilo.hawaii.edu/academics/hohonu/writing.php?id=91.

Gonzalez, R., and Ruiz, A. 2002. *My First Book of Proverbs/Mi primer libro de dichos.* San Francisco, CA: Children's Book Press.

Güereña, S. 1990. *Latino Librarianship: A Handbook for Professionals.* Jefferson, NC: McFarland and Company.

Güereña, S., ed. 2000. *Library Service to Latinos: An Anthology.* Jefferson, NC: McFarland and Company.

Hakimzadeh, S., and Cohn, D'V. 2007. "English Usage among Hispanics in the United States," November 2. Washington DC: Pew Hispanic Center, a Pew Research Center project. http://pewhispanic.org/reports/report.php?ReportID=82.

Hall, E. T. 1976. *Beyond Culture.* New York: Anchor Books Editions.

Haugen, E. 1987. *Blessings of Babel: Bilingualism and Language Planning: Problems and pleasures.* Berlin: Walter de Gruyter and Co.

Headland, T., Pike, K., and Harris, M., eds. 1990. *Emics and Etics: The Insider/Outsider Debate.* Thousand Oaks, CA: Sage Publications.

Hiebing, R. G., Jr., and Cooper, S. W. 1997. *The Successful Marketing Plan: A Disciplined and Comprehensive Approach,* 2nd ed. Chicago, IL: NTC Business Books.

Hirschman, E. C. 1986. "The Effect of Verbal and Pictorial Advertising Stimuli on Aesthetic, Utilitarian, and Familiarity Perceptions." *Journal of Advertising* 15 (2): 27–34.

Hofstede, G. 2005. *Cultures and Organizations: Software of the Mind,* 2nd ed. New York: McGraw-Hill.

Holt, G. E. 1999. *Public Library Partnerships: Mission-Driven Tools for 21st Century Success.* Gütersloh, Germany: Bertelsmann Foundation Publishers. http://www.public-libraries.net/html/x_media/pdf/holt6en.pdf.

"How Immigrants Saved Social Security." 2008. *New York Times* [Editorial], April 2. http://www.nytimes.com/2008/04/02/opinion/02wed3.html?_r=2&ref=opinion&oref=slogin.

Hughes, M. 2005. *Buzzmarketing: Get People to Talk about Your Stuff.* New York: Portfolio, Penguin Group.

Immroth, B., and de la Peña McCook, K., eds. 2000. *Library Services to Youth of Hispanic Heritage.* Jefferson, NC: McFarland and Company.

Kahn, J. R., and Berkowitz, R. E. 1995. "Sources of Support for Young Latina Mothers: Executive Summary," August 16. The Urban Institute. Prepared for the Office of the Assistant Secretary for Planning and Evaluation, U.S. Department of Health and Human Services. http://aspe.hhs.gov/hsp/cyp/xslatina.htm.

Kaiser Family Foundation. 2004. "Latinos in California, Texas, New York, Florida, and New Jersey—2002 National Survey of Latinos Survey Brief." Publication #7056, Menlo Park, CA: Kaiser Family Foundation and Washington DC: Pew Hispanic Center. http://www.kff.org/kaiserpolls/7056.cfm.

Kaneko, M. A. 2003. "Spanish-Language Videos and DVDs: A Resourceful Librarian's Tips for Starting a Collection." *Críticas Magazine,* March/April, 68–70.

Kasarda J. D., and Johnson J. H., Jr. 2007. "The Economic Impact of the Hispanic Population on the State of North Carolina." Chapel Hill, NC: Frank Hawkins Kenan Institute of Private Enterprise at Kenan-Flager Business School, University of North Carolina at Chapel Hill. http://www.ime.gob.mx/investigaciones/2006/estudios/migracion/economic_impact_hispanic_population_north_carolina.pdf.

Keefe, S. E., and Padilla, A. M. 1987. *Chicano Ethnicity.* Albuquerque, NM: University of New Mexico Press.

Kivisto, Peter. 2004. "What is the Canonical Theory of Assimilation?" *Journal of the History of the Behavioral Sciences* 40 (2): 149–63.

Kline Weinreich, N. 2005. *Hands-On Social Marketing: A Step-by-Step Guide.* Thousand Oaks, CA: Sage Publications.

Kochhar, R. 2005. "The Occupational Status and Mobility of Hispanics," December 15. Washington DC: Pew Hispanic Center, a Pew Research Center project. http://pewhispanic.org/files/reports/59.pdf.

Kochhar, R. 2007. "1995–2005: Foreign-Born Latinos Make Progress on Wages," August 21. Washington DC: Pew Hispanic Center, a Pew Research Center project. http://pewhispanic.org/files/reports/78.pdf.

Korzenny, F., and Korzenny, B. A. 2005. *Hispanic Marketing: A Cultural Perspective.* Boston, MA: Elsevier.

Kotler, P. 1987. *Strategic Marketing for Non-Profit Organizations,* 3rd ed. Upper Saddle River, NJ: Prentice-Hall.

Kotler, P., and Fox, K.F.A. 1995. *Strategic Marketing for Educational Institutions.* Upper Saddle River, NJ: Prentice-Hall.

Kotler, P., Roberto, N., and Lee, N. 2002. *Social Marketing: Improving the Quality of Life,* 2nd ed. Thousand Oaks, CA: Sage Publications.

Kotler, P., and Zaltman, G. 1971. "Social Marketing: An Approach to Planned Change." *Journal of Marketing* 35 (July): 3–12.

Kottak, C. P., and Kozaitis, K. A. 1999. *On Being Different: Diversity and Multiculturalism in the North American Mainstream.* Blacklick, OH: McGraw-Hill Humanities/Social Sciences/Languages.

Kummerow, J. 2000. *New Directions in Career Planning and the Workplace.* Palo Alto, CA: Davies-Black Publishing, an imprint of Consulting Psychologists Press.

Labov, W. 1973. *Language in the Inner City: Studies in Black English Vernacular.* Philadelphia, PA: University of Pennsylvania Press.

LaFromboise, T. D., Coleman, H.L.K., and Gerton, J. 1993. "Psychological Impact of Biculturalism: Evidence and Theory." *Psychological Bulletin* 114 (3): 395–412.

Laubeova, L. 2000. "Melting Pot vs. Ethnic Stew." *Encyclopedia of the World's Minorities.* http://www.tolerance.cz/courses/texts/melting.htm.

Levine, E. S., and Padilla, A. M. 1980. *Crossing Cultures in Therapy: Pluralistic Counseling for the Hispanic.* Monterey, CA: Brooks/Cole Publishing.

Livesey, C. 2005. *AS Sociology for AQA.* London: Hodder Arnold Publisher.

Livingston, G., Parker, K., and Fox, S. 2009. "Latinos Online, 2006–2008: Narrowing the Gap." Pew Research Center, Pew Internet and American Life Project, http://www.pewinternet.org/Commentary/2009/December/Latinos-Online-20062008.aspx.

Lopez, E., Ramirez, E., and Rochin, R. 1999. "Latinos and Economic Development in California." Sacramento, CA: California Research Bureau, California State Library.

Lopez, M. H. 2009. "Latinos and Education: Explaining the Attainment Gap," October 7. Washington DC: Pew Hispanic Center, a Pew Research Center project. http://pewhispanic.org/reports/report.php?ReportID=115.

Lytwak, E. 1999. "A Tale of Two Futures: Changing Shares of U.S. Population Growth." *NPG Forum,* March. http://www.npg.org/forum_series/two_futures.htm.

Marín, G., and Triandis, H. C. 1985. "Allocentrism as an Important Characteristic of the Behavior of Latin American and Hispanics." In *Cross-cultural and National Studies in Social Psychology,* ed. R. Diaz, 85–104. Amsterdam, NY: Elsevier Science Publishers.

Marshall Orange, S., and Osborne, R. 2004. "Introduction." In *From Outreach to Equity*, ed. Robin Osborne. Office for Literacy and Outreach Services. Chicago, IL: ALA Editions.

Massey, D. S. 2005. Cited in "Five Myths about Immigration: Common Misconceptions Underlying U.S. Border-Enforcement Policy." *The American Immigration Law Foundation* 4 (6). http://www.ailf.org.

Mayer, R. E., and Anderson, R. B. 1991. "Animations Need Narrations: An Experimental Test of a Dual-coding Hypothesis." *Journal of Educational Psychology* 83: 484–90.

McKinley Jr., J. C. 2010. "An Arizona Morgue Grows Crowded." *New York Times,* July 28. http://www.nytimes.com/2010/07/29/us/29border.html?ref=james_c_jr_mckinley.

Michman, R. D. 1991. *Lifestyle Market Segmentation.* New York: Praeger Publishers.

Morales, E. 2002. *Living in Spanglish: The Search for Latino Identity in America.* New York: LA Weekly Books/Saint Martin's Press.

Moure-Eraso, R., and Friedman-Jiménez, G. 2001. "Occupational Health among Latino Workers in the Urban Setting." In *Health Issues in the Latinos Community,* ed. M. Aguirre-Molina, C. W. Molina, and R. E. Zambrana, 327. San Francisco, CA: Jossey-Bass.

Murray, D. D. 2007. "A Brief History of U.S. Immigration." ILW.com. http://www.ilw.com/articles/2007,0829-murray.shtm.

Najjar, L. J. 1998. "Principles of Educational Multimedia User Interface Design." *Human Factors* 40 (2): 311–323.

Nava, Y. 2000. *It's All in the Frijoles: 100 Famous Latinos Share Real Life Stories, Time-Tested Dichos, Favorite Folktales, and Inspiring Words of Wisdom.* New York: Fireside Books.

Nguyen, M., ed. 2005. *Hispanic Americans: A Statistical Sourcebook.* Woodside, CA: Information Publications.

Novotny, E. 2003. "Library Services to Immigrants: The Debate in the Library Literature. 1900–1920, and a Chicago Case Study." In *Reference and User Services Quarterly* 42 (4): 342–352.

OCLC Online Computer Library Center, Inc. 2005. *Perceptions of Libraries and Information Resources,* a report to the OCLC membership. Dublin, OH: OCLC Online Computer Library Center, Inc.

O'Connell, J., ed. 1997. *The Blackwell Encyclopedic Dictionary of International Management,* vol. 7. Malden, MA: Blackwell Publishers.

Ortiz, F. 1983. *El Contrapunteo cubano del azúcar y del tabaco.* La Habana: Editorial de Ciencias Sociales (Orig. pub. 1940).

Passel, J. S. 2005. "Estimates of the Size and Characteristics of the Undocumented Population," March 21. Washington DC: Pew Hispanic Center, a Pew Research Center project. http://pewhispanic.org/files/reports/44.pdf.

Passel, J. S. 2007. "Growing Share of Immigrants Choosing Naturalization," March 28. Washington DC: Pew Hispanic Center, a Pew Research Center project. http://pewhispanic.org/files/reports/74.pdf.

Passel, J. S., and Suro, R. 2005. "Rise, Peak, and Decline: Trends in U.S. Immigration 1992–2004," September 27. Washington DC: Pew Hispanic Center, a Pew Research Center project. http://pewhispanic.org/files/reports/53.pdf.

Pew Hispanic Center. 2005. "Estimates of the Size and Characteristics of the Undocumented Population," March 21. http://pewhispanic.org/files/reports/44.pdf.

Pew Hispanic Center. 2006. "Estimates of the Unauthorized Migrant Population for States Based on the March 2005 CPS," a Pew Research Center project. April 26. http://pewhispanic.org/files/factsheets/17.pdf.

Pew Hispanic Center. 2008. "Hispanic Women in the United States, 2007." http://pewhispanic.org/files/factsheets/42.pdf.

Pew Hispanic Center, a Pew Research Center project. 2004. "Latino Teens Staying in High School: A Challenge for All Generations." January. http://pewhispanic.org/files/factsheets/7.3.pdf.

Pew Hispanic Center, a Pew Research Center project. 2006. "From 200 Million to 300 Million: The Numbers behind Population Growth," October 10. http://pewhispanic.org/files/factsheets/25.pdf.

Pew Hispanic Center, a Pew Research Center project. 2006. "Table 19: Language Spoken at Home and English-Speaking Ability by Age, Race, and Ethnicity: 2006." In "Statistical Portrait of Hispanics in the United States, 2006," http://pewhispanic.org/files/factsheets/hispanics2006/Table-19.pdf.

Pew Hispanic Center, a Pew Research Center project. 2009. "Statistical Portrait of Hispanics in the United States, 2007," March 5. http://pewhispanic.org/factsheets/factsheet.php?FactsheetID=46.

Pew Hispanic Center/Kaiser Family Foundation. 2004. "National Survey of Latinos: Education," January 26. http://pewhispanic.org/files/reports/25.pdf.

Portes, A., and Hoffman, K. 2003. "Latin American Class Structures: Their Composition and Change during the Neoliberal Era." *Latin American Research Review* 38 (1): 41–82.

Pulvino, C. J., and Lee, J. L. 1991. *Financial Counseling: A Strategic Approach.* Madison, WI: Instructional Enterprises.

Quezada, S. 1991. "The Role of Libraries in Providing Services to Adults in Learning English," *ERIC Digest.* Washington, DC: National Clearinghouse of Literacy Education, Office of Educational Research and Improvement [ED]. http://www.ericdigests.org/pre-9220/libraries.htm.

Ramirez, R. R. 2004. "We the People: Hispanics in the United States," December. Census 2000 Special Reports. http://www.census.gov/prod/2004pubs/censr-18.pdf.

Ramírez Wohlmuth, S. 2000. "Breaking through the Linguistic Barrier." In *Library Services to Latinos,* ed. Salvador Güereña. Jefferson, NC: McFarland and Company.

Ríos Kravitz, R. 2000. "Battling the Adobe Ceiling: Barriers to Professional Advancement for Academic Librarians of Color." In *Library Services to Latinos,* ed. Salvador Güereña. Jefferson, NC: McFarland and Company.

Rodriguez, G. 1996. "The Emerging Latinos Middle Class." *Research Reports.* Davenport Institute. http://publicpolicy.pepperdine.edu/davenport-institute/reports/latino.

Rodriguez, J. 2000. "Parent's Workshops." In *Library Services to Youth of Hispanic Heritage,* ed. B. Immroth and K. de la Peña McCook. Jefferson, NC: McFarland and Company.

Sabogal, F., Marín, G., Otero-Sabogal, R., Marín, B., and Pérez-Stable, E. J. 1987. "Hispanic Familism and Acculturation: What Changes and What Doesn't?" *Hispanic Journal of Behavioral Sciences* 9: 397–412.

Saenz, R. 2004. "Latinos and the Changing Face of America." Russell Sage Foundation and Population Reference Bureau. http://www.prb.org/Articles/2004/LatinosandtheChangingFaceofAmerica.aspx.

Samovar, L. A., and Porter, R. E. 2001. *Communication between Cultures,* 4th ed. Belmont, CA: Wadsworth/Thomson Learning.

Samovar, L. A., Porter, R. E., and McDaniel, E. R. 2007. *Communication between Cultures,* 7th ed. Boston, MA: Wadsworth/Cengage Learning.

Sánchez Ruiz, E. 2003. "La industria editorial y el libre comercio." In *X Anuario de Investigación de la Comunicación,* ed. Bernardo Russi Alzaga. San Luis Potosí: CONEICC/Universidad Intercontinental.

Santiago, D. A., and Brown, S. 2004. "Federal Policy and Latinos in Higher Education," June 23. Washington DC: Pew Hispanic Center, a Pew Research Center project. http://pewhispanic.org/files/reports/32.pdf.

Santiago-Rivera, A. L., Arredondo, P., and Gallardo-Cooper, M. 2002. *Counseling Latinos and la Familia.* Multicultural Aspects of Counseling Series 17. Thousand Oaks, CA: Sage Publications.

Seda-Santana, I. 2000. "Literacy Research in Latin America: Context, Characteristics, and Applications" ["Investigación Sobre Alfabetización en América Latina: Contexto, Características, y Aplicaciones"]. *Reading Online* 4 (4). http://www.readingonline.org/articles/art_index.asp?HREF=/articles/handbook/seda/index.html.

Seltzer, M. 2001. *Securing Your Organization's Future: A Complete Guide to Fundraising Strategies.* New York: The Foundation Center.

Shorris, E. 1992. *Latinos: A Biography of the People.* New York: W. W. Norton and Company.

Smith O'Brien, D. 2004. "Outreach Starts at the Top: Advice from a Library Director." In *From Outreach To Equity,* ed. T. Osborne. Office for Literacy and Outreach Services. Chicago, IL: ALA Editions.

Sobrino, M. L. 2007. *Thriving Latina Entrepreneurs in America.* El Monte, CA: W Business Books.

Soto, T. J. 2006. *Marketing to Hispanics: A Strategic Approach to Assessing and Planning Your Initiative.* Chicago, IL: Kaplan Publishing.

Spitta, S. 1995. *Between Two Waters: Narratives of Transculturation in Latin America.* Houston, TX: Rice University Press.

Spradley, J. P. 1979. *The Ethnographic Interview.* Fort Worth, TX: Harcourt Brace Jovanovich College Publishers.

Spradley, J. P., and McCurdy, David W. 1972. *The Cultural Experience: Ethnography in Complex Society.* Chicago, IL: Science Research Associates, a subsidiary of IBM.

Spradley, J. P., and McCurdy, David W. 1988. *The Cultural Experience: Ethnography in Complex Society.* Prospect Hills, IL: Waveland Press.

Suárez-Orozco, M. M., and Páez, M. M., eds. 2002. *Latinos Remaking America.* Berkeley, CA: University of California Press.

Sundell, J. 2000. "Library Service to Hispanic Immigrants of Forsyth County, North Carolina: A Community Collaboration." In *Library Service to Latinos, An Anthology,* ed. Salvador Güereña, 143–68. Jefferson, NC: McFarland and Company.

Suro, R. 1999. *Strangers among US: Latino Lives in a Changing America.* New York: Vintage Books.

Tafoya, S. 2004. "Shades of Belonging: Latinos and Racial Identity." Washington DC: Pew Hispanic Center, a Pew Research Center project. http://pewhispanic.org/files/reports/35.pdf.

Takaki, R. 1994. *A Different Mirror: A History of Multicultural America.* New York: Back Bay Books.

Teinowitz, I., and Cardona, M. M. 1999. "Sharpton Sets Timetable for Minority Ad Changes." *Advertising Age,* January 25, 18.

Thomas, R. R., Jr. 1996. *Redefining Diversity.* New York: AMACOM.

Torres-Rivas, E. 1983. "Central America Today: A Study in Regional Dependency." In *Trouble in Our Backyard,* ed. M. Diskin. New York: Pantheon Books/Random House.

Toussaint-Comeau, M., Smith, T., and Comeau, L., Jr. 2005. "Occupational Attainment and Mobility of Hispanics in a Changing Economy," September. Washington DC: Pew Hispanic Center, a Pew Research Center project. http://pewhispanic.org/files/reports/59.1.pdf.

Trumpbour, J., and Bernard, E. 2002. "Unions and Latinos: Mutual Transformation." In *Latinos Remaking America,* ed. M. M. Suárez-Orozco and M. M. Páez. Berkeley, CA: University of California Press.

Turner, B., ed. 2000. *Latin America Profiled.* New York: Saint Martin's Press.

United Nations Educational, Scientific, and Cultural Organization (UNESCO). 2000. *Facts and Figures 2000.* Paris: UNESCO Institute for Statistics.

Valdés, M. I. 2000. *Marketing to American Latinos.* Part 1. New York: Paramount Market Publishing.

Valle, F. J., and Mandel, J. M. 2003. *How to Win the Hispanic Rush Gold.* Lincoln, NE: iUniverse.

Vega, W. A., Zimmerman, R., Gil, A., Warheit, G. J., and Apospori, E. 1993. "Acculturation Strain Theory: Its Application in Explaining Drug Use Behavior Among Cuban and Other Hispanic Youth." In *Drug Abuse Among Minority Youth*: *Methodological Issues and Recent Research Advance,* ed. M. De La Rosa and J. L. Recio Adrados. National Institute of Drug Abuse Research Monograph Series. http://archives.drugabuse.gov/pdf/monographs/130.pdf.

Waldinger, R. 2007. "Between Here and There: How Attached Are Latino Immigrants to Their Native Country?" October 25. Washington DC: Pew Hispanic Center, a Pew Research Center project. http://pewhispanic.org/reports/report.php?ReportID=80.

Weaver, Gary. 1986. *Cross-Cultural Orientation: New Conceptualizations and Applications,* ed. R. M. Paige. Lanham, MD: Rowman and Littlefield.

Webster, B. H., Jr., and Bishaw, A. 2007. "Income, Earnings, and Poverty Data from the 2006 American Community Survey," August. American Community Survey Reports, U.S. Census Bureau. http://www.census.gov/prod/2007pubs/acs-08.pdf.

White, C. M. 1969. *Mexico's Library and Information Services.* Totowa, NJ: Bedminster Press.

Wilson, W. J. 2003. *The Roots of Racial Tension: Urban Ethnic Neighborhoods.* Harvard University. http://www.hks.harvard.edu/inequality/Summer/Summer04/papers/Wilson 2004.pdf.

Wolcott, H. F. 2008. *Ethnography: A Way of Seeing,* 2nd ed. Landham, MD: AltaMira Press.

Zehr, M. A. 2009. "Scholars Mull the 'Paradox' of Immigrants: Academic Success Declines From 1st to 3rd Generation." *Education Week* 28 (25): 1, 12.

Zona, G. 1970. *Eyes That See Do Not Grow Old: The Proverbs of Mexico, Central, and South America.* New York: Touchstone Publishers.

Index

Hovius, Beth, 55
Humorous communication style,
    241

Idaho Public Library, 201
Identified behaviors, limiting beliefs, and
    opposing messages/cost, in creative
    briefs, 239–40
Identity and self-image, 119–20
IFLA (International Federation of Library
    Associations and Institutions), 4–5
Image, creating, 225, 229
Images (visuals), 245–48, 249
Immigrants: acculturation, 8–9; assimila-
    tion, 8; recent, 46–47
Immigration status: generations and,
    71–72; national trends summary,
    70–72, 90; significance and relation to
    other variables, 72; suggested research
    questions, 72; worksheets with other
    variables, 110, 338
Implementation plan, 192
Incentives, 188–92, 211, 251, 359
Income: national trends summary, 83–84,
    91; significance and relation to other
    variables, 84; suggested research ques-
    tions, 84–85; worksheets with other
    variables, 107, 335
Indicators: in communication stages,
    278–79, 286, 384; diversity goals and,
    276; external outcome, 278–79, 286,
    384; goals of outreach activities and,
    277; internal outcome, 277–78; over-
    view, 276–77; promotional campaign,
    279, 286, 384; promotion and, 277;
    strategic partnerships and, 276; using
    numbers and amounts, 278, 286, 384;
    worksheets, 286, 384
Individualism, 120
Influencers: identifying, 182, 224, 228, 356;
    market segmentation and, 187; social
    pressure and, 153, 154; worksheets, 182,
    356
Information centers, libraries as, 4
Information gathering, informal, 99
Information sources for demographic data,
    94–99; primary sources, 94–95, 95–96,
    98–99; qualitative information, 94,

95–96; quantitative information, 94–95,
    96; secondary sources, 95, 96–98, 99
Infrastructure, 52
Intercultural communication, 127
Internal execution plan, 250, 252, 268–69,
    373–78
Internal outcome indicators, 277–78
Internal resources subcommittee, 29
International Federation of Library Associ-
    ations and Institutions (IFLA), 4–5
Internet: classes, 193; as secondary data
    source, 97, 99; use by Latinos, 79
Inter-University Consortium for Political
    and Social Research, 119–20
Intervention, organizing, 53
Interviews: community leader, 47–48,
    325–29; ethnographic, 128–29, 141,
    341–44; intercept, 96; one-on-one, 98,
    258; qualitative information from pri-
    mary sources, 95–96
Introductions, 121

Judgment, trusted, 52

"Key Findings from the 2006 Latino
    National Survey," 71–72
Konstanki, Mary, 227
Kummerow, Jean, 35–36

LAB (Latino Advisory Board), 30
Lake County Public Library (Colorado),
    162–63
Language: culture and, 133; issues regard-
    ing, 7–8, 127; in Latin America, 135–36
Language ability: market segmentation
    and, 185, 186; national trends sum-
    mary, 80, 90; significance and relation
    to other variables, 80–81; suggested
    research questions, 81; worksheets
    with other variables, 109, 111, 337
Lantino outreach: youth, 200–202
Lara, Elena, 193
LaRed Latina, 55
Latin America: cultural experience, 117;
    languages spoken in, 135–36; publish-
    ing industry, 137
Latino adults and seniors, outreach activi-
    ties for, 193–200

Plan for Latino Outreach: benefits, 19–20; elements, essential, 20–21; necessity for, 18–19. *See also* Worksheets

Planning activity or event logistics checklist, 360–61

Planning and implementing outreach activities, 183–211; implementation plan, 192; incentives, creating, 188–92, 211, 359; Latino adult/senior activities, 193–200; Latino children's activities, 202–4; Latino youth activities, 200–202; market segments, 184–88, 210, 358; outreach activities, 192–204; outreach strategy as benefit-oriented strategy, 189–92; overview, 183–84; planning internal logistics, 206–8; referrals, getting, 204–6; worksheets, 210–11, 358–64

Planning internal logistics, 206–8

Planning promotional tactics, 262, 367

Plans: external distribution, 250–52, 266–67, 372; implementation, 192; internal execution, 250, 252, 268–69, 373–78; marketing, 214–15. *See also* Media plan

Policy, in marketing mix, 166–67

Population growth, Latino, 59, 62–64

Positioning library/resources, 143–82; competition, 151–56; due diligence, 156; Latino community needs, 149–51, 176, 351–52; marketing goals and strategies, 148–49, 174–75, 350; marketing mix, 156–68; overview, 143–44, 167–68; preparation stage, 144–45; SWOT analysis, 145–48, 170–73, 347–49; worksheets, 170–82, 347–56

Positioning statements, 154, 181, 211, 355, 359

Post-campaign evaluation, 255–56, 273, 382

Post-evaluation of marketing strategy, 282, 287, 385

Pre-campaign tactics evaluation, 253–55, 270–72, 379–81

Press releases, 218

Pretesting campaign, 248–50

Price, in marketing mix, 160–61

Primary information sources, 94–95, 95–96, 98–99

Printed materials, 220–21, 222, 251. *See also* Flyers

Procedures: comparing with outcomes, 256–57; evaluating changes in, 276, 280

Product, describing, 227–28

Product choices, in marketing mix, 157–60; collecting Spanish-language material on regular basis, 160; fiction, 158; nonfiction, 158–59; suppliers, 159–60; trends, 159

Professional development training, 33

Programming subcommittee, 29

Promotion, 213–73; communication model, 230–33; evaluating, 252–58; goals, 216–17; indicators related to, 277; in marketing mix, 165; marketing plan *versus* promotional campaign, 214–15; media plan, building, 233–34; messages, creating effective, 235–50; overview, 213–14, 258–59; promotional campaign, implementing, 250–52; promotional campaign, starting, 222–30; strategies, 215–16; tactics, 217–22, 270, 273, 379, 382; timing and scheduling, 234–35, 264, 369; worksheets, 261–73, 366–82

Promotional campaigns: branding, 216, 223–27; evaluating, 281; indicators, 279, 286, 384; marketing plan *versus*, 214–15; mini-campaigns, 216, 227–30; objectives, 224–25, 228–29; starting, 222–30; worksheets, 261–62, 366–67

Promotional items, 221, 222

Promotional pieces, bilingual, 241–42

Promotional products, celebrity, 202

Promotional strategies subcommittee, 29

Property taxes, 7

Proxemics, 120–22, 130

PSAs (public service announcements), 219, 222

Publications, as secondary data source, 97, 99

Publicity, 218, 222

Public Library of Charlotte and Mecklenburg County (North Carolina), 203

Standard Spanish, 136

Stereotypes: about Latinos, 114–15, 131, 132; avoiding in images, 246–47

Strategic partnerships, 43–58; advantages of, 44–45; assessing potential, 321–24; challenges of, 45; community activities, participating in/supporting, 54; community leaders, 46–48, 325–29; defined, 44; facilities, lending your, 53–54; follow-up, 269, 374, 377; getting started, 45; indicators related to, 276; learning from existing efforts, 54–55; logistical help for community activities, 52–53; market channels, 49, 50–51; in marketing mix, 166; media, talking to the, 51; organizing an intervention, 53; overview, 43–44; participation ideas, 51–54; proceeding with, 49–51; researching potential partners worksheets, 58, 320; as secondary data source, 97, 99; staff and, 52, 55–56; types of, 45–46

Strategic partners subcommittee, 28–29

Strengths, in SWOT analysis, 146–47, 170–72, 347–48

Subcommittees, 28–29

Substance Abuse and Mental Health Services Administration, 197

Summer reading programs, 134–35

Suppliers, 159–60

Support statement/third-party credibility, in creative briefs, 240–41

Surveys, 96, 98, 99, 258, 317–18

Survival skills, 194

SWOT analysis: described, 145–46; opportunities and threats worksheets, 173, 349; performing, 146–47; strengths and weaknesses worksheets, 170–72, 347–48; working with results, 147–48

Tafoya, Sonya, 120

Talking, 131, 132

Target audience: in creative briefs, 237; identifying, 224, 228; images for, 246; timing and scheduling promotional efforts, 235

Taxes paid by Latinos, 6–7

Technical problems, 283–84

Teens, outreach activities for, 155–56, 178, 180, 200–202

Templates: end of marketing campaign report, 386; ethnographic interviews, 141, 341–44

Temporary protected status (TPS), 72

Themes, 225

Threats, in SWOT analysis, 145, 147, 173, 349

Time, perception and use of, 122

Time in the United States: national trends summary, 87–89, 91; significance and relation to other variables, 89; suggested research questions, 89; worksheets with other variables, 106–9, 334–37

Timing: of evaluation, 281–82; of promotional efforts, 234–35, 264, 369

Tone/language, in creative briefs, 241–42

Touching, 130–31

Tours, guided library, 47

TPS (temporary protected status), 72

Traditional career factors, in career selection, 36

Translations, 134, 158

Treasurer/administrator, Committee for Latin Outreach, 28

Trial and error with an educated guess, 99–100

Tucson-Pima Public Library, 227

TV, local, 218

Undocumented Latinos, 6–7

University City Regional Library (North Carolina), 203

U.S. Census, 62–64, 97, 120

Values, 23

Video crates, 253

Videos, 191

Vision statements: about, 21; outreach activities based on, 184; Queens Library (New York), 22–23; worksheets, 38, 302–3

Vos (Spanish pronoun), 135

Water, marketing of, 189

Weaknesses, in SWOT analysis, 146–47, 170–72, 347–48

White people, as diversity leaders, 36

About the Author

SUSANA G. BAUMANN is the director of LCSWorldwide Language and Multicultural Marketing Communications, a consulting company currently located in New Brunswick, New Jersey. Since 1996, LCSWorldwide has developed community outreach initiatives for organizations in health care, education, and public service.

Baumann, a former tenured professor at the National University of Rosario, Argentina, emigrated from Argentina in 1990. She obtained an MA in Liberal Studies at Monmouth University, New Jersey, and pursued a career in publishing and communications. In addition to her experience in multicultural marketing, community outreach, and organizational staff development, Baumann was the publisher of the first bilingual newspaper in New Jersey.

She has been an active member of the New Jersey Latino Chamber of Commerce; the American Association of University Women, Spanish Chapter; the American Translators Association; and the Red Bank Education and Development Initiative; among others. She was a board member and chair of the Planning and Programming Committee of the Hispanic Affairs and Resource Center of Monmouth County for several years. She was appointed as the first Latino member of the Red Bank Borough Human Relations Committee. She also became the first Latino member of the Monmouth County Arts Council Diversity Committee. She was recently honored as a 2009 Clarion Awards Judge for the Association of Women in Communications.